The absorbing personal story of the man who rose from hoodlum, thief, dope peddler, and pimp to become the most dynamic leader of the Black Revolution. It is, too, a testament of great emotional power from which every American can learn much. But, above all, this book shows the Malcolm X that very few people knew, the man behind the stereotyped image of the hate-preacher—a sensitive, proud, highly intelligent man whose plan to move into the mainstream of the Black Revolution was cut short by a hail of assassins' bullets, a man who felt certain he would not live long enough to see this book appear.

"In the agony of this brilliant Negro's self-creation [is] the agony of an entire people in their search for identity. No man has better expressed his people's trapped anguish."
—The New York Review of Books

THE AUTOBIOGRAPHY OF
MALCOLM X

With the assistance of Alex Haley
Introduction by M. S. Handler
Epilogue by Alex Haley

BALLANTINE BOOKS • NEW YORK

This book I dedicate to my beloved wife Betty and to our children whose understanding and whose sacrifices made it possible for me to do my work.

CONTENTS

INTRODUCTION

The Sunday before he was to officially announce his rupture with Elijah Muhammad, Malcolm X came to my home to discuss his plans and give me some necessary documentation.

Mrs. Handler had never met Malcolm before this fateful visit. She served us coffee and cakes while Malcolm spoke in the courteous, gentle manner that was his in private. It was obvious to me that Mrs. Handler was impressed by Malcolm. His personality filled our living room.

Malcolm's attitude was that of a man who had reached a crossroads in his life and was making a choice under an inner compulsion. A wistful smile illuminated his countenance from time to time—a smile that said many things. I felt uneasy because Malcolm was evidently trying to say something which his pride and dignity prevented him from expressing. I sensed that Malcolm was not confident he would succeed in escaping from the shadowy world which had held him in thrall.

Mrs. Handler was quiet and thoughtful after Malcolm's departure. Looking up suddenly, she said:

"You know, it was like having tea with a black panther."

The description startled me. The black panther is an aristocrat in the animal kingdom. He is beautiful. He is dangerous. As a man, Malcolm X had the physical bearing and the inner self-confidence of a born aristocrat. And he was potentially dangerous. No man in our time aroused fear and hatred in the white man as did Malcolm, because in him the white man sensed an implacable foe who could not be had for any price —a man unreservedly committed to the cause of liberating the black man in American society rather than integrating the black man into that society.

My first meeting with Malcolm X took place in March 1963

in the Muslim restaurant of Temple Number Seven on Lenox Avenue. I had been assigned by *The New York Times* to investigate the growing pressures within the Negro community. Thirty years of experience as a reporter in Western and Eastern Europe had taught me that the forces in a developing social struggle are frequently buried beneath the visible surface and make themselves felt in many ways long before they burst out into the open. These generative forces make themselves felt through the power of an idea long before their organizational forms can openly challenge the establishment. It is the merit of European political scientists and sociologists to give a high priority to the power of ideas in a social struggle. In the United States, it is our weakness to confuse the numerical strength of an organization and the publicity attached to leaders with the germinating forces that sow the seeds of social upheaval in our community.

In studying the growing pressures within the Negro community, I had not only to seek the opinions of the established leaders of the civil rights organizations but the opinions of those working in the penumbra of the movement—"underground," so to speak. This is why I sought out Malcolm X, whose ideas had reached me through the medium of Negro integrationists. Their thinking was already reflecting a high degree of nascent Negro nationalism.

I did not know what to expect as I waited for Malcolm. I was the only white person in the restaurant, an immaculate establishment tended by somber, handsome, uncommunicative Negroes. Signs reading "Smoking Forbidden" were pasted on the highly polished mirrors. I was served coffee but became uneasy in this aseptic, silent atmosphere as time passed. Malcolm finally arrived. He was very tall, handsome, of impressive bearing. His skin had a bronze hue.

I rose to greet him and extended my hand. Malcolm's hand came up slowly. I had the impression it was difficult for him to take my hand, but, *noblesse oblige,* he did. Malcolm then did a curious thing which he always repeated whenever we met in public in a restaurant in New York or Washington. He asked whether I would mind if he took a seat facing the door. I had had similar requests put to me in Eastern European capitals. Malcolm was on the alert, he wished to see every person who entered the restaurant. I quickly realized that Malcolm constantly walked in danger.

We spoke for more than three hours at this first encounter.

His views about the white man were devastating, but at no time did he transgress against my own personality and make me feel that I, as an individual, shared in the guilt. He attributed the degradation of the Negro people to the white man. He denounced integration as a fraud. He contended that if the leaders of the established civil rights organizations persisted, the social struggle would end in bloodshed because he was certain the white man would never concede full integration. He argued the Muslim case for separation as the only solution in which the Negro could achieve his own identity, develop his own culture, and lay the foundations for a self-respecting productive community. He was vague about where the Negro state could be established.

Malcolm refused to see the impossibility of the white man conceding secession from the United States; at this stage in his career he contended it was the only solution. He defended Islam as a religion that did not recognize color bars. He denounced Christianity as a religion designed for slaves and the Negro clergy as the curse of the black man, exploiting him for their own purposes instead of seeking to liberate him, and acting as handmaidens of the white community in its determination to keep the Negroes in a subservient position.

During this first encounter Malcolm also sought to enlighten me about the Negro mentality. He repeatedly cautioned me to beware of Negro affirmations of good will toward the white man. He said that the Negro had been trained to dissemble and conceal his real thoughts, as a matter of survival. He argued that the Negro only tells the white man what he believes the white man wishes to hear, and that the art of dissembling reached a point where even Negroes cannot truthfully say they understand what their fellow Negroes believe. The art of deception practiced by the Negro was based on a thorough understanding of the white man's mores, he said; at the same time the Negro has remained a closed book to the white man, who has never displayed any interest in understanding the Negro.

Malcolm's exposition of his social ideas was clear and thoughtful, if somewhat shocking to the white initiate, but most disconcerting in our talk was Malcolm's belief in Elijah Muhammad's history of the origins of man, and in a genetic theory devised to prove the superiority of black over white—a theory stunning to me in its sheer absurdity.

After this first encounter, I realized that there were two

Malcolms—the private and the public person. His public performances on television and at meeting halls produced an almost terrifying effect. His implacable marshaling of facts and his logic had something of a new dialectic, diabolic in its force. He frightened white television audiences, demolished his Negro opponents, but elicited a remarkable response from Negro audiences. Many Negro opponents in the end refused to make any public appearances on the same platform with him. The troubled white audiences were confused, disturbed, felt themselves threatened. Some began to consider Malcolm evil incarnate.

Malcolm appealed to the two most disparate elements in the Negro community—the depressed mass, and the galaxy of Negro writers and artists who have burst on the American scene in the past decade. The Negro middle class—the Negro "establishment"—abhorred and feared Malcolm as much as he despised it.

The impoverished Negroes respected Malcolm in the way that wayward children respect the grandfather image. It was always a strange and moving experience to walk with Malcolm in Harlem. He was known to all. People glanced at him shyly. Sometimes Negro youngsters would ask for his autograph. It always seemed to me that their affection for Malcolm was inspired by the fact that although he had become a national figure, he was still a man of the people who, they felt, would never betray them. The Negroes have suffered too long from betrayals and in Malcolm they sensed a man of mission. They knew his origins, with which they could identify. They knew his criminal and prison record, which he had never concealed. They looked upon Malcolm with a certain wonderment. Here was a man who had come from the lower depths which they still inhabited, who had triumphed over his own criminality and his own ignorance to become a forceful leader and spokesman, an uncompromising champion of his people.

Although many could not share his Muslim religious beliefs, they found in Malcolm's puritanism a standing reproach to their own lives. Malcolm had purged himself of all the ills that afflict the depressed Negro mass: drugs, alcohol, tobacco, not to speak of criminal pursuits. His personal life was impeccable—of a puritanism unattainable for the mass. Human redemption—Malcolm had achieved it in his own lifetime, and this was known to the Negro community.

In his television appearances and at public meetings Malcolm articulated the woes and the aspirations of the depressed Negro mass in a way it was unable to do for itself. When he attacked the white man, Malcolm did for the Negroes what they couldn't do for themselves—he attacked with a violence and anger that spoke for the ages of misery. It was not an academic exercise of just giving hell to "Mr. Charlie."

Many of the Negro writers and artists who are national figures today revered Malcolm for what they considered his ruthless honesty in stating the Negro case, his refusal to compromise, and his search for a group identity that had been destroyed by the white man when he brought the Negroes in chains from Africa. The Negro writers and artists regarded Malcolm as the great catalyst, the man who inspired self-respect and devotion in the downtrodden millions.

A group of these artists gathered one Sunday in my home, and we talked about Malcolm. Their devotion to him as a man was moving. One said: "Malcolm will never betray us. We have suffered too much from betrayals in the past."

Malcolm's attitude toward the white man underwent a marked change in 1964—a change that contributed to his break with Elijah Muhammad and his racist doctrines. Malcolm's meteoric eruption on the national scene brought him into wider contact with white men who were not the "devils" he had thought they were. He was much in demand as a speaker at student forums in Eastern universities and had appeared at many by the end of his short career as a national figure. He always spoke respectfully and with a certain surprise of the positive response of white students to his lectures.

A second factor that contributed to his conversion to wider horizons was a growing doubt about the authenticity of Elijah Muhammad's version of the Muslim religion—a doubt that grew into a certainty with more knowledge and more experience. Certain secular practices at the Chicago headquarters of Elijah Muhammad had come to Malcolm's notice and he was profoundly shocked.

Finally, he embarked on a number of prolonged trips to Mecca and the newly independent African states through the good offices of the representatives of the Arab League in the United States. It was on his first trip to Mecca that he came to the conclusion that he had yet to discover Islam.

Assassins' bullets ended Malcolm's career before he was able to develop this new approach, which in essence recognized the Negroes as an integral part of the American community—a far cry from Elijah Muhammad's doctrine of separation. Malcolm had reached the midpoint in redefining his attitude to this country and the white-black relationship. He no longer inveighed against the United States but against a segment of the United States represented by overt white supremacists in the South and covert white supremacists in the North.

It was Malcolm's intention to raise Negro militancy to a new high point with the main thrust aimed at both the Southern and Northern white supremacists. The Negro problem, which he had always said should be renamed "the white man's problem," was beginning to assume new dimensions for him in the last months of his life.

To the very end, Malcolm sought to refashion the broken strands between the American Negroes and African culture. He saw in this the road to a new sense of group identity, a self-conscious role in history, and above all a sense of man's own worth which he claimed the white man had destroyed in the Negro.

American autobiographical literature is filled with numerous accounts of remarkable men who pulled themselves to the summit by their bootstraps. Few are as poignant as Malcolm's memoirs. As testimony to the power of redemption and the force of human personality, the autobiography of Malcolm X is a revelation.

New York, June 1965

THE AUTOBIOGRAPHY OF
MALCOLM X

CHAPTER ONE

NIGHTMARE

When my mother was pregnant with me, she told me later, a party of hooded Ku Klux Klan riders galloped up to our home in Omaha, Nebraska, one night. Surrounding the house, brandishing their shotguns and rifles, they shouted for my father to come out. My mother went to the front door and opened it. Standing where they could see her pregnant condition, she told them that she was alone with her three small children, and that my father was away, preaching, in Milwaukee. The Klansmen shouted threats and warnings at her that we had better get out of town because "the good Christian white people" were not going to stand for my father's "spreading trouble" among the "good" Negroes of Omaha with the "back to Africa" preachings of Marcus Garvey.

My father, the Reverend Earl Little, was a Baptist minister, a dedicated organizer for Marcus Aurelius Garvey's U.N.I.A. (Universal Negro Improvement Association). With the help of such disciples as my father, Garvey, from his headquarters in New York City's Harlem, was raising the banner of black-race purity and exhorting the Negro masses to return to their ancestral African homeland—a cause which had made Garvey the most controversial black man on earth.

Still shouting threats, the Klansmen finally spurred their horses and galloped around the house, shattering every window pane with their gun butts. Then they rode off into the night, their torches flaring, as suddenly as they had come.

My father was enraged when he returned. He decided to wait until I was born—which would be soon—and then the family would move. I am not sure why he made this decision, for he was not a frightened Negro, as most then were, and many still are today. My father was a big, six-foot-four, very

1

black man. He had only one eye. How he had lost the other one I have never known. He was from Reynolds, Georgia, where he had left school after the third or maybe fourth grade. He believed, as did Marcus Garvey, that freedom, independence and self-respect could never be achieved by the Negro in America, and that therefore the Negro should leave America to the white man and return to his African land of origin. Among the reasons my father had decided to risk and dedicate his life to help disseminate this philosophy among his people was that he had seen four of his six brothers die by violence, three of them killed by white men, including one by lynching. What my father could not know then was that of the remaining three, including himself, only one, my Uncle Jim, would die in bed, of natural causes. Northern white police were later to shoot my Uncle Oscar. And my father was finally himself to die by the white man's hands.

It has always been my belief that I, too, will die by violence. I have done all that I can to be prepared.

I was my father's seventh child. He had three children by a previous marriage—Ella, Earl, and Mary, who lived in Boston. He had met and married my mother in Philadelphia, where their first child, my oldest full brother, Wilfred, was born. They moved from Philadelphia to Omaha, where Hilda and then Philbert were born.

I was next in line. My mother was twenty-eight when I was born on May 19, 1925, in an Omaha hospital. Then we moved to Milwaukee, where Reginald was born. From infancy, he had some kind of hernia condition which was to handicap him physically for the rest of his life.

Louise Little, my mother, who was born in Grenada, in the British West Indies, looked like a white woman. Her father *was* white. She had straight black hair, and her accent did not sound like a Negro's. Of this white father of hers, I know nothing except her shame about it. I remember hearing her say she was glad that she had never seen him. It was, of course, because of him that I got my reddish-brown "mariny" color of skin, and my hair of the same color. I was the lightest child in our family. (Out in the world later on, in Boston and New York, I was among the millions of Negroes who were insane enough to feel that it was some kind of status symbol to be light-complexioned—that one was actually fortunate to be born thus. But, still later, I learned to hate every drop of that white rapist's blood that is in me.)

Our family stayed only briefly in Milwaukee, for my father wanted to find a place where he could raise our own food and perhaps build a business. The teaching of Marcus Garvey stressed becoming independent of the white man. We went next, for some reason, to Lansing, Michigan. My father bought a house and soon, as had been his pattern, he was doing free-lance Christian preaching in local Negro Baptist churches, and during the week he was roaming about spreading word of Marcus Garvey.

He had begun to lay away savings for the store he had always wanted to own when, as always, some stupid local Uncle Tom Negroes began to funnel stories about his revolutionary beliefs to the local white people. This time, the get-out-of-town threats came from a local hate society called The Black Legion. They wore black robes instead of white. Soon, nearly everywhere my father went, Black Legionnaires were reviling him as an "uppity nigger" for wanting to own a store, for living outside the Lansing Negro district, for spreading unrest and dissension among "the good niggers."

As in Omaha, my mother was pregnant again, this time with my youngest sister. Shortly after Yvonne was born came the nightmare night in 1929, my earliest vivid memory. I remember being suddenly snatched awake into a frightening confusion of pistol shots and shouting and smoke and flames. My father had shouted and shot at the two white men who had set the fire and were running away. Our home was burning down around us. We were lunging and bumping and tumbling all over each other trying to escape. My mother, with the baby in her arms, just made it into the yard before the house crashed in, showering sparks. I remember we were outside in the night in our underwear, crying and yelling our heads off. The white police and firemen came and stood around watching as the house burned down to the ground.

My father prevailed on some friends to clothe and house us temporarily; then he moved us into another house on the outskirts of East Lansing. In those days Negroes weren't allowed after dark in East Lansing proper. There's where Michigan State University is located; I related all of this to an audience of students when I spoke there in January, 1963 (and had the first reunion in a long while with my younger brother, Robert, who was there doing postgraduate studies in psychology). I told them how East Lansing harassed us so much that we had to move again, this time two miles out of town, into the country. This was where my father built for us with his own hands a four-room house. This is where I really begin to remember things—this home where I started to grow up.

After the fire, I remember that my father was called in and questioned about a permit for the pistol with which he had shot at the white men who set the fire. I remember that the police were always dropping by our house, shoving things around, "just checking" or "looking for a gun." The pistol they were looking for—which they never found, and for which they wouldn't issue a permit—was sewed up inside a pillow. My father's .22 rifle and his shotgun, though, were right out in the open; everyone had them for hunting birds and rabbits and other game.

After that, my memories are of the friction between my father and mother. They seemed to be nearly always at odds. Sometimes my father would beat her. It might have had something to do with the fact that my mother had a pretty good education. Where she got it I don't know. But an educated woman, I suppose, can't resist the temptation to correct an uneducated man. Every now and then, when she put those smooth words on him, he would grab her.

My father was also belligerent toward all of the children, except me. The older ones he would beat almost savagely if they broke any of his rules—and he had so many rules it was hard to know them all. Nearly all my whippings came from my mother. I've thought a lot about why. I actually believe that as anti-white as my father was, he was subconsciously so afflicted with the white man's brainwashing of Negroes that he inclined to favor the light ones, and I was his lightest child. Most Negro parents in those days would almost instinctively treat any lighter children better than they did the darker ones. It came directly from the slavery tradition that the "mulatto," because he was visibly nearer to white, was therefore "better."

My two other images of my father are both outside the home. One was his role as a Baptist preacher. He never pastored in any regular church of his own; he was always a "visiting preacher." I remember especially his favorite sermon: "That little *black* train is a-comin' . . . an' you better get all your business right!" I guess this also fit his association with the back-to-Africa movement, with Marcus Garvey's "Black Train Homeward." My brother Philbert, the one just older than me, loved church, but it confused and amazed me. I would sit goggle-eyed at my father jumping and shouting as he preached, with the congregation jumping and shouting behind him, their souls and bodies devoted to singing and praying. Even at that young age, I just couldn't believe in the Christian concept of Jesus as someone divine. And no religious person, until I was a man in my twenties—and then in prison —could tell me anything. I had very little respect for most people who represented religion.

It was in his role as a preacher that my father had most contact with the Negroes of Lansing. Believe me when I tell you that those Negroes were in bad shape then. They are still in bad shape—though in a different way. By that I mean that I don't know a town with a higher percentage of complacent and misguided so-called "middle-class" Negroes—the typical status-symbol-oriented, integration-seeking type of Negroes. Just recently, I was standing in a lobby at the United Nations talking with an African ambassador and his wife, when a Negro came up to me and said, "You know me?" I was a little embarrassed because I thought he was someone I should remember. It turned out that he was one of those bragging, self-satisfied, "middle-class" Lansing Negroes. I wasn't ingratiated. He was the type who would never have been associated with Africa, until the fad of having African friends became a status-symbol for "middle-class" Negroes.

Back when I was growing up, the "successful" Lansing Negroes were such as waiters and bootblacks. To be a janitor at some downtown store was to be highly respected. The real "elite," the "big shots," the "voices of the race," were the waiters at the Lansing Country Club and the shoeshine boys at the state capitol. The only Negroes who really had any money were the ones in the numbers racket, or who ran the gambling houses, or who in some other way lived parasitically off the poorest ones, who were the masses. No Negroes were hired then by Lansing's big Oldsmobile plant, or the Reo plant. (Do you remember the Reo? It was manufactured in Lansing, and R. E. Olds, the man after whom it was named, also lived in Lansing. When the war came along, they hired some Negro janitors.) The bulk of the Negroes were either on Welfare, or W.P.A., or they starved.

The day was to come when our family was so poor that we would eat the hole out of a doughnut; but at that time we were much better off than most town Negroes. The reason was we raised much of our own food out there in the country where we were. We were much better off than the town Negroes who would shout, as my father preached, for the pie-in-the-sky and their heaven in the hereafter while the white man had his here on earth.

I knew that the collections my father got for his preaching were mainly what fed and clothed us, and he also did other odd jobs, but still the image of him that made me proudest was his crusading and militant campaigning with the words of Marcus Garvey. As young as I was then, I knew from what I overheard that my father was saying something that made him a "tough" man. I remember an old lady, grinning and saying to my father, "You're scaring these white folks to death!"

One of the reasons I've always felt that my father favored me was that to the best of my remembrance, it was only me that he sometimes took with him to the Garvey U.N.I.A. meetings which he held quietly in different people's homes. There were never more than a few people at any one time—twenty at most. But that was a lot, packed into someone's living room. I noticed how differently they all acted, although sometimes they were the same people who jumped and shouted in church. But in these meetings both they and my father were more intense, more intelligent and down to earth. It made me feel the same way.

I can remember hearing of "Adam driven out of the garden into the caves of Europe," "Africa for the Africans," "Ethiopians, Awake!" And my father would talk about how it would not be much longer before Africa would be completely run by Negroes—"by black men," was the phrase he always used. "No one knows when the hour of Africa's redemption cometh. It is in the wind. It is coming. One day, like a storm, it will be here."

I remember seeing the big, shiny photographs of Marcus Garvey that were passed from hand to hand. My father had a big envelope of them that he always took to these meetings. The pictures showed what seemed to me millions of Negroes thronged in parade behind Garvey riding in a fine car, a big black man dressed in a dazzling uniform with gold braid on it, and he was wearing a thrilling hat with tall plumes. I remember hearing that he had black followers not only in the United States but all around the world, and I remember how the meetings always closed with my father saying, several times, and the people chanting after him, "Up, you mighty race, you can accomplish what you will!"

I have never understood why, after hearing as much as I did of these kinds of things, I somehow never thought, then, of the black people in Africa. My image of Africa, at that time, was of naked savages, cannibals, monkeys and tigers and steaming jungles.

My father would drive in his old black touring car, sometimes taking me, to meeting places all around the Lansing area. I remember one daytime meeting (most were at night) in the town of Owosso, forty miles from Lansing, which the Negroes called "White City." (Owosso's greatest claim to fame is that it is the home town of Thomas E. Dewey.) As in East Lansing, no Negroes were allowed on the streets there after dark—hence the daytime meeting. In point of fact, in those days lots of Michigan towns were like that. Every town had a few "home" Negroes who lived there. Sometimes it would be just one family, as in the nearby county seat, Mason, which had a single Negro family named Lyons. Mr. Lyons had been a famous football star at Mason High School, was highly thought of in Mason, and consequently he now worked around that town in menial jobs.

My mother at this time seemed to be always working—cooking, washing, ironing, cleaning, and fussing over us eight children. And she was usually either arguing with or not speaking to my father. One cause of friction was that she had strong ideas about what she wouldn't eat—and didn't want *us* to eat—including pork and rabbit, both of which my father loved dearly. He was a real Georgia Negro, and he believed in eating plenty of what we in Harlem today call "soul food."

I've said that my mother was the one who whipped me—at least she did whenever she wasn't ashamed to let the neighbors think she was killing me. For if she even acted as though she was about to raise her hand to me, I would open my mouth and let the world know about it. If anybody was passing by out on the road, she would either change her mind or just give me a few licks.

Thinking about it now, I feel definitely that just as my father favored me for being lighter than the other children, my mother gave me more hell for the same reason. She was very light herself but she favored the ones who were darker.

Wilfred, I know, was particularly her angel. I remember that she would tell me to get out of the house and "Let the sun shine on you so you can get some color." She went out of her way never to let me become afflicted with a sense of color-superiority. I am sure that she treated me this way partly because of how she came to be light herself.

I learned early that crying out in protest could accomplish things. My older brothers and sister had started to school when, sometimes, they would come in and ask for a buttered biscuit or something and my mother, impatiently, would tell them no. But I would cry out and make a fuss until I got what I wanted. I remember well how my mother asked me why I couldn't be a nice boy like Wilfred; but I would think to myself that Wilfred, for being so nice and quiet, often stayed hungry. So early in life, I had learned that if you want something, you had better make some noise.

Not only did we have our big garden, but we raised chickens. My father would buy some baby chicks and my mother would raise them. We all loved chicken. That was one dish there was no argument with my father about. One thing in particular that I remember made me feel grateful toward my mother was that one day I went and asked her for my own garden, and she did let me have my own little plot. I loved it and took care of it well. I loved especially to grow peas. I was proud when we had them on our table. I would pull out the grass in my garden by hand when the first little blades came up. I would patrol the rows on my hands and knees for any worms and bugs, and I would kill and bury them. And sometimes when I had everything straight and clean for my things to grow, I would lie down on my back between two rows, and I would gaze up in the blue sky at the clouds moving and think all kinds of things.

At five, I, too, began to go to school, leaving home in the morning along with Wilfred, Hilda, and Philbert. It was the Pleasant Grove School that went from kindergarten through the eighth grade. It was two miles outside the city limits, and I guess there was no problem about our attending because we were the only Negroes in the area. In those days white people in the North usually would "adopt" just a few Negroes; they didn't see them as any threat. The white kids didn't make any great thing about us, either. They called us "nigger" and "darkie" and "Rastus" so much that we thought those were our natural names. But they didn't think of it as an insult; it was just the way they thought about us.

One afternoon in 1931 when Wilfred, Hilda, Philbert, and I came home, my mother and father were having one of their arguments. There had lately been a lot of tension around the house because of Black Legion threats. Anyway, my father had taken one of the rabbits which we were raising, and ordered my mother to cook it. We raised rabbits, but sold them to whites. My father had taken a rabbit from the rabbit pen. He had pulled off the rabbit's head. He was so strong, he needed no knife to behead chickens or rabbits. With one twist of his big black hands he simply twisted off the head and threw the bleeding-necked thing back at my mother's feet.

My mother was crying. She started to skin the rabbit, preparatory to cooking it. But my father was so angry he slammed on out of the front door and started walking up the road toward town.

It was then that my mother had this vision. She had always been a strange woman in this sense, and had always had a strong intuition of things about to happen. And most of her children are the same way, I think. When something is about to happen, I can feel something, sense something. I never have known something to happen that has caught me completely off guard—except once. And that was when, years later, I discovered facts I couldn't believe about a man who, up until that discovery, I would gladly have given my life for.

My father was well up the road when my mother ran screaming out onto the porch. "Early! Early!" She screamed his name. She clutched up her apron in one hand, and ran down across the yard and into the road. My father turned around. He saw her. For some reason, considering how angry he had been when he left, he waved at her. But he kept on going.

She told me later, my mother did, that she had a vision of my father's end. All the rest of the afternoon, she was not herself, crying and nervous and upset. She finished cooking the rabbit and put the whole thing in the warmer part of the black stove. When my father was not back home by our bedtime, my mother hugged and clutched us, and we felt strange, not knowing what to do, because she had never acted like that.

I remember waking up to the sound of my mother's screaming again. When I scrambled out, I saw the police in the living room; they were trying to calm her down. She had snatched on her clothes to go with them. And all of us children who were staring knew without anyone having to say it that something terrible had happened to our father.

My mother was taken by the police to the hospital, and to a room where a sheet was over my father in a bed, and she wouldn't look, she was afraid to look. Probably it was wise that she didn't. My father's skull, on one side, was crushed in, I was told later. Negroes in Lansing have always whispered that he was attacked, and then laid across some tracks for a streetcar to run over him. His body was cut almost in half.

He lived two and a half hours in that condition. Negroes then were stronger than they are now, especially Georgia Negroes. Negroes born in Georgia had to be strong simply to survive.

It was morning when we children at home got the word that he was dead. I was six. I can remember a vague commotion, the house filled up with people crying, saying bitterly that the white Black Legion had finally gotten him. My mother was hysterical. In the bedroom, women were holding smelling salts under her nose. She was still hysterical at the funeral.

I don't have a very clear memory of the funeral, either. Oddly, the main thing I remember is that it wasn't in a church, and that surprised me, since my father was a preacher, and I had been where he preached people's funerals in churches. But his was in a funeral home.

And I remember that during the service a big black fly came down and landed on my father's face, and Wilfred sprang up from his chair and he shooed the fly away, and he came groping back to his chair—there were folding chairs for us to sit on—and the tears were streaming down his face. When we went by the casket, I remember that I thought that it looked as if my father's strong black face had been dusted with flour, and I wished they hadn't put on such a lot of it.

Back in the big four-room house, there were many visitors for another week or so. They were good friends of the family, such as the Lyons from Mason, twelve miles away, and the Walkers, McGuires, Liscoes, the Greens, Randolphs, and the Turners, and others from Lansing, and a lot of people from other towns, whom I had seen at the Garvey meetings.

We children adjusted more easily than our mother did. We couldn't see, as clearly as she did, the trials that lay ahead. As the visitors tapered off, she became very concerned about collecting the two insurance policies that my father had always been proud he carried. He had always said that families should be protected in case of death. One policy apparently paid off without any problem—the smaller one. I don't know the amount of it. I would imagine it was not more than a thousand dollars, and maybe half of that.

But after that money came, and my mother had paid out a lot of it for the funeral and expenses, she began going into town and returning very upset. The company that had issued the bigger policy was balking at paying off. They were claiming that my father had committed suicide. Visitors came again, and there was bitter talk about white people: how could my father bash himself in the head, then get down across the streetcar tracks to be run over?

So there we were. My mother was thirty-four years old now, with no husband, no provider or protector to take care of her eight children. But some kind of a family routine got going again. And for as long as the first insurance money lasted, we did all right.

Wilfred, who was a pretty stable fellow, began to act older than his age. I think he had the sense to see, when the rest of us didn't, what was in the wind for us. He quietly quit school and went to town in search of work. He took any kind of job he could find and he would come home, dog-tired, in the evenings, and give whatever he had made to my mother.

Hilda, who always had been quiet, too, attended to the babies. Philbert and I didn't contribute anything. We just fought all the time—each other at home, and then at school we would team up and fight white kids. Sometimes the fights would be racial in nature, but they might be about anything.

Reginald came under my wing. Since he had grown out of the toddling stage, he and I had become very close. I suppose I enjoyed the fact that he was the little one, under me, who looked up to me.

My mother began to buy on credit. My father had always been very strongly against credit. "Credit is the first step into debt and back into slavery," he had always said. And then she went to work herself. She would go into Lansing and find different jobs—in housework, or sewing—for white people. They didn't realize, usually, that she was a Negro. A lot of white people around there didn't want Negroes in their houses.

She would do fine until in some way or other it got to people who she was, whose widow she was. And then she would be let go. I remember how she used to come home crying, but trying to hide it, because she had lost a job that she needed so much.

Once when one of us—I cannot remember which—had to go for something to where she was working, and the people saw us, and realized she was actually a Negro, she was fired on the spot, and she came home crying, this time not hiding it.

When the state Welfare people began coming to our house, we would come from school sometimes and find them talking with our mother, asking a thousand questions. They acted and looked at her, and at us, and around in our house, in a way that had about it the feeling—at least for me—that we were not people. In their eyesight we were just *things*, that was all.

My mother began to receive two checks—a Welfare check and, I believe, a widow's pension. The checks helped. But they weren't enough, as many of us as there were. When they came, about the first of the month, one always was already owed in full, if not more, to the man at the grocery store. And, after that, the other one didn't last long.

We began to go swiftly downhill. The physical downhill wasn't as quick as the psychological. My mother was, above everything else, a proud woman, and it took its toll on her that she was accepting charity. And her feelings were communicated to us.

She would speak sharply to the man at the grocery store for padding the bill, telling him that she wasn't ignorant, and he didn't like that. She would talk back sharply to the state Welfare people, telling them that she was a grown woman, able to raise her children, that it wasn't necessary for them to keep coming around so much, meddling in our lives. And they didn't like that.

But the monthly Welfare check was their pass. They acted as if they owned us, as if we were their private property. As much as my mother would have liked to, she couldn't keep them out. She would get particularly incensed when they began insisting upon drawing us older children aside, one at a time, out on the porch or somewhere, and asking us questions, or telling us things—against our mother and against each other.

We couldn't understand why, if the state was willing to give us packages of meat, sacks of potatoes and fruit, and cans of all kinds of things, our mother obviously hated to accept. We really couldn't understand. What I later understood was that my mother was making a desperate effort to preserve her pride—and ours.

Pride was just about all we had to preserve, for by 1934, we really began to suffer. This was about the worst depression year, and no one we knew had enough to eat or live on. Some old family friends visited us now and then. At first they brought food. Though it was charity, my mother took it.

Wilfred was working to help. My mother was working, when she could find any kind of job. In Lansing, there was a bakery where, for a nickel, a couple of us children would buy a tall flour sack of day-old bread and cookies, and then walk the two miles back out into the country to our house. Our mother knew, I guess, dozens of ways to cook things with bread and out of bread. Stewed tomatoes with bread, maybe that would be a meal. Something like French toast, if we had any eggs. Bread pudding, sometimes with raisins in it. If we got hold of some hamburger, it came to the table more bread than meat. The cookies that were always in the sack with the bread, we just gobbled down straight.

But there were times when there wasn't even a nickel and we would be so hungry we were dizzy. My mother would boil a big pot of dandelion greens, and we would eat that. I remember that some small-minded neighbor put it out, and children would tease us, that we ate "fried grass." Sometimes, if we were lucky, we would have oatmeal or cornmeal mush three times a day. Or mush in the morning and cornbread at night.

Philbert and I were grown up enough to quit fighting long

enough to take the .22 caliber rifle that had been our father's, and shoot rabbits that some white neighbors up or down the road would buy. I know now that they just did it to help us, because they, like everyone, shot their own rabbits. Sometimes, I remember, Philbert and I would take little Reginald along with us. He wasn't very strong, but he was always so proud to be along. We would trap muskrats out in the little creek in back of our house. And we would lie quiet until unsuspecting bullfrogs appeared, and we would spear them, cut off their legs, and sell them for a nickel a pair to people who lived up and down the road. The whites seemed less restricted in their dietary tastes.

Then, about in late 1934, I would guess, something began to happen. Some kind of psychological deterioration hit our family circle and began to eat away our pride. Perhaps it was the constant tangible evidence that we were destitute. We had known other families who had gone on relief. We had known without anyone in our home ever expressing it that we had felt prouder not to be at the depot where the free food was passed out. And, now, we were among them. At school, the "on relief" finger suddenly was pointed at us, too, and sometimes it was said aloud.

It seemed that everything to eat in our house was stamped Not To Be Sold. All Welfare food bore this stamp to keep the recipients from selling it. It's a wonder we didn't come to think of Not To Be Sold as a brand name.

Sometimes, instead of going home from school, I walked the two miles up the road into Lansing. I began drifting from store to store, hanging around outside where things like apples were displayed in boxes and barrels and baskets, and I would watch my chance and steal me a treat. You know what a treat was to me? Anything!

Or I began to drop in about dinnertime at the home of some family that we knew. I knew that they knew exactly why I was there, but they never embarrassed me by letting on. They would invite me to stay for supper, and I would stuff myself.

Especially, I liked to drop in and visit at the Gohannas' home. They were nice, older people, and great churchgoers. I had watched them lead the jumping and shouting when my father preached. They had, living with them—they were raising him—a nephew whom everyone called "Big Boy," and he and I got along fine. Also living with the Gohannas was old Mrs. Adcock, who went with them to church. She was always trying to help anybody she could, visiting anyone she heard was sick, carrying them something. She was the one who, years later, would tell me something that I remembered a long time: "Malcolm, there's one thing I like about you. You're no good, but you don't try to hide it. You are not a hypocrite."

The more I began to stay away from home and visit people and steal from the stores, the more aggressive I became in my inclinations. I never wanted to wait for anything.

I was growing up fast, physically more so than mentally. As I began to be recognized more around the town, I started to become aware of the peculiar attitude of white people toward me. I sensed that it had to do with my father. It was an adult version of what several white children had said at school, in hints, or sometimes in the open, which really expressed what their parents had said—that the Black Legion or the Klan had killed my father, and the insurance company had pulled a fast one in refusing to pay my mother the policy money.

When I began to get caught stealing now and then, the state Welfare people began to focus on me when they came to our house. I can't remember how I first became aware that they were talking of taking me away. What I first remember along that line was my mother raising a storm about being able to bring up her own children. She would whip me for stealing, and I would try to alarm the neighborhood with my yelling. One thing I have always been proud of is that I never raised my hand against my mother.

In the summertime, at night, in addition to all the other things we did, some of us boys would slip out down the road, or across the pastures, and go "cooning" watermelons. White people always associated watermelons with Negroes, and they sometimes called Negroes "coons" among all the other names, and so stealing watermelons became "cooning" them. If white boys were doing it, it implied that they were only acting like Negroes. Whites have always hidden or justified all of the guilts they could by ridiculing or blaming Negroes.

One Halloween night, I remember that a bunch of us were out tipping over those old country outhouses, and one old farmer—I guess he had tipped over enough in his day—had set a trap for us. Always, you sneak up from behind the outhouse, then you gang together and push it, to tip it over. This farmer had taken his outhouse off the hole, and set it just in *front* of the hole. Well, we came sneaking up in single file, in the darkness, and the two white boys in the lead fell down into the outhouse hole neck deep. They smelled so bad it was all we could stand to get them out, and that finished us all for that Halloween. I had just missed falling in myself. The whites were so used to taking the lead, this time it had really gotten them in the hole.

Thus, in various ways, I learned various things. I picked strawberries, and though I can't recall what I got per crate for picking, I remember that after working hard all one day, I wound up with about a dollar, which was a whole lot of money in those times. I was so hungry, I didn't know what to do. I was walking away toward town with visions of buying something good to eat, and this older white boy I knew, Richard Dixon, came up and asked me if I wanted to match nickels. He had plenty of change for my dollar. In about a half hour, he had all the change back, including my dollar, and instead of going to town to buy something, I went home with nothing, and I was bitter. But that was nothing compared to what I felt when I found out later that he had cheated. There is a way that you can catch and hold the nickel and make it come up the way you want. This was my first lesson about gambling: if you see somebody winning all the time, he isn't gambling, he's cheating. Later on in life, if I were continuously losing in any gambling situation, I would watch very closely. It's like the Negro in America seeing the white man win all the time. He's a professional gambler; he has all the cards and the odds stacked on his side, and he has always dealt to our people from the bottom of the deck.

About this time, my mother began to be visited by some Seventh Day Adventists who had moved into a house not too far down the road from us. They would talk to her for hours at a time, and leave booklets and leaflets and magazines for her to read. She read them, and Wilfred, who had started back to school after we had begun to get the relief food supplies, also read a lot. His head was forever in some book.

Before long, my mother spent much time with the Adventists. It's my belief that what mostly influenced her was that they had even more diet restrictions than she always had taught and practiced with us. Like us, they were against eating rabbit and pork; they followed the Mosaic dietary laws. They ate nothing of the flesh without a split hoof, or that didn't chew a cud. We began to go with my mother to the Adventist meetings that were held further out in the country. For us children, I know that the major attraction was the good food they served. But we listened, too. There were a handful of Negroes, from small towns in the area, but I would say that it was ninety-nine percent white people. The Adventists felt that we were living at the end of time, that the world soon was coming to an end. But they were the friendliest white people I had ever seen. In some ways, though, we children noticed, and, when we were back at home, discussed, that they were different from us—such as the lack of enough seasoning in their food, and the different way that white people smelled.

Meanwhile, the state Welfare people kept after my mother. By now, she didn't make it any secret that she hated them, and didn't want them in her house. But they exerted their right to come, and I have many, many times reflected upon how, talking to us children, they began to plant the seeds of division in our minds. They would ask such things as who was smarter than the other. And they would ask me why I was "so different."

I think they felt that getting children into foster homes was a legitimate part of their function, and the result would be less troublesome, however they went about it.

And when my mother fought them, they went after her—first, through me. I was the first target. I stole; that implied that I wasn't being taken care of by my mother.

All of us where mischievous at some time or another, I more so than any of the rest. Philbert and I kept a battle going. And this was just one of a dozen things that kept building up the pressure on my mother.

I'm not sure just how or when the idea was first dropped by the Welfare workers that our mother was losing her mind.

But I can distinctly remember hearing "crazy" applied to her by them when they learned that the Negro farmer who was in the next house down the road from us had offered to give us some butchered pork—a whole pig, maybe even two of them—and she had refused. We all heard them call my mother "crazy" to her face for refusing good meat. It meant nothing to them even when she explained that we had never eaten pork, that it was against her religion as a Seventh Day Adventist.

They were as vicious as vultures. They had no feelings, understanding, compassion, or respect for my mother. They told us, "She's crazy for refusing food." Right then was when our home, our unity, began to disintegrate. We were having a hard time, and I wasn't helping. But we could have made it, we could have stayed together. As bad as I was, as much trouble and worry as I caused my mother, I loved her.

The state people, we found out, had interviewed the Gohannas family, and the Gohannas' had said that they would take me into their home. My mother threw a fit, though, when she heard that—and the home wreckers took cover for a while.

It was about this time that the large, dark man from Lansing began visiting. I don't remember how or where he and my mother met. It may have been through some mutual friends. I don't remember what the man's profession was. In 1935, in Lansing, Negroes didn't have anything you could call a profession. But the man, big and black, looked something like my father. I can remember his name, but there's no need to mention it. He was a single man, and my mother was a widow only thirty-six years old. The man was independent; naturally she admired that. She was having a hard time disciplining us, and a big man's presence alone would help. And if she had a man to provide, it would send the state people away forever.

We all understood without ever saying much about it. Or at least we had no objection. We took it in stride, even with some amusement among us, that when the man came, our mother would be all dressed up in the best that she had—she still was a good-looking woman—and she would act differently, lighthearted and laughing, as we hadn't seen her act in years.

It went on for about a year, I guess. And then, about 1936, or 1937, the man from Lansing jilted my mother suddenly. He just stopped coming to see her. From what I later understood, he finally backed away from taking on the responsibility of those eight mouths to feed. He was afraid of so many of us. To this day, I can see the trap that Mother was in, saddled with all of us. And I can also understand why he would shun taking on such a tremendous responsibility.

But it was a terrible shock to her. It was the beginning of the end of reality for my mother. When she began to sit around and walk around talking to herself—almost as though she was unaware that we were there—it became increasingly terrifying.

The state people saw her weakening. That was when they began the definite steps to take me away from home. They began to tell me how nice it was going to be at the Gohannas' home, where the Gohannas' and Big Boy and Mrs. Adcock had all said how much they liked me, and would like to have me live with them.

I liked all of them, too. But I didn't want to leave Wilfred. I looked up to and admired my big brother. I didn't want to leave Hilda, who was like my second mother. Or Philbert; even in our fighting, there was a feeling of brotherly union. Or Reginald, especially, who was weak with his hernia condition, and who looked up to me as his big brother who looked out for him, as I looked up to Wilfred. And I had nothing, either, against the babies, Yvonne, Wesley, and Robert.

As my mother talked to herself more and more, she gradually became less responsive to us. And less responsible. The house became less tidy. We began to be more unkempt. And usually, now, Hilda cooked.

We children watched our anchor giving way. It was something terrible that you couldn't get your hands on, yet you couldn't get away from. It was a sensing that something bad was going to happen. We younger ones leaned more and more heavily on the relative strength of Wilfred and Hilda, who were the oldest.

When finally I was sent to the Gohannas' home, at least in a surface way I was glad. I remember that when I left home with the state man, my mother said one thing: "Don't let them feed him any pig."

It was better, in a lot of ways, at the Gohannas'. Big Boy and I shared his room together, and we hit it off nicely. He just wasn't the same as my blood brothers. The Gohannas' were very religious people. Big Boy and I attended church with them. They were sanctified Holy Rollers now. The preachers and congregations jumped even higher and shouted even louder than the Baptists I had known. They sang at the top of their lungs, and swayed back and forth and cried and moaned and beat on tambourines and chanted. It was spooky, with ghosts and spirituals and "ha'nts" seeming to be in the very atmosphere when finally we all came out of the church, going back home.

The Gohannas' and Mrs. Adcock loved to go fishing, and

some Saturdays Big Boy and I would go along. I had changed schools now, to Lansing's West Junior High School. It was right in the heart of the Negro community, and a few white kids were there, but Big Boy didn't mix much with any of our schoolmates, and I didn't either. And when we went fishing, neither he nor I liked the idea of just sitting and waiting for the fish to jerk the cork under the water—or make the tight line quiver, when we fished that way. I figured there should be some smarter way to get the fish—though we never discovered what it might be.

Mr. Gohannas was close cronies with some other men who, some Saturdays, would take me and Big Boy with them hunting rabbits. I had my father's .22 caliber rifle; my mother had said it was all right for me to take it with me. The old men had a set rabbit-hunting strategy that they had always used. Usually when a dog jumps a rabbit, and the rabbit gets away, that rabbit will always somehow instinctively run in a circle and return sooner or later past the very spot where he originally was jumped. Well, the old men would just sit and wait in hiding somewhere for the rabbit to come back, then get their shots at him. I got to thinking about it, and finally I thought of a plan. I would separate from them and Big Boy and I would go to a point where I figured that the rabbit, returning, would have to pass me first.

It worked like magic. I began to get three and four rabbits before they got one. The astonishing thing was that none of the old men ever figured out why. They outdid themselves exclaiming what a sure shot I was. I was about twelve, then. All I had done was to improve on their strategy, and it was the beginning of a very important lesson in life—that anytime you find someone more successful than you are, especially when you're both engaged in the same business—you know they're doing something that you aren't.

I would return home to visit fairly often. Sometimes Big Boy and one or another, or both, of the Gohannas' would go with me—sometimes not. I would be glad when some of them did go, because it made the ordeal easier.

Soon the state people were making plans to take over all of my mother's children. She talked to herself nearly all of the time now, and there was a crowd of new white people entering the picture—always asking questions. They would even visit me at the Gohannas'. They would ask me questions out on the porch, or sitting out in their cars.

Eventually my mother suffered a complete breakdown, and the court orders were finally signed. They took her to the State Mental Hospital at Kalamazoo.

It was seventy-some miles from Lansing, about an hour and a half on the bus. A Judge McClellan in Lansing had authority over me and all of my brothers and sisters. We were "state children," court wards; he had the full say-so over us. A white man in charge of a black man's children! Nothing but legal, modern slavery—however kindly intentioned.

My mother remained in the same hospital at Kalamazoo for about twenty-six years. Later, when I was still growing up in Michigan, I would go to visit her every so often. Nothing that I can imagine could have moved me as deeply as seeing her pitiful state. In 1963, we got my mother out of the hospital, and she now lives there in Lansing with Philbert and his family.

It was so much worse than if it had been a physical sickness, for which a cause might be known, medicine given, a cure effected. Every time I visited her, when finally they led her—a case, a number—back inside from where we had been sitting together, I felt worse.

My last visit, when I knew I would never come to see her again—there—was in 1952. I was twenty-seven. My brother Philbert had told me that on his last visit, she had recognized him somewhat. "In spots," he said.

But she didn't recognize me at all.

She stared at me. She didn't know who I was.

Her mind, when I tried to talk, to reach her, was somewhere else. I asked, "Mama, do you know what day it is?"

She said, staring, "All the people have gone."

I can't describe how I felt. The woman who had brought me into the world, and nursed me, and advised me, and chastised me, and loved me, didn't know me. It was as if I was trying to walk up the side of a hill of feathers. I looked at her. I listened to her "talk." But there was nothing I could do.

I truly believe that if ever a state social agency destroyed a family, it destroyed ours. We wanted and tried to stay together. Our home didn't have to be destroyed. But the Welfare, the courts, and their doctor, gave us the one-two-three punch. And ours was not the only case of this kind.

I knew I wouldn't be back to see my mother again because

it could make me a very vicious and dangerous person—knowing how they had looked at us as numbers and as a case in their book, not as human beings. And knowing that my mother in there was a statistic that didn't have to be, that existed because of a society's failure, hypocrisy, greed, and lack of mercy and compassion. Hence I have no mercy or compassion in me for a society that will crush people, and then penalize them for not being able to stand up under the weight.

I have rarely talked to anyone about my mother, for I believe that I am capable of killing a person, without hesitation, who happened to make the wrong kind of remark about my mother. So I purposely don't make any opening for some fool to step into.

Back then when our family was destroyed, in 1937, Wilfred and Hilda were old enough so that the state let them stay on their own in the big four-room house that my father had built. Philbert was placed with another family in Lansing, a Mrs. Hackett, while Reginald and Wesley went to live with a family called Williams, who were friends of my mother's. And Yvonne and Robert went to live with a West Indian family named McGuire.

Separated though we were, all of us maintained fairly close touch around Lansing—in school and out—whenever we could get together. Despite the artificially created separation and distance between us, we still remained very close in our feelings toward each other.

CHAPTER TWO

MASCOT

On June twenty-seventh of that year, nineteen thirty-seven, Joe Louis knocked out James J. Braddock to become the heavyweight champion of the world. And all the Negroes in Lansing, like Negroes everywhere, went wildly happy with the greatest celebration of race pride our generation had ever known. Every Negro boy old enough to walk wanted to be the next Brown Bomber. My brother Philbert, who had already become a pretty good boxer in school, was no exception. (I was trying to play basketball. I was gangling and tall, but I wasn't very good at it—too awkward.) In the fall of that year, Philbert entered the amateur bouts that were held in Lansing's Prudden Auditorium.

He did well, surviving the increasingly tough eliminations. I would go down to the gym and watch him train. It was very exciting. Perhaps without realizing it I became secretly envious; for one thing, I know I could not help seeing some of my younger brother Reginald's lifelong admiration for me getting siphoned off to Philbert.

People praised Philbert as a natural boxer. I figured that since we belonged to the same family, maybe I would become one, too. So I put myself in the ring. I think I was thirteen when I signed up for my first bout, but my height and raw-boned frame let me get away with claiming that I was sixteen, the minimum age—and my weight of about 128 pounds got me classified as a bantamweight.

They matched me with a white boy, a novice like myself, named Bill Peterson. I'll never forget him. When our turn in the next amateur bouts came up, all of my brothers and sisters were there watching, along with just about everyone else I knew in town. They were there not so much because of me but because of Philbert, who had begun to build up a pretty good following, and they wanted to see how his brother would do.

I walked down the aisle between the people thronging the rows of seats, and climbed in the ring. Bill Peterson and I were introduced, and then the referee called us together and mumbled all of that stuff about fighting fair and breaking clean. Then the bell rang and we came out of our corners. I knew I was scared, but I didn't know, as Bill Peterson told me later on, that he was scared of me, too. He was so scared I was going to hurt him that he knocked me down fifty times if he did once.

He did such a job on my reputation in the Negro neighborhood that I practically went into hiding. A Negro just can't be whipped by somebody white and return with his head up to the neighborhood, especially in those days, when sports and, to a lesser extent show business, were the only fields open to Negroes, and when the ring was the only place a Negro could whip a white man and not be lynched. When I did show my face again, the Negroes I knew rode me so badly I knew I had to do something.

But the worst of my humiliations was my younger brother Reginald's attitude: he simply never mentioned the fight. It was the way he looked at me—and avoided looking at me. So I went back to the gym, and I trained—hard. I beat bags and skipped rope and grunted and sweated all over the place. And finally I signed up to fight Bill Peterson again. This time, the bouts were held in his hometown of Alma, Michigan.

The only thing better about the rematch was that hardly anyone I knew was there to see it; I was particularly grateful for Reginald's absence. The moment the bell rang, I saw a fist, then the canvas coming up, and ten seconds later the referee was saying *"Ten!"* over me. It was probably the shortest "fight" in history. I lay there listening to the full count, but I couldn't move. To tell the truth, I'm not sure I wanted to move.

That white boy was the beginning and the end of my fight career. A lot of times in these later years since I became a Muslim, I've thought back to that fight and reflected that it was Allah's work to stop me: I might have wound up punchy.

Not long after this, I came into a classroom with my hat on. I did it deliberately. The teacher, who was white, ordered me to keep the hat on, and to walk around and around the room until he told me to stop. "That way," he said, "everyone can see you. Meanwhile, we'll go on with class for those who are here to learn something."

I was still walking around when he got up from his desk and turned to the blackboard to write something on it. Everyone in the classroom was looking when, at this moment, I passed behind his desk, snatched up a thumbtack and deposited it in his chair. When he turned to sit back down, I was far from the scene of the crime, circling around the rear of the room. Then he hit the tack, and I heard him holler and caught a glimpse of him spraddling up as I disappeared though the door.

With my deportment record, I wasn't really shocked when the decision came that I had been expelled.

I guess I must have had some vague idea that if I didn't have to go to school, I'd be allowed to stay on with the Gohannas' and wander around town, or maybe get a job if I wanted one for pocket money. But I got rocked on my heels when a state man whom I hadn't seen before came and got me at the Gohannas' and took me down to court.

They told me I was going to go to a reform school. I was still thirteen years old.

But first I was going to the detention home. It was in Mason, Michigan, about twelve miles from Lansing. The detention home was where all the "bad" boys and girls from Ingham County were held, on their way to reform school—waiting for their hearings.

The white state man was a Mr. Maynard Allen. He was nicer to me than most of the state Welfare people had been. He even had consoling words for the Gohannas' and Mrs. Adcock and Big Boy; all of them were crying. But I wasn't. With the few clothes I owned stuffed into a box, we rode in his car to Mason. He talked as he drove along, saying that my school marks showed that if I would just straighten up, I could make something of myself. He said that reform school had the wrong reputation; he talked about what the word "reform" meant—to change and become better. He said the school was really a place where boys like me could have time to see their mistakes and start a new life and become somebody everyone would be proud of. And he told me that the lady in charge of the detention home, a Mrs. Swerlin, and her husband were very good people.

They were good people. Mrs. Swerlin was bigger than her husband, I remember, a big, buxom, robust, laughing woman, and Mr. Swerlin was thin, with black hair, and a black mustache and a red face, quiet and polite, even to me.

They liked me right away, too. Mrs. Swerlin showed me to my room, my own room—the first in my life. It was in one of those huge dormitory-like buildings where kids in detention were kept in those days—and still are in most places. I discovered next, with surprise, that I was allowed to eat with the Swerlins. It was the first time I'd eaten with white people—at least with grown white people—since the Seventh Day Adventist country meetings. It wasn't my own exclusive privilege, of course. Except for the very troublesome boys and girls at the detention home, who were kept locked up—those who had run away and been caught and brought back, or something like that—all of us ate with the Swerlins sitting at the head of the long tables.

They had a white cook-helper, I recall—Lucille Lathrop. (It amazes me how these names come back, from a time I haven't thought about for more than twenty years.) Lucille treated me well, too. Her husband's name was Duane Lathrop. He worked somewhere else, but he stayed there at the detention home on the weekends with Lucille.

I noticed again how white people smelled different from us, and how their food tasted different, not seasoned like Negro cooking. I began to sweep and mop and dust around in the Swerlins' house, as I had done with Big Boy at the Gohannas'.

They all liked my attitude, and it was out of their liking for me that I soon became accepted by them—as a mascot, I know now. They would talk about anything and everything with me standing right there hearing them, the same way people would talk freely in front of a pet canary. They would even talk about me, or about "niggers," as though I wasn't there, as if I wouldn't understand what the word meant. A hundred times a day, they used the word "nigger." I suppose that in their own minds, they meant no harm; in fact they probably meant well. It was the same with the cook, Lucille, and her husband, Duane. I remember one day when Mr. Swerlin, as nice as he was, came in from Lansing, where he had been through the Negro section, and said to Mrs. Swerlin right in front of me, "I just can't see how those niggers can be so happy and be so poor." He talked about how they lived in shacks, but had those big, shining cars out front.

And Mrs. Swerlin said, me standing right there, "Niggers are just that way. . . ." That scene always stayed with me.

It was the same with the other white people. most of them local politicians. when they would come visiting the Swerlins. One of their favorite parlor topics was "niggers." One of them was the judge who was in charge of me in Lansing. He was a close friend of the Swerlins. He would ask about me when he came, and they would call me in. and he would look me up and down, his expression approving, like he was examining a fine colt, or a pedigreed pup. I knew they must have told him how I acted and how I worked.

What I am trying to say is that it just never dawned upon them that I could understand. that I wasn't a pet, but a human being. They didn't give me credit for having the same sensitivity, intellect, and understanding that they would have been ready and willing to recognize in a white boy in my position. But it has historically been the case with white people, in their regard for black people. that even though we might be *with* them, we weren't considered *of* them. Even though they appeared to have opened the door, it was still closed. Thus they never did really see *me*.

This is the sort of kindly condescension which I try to clarify today, to these integration-hungry Negroes, about their "liberal" white friends, these so-called "good white people"—most of them anyway. I don't care how nice one is to you; the thing you must always remember is that almost never does he really see you as he sees himself, as he sees his own kind. He may stand with you through thin, but not thick: when the chips are down, you'll find that as fixed in him as his bone structure is his sometimes subconscious conviction that he's better than anybody black.

But I was no more than vaguely aware of anything like that in my detention-home years. I did my little chores around the house, and everything was fine. And each weekend, they didn't mind my catching a ride over to Lansing for the afternoon or evening. If I wasn't old enough, I sure was big enough by then, and nobody ever questioned my hanging out, even at night, in the streets of the Negro section.

I was growing up to be even bigger than Wilfred and Philbert. who had begun to meet girls at the school dances, and other places, and introduced me to a few. But the ones who seemed to like me, I didn't go for—and vice versa. I couldn't dance a lick, anyway, and I couldn't see squandering my few dimes on girls. So mostly I pleasured myself these Saturday nights by gawking around the Negro bars and restaurants. The jukeboxes were wailing Erskine Hawkins' "Tuxedo Junction," Slim and Slam's "Flatfoot Floogie," things like that. Sometimes, big bands from New York, out touring the one-night stands in the sticks, would play for big dances in Lansing. Everybody with legs would come out to see any performer who bore the magic name "New York." Which is how I first heard Lucky Thompson and Milt Jackson, both of whom I later got to know well in Harlem.

Many youngsters from the detention home, when their dates came up, went off to the reform school. But when mine came up—two or three times—it was always ignored. I saw new youngsters arrive and leave. I was glad and grateful. I knew it was Mrs. Swerlin's doing. I didn't want to leave.

She finally told me one day that I was going to be entered in Mason Junior High School. It was the only school in town. No ward of the detention home had ever gone to school there, at least while still a ward. So I entered their seventh grade. The only other Negroes there were some of the Lyons children, younger than I was, in the lower grades. The Lyons and I, as it happened, were the town's only Negroes. They were, as Negroes, very much respected. Mr. Lyons was a smart, hardworking man, and Mrs. Lyons was a very good woman. She and my mother, I had heard my mother say, were two of the four West Indians in that whole section of Michigan.

Some of the white kids at school, I found, were even friendlier than some of those in Lansing had been. Though some, including the teachers, called me "nigger," it was easy to see that they didn't mean any more harm by it than the Swerlins. As the "nigger" of my class, I was in fact extremely popular—I suppose partly because I was kind of a novelty. I was in demand, I had top priority. But I also benefited from the special prestige of having the seal of approval from that Very Important Woman about the town of Mason, Mrs. Swerlin. Nobody in Mason would have dreamed of getting on the wrong side of her. It became hard for me to get through a school day without someone after me to join this or head up that—the debating society, the Junior High basketball team, or some other extracurricular activity. I never turned them down.

And I hadn't been in the school long when Mrs. Swerlin, knowing I could use spending money of my own, got me a job after school washing the dishes in a local restaurant. My boss there was the father of a white classmate whom I spent a lot of time with. His family lived over the restaurant. It was fine working there. Every Friday night when I got paid, I'd feel at least ten feet tall. I forget how much I made, but it seemed like a lot. It was the first time I'd ever had any money to speak of, all my own, in my whole life. As soon as I could afford it, I bought a green suit and some shoes, and at school I'd buy treats for the others in my class— at least as much as any of them did for me.

English and history were the subjects I liked most. My English teacher, I recall—a Mr. Ostrowski—was always giving advice about how to become something in life. The one thing I didn't like about history class was that the teacher, Mr. Williams, was a great one for "nigger" jokes. One day during my first week at school, I walked into the room and he started singing to the class, as a joke, " 'Way down yonder in the cotton field, some folks say that a nigger won't steal." Very funny. I liked history, but I never thereafter had much liking for Mr. Williams. Later, I remember, we came to the textbook section on Negro history. It was exactly one paragraph long. Mr. Williams laughed through it practically in a single breath, reading aloud how the Negroes had been slaves and then were freed, and how they were usually lazy and dumb and shiftless. He added, I remember, an anthropological footnote on his own, telling us between laughs how Negroes' feet were "so big that when they walk, they don't leave tracks, they leave a hole in the ground."

I'm sorry to say that the subject I most disliked was mathematics. I have thought about it. I think the reason was that mathematics leaves no room for argument. If you made a mistake, that was all there was to it.

Basketball was a big thing in my life, though. I was on the team; we traveled to neighboring towns such as Howell and Charlotte, and wherever I showed my face, the audiences in the gymnasiums "niggered" and "cooned" me to death. Or called me "Rastus." It didn't bother my teammates or my coach at all, and to tell the truth, it bothered me only vaguely. Mine was the same psychology that makes Negroes even today, though it bothers them down inside, keep letting the white man tell them how much "progress" they are making. They've heard it so much they've almost gotten brainwashed into believing it—or at least accepting it.

After the basketball games, there would usually be a school

dance. Whenever our team walked into another school's gym for the dance, with me among them, I could feel the freeze. It would start to ease as they saw that I didn't try to mix, but stuck close to someone on our team, or kept to myself. I think I developed ways to do it without making it obvious. Even at our own school, I could sense it almost as a physical barrier, that despite all the beaming and smiling, the mascot wasn't supposed to dance with any of the white girls.

It was some kind of psychic message—not just from them, but also from within myself. I am proud to be able to say that much for myself, at least. I would just stand around and smile and talk and drink punch and eat sandwiches, and then I would make some excuse and get away early.

They were typical small-town school dances. Sometimes a little white band from Lansing would be brought in to play. But most often, the music was a phonograph set up on a table, with the volume turned up high, and the records scratchy, blaring things like Glenn Miller's "Moonlight Serenade"—his band was riding high then—or the Ink Spots, who were also very popular, singing "If I Didn't Care."

I used to spend a lot of time thinking about a peculiar thing. Many of these Mason white boys, like the ones at the Lansing school—especially if they knew me well, and if we hung out a lot together—would get me off in a corner somewhere and push me to proposition certain white girls, sometimes their own sisters. They would tell me that they'd already had the girls themselves—including their sisters—or that they were trying to and couldn't. Later on, I came to understand what was going on: If they could get the girls into the position of having broken the terrible taboo by slipping off with me somewhere, they would have that hammer over the girls' heads, to make them give in to them.

It seemed that the white boys felt that I, being a Negro, just naturally knew more about "romance," or sex, than they did—that I instinctively knew more about what to do and say with their own girls. I never did tell anybody that I really went for some of the white girls, and some of them went for me, too. They let me know in many ways. But anytime we found ourselves in any close conversations or potentially intimate situations, always there would come up between us some kind of a wall. The girls I really wanted to have were a couple of Negro girls whom Wilfred or Philbert had introduced me to in Lansing. But with these girls, somehow, I lacked the nerve.

From what I heard and saw on the Saturday nights I spent hanging around in the Negro district I knew that race-mixing went on in Lansing. But strangely enough, this didn't have any kind of effect on me. Every Negro in Lansing, I guess, knew how white men would drive along certain streets in the black neighborhoods and pick up Negro streetwalkers who patrolled the area. And, on the other hand, there was a bridge that separated the Negro and Polish neighborhoods, where white women would drive or walk across and pick up Negro men, who would hang around in certain places close to the bridge, waiting for them. Lansing's white women, even in those days, were famous for chasing Negro men. I didn't yet appreciate how most whites accord to the Negro this reputation for prodigious sexual prowess. There in Lansing, I never heard of any trouble about this mixing, from either side. I imagine that everyone simply took it for granted, as I did.

Anyway, from my experience as a little boy at the Lansing school, I had become fairly adept at avoiding the white-girl issue—at least for a couple of years yet.

Then, in the second semester of the seventh grade, I was elected class president. It surprised me even more than other people. But I can see now why the class might have done it. My grades were among the highest in the school. I was unique in my class, like a pink poodle. And I was proud; I'm not going to say I wasn't. In fact, by then, I didn't really have much feeling about being a Negro, because I was trying so hard, in every way I could, to be white. Which is why I am spending much of my life today telling the American black man that he's wasting his time straining to "integrate." I know from personal experience. I tried hard enough.

"Malcolm, we're just so *proud* of you!" Mrs. Swerlin exclaimed when she heard about my election. It was all over the restaurant where I worked. Even the state man, Maynard Allen, who still dropped by to see me once in a while, had a word of praise. He said he never saw anybody prove better exactly what "reform" meant. I really liked him—except for one thing: he now and then would drop something that hinted my mother had let us down somehow.

Fairly often, I would go and visit the Lyons, and they acted as happy as though I was one of their children. And it was the same warm feeling when I went into Lansing to visit my brothers and sisters, and the Gohannas'.

I remember one thing that marred this time for me: the movie "Gone with the Wind." When it played in Mason, I was the only Negro in the theater, and when Butterfly McQueen went into her act, I felt like crawling under the rug.

Every Saturday, just about, I would go into Lansing. I was going on fourteen, now. Wilfred and Hilda still lived out by themselves at the old family home. Hilda kept the house very clean. It was easier than my mother's plight, with eight of us always under foot or running around. Wilfred worked wherever he could, and he still read every book he could get his hands on. Philbert was getting a reputation as one of the better amateur fighters in this part of the state; everyone really expected that he was going to become a professional.

Reginald and I, after my fighting fiasco, had finally gotten back on good terms. It made me feel great to visit him and Wesley over at Mrs. Williams'. I'd offhandedly give them each a couple of dollars to just stick in their pockets, to have something to spend. And little Yvonne and Robert were doing okay, too, over at the home of the West Indian lady, Mrs. McGuire. I'd give them about a quarter apiece; it made me feel good to see how they were coming along.

None of us talked much about our mother. And we never mentioned our father. I guess none of us knew what to say. We didn't want anybody else to mention our mother either, I think. From time to time, though, we would all go over to Kalamazoo to visit her. Most often we older ones went singly, for it was something you didn't want to have to experience with anyone else present, even your brother or sister.

During this period, the visit to my mother that I most remember was toward the end of that seventh-grade year, when our father's grown daughter by his first marriage, Ella, came from Boston to visit us. Wilfred and Hilda had exchanged some letters with Ella, and I, at Hilda's suggestion, had written to her from the Swerlins'. We were all excited and happy when her letter told us that she was coming to Lansing.

I think the major impact of Ella's arrival, at least upon me, was that she was the first really proud black woman I had ever seen in my life. She was plainly proud of her very dark skin. This was unheard of among Negroes in those days, especially in Lansing.

I hadn't been sure just what day she would come. And then one afternoon I got home from school and there she was. She hugged me, stood me away, looked me up and down. A commanding woman, maybe even bigger than Mrs. Swerlin, Ella wasn't just black, but like our father, she was jet black. The way she sat, moved, talked, did everything, bespoke somebody who did and got exactly what she wanted. This was the woman my father had boasted of so often for having brought so many of their family out of Georgia to Boston. She owned some property, he would say, and she was "in society." She had come North with nothing, and she had worked and saved and had invested in property that she built up in value, and then she started sending money to Georgia for another sister, brother, cousin, niece or nephew to come north to Boston. All that I had heard was reflected in Ella's appearance and bearing. I had never been so impressed with anybody. She was in her second marriage; her first husband had been a doctor.

Ella asked all kinds of questions about how I was doing; she had already heard from Wilfred and Hilda about my election as class president. She asked especially about my grades, and I ran and got my report cards. I was then one of the three highest in the class. Ella praised me. I asked her about her brother, Earl, and her sister, Mary. She had the exciting news that Earl was a singer with a band in Boston. He was singing under the name of Jimmy Carleton. Mary was also doing well.

Ella told me about other relatives from that branch of the family. A number of them I'd never heard of; she had helped them up from Georgia. They, in their turn, had helped up others. "We Littles have to stick together," Ella said. It thrilled me to hear her say that, and even more, the way she said it. I had become a mascot; our branch of the family was split to pieces; I had just about forgotten about being a Little in any family sense. She said that different members of the family were working in good jobs, and some even had small businesses going. Most of them were homeowners.

When Ella suggested that all of us Littles in Lansing accompany her on a visit to our mother, we all were grateful. We all felt that if anyone could do anything that could help our mother, that might help her get well and come back, it would be Ella. Anyway, all of us, for the first time together, went with Ella to Kalamazoo.

Our mother was smiling when they brought her out. She

was extremely surprised when she saw Ella. They made a striking contrast, the thin near-white woman and the big black one hugging each other. I don't remember much about the rest of the visit, except that there was a lot of talking, and Ella had everything in hand, and we left with all of us feeling better than we ever had about the circumstances. I know that for the first time, I felt as though I had visited with someone who had some kind of physical illness that had just lingered on.

A few days later, after visiting the homes where each of us were staying, Ella left Lansing and returned to Boston. But before leaving, she told me to write to her regularly. And she had suggested that I might like to spend my summer holiday visiting her in Boston. I jumped at that chance.

That summer of 1940, in Lansing, I caught the Greyhound bus for Boston with my cardboard suitcase, and wearing my green suit. If someone had hung a sign, "HICK," around my neck, I couldn't have looked much more obvious. They didn't have the turnpikes then; the bus stopped at what seemed every corner and cowpatch. From my seat in—you guessed it—the back of the bus, I gawked out of the window at white man's America rolling past for what seemed a month, but must have been only a day and a half.

When we finally arrived, Ella met me at the terminal and took me home. The house was on Waumbeck Street in the Sugar Hill section of Roxbury, the Harlem of Boston. I met Ella's second husband, Frank, who was now a soldier; and her brother Earl, the singer who called himself Jimmy Carleton; and Mary, who was very different from her older sister. It's funny how I seemed to think of Mary as Ella's sister, instead of her being, just as Ella is, my own half-sister. It's probably because Ella and I always were much closer as basic types; we're dominant people, and Mary has always been mild and quiet, almost shy.

Ella was busily involved in dozens of things. She belonged to I don't know how many different clubs; she was a leading light of local so-called "black society." I saw and met a hundred black people there whose big-city talk and ways left my mouth hanging open.

I couldn't have feigned indifference if I had tried to. People talked casually about Chicago, Detroit, New York. I didn't know the world contained as many Negroes as I saw thronging downtown Roxbury at night, especially on Saturdays.

Neon lights, nightclubs, poolhalls, bars, the cars they drove! Restaurants made the streets smell—rich, greasy, down-home black cooking! Jukeboxes blared Erskine Hawkins, Duke Ellington, Cootie Williams, dozens of others. If somebody had told me then that some day I'd know them all personally, I'd have found it hard to believe. The biggest bands, like these, played at the Roseland State Ballroom, on Boston's Massachusetts Avenue—one night for Negroes, the next night for whites.

I saw for the first time occasional black-white couples strolling around arm in arm. And on Sundays, when Ella, Mary, or somebody took me to church, I saw churches for black people such as I had never seen. They were many times finer than the white church I had attended back in Mason, Michigan. There, the white people just sat and worshiped with words; but the Boston Negroes, like all other Negroes I had ever seen at church, threw their souls and bodies wholly into worship.

Two or three times, I wrote letters to Wilfred intended for everybody back in Lansing. I said I'd try to describe it when I got back.

But I found I couldn't.

My restlessness with Mason—and for the first time in my life a restlessness with being around white people—began as soon as I got back home and entered eighth grade.

I continued to think constantly about all that I had seen in Boston, and about the way I had felt there. I know now that it was the sense of being a real part of a mass of my own kind, for the first time.

The white people—classmates, the Swerlins, the people at the restaurant where I worked—noticed the change. They said, "You're acting so strange. You don't seem like yourself, Malcolm. What's the matter?"

I kept close to the top of the class, though. The topmost scholastic standing, I remember, kept shifting between me, a girl named Audrey Slaugh, and a boy named Jimmy Cotton.

It went on that way, as I became increasingly restless and disturbed through the first semester. And then one day, just about when those of us who had passed were about to move up to 8-A, from which we would enter high school the next year, something happened which was to become the first major turning point of my life.

Somehow, I happened to be alone in the classroom with

Mr. Ostrowski, my English teacher. He was a tall, rather reddish white man and he had a thick mustache. I had gotten some of my best marks under him, and he had always made me feel that he liked me. He was, as I have mentioned, a natural-born "advisor," about what you ought to read, to do, or think—about any and everything. We used to make unkind jokes about him: why was he teaching in Mason instead of somewhere else, getting for himself some of the "success in life" that he kept telling us how to get?

I know that he probably meant well in what he happened to advise me that day. I doubt that he meant any harm. It was just in his nature as an American white man. I was one of his top students, one of the school's top students—but all he could see for me was the kind of future "in your place" that almost all white people see for black people.

He told me, "Malcolm, you ought to be thinking about a career. Have you been giving it thought?"

The truth is, I hadn't. I never have figured out why I told him, "Well, yes, sir, I've been thinking I'd like to be a lawyer." Lansing certainly had no Negro lawyers—or doctors either—in those days, to hold up an image I might have aspired to. All I really knew for certain was that a lawyer didn't wash dishes, as I was doing.

Mr. Ostrowski looked surprised, I remember, and leaned back in his chair and clasped his hands behind his head. He kind of half-smiled and said, "Malcolm, one of life's first needs is for us to be realistic. Don't misunderstand me, now. We all here like you, you know that. But you've got to be realistic about being a nigger. A lawyer—that's no realistic goal for a nigger. You need to think about something you *can* be. You're good with your hands—making things. Everybody admires your carpentry shop work. Why don't you plan on carpentry? People like you as a person— you'd get all kinds of work."

The more I thought afterwards about what he said, the more uneasy it made me. It just kept treading around in my mind.

What made it really begin to disturb me was Mr. Ostrowski's advice to others in my class—all of them white. Most of them had told him they were planning to become farmers. But those who wanted to strike out on their own, to try something new, he had encouraged. Some, mostly girls, wanted to be teachers. A few wanted other professions, such as one boy who wanted to become a county agent; another, a veterinarian; and one girl wanted to be a nurse. They all reported that Mr. Ostrowski had encouraged what they had wanted. Yet nearly none of them had earned marks equal to mine.

It was a surprising thing that I had never thought of it that way before, but I realized that whatever I wasn't, I *was* smarter than nearly all of those white kids. But apparently I was still not intelligent enough, in their eyes, to become whatever *I* wanted to be.

It was then that I began to change—inside.

I drew away from white people. I came to class, and I answered when called upon. It became a physical strain simply to sit in Mr. Ostrowski's class.

Where "nigger" had slipped off my back before, wherever I heard it now, I stopped and looked at whoever said it. And they looked surprised that I did.

I quit hearing so much "nigger" and "What's wrong?"—which was the way I wanted it. Nobody, including the teachers, could decide what had come over me. I knew I was being discussed.

In a few more weeks, it was that way, too, at the restaurant where I worked washing dishes, and at the Swerlins'.

One day soon after, Mrs. Swerlin called me into the living room, and there was the state man, Maynard Allen. I knew from their faces that something was about to happen. She told me that none of them could understand why—after I had done so well in school, and on my job, and living with them, and after everyone in Mason had come to like me—I had lately begun to make them all feel that I wasn't happy there anymore.

She said she felt there was no need for me to stay at the detention home any longer, and that arrangements had been made for me to go and live with the Lyons family, who liked me so much.

She stood up and put out her hand. "I guess I've asked you a hundred times, Malcolm—do you want to tell me what's wrong?"

I shook her hand, and said, "Nothing, Mrs. Swerlin." Then I went and got my things, and came back down. At the living room door I saw her wiping her eyes. I felt very bad. I thanked her and went out in front to Mr. Allen, who took me over to the Lyons'.

Mr. and Mrs. Lyons, and their children, during the two

months I lived with them—while finishing eighth grade—also tried to get me to tell them what was wrong. But somehow I couldn't tell them, either.

I went every Saturday to see my brothers and sisters in Lansing, and almost every other day I wrote to Ella in Boston. Not saying why, I told Ella that I wanted to come there and live.

I don't know how she did it, but she arranged for official custody of me to be transferred from Michigan to Massachusetts, and the very week I finished the eighth grade, I again boarded the Greyhound bus for Boston.

I've thought about that time a lot since then. No physical move in my life has been more pivotal or profound in its repercussions.

If I had stayed on in Michigan, I would probably have married one of those Negro girls I knew and liked in Lansing. I might have become one of those state capitol building shoeshine boys, or a Lansing Country Club waiter, or gotten one of the other menial jobs which, in those days, among Lansing Negroes, would have been considered "successful"—or even become a carpenter.

Whatever I have done since then, I have driven myself to become a success at it. I've often thought that if Mr. Ostrowski had encouraged me to become a lawyer, I would today probably be among some city's professional black bourgeoisie, sipping cocktails and palming myself off as a community spokesman for and leader of the suffering black masses, while my primary concern would be to grab a few more crumbs from the groaning board of the two-faced whites with whom they're begging to "integrate."

All praise is due to Allah that I went to Boston when I did. If I hadn't, I'd probably still be a brainwashed black Christian.

CHAPTER THREE

"HOMEBOY"

I looked like Li'l Abner. Mason, Michigan, was written all over me. My kinky, reddish hair was cut hick style, and I didn't even use grease in it. My green suit's coat sleeves stopped above my wrists, the pants legs showed three inches of socks. Just a shade lighter green than the suit was my narrow-collared, three-quarter length Lansing department store topcoat. My appearance was too much for even Ella. But she told me later she had seen countrified members of the Little family come up from Georgia in even worse shape than I was.

Ella had fixed up a nice little upstairs room for me. And she was truly a Georgia Negro woman when she got into the kitchen with her pots and pans. She was the kind of cook who would heap up your plate with such as ham hock, greens, black-eyed peas, fried fish, cabbage, sweet potatoes, grits and gravy, and cornbread. And the more you put away, the better she felt. I worked out at Ella's kitchen table like there was no tomorrow.

Ella still seemed to be as big, black, outspoken and impressive a woman as she had been in Mason and Lansing. Only about two weeks before I arrived, she had split up with her second husband—the soldier, Frank, whom I had met there the previous summer; but she was taking it right in stride. I could see, though I didn't say, how any average man would find it almost impossible to live for very long with a woman whose every instinct was to run everything and everybody she had anything to do with—including me. About my second day there in Roxbury, Ella told me that she didn't want me to start hunting for a job right away, like most newcomer Negroes did. She said that she had told all those she'd brought North to take their time, to walk around, to travel the buses and the subway, and get the feel of Boston, before they tied themselves down working somewhere, because they would never again have the time to really see and get to know anything about the city t'ey were living in. Ella said she'd help me find a job when it was time for me to go to work.

So I went gawking around the neighborhood—the Waumbeck and Humboldt Avenue Hill section of Roxbury, which is something like Harlem's Sugar Hill, where I'd later live. I saw those Roxbury Negroes acting and living differently from any black people I'd ever dreamed of in my life. This was the snooty-black neighborhood; they called themselves the "Four Hundred," and looked down their noses at the Negroes of the black ghetto, or so-called "town" section where Mary, my other half-sister, lived.

What I thought I was seeing there in Roxbury were high-class, educated, important Negroes, living well, working in big jobs and positions. Their quiet homes sat back in their mowed yards. These Negroes walked along the sidewalks looking haughty and dignified, on their way to work, to shop, to visit, to church. I know now, of course, that what I was really seeing was only a big-city version of those "successful" Negro bootblacks and janitors back in Lansing. The only difference was that the ones in Boston had been brainwashed even more thoroughly. They prided themselves on being incomparably more "cultured," "cultivated," "dignified," and better off than their black brethren down in the ghetto, which was no further away than you could throw a rock. Under the pitiful misapprehension that it would make them "better," these Hill Negroes were breaking their backs trying to imitate white people.

Any black family that had been around Boston long enough to own the home they lived in was considered among the Hill elite. It didn't make any difference that they had to rent out rooms to make ends meet. Then the native-born New Englanders among them looked down upon recently migrated Southern home-owners who lived next door, like Ella. And a big percentage of the Hill dwellers were in Ella's category—Southern strivers and scramblers, and West Indian Negroes, whom both the New Englanders and the Southerners called "Black Jews." Usually it was the Southerners and the West Indians who not only managed to own the places where they lived, but also at least one other house which they rented as income property. The snooty New Englanders usually owned less than they.

In those days on the Hill, any who could claim "professional" status—teachers, preachers, practical nurses—also considered themselves superior. Foreign diplomats could have modeled their conduct on the way the Negro postmen, Pullman porters, and dining car waiters of Roxbury acted, striding around as if they were wearing top hats and cutaways.

I'd guess that eight out of ten of the Hill Negroes of Roxbury, despite the impressive-sounding job titles they affected, actually worked as menials and servants. "He's in banking," or "He's in securities." It sounded as though they were discussing a Rockefeller or a Mellon—and not some gray-headed, dignity-posturing bank janitor, or bond-house messenger. "I'm with an old family" was the euphemism used to dignify the professions of white folks' cooks and maids who talked so affectedly among their own kind in Roxbury that you couldn't even understand them. I don't know how many forty- and fifty-year-old errand boys went down the Hill dressed like ambassadors in black suits and white collars, to downtown jobs "in government," "in finance," or "in law." It has never ceased to amaze me how so many Negroes, then and now, could stand the indignity of that kind of self-delusion.

Soon I ranged out of Roxbury and began to explore Boston proper. Historic buildings everywhere I turned, and plaques and markers and statues for famous events and men. One statue in the Boston Commons astonished me: a Negro named Crispus Attucks, who had been the first man to fall in the Boston Massacre. I had never known anything like that.

I roamed everywhere. In one direction, I walked as far as Boston University. Another day, I took my first subway ride. When most of the people got off, I followed. It was Cambridge, and I circled all around in the Harvard University campus. Somewhere, I had already heard of Harvard—though I didn't know much more about it. Nobody that day could have told me I would give an address before the Harvard Law School Forum some twenty years later.

I also did a lot of exploring downtown. Why a city would have *two* big railroad stations—North Station and South

Station—I couldn't understand. At both of the stations, I stood around and watched people arrive and leave. And I did the same thing at the bus station where Ella had met me. My wanderings even led me down along the piers and docks where I read plaques telling about the old sailing ships that used to put into port there.

In a letter to Wilfred, Hilda, Philbert, and Reginald back in Lansing, I told them about all this, and about the winding, narrow, cobblestoned streets, and the houses that jammed up against each other. Downtown Boston, I wrote them, had the biggest stores I'd ever seen, and white people's restaurants and hotels. I made up my mind that I was going to see every movie that came to the fine, air-conditioned theaters.

On Massachusetts Avenue, next door to one of them, the Loew's State Theater, was the huge, exciting Roseland State Ballroom. Big posters out in front advertised the nationally famous bands, white and Negro, that had played there. "COMING NEXT WEEK," when I went by that first time, was Glenn Miller. I remember thinking how nearly the whole evening's music at Mason High School dances had been Glenn Miller's records. What wouldn't that crowd have given, I wondered, to be standing where Glenn Miller's band was actually going to play? I didn't know how familiar with Roseland I was going to become.

Ella began to grow concerned, because even when I had finally had enough sight-seeing, I didn't stick around very much on the Hill. She kept dropping hints that I ought to mingle with the "nice young people my age" who were to be seen in the Townsend Drugstore two blocks from her house, and a couple of other places. But even before I came to Boston, I had always felt and acted toward anyone my age as if they were in the "kid" class, like my younger brother Reginald. They had always looked up to me as if I were considerably older. On weekends back in Lansing where I'd go to get away from the white people in Mason, I'd hung around in the Negro part of town with Wilfred's and Philbert's set. Though all of them were several years older than me, I was bigger, and I actually looked older than most of them.

I didn't want to disappoint or upset Ella, but despite her advice, I began going down into the town ghetto section. That world of grocery stores, walk-up flats, cheap restaurants, poolrooms, bars, storefront churches, and pawnshops seemed to hold a natural lure for me.

Not only was this part of Roxbury much more exciting, but I felt more relaxed among Negroes who were being their natural selves and not putting on airs. Even though I did live on the Hill, my instincts were never—and still aren't—to feel myself any better than any other Negro.

I spent my first month in town with my mouth hanging open. The sharp-dressed young "cats" who hung on the corners and in the poolrooms, bars and restaurants, and who obviously didn't work anywhere, completely entranced me. I couldn't get over marveling at how their hair was straight and shiny like white men's hair; Ella told me this was called a "conk." I had never tasted a sip of liquor, never even smoked a cigarette, and here I saw little black children, ten and twelve years old, shooting craps, playing cards, fighting, getting grown-ups to put a penny or a nickel on their number for them, things like that. And these children threw around swear words I'd never heard before, even, and slang expressions that were just as new to me, such as "stud" and "cat" and "chick" and "cool" and "hip." Every night as I lay in bed I turned these new words over in my mind. It was shocking to me that in town, especially after dark, you'd occasionally see a white girl and a Negro man strolling arm in arm along the sidewalk, and mixed couples drinking in the neon-lighted bars—not slipping off to some dark corner, as in Lansing. I wrote Wilfred and Philbert about that, too.

I wanted to find a job myself, to surprise Ella. One afternoon, something told me to go inside a poolroom whose window I was looking through. I had looked through that window many times. I wasn't yearning to play pool; in fact, I had never held a cue stick. But I was drawn by the sight of the cool-looking "cats" standing around inside, bending over the big, green, felt-topped tables, making bets and shooting the bright-colored balls into the holes. As I stared though the window this particular afternoon, something made me decide to venture inside and talk to a dark, stubby, conk-headed fellow who racked up balls for the pool-players, whom I'd heard called "Shorty." One day he had come outside and seen me standing there and said "Hi, Red," so that made me figure he was friendly.

As inconspicuously as I could, I slipped inside the door and around the side of the poolroom, avoiding people, and on to the back, where Shorty was filling an aluminum can with the powder that pool players dust on their hands. He looked up at me. Later on, Shorty would enjoy teasing me about how with that first glance he knew my whole story. "Man, that cat still *smelled* country!" he'd say, laughing. "Cat's legs was so long and his pants so short his knees showed—an' his head looked like a briar patch!"

But that afternoon Shorty didn't let it show in his face how "country" I appeared when I told him I'd appreciate it if he'd tell me how could somebody gò about getting a job like his.

"If you mean racking up balls," said Shorty, "I don't know of no pool joints around here needing anybody. You mean you just want any slave you can find?" A "slave" meant work, a job.

He asked what kind of work I had done. I told him that I'd washed restaurant dishes in Mason, Michigan. He nearly dropped the powder can. "My homeboy! Man, gimme some skin! I'm from Lansing!"

I never told Shorty—and he never suspected—that he was about ten years older than I. He took us to be about the same age. At first I would have been embarrassed to tell him, later I just never bothered. Shorty had dropped out of first-year high school in Lansing, lived a while with an uncle and aunt in Detroit, and had spent the last six years living with his cousin in Roxbury. But when I mentioned the names of Lansing people and places, he remembered many, and pretty soon we sounded as if we had been raised in the same block. I could sense Shorty's genuine gladness, and I don't have to say how lucky I felt to find a friend as hip as he obviously was.

"Man, this is a swinging town if you dig it," Shorty said. "You're my homeboy—I'm going to school you to the happenings." I stood there and grinned like a fool. "You got to go anywhere now? Well, stick around until I get off."

One thing I liked immediately about Shorty was his frankness. When I told him where I lived, he said what I already knew—that nobody in town could stand the Hill Negroes. But he thought a sister who gave me a "pad," not charging me rent, not even running me out to find "some slave," couldn't be all bad. Shorty's slave in the poolroom, he said, was just to keep ends together while he learned his horn. A couple of years before, he'd hit the numbers and bought a saxophone. "Got it right in there in the closet now, for my lesson tonight." Shorty was taking lessons "with some other studs," and he intended one day to organize his own small band. "There's a lot of bread to be made gigging right around here in Roxbury," Shortly explained to me. "I don't dig joining some big band, one-nighting all over just to say I played with Count or Duke or somebody." I thought that was smart. I wished I had studied a horn; but I never had been exposed to one.

All afternoon, between trips up front to rack balls, Shorty talked to me out of the corner of his mouth: which hustlers —standing around, or playing at this or that table—sold "reefers," or had just come out of prison, or were "second-story men." Shorty told me that he played at least a dollar a day on the numbers. He said as soon as he hit a number, he would use the winnings to organize his band.

I was ashamed to have to admit that I had never played the numbers. "Well, you ain't never had nothing to play with," he said, excusing me, "but you start when you get a slave, and if you hit, you got a stake for something."

He pointed out some gamblers and some pimps. Some of them had white whores, he whispered. "I ain't going to lie— I dig them two-dollar white chicks," Shorty said. "There's a lot of that action around here, nights: you'll see it." I said I already had seen some. "You ever had one?" he asked.

My embarrassment at my inexperience showed. "Hell, man," he said, "don't be ashamed. I had a few before I left Lansing—them Polack chicks that used to come over the bridge. Here, they're mostly Italians and Irish. But it don't matter what kind, they're something else! Ain't no different nowhere—there's nothing they love better than a black stud."

Through the afternoon, Shorty introduced me to players and loungers. "My homeboy," he'd say, "he's looking for a slave if you hear anything." They all said they'd look out.

At seven o'clock, when the night ball-racker came on, Shorty told me he had to hurry to his saxophone lesson. But before he left, he held out to me the six or seven dollars he had collected that day in nickel and dime tips. "You got enough bread, homeboy?"

I was okay, I told him—I had two dollars. But Shorty made me take three more. "Little fattening for your pocket," he said. Before we went out, he opened his saxophone case and showed me the horn. It was gleaming brass against the green velvet, an alto sax. He said, "Keep cool, homeboy, and come back tomorrow. Some of the cats will turn you up a slave."

When I got home, Ella said there had been a telephone call from somebody named Shorty. He had left a message that over at the Roseland State Ballroom, the shoeshine boy was quitting that night, and Shorty had told him to hold the job for me.

"Malcolm, you haven't had any experience shining shoes," Ella said. Her expression and tone of voice told me she wasn't happy about my taking that job. I didn't particularly care, because I was already speechless thinking about being somewhere close to the greatest bands in the world. I didn't even wait to eat any dinner.

The ballroom was all lighted when I got there. A man at the front door was letting in members of Benny Goodman's band. I told him I wanted to see the shoeshine boy, Freddie.

"You're going to be the new one?" he asked. I said I thought I was, and he laughed, "Well, maybe you'll hit the numbers and get a Cadillac, too." He told me that I'd find Freddie upstairs in the men's room on the second floor.

But downstairs before I went up, I stepped over and snatched a glimpse inside the ballroom. I just couldn't believe the size of that waxed floor! At the far end, under the soft, rose-colored lights, was the bandstand with the Benny Goodman musicians moving around, laughing and talking, arranging their horns and stands.

A wiry, brown-skinned, conked fellow upstairs in the men's room greeted me. "You Shorty's homeboy?" I said I was, and he said he was Freddie. "Good old boy," he said. "He called me, he just heard I hit the big number, and he figured right I'd be quitting." I told Freddie what the man at the front door had said about a Cadillac. He laughed and said, "Burns them white cats up when you get yourself something. Yeah, I told them I was going to get me one— just to bug them."

Freddie then said for me to pay close attention, that he was going to be busy and for me to watch but not get in the way, and he'd try to get me ready to take over at the next dance, a couple of nights later.

As Freddie busied himself setting up the shoeshine stand, he told me, "Get here early . . . your shoeshine rags and brushes by this footstand . . . your polish bottles, paste wax, suede brushes over here . . . everything in place, you get rushed, you never need to waste motion. . . ."

While you shined shoes, I learned, you also kept watch on customers inside, leaving the urinals. You darted over and offered a small white hand towel. "A lot of cats who ain't planning to wash their hands, sometimes you can run up with a towel and shame them. Your towels are really your best hustle in here. Cost you a penny apiece to launder —you always get at least a nickel tip."

The shoeshine customers, and any from the inside rest room who took a towel, you whiskbroomed a couple of licks. "A nickel or a dime tip, just give 'em that," Freddie said. "But for two bits, Uncle Tom a little—white cats especially like that. I've had them to come back two, three times a dance."

From down below, the sound of the music had begun floating up. I guess I stood transfixed. "You never seen a big dance?" asked Freddie. "Run on awhile, and watch."

There were a few couples already dancing under the rose-colored lights. But even more exciting to me was the crowd thronging in. The most glamorous-looking white women I'd ever seen—young ones, old ones, white cats buying tickets at the window, sticking big wads of green bills back into their pockets, checking the women's coats, and taking their arms and squiring them inside.

Freddie had some early customers when I got back upstairs. Between the shoeshine stand and thrusting towels to me just as they approached the wash basin, Freddie seemed to be doing four things at once. "Here, you can take over the whiskbroom," he said, "just two or three licks —but let 'em feel it."

When things slowed a little, he said, "You ain't seen nothing tonight. You wait until you see a spooks' dance! Man, our own people carry *on!*" Whenever he had a moment, he kept schooling me. "Shoelaces, this drawer here. You just starting out, I'm going to make these to you as a present. Buy them for a nickel a pair, tell cats they need laces if they do, and charge two bits."

Every Benny Goodman record I'd ever heard in my life, it seemed, was filtering faintly into where we were. During another customer lull, Freddie let me slip back outside again to listen. Peggy Lee was at the mike singing. Beautiful! She had just joined the band and she was from North Dakota and had been singing with a group in Chicago when Mrs. Benny Goodman discovered her, we had heard some customers say. She finished the song and the crowd burst into applause. She was a big hit.

"It knocked me out, too, when I first broke in here," Freddie said, grinning, when I went back in there. "But, look, you ever shined any shoes?" He laughed when I said I hadn't, excepting my own. "Well, let's get to work. I never had neither." Freddie got on the stand and went to work on his own shoes. Brush, liquid polish, brush, paste wax, shine rag, lacquer sole dressing . . . step by step, Freddie showed me what to do.

"But you got to get a whole lot faster. You can't waste time!" Freddie showed me how fast on my own shoes. Then, because business was tapering off, he had time to give me a demonstration of how to make the shine rag pop like a firecracker. "Dig the action?" he asked. He did it in slow motion. I got down and tried it on his shoes. I had the principle of it. "Just got to do it faster," Freddie said. "It's a jive noise, that's all. Cats tip better, they figure you're knocking yourself out!"

By the end of the dance, Freddie had let me shine the shoes of three or four stray drunks he talked into having shines, and I had practiced picking up my speed on Freddie's shoes until they looked like mirrors. After we had helped the janitors to clean up the ballroom after the dance, throwing out all the paper and cigarette butts and empty liquor bottles, Freddie was nice enough to drive me all the way home to Ella's on the Hill in the second-hand maroon Buick he said he was going to trade in on his Cadillac. He talked to me all the way. "I guess it's all right if I tell you, pick up a couple of dozen packs of rubbers, two-bits apiece. You notice some of those cats that came up to me around the end of the dance? Well, when some have new chicks going right, they'll come asking you for rubbers. Charge a dollar, generally you'll get an extra tip."

He looked across at me. "Some hustles you're too new for. Cats will ask you for liquor, some will want reefers. But you don't need to have nothing except rubbers—until you can dig who's a cop.

"You can make ten, twelve dollars a dance for yourself if you work everything right," Freddie said, before I got out of the car in front of Ella's. "The main thing you got to remember is that everything in the world is a hustle. So long, Red."

The next time I ran into Freddie I was downtown one night a few weeks later. He was parked in his pearl gray Cadillac, sharp as a tack, "cooling it."

"Man, you sure schooled me!" I said, and he laughed; he knew what I meant. It hadn't taken me long on the job to find out that Freddie had done less shoeshining and towel-hustling than selling liquor and reefers, and putting white "Johns" in touch with Negro whores. I also learned that white girls always flocked to the Negro dances—some of them whores whose pimps brought them to mix business and pleasure, others who came with their black boy friends, and some who came in alone, for a little freelance lusting among a plentiful availability of enthusiastic Negro men.

At the white dances, of course, nothing black was allowed, and that's where the black whores' pimps soon showed a new shoeshine boy what he could pick up on the side by slipping a phone number or address to the white Johns who came around the end of the dance looking for "black chicks."

Most of Roseland's dances were for whites only, and they had white bands only. But the only white band ever to play there at a Negro dance to my recollection, was Charlie Barnet's. The fact is that very few white bands could have satisfied the Negro dancers. But I know that Charlie Barnet's "Cherokee" and his "Redskin Rhumba" drove those Negroes wild. They'd jampack that ballroom, the black girls in way-out silk and satin dresses and shoes, their hair done in all kinds of styles, the men sharp in their zoot suits and crazy conks, and everybody grinning and greased and gassed.

Some of the bandsmen would come up to the men's room at about eight o'clock and get shoeshines before they went to work. Duke Ellington, Count Basie, Lionel Hampton, Cootie Williams, Jimmie Lunceford were just a few of those who sat in my chair. I would really make my shine rag sound like someone had set off Chinese firecrackers. Duke's great alto saxman, Johnny Hodges—he was Shorty's idol—still owes me for a shoeshine I gave him. He was in the chair one night, having a friendly argument with the drummer, Sonny Greer, who was standing there, when I tapped the bottom of his shoes to signal that I was finished. Hodges stepped down, reaching his hand in his pocket to pay me, but then snatched his hand out to gesture, and just forgot me, and walked away. I wouldn't have dared to bother the man who could do what he did with "Daydream" by asking him for fifteen cents.

I remember that I struck up a little shoeshine-stand conversation with Count Basie's great blues singer, Jimmie Rushing. (He's the one famous for "Sent For You Yesterday, Here You Come Today" and things like that.) Rushing's feet, I remember, were big and funny-shaped—not long like most big feet, but they were round and roly-poly like Rushing. Anyhow, he even introduced me to some of the other Basie cats, like Lester Young, Harry Edison, Buddy Tate, Don Byas, Dickie Wells, and Buck Clayton. They'd walk in the rest room later, by themselves. "Hi, Red." They'd be up there in my chair, and my shine rag was popping to the beat of all of their records, spinning in my head. Musicians never have had, anywhere, a greater shoeshine-boy fan than I was. I would write to Wilfred and Hilda and Philbert and Reginald back in Lansing, trying to describe it.

I never got any decent tips until the middle of the Negro dances, which is when the dancers started feeling good and getting generous. After the white dances, when I helped to clean out the ballroom, we would throw out perhaps a dozen empty liquor bottles. But after the Negro dances, we would have to throw out cartons full of empty fifth bottles—not rotgut, either, but the best brands, and especially Scotch.

During lulls up there in the men's room, sometimes I'd get in five minutes of watching the dancing. The white people danced as though somebody had trained them—left, one, two; right, three, four—the same steps and patterns over and over, as though somebody had wound them up. But those Negroes—nobody in the world could have choreographed the way they did whatever they felt—just grabbing partners, even the white chicks who came to the Negro dances. And my black brethren today may hate me for saying it, but a lot of black girls nearly got run over by some of those Negro males scrambling to get at those white women; you would have thought God had lowered some of his angels. Times have sure changed; if it happened today, those same black girls would go after those Negro men—and the white women, too.

Anyway, some couples were so abandoned—flinging high

and wide, improvising steps and movements—that you couldn't believe it. I could feel the beat in my bones, even though I had never danced.

"Showtime!" people would start hollering about the last hour of the dance. Then a couple of dozen really wild couples would stay on the floor, the girls changing to low white sneakers. The band now would really be blasting, and all the other dancers would form a clapping, shouting circle to watch that wild competition as it began, covering only a quarter or so of the ballroom floor. The band, the spectators and the dancers, would be making the Roseland Ballroom feel like a big rocking ship. The spotlight would be turning, pink, yellow, green, and blue, picking up the couples lindy-hopping as if they had gone mad. *"Wail, man, wail!"* people would be shouting at the band; and it *would* be wailing, until first one and then another couple just ran out of strength and stumbled off toward the crowd, exhausted and soaked with sweat. Sometimes I would be down there standing inside the door jumping up and down in my gray jacket with the whiskbroom in the pocket, and the manager would have to come and shout at me that I had customers upstairs.

The first liquor I drank, my first cigarettes, even my first reefers, I can't specifically remember. But I know they were all mixed together with my first shooting craps, playing cards, and betting my dollar a day on the numbers, as I started hanging out at night with Shorty and his friends. Shorty's jokes about how country I had been made us all laugh. I still was country, I know now, but it all felt so great because I was accepted. All of us would be in somebody's place, usually one of the girls', and we'd be turning on, the reefers making everybody's head light, or the whisky aglow in our middles. Everybody understood that my head had to stay kinky a while longer, to grow long enough for Shorty to conk it for me. One of these nights, I remarked that I had saved about half enough to get a zoot.

"Save?" Shorty couldn't believe it. "Homeboy, you never heard of credit?" He told me he'd call a neighborhood clothing store the first thing in the morning, and that I should be there early.

A salesman, a young Jew, met me when I came in. "You're Shorty's friend?" I said I was; it amazed me—all of Shorty's contacts. The salesman wrote my name on a form, and the Roseland as where I worked, and Ella's address as where

I lived. Shorty's name was put down as recommending me. The salesman said, "Shorty's one of our best customers."

I was measured, and the young salesman picked off a rack a zoot suit that was just wild: sky-blue pants thirty inches in the knee and angle-narrowed down to twelve inches at the bottom, and a long coat that pinched my waist and flared out below my knees.

As a gift, the salesman said, the store would give me a narrow leather belt with my initial "L" on it. Then he said I ought to also buy a hat, and I did—blue, with a feather in the four-inch brim. Then the store gave me another present: a long, thick-linked, gold-plated chain that swung down lower than my coat hem. I was sold forever on credit.

When I modeled the zoot for Ella, she took a long look and said, "Well, I guess it had to happen." I took three of those twenty-five-cent sepia-toned, while-you-wait pictures of myself, posed the way "hipsters" wearing their zoots would "cool it"—hat dangled, knees drawn close together, feet wide apart, both index fingers jabbed toward the floor. The long coat and swinging chain and the Punjab pants were much more dramatic if you stood that way. One picture, I autographed and airmailed to my brothers and sisters in Lansing, to let them see how well I was doing. I gave another one to Ella, and the third to Shorty, who was really moved: I could tell by the way he said, "Thanks, homeboy." It was part of our "hip" code not to show that kind of affection.

Shorty soon decided that my hair was finally long enough to be conked. He had promised to school me in how to beat the barbershops' three- and four-dollar price by making up congolene, and then conking ourselves.

I took the little list of ingredients he had printed out for me, and went to a grocery store, where I got a can of Red Devil lye, two eggs, and two medium-sized white potatoes. Then at a drugstore near the poolroom, I asked for a large jar of vaseline, a large bar of soap, a large-toothed comb and a fine-toothed comb, one of those rubber hoses with a metal spray-head, a rubber apron and a pair of gloves.

"Going to lay on that first conk?" the drugstore man asked me. I proudly told him, grinning, "Right!"

Shorty paid six dollars a week for a room in his cousin's shabby apartment. His cousin wasn't at home. "It's like the pad's mine, he spends so much time with his woman," Shorty said. "Now, you watch me—"

He peeled the potatoes and thin-sliced them into a quart-sized Mason fruit jar, then started stirring them with a wooden spoon as he gradually poured in a little over half the can of lye. "Never use a metal spoon; the lye will turn it black," he told me.

A jelly-like, starchy-looking glop resulted fom the lye and potatoes, and Shorty broke in the two eggs, stirring real fast—his own conk and dark face bent down close. The congolene turned pale-yellowish. "Feel the jar," Shorty said. I cupped my hand against the outside, and snatched it away. "Damn right, it's hot, that's the lye," he said. "So you know it's going to burn when I comb it in—it burns *bad*. But the longer you can stand it, the straighter the hair."

He made me sit down, and he tied the string of the new rubber apron tightly around my neck, and combed up my bush of hair. Then, from the big vaseline jar, he took a handful and massaged it hard all through my hair and into the scalp. He also thickly vaselined my neck, ears and forehead. "When I get to washing out your head, be sure to tell me anywhere you feel any little stinging," Shorty warned me, washing his hands, then pulling on the rubber gloves, and tying on his own rubber apron. "You always got to remember that any congolene left in burns a sore into your head."

The congolene just felt warm when Shorty started combing it in. But then my head caught fire.

I gritted my teeth and tried to pull the sides of the kitchen table together. The comb felt as if it was raking my skin off.

My eyes watered, my nose was running. I couldn't stand it any longer; I bolted to the washbasin. I was cursing Shorty with every name I could think of when he got the spray going and started soap-lathering my head.

He lathered and spray-rinsed, lathered and spray-rinsed, maybe ten or twelve times, each time gradually closing the hot-water faucet, until the rinse was cold, and that helped some.

"You feel any stinging spots?"

"No," I managed to say. My knees were trembling.

"Sit back down, then. I think we got it all out okay."

The flame came back as Shorty, with a thick towel, started drying my head, rubbing hard. *"Easy, man, easy!"* I kept shouting.

"The first time's always worst. You get used to it better

before long. You took it real good, homeboy. You got a good conk."

When Shorty let me stand up and see in the mirror, my air hung down in limp, damp strings. My scalp still flamed, but not as badly; I could bear it. He draped the towel around my shoulders, over my rubber apron, and began again vaselining my hair.

I could feel him combing, straight back, first the big comb, then the fine-tooth one.

Then, he was using a razor, very delicately, on the back of my neck. Then, finally, shaping the sideburns.

My first view in the mirror blotted out the hurting. I'd seen some pretty conks, but when it's the first time, on your *own* head, the transformation, after the lifetime of kinks, is staggering.

The mirror reflected Shorty behind me. We both were grinning and sweating. And on top of my head was this thick, smooth sheen of shining red hair—real red—as straight as any white man's.

How ridiculous I was! Stupid enough to stand there simply lost in admiration of my hair now looking "white," reflected in the mirror in Shorty's room. I vowed that I'd never again be without a conk, and I never was for many years.

This was my first really big step toward self-degradation: when I endured all of that pain, literally burning my flesh to have it look like a white man's hair. I had joined that multitude of Negro men and women in America who are brainwashed into believing that the black people are "inferior"—and white people "superior"—that they will even violate and mutilate their God-created bodies to try to look "pretty" by white standards.

Look around today, in every small town and big city, from two-bit catfish and soda-pop joints into the "integrated" lobby of the Waldorf-Astoria, and you'll see conks on black men. And you'll see black women wearing these green and pink and purple and red and platinum-blonde wigs. They're all more ridiculous than a slapstick comedy. It makes you wonder if the Negro has completely lost his sense of identity, lost touch with himself.

You'll see the conk worn by many, many so-called "upper class" Negroes, and, as much as I hate to say it about them, on all too many Negro entertainers. One of the reasons that I've especially admired some of them, like Lionel

Hampton and Sidney Poitier, among others, is that they have kept their natural hair and fought to the top. I admire any Negro man who has never had himself conked, or who has had the sense to get rid of it—as I finally did.

I don't know which kind of self-defacing conk is the greater shame—the one you'll see on the heads of the black so-called "middle class" and "upper class," who ought to know better, or the one you'll see on the heads of the poorest, most downtrodden, ignorant black men. I mean the legal-minimum-wage ghetto-dwelling kind of Negro, as I was when I got my first one. It's generally among these poor fools that you'll see a black kerchief over the man's head, like Aunt Jemima; he's trying to make his conk last longer, between trips to the barbershop. Only for special occasions is this kerchief-protected conk exposed—to show off how "sharp" and "hip" its owner is. The ironic thing is that I have never heard any woman, white or black, express any admiration for a conk. Of course, any white woman with a black man isn't thinking about his hair. But I don't see how on earth a black woman with any race pride could walk down the street with any black man wearing a conk—the emblem of his shame that he is black.

To my own shame, when I say all of this I'm talking first of all about myself—because you can't show me any Negro who ever conked more faithfully than I did. I'm speaking from personal experience when I say of any black man who conks today, or any white-wigged black woman, that if they gave the brains in their heads just half as much attention as they do their hair, they would be a thousand times better off.

CHAPTER FOUR

LAURA

Shorty would take me to groovy, frantic scenes in different chicks' and cats' pads, where with the lights and juke down mellow, everybody blew gage and juiced back and jumped. I met chicks who were fine as May wine, and cats who were hip to all happenings.

That paragraph is deliberate, of course; it's just to display a bit more of the slang that was used by everyone I respected as "hip" in those days. And in no time at all, I was talking the slang like a lifelong hipster.

Like hundreds of thousands of country-bred Negroes who had come to the Northern black ghetto before me, and have come since, I'd also acquired all the other fashionable ghetto adornments—the zoot suits and conk that I have described, liquor, cigarettes, then reefers—all to erase my embarrassing background. But I still harbored one secret humiliation: I couldn't dance.

I can't remember when it was that I actually learned how —that is to say, I can't recall the specific night or nights. But dancing was the chief action at those "pad parties," so I've no doubt about how and why my initiation into lindy-hopping came about. With alcohol or marijuana lightening my head, and that wild music wailing away on those portable record players, it didn't take long to loosen up the dancing instincts in my African heritage. All I remember is that during some party around this time, when nearly everyone but me was up dancing, some girl grabbed me—they often would take the initiative and grab a partner, for no girl at those parties ever would dream that anyone present couldn't dance—and there I was out on the floor.

I was up in the jostling crowd—and suddenly, unexpectedly, I got the idea. It was as though somebody had clicked on a light. My long-suppressed African instincts broke through, and loose.

Having spent so much time in Mason's white environment, I had always believed and feared that dancing involved a certain order or pattern of specific steps—as dancing *is* done by whites. But here among my own less-inhibited people, I discovered it was simply letting your feet, hands and body spontaneously act out whatever impulses were stirred by the music.

From then on, hardly a party took place without me turning up—inviting myself, if I had to—and lindy-hopping my head off.

I'd always been fast at picking up new things. I made up for lost time now so fast, that soon girls were asking me to dance with them. I worked my partners hard; that's why they liked me so much.

When I was at work, up in the Roseland men's room, I just couldn't keep still. My shine rag popped with the rhythm of those great bands rocking the ballroom. White customers on the shine stand, especially, would laugh to see my feet suddenly break loose on their own and cut a few steps. Whites are correct in thinking that black people are natural dancers. Even little kids are—except for those Negroes today who are so "integrated," as I had been, that their instincts are inhibited. You know those "dancing jigaboo" toys that you wind up? Well, I was like a live one—music just wound me up.

By the next dance for the Boston black folk—I remember that Lionel Hampton was coming in to play—I had given my notice to the Roseland's manager.

When I told Ella why I had quit, she laughed aloud: I told her I couldn't find time to shine shoes and dance, too. She was glad, because she had never liked the idea of my working at that no-prestige job. When I told Shorty, he said he'd known I'd soon outgrow it anyway.

Shorty could dance all right himself but, for his own reasons, he never cared about going to the big dances. He loved just the music-making end of it. He practiced his saxophone and listened to records. It astonished me that Shorty didn't care to go and hear the big bands play. He had his alto sax idol, Johnny Hodges, with Duke Ellington's band, but he said he thought too many young musicians were only carbon-copying the big-band names on the same instrument. Anyway, Shorty was really serious about nothing except his music, and about working for the day when he could start his own little group to gig around Boston.

The morning after I quit Roseland, I was down at the men's clothing store bright and early. The salesman checked and found that I'd missed only one weekly payment: I had "A-1" credit. I told him I'd just quit my job, but he said that didn't make any difference; I could miss paying them for a couple of weeks if I had to; he knew I'd get straight.

This time, I studied carefully everything in my size on the racks. And finally I picked out my second zoot. It was a sharkskin gray, with a big, long coat, and pants ballooning out at the knees and then tapering down to cuffs so narrow that I had to take off my shoes to get them on and off. With the salesman urging me on, I got another shirt, and a hat, and new shoes—the kind that were just comnig into hipster style; dark orange colored, with paper-thin soles and knob style toes. It all added up to seventy or eighty dollars.

It was such a red-letter day that I even went and got my first barbershop conk. This time it didn't hurt so much, just as Shorty had predicted.

That night, I timed myself to hit Roseland as the thick of the crowd was coming in. In the thronging lobby, I saw some of the real Roxbury hipsters eyeing my zoot, and some fine women were giving me that look. I sauntered up to the men's room for a short drink from the pint in my inside coat-pocket. My replacement was there—a scared, narrow-faced, hungry-looking little brown-skinned fellow just in town from Kansas City. And when he recognized me, he couldn't keep down his admiration and wonder. I told him to "keep cool," that he'd soon catch on to the happenings. Everything felt right when I went into the ballroom.

Hamp's band was working, and that big, waxed floor was packed with people lindy-hopping like crazy. I grabbed some girl I'd never seen, and the next thing I knew we were out there lindying away and grinning at each other. It couldn't have been finer.

I'd been lindying previously only in cramped little apartment living rooms, and now I had room to maneuver. Once I really got myself warmed and loosened up, I was snatching partners from among the hundreds of unattached, free-lancing girls along the sidelines—almost every one of them could really dance—and I just about went wild! Hamp's band wailing. I was whirling girls so fast their skirts were snapping. Black girls, brownskins, high yellows, even a couple of the white girls there. Boosting them over my hips, my shoulders, into the air. Though I wasn't quite sixteen then, I was tall and rawboned and looked like twenty-one; I was also pretty strong for my age. Circling, tap-dancing, I was underneath them when they landed—doing the "flapping eagle," "the kangaroo" and the "split."

After that, I never missed a Roseland lindy-hop as long as I stayed in Boston.

The greatest lindy-dancing partner I had, everything considered, was a girl named Laura. I met her at my next job. When I quit shoeshining, Ella was so happy that she went around asking about a job for me—one she would approve. Just two blocks from her house, the Townsend Drug Store was about to replace its soda fountain clerk, a fellow who was leaving to go off to college.

When Ella told me, I didn't like it. She knew I couldn't stand those Hill characters. But speaking my mind right then would have made Ella mad. I didn't want that to happen, so I put on the white jacket and started serving up sodas, sundaes, splits, shakes and all the rest of that fountain stuff to those fancy-acting Negroes.

Every evening when I got off at eight and came home, Ella would keep saying, "I hope you'll meet some of these nice young people your age here in Roxbury." But those penny-ante squares who came in there putting on their millionaires' airs, the young ones and the old ones both, only annoyed me. People like the sleep-in maid for Beacon Hill white folks who used to come in with her "ooh, my deah" manners and order corn plasters in the Jew's drugstore for black folks. Or the hospital cafeteria-line serving woman sitting there on her day off with a cat fur around her neck, telling the proprietor she was a "dietitian"—both of them knowing she was lying. Even the young ones, my age, whom Ella was always talking about. The soda fountain was one of their hang-outs. They soon had me ready to quit, with their accents so phonied up that if you just heard them and didn't see them, you wouldn't even know they were Negroes. I couldn't wait for eight o'clock to get home to eat out of those soul-food pots of Ella's, then get dressed in my zoot and head for some of my friends' places in town, to lindy-hop and get high, or something, for relief from those Hill clowns.

Before long, I didn't see how I was going to be able to stick it out there eight hours a day; and I nearly didn't. I remember one night, I nearly quit because I had hit the numbers for ten cents—the first time I had ever hit—on one of the sideline bets that I'd made in the drugstore. (Yes, there were several runners on the Hill; even dignified Negroes played the numbers.) I won sixty dollars, and Shorty and I had a ball with it. I wished I had hit for the daily dollar that I played with my town man, paying him by the week. I would surely have quit the drugstore. I could have bought a car.

Anyway, Laura lived in a house that was catercorner across the street from the drugstore. After a while, as soon as I saw her coming in, I'd start making up a banana split. She was a real bug for them, and she came in late every afternoon—after school. I imagine I'd been shoving that ice cream dish under her nose for five or six weeks before somehow it began to sink in that she wasn't like the rest. She was certainly the only Hill girl that came in there and acted in any way friendly and natural.

She always had some book with her, and poring over it, she would make a thirty-minute job of that daily dish of banana split. I began to notice the books she read. They were pretty heavy school stuff—Latin, algebra, things like that. Watching her made me reflect that I hadn't read even a newspaper since leaving Mason.

Laura. I heard her name called by a few of the others who came in when she was there. But I could see they didn't know her too well; they said "hello"—that was about the extent of it. She kept to herself, and she never said more than "Thank you" to me. Nice voice. Soft. Quiet. Never another word. But no airs like the others, no black Bostonese. She was just herself.

I liked that. Before too long, I struck up a conversation. Just what subject I got off on I don't remember, but she readily opened up and began talking, and she was very friendly. I found out that she was a high school junior, an honor student. Her parents had split up when she was a baby, and she had been raised by her grandmother, an old lady on a pension, who was very strict and old-fashioned and religious. Laura had just one close friend, a girl who lived over in Cambridge, whom she had gone to school with. They talked on the telephone every day. Her grandmother scarcely ever let her go to the movies, let alone on dates.

But Laura really liked school. She said she wanted to go on to college. She was keen for algebra, and she planned to major in science. Laura never would have dreamed that she was a year older than I was. I gauged that indirectly. She looked up to me as though she felt I had a world of experience more than she did—which really was the truth. But sometimes, when she had gone, I felt let down, thinking how I had turned away from the books I used to like when I was back in Michigan.

I got to the point where I looked forward to her coming in every day after school. I stopped letting her pay, and gave her extra ice cream. And she wasn't hiding the fact that she liked me.

It wasn't long before she had stopped reading her books when she came in, and would just sit and eat and talk with me. And soon she began trying to get me to talk about myself. I was immediately sorry when I dropped that I had once thought about becoming a lawyer. She didn't want to let me rest about that. "Malcolm, there's no reason you can't pick up right where you are and become a lawyer." She had the idea that my sister Ella would help me as much as she could. And if Ella had ever thought that she could help any member of the Little family put up any kind of professional shingle—as a teacher, a foot-doctor, anything—why, you would have had to tie her down to keep her from taking in washing.

I never mentioned Laura to Shorty. I just knew she never would have understood him, or that crowd. And they wouldn't have understood her. She had never been touched, I'm certain she hadn't, or even had a drink, and she wouldn't even have known what a reefer was.

It was a great surprise to me when one afternoon Laura happened to let drop that she "just loved" lindy-hopping. I asked her how had she been able to go out dancing. She said she'd been introduced to lindy-hopping at a party given by the parents of some Negro friend just accepted by Harvard.

It was just about time to start closing down the soda fountain, and I said that Count Basie was playing the Rose-land that weekend, and would she like to go?

Laura's eyes got wide. I thought I'd have to catch her, she was so excited. She said she'd never been there, she'd heard so much about it, she'd imagined what it was like, she'd just give anything—but her grandma would have a fit.

So I said maybe some other time.

But the afternoon before the dance, Laura came in full of excitement. She whispered that she'd never lied to her grandma before, but she had told her she had to attend some school function that evening. If I'd get her home early, she'd meet me—if I'd still take her.

I told her we'd have to go by for me to change clothes at the house. She hesitated, but said okay. Before we left, I telephoned Ella to say I'd be bringing a girl by on the way to the dance. Though I'd never before done anything like it, Ella covered up her surprise.

I laughed to myself a long time afterward about how Ella's mouth flew open when we showed up at the front door—me and a well-bred Hill girl. Laura, when I introduced her, was warm and sincere. And Ella, you would have thought she was closing in on her third husband.

While they sat and talked downstairs, I dressed upstairs in my room. I remember changing my mind about the wild sharkskin gray zoot I had planned to wear, and deciding instead to put on the first one I'd gotten, the blue zoot. I knew I should wear the most conservative thing I had.

They were like old friends when I came back down. Ella had even made tea. Ella's hawk-eye just about raked my zoot right off my back. But I'm sure she was grateful that I'd at least put on the blue one. Knowing Ella, I knew that she had already extracted Laura's entire life story—and all but had the wedding bells around my neck. I grinned all the way to the Roseland in the taxi, because I had showed Ella I could hang out with Hill girls if I wanted to.

Laura's eyes were so big. She said almost none of her acquaintances knew her grandmother, who never went anywhere but to church, so there wasn't much danger of it getting back to her. The only person she had told was her girl friend, who had shared her excitement.

Then, suddenly, we were in the Roseland's jostling lobby. And I was getting waves and smiles and greetings. They shouted "My man!" and "Hey, Red!" and I answered "Daddy-o."

She and I never before had danced together, but that

certainly was no problem. Any two people who can lindy at all can lindy together. We just started out there on the floor among a lot of other couples.

It was maybe halfway in the number before I became aware of how she danced.

If you've ever lindy-hopped, you'll know what I'm talking about. With most girls, you kind of work opposite them, circling, side-stepping, leading. Whichever arm you lead with is half-bent out there, your hands are giving that little pull, that little push, touching her waist, her shoulders, her arms. She's in, out, turning, whirling, wherever you guide her. With poor partners, you feel their weight. They're slow and heavy. But with really good partners, all you need is just the push-pull suggestion. They guide nearly effortlessly, even off the floor and into the air, and your little solo maneuver is done on the floor before they land, when they join you, whirling, right in step.

I'd danced with plenty of good partners. But what I became suddenly aware of with Laura was that I'd never before felt so little weight! I'd nearly just *think* a maneuver, and she'd respond.

Anyway, as she danced up, down, under my arm, flinging out, while I felt her out and examined her style, I glimpsed her footwork. I can close my eyes right now and see it, like some blurring ballet—beautiful! And her lightness, like a shadow! My perfect partner, if somebody had asked me, would have been one who handled as lightly as Laura and who would have the strength to last through a long, tough showtime. But I knew that Laura wouldn't begin to be that strong.

In Harlem, years later, a friend of mine called "Sammy The Pimp" taught me something I wish I had known then to look for in Laura's face. It was what Sammy declared was his infallible clue for determining the "unconscious, true personality" of women. Considering all the women he had picked out of crowds and turned into prostitutes, Sammy qualified as an expert. Anyway, he swore that if a woman, any woman, gets really carried away while dancing, what she truly is—at least potentially—will surface and show on her face.

I'm not suggesting that a lady-of-easy-virtue look danced to the surface in Laura—although life did deal her cruel blows, starting with her meeting me. All I am saying is that it may be that if I had been equipped with Sammy's ability, I might have spotted in Laura then some of the subsurface potential, destined to become real, that would have shocked her grandma.

A third of the way or so through the evening the main vocalizing and instrumental stylings would come—and then showtime, when only the greatest lindy-hoppers would stay on the floor, to try and eliminate each other. All the other dancers would form a big "U" with the band at the open end.

The girls who intended to compete would slip over to the sidelines and change from high heels into low white sneakers. In competition, they never could survive in heels. And always among them were four or five unattached girls who would run around trying to hook up with some guy they knew could really lindy.

Now Count Basie turned on the showtime blast, and the other dancers moved off the floor, shifting for good watching positions, and began their hollering for their favorites. "All right now, Red!" they shouted to me, "Go get 'em, Red." And then a free-lancing lindy-girl I'd danced with before, Mamie Bevels, a waitress and a wild dancer ran up to me, with Laura standing right there. I wasn't sure what to do. But Laura started backing away toward the crowd, still looking at me.

The Count's band was wailing. I grabbed Mamie and we started to work. She was a big, rough, strong gal, and she lindied like a bucking horse. I remember the very night that she became known as one of the showtime favorites there at the Roseland. A band was screaming when she kicked off her shoes and got barefooted, and shouted, and shook herself as if she were in some African jungle frenzy, and then she let loose with some dancing, shouting with every step, until the guy that was out there with her nearly had to fight her to control her. The crowd loved any way-out lindying style that made a colorful show like that. It was how Mamie had become known.

Anyway, I started driving her like a horse, the way she liked. When we came off the floor after the first number, we both were wringing wet with sweat, and people were shouting and pounding our backs.

I remember leaving early with Laura, to get her home

in time. She was very quiet. And she didn't have much to say for the next week or so when she came into the drugstore. Even then, I had learned enough about women to know not to pressure them when they're thinking something out; they'll tell you when they're ready.

Every time I saw Ella, even brushing my teeth in the morning, she turned on the third degree. When was I seeing Laura again? Was I going to bring her by again? "What a nice girl she is!" Ella had picked her out for me.

But in that kind of way, I thought hardly anything about the girl. When it came to personal matters, my mind was strictly on getting "sharp" in my zoot as soon as I left work, and racing downtown to hang out with Shorty and the other guys—and with the girls they knew—a million miles away from the stuck-up Hill.

I wasn't even thinking about Laura when she came up to me in the drugstore and asked me to take her to the next Negro dance at the Roseland. Duke Ellington was going to play, and she was beside herself with excitement. I had no way to know what was going to happen.

She asked me to pick her up at her house this time. I didn't want any contact with the old grandma she had described, but I went. Grandma answered the door—an old-fashioned, wrinkled, black woman, with fuzzy gray hair. She just opened the door enough for me to get in, not even saying as much as "Come in, dog." I've faced armed detectives and gangsters less hostile than she was.

I remember the musty living room, full of those old Christ pictures, prayers woven into tapestries, statuettes of the crucifixion, other religious objects on the mantel, shelves, table tops, walls, everywhere.

Since the old lady wasn't speaking to me, I didn't speak to her, either. I completely sympathize with her now, of course. What could she have thought of me in my zoot and conk and orange shoes? She'd have done us all a favor if she had run screaming for the police. If something looked as I did then ever came knocking at my door today, asking to see one of my four daughters, I know I would explode.

When Laura rushed into the room, jerking on her coat, I could see that she was upset and angry and embarrassed. And in the taxi, she started crying. She had hated herself for lying before; she had decided to tell the truth about where she was going, and there had been a screaming battle with grandma. Laura had told the old lady that she was going to start going out when and where she wanted to, or she would quit school and get a job and move out on her own—and her grandma had pitched a fit. Laura just walked out.

When we got to the Roseland, we danced the early part of the evening with each other and with different partners. And finally the Duke kicked off showtime.

I knew, and Laura knew, that she couldn't match the veteran showtime girls, but she told me that she wanted to compete. And the next thing I knew, she was among those girls over on the sidelines changing into sneakers. I shook my head when a couple of the free-lancing girls ran up to me.

As always, the crowd clapped and shouted in time with the blasting band. "Go, Red, go!" Partly it was my reputation, and partly Laura's ballet style of dancing that helped to turn the spotlight—and the crowd's attention—to us. They never had seen the feather-lightness that she gave to lindying, a completely fresh style—and they were connoisseurs of styles. I turned up the steam, Laura's feet were flying; I had her in the air, down, sideways, around; backwards, up again, down, whirling. . . .

The spotlight was working mostly just us. I caught glimpses of the four or five other couples, the girls jungle-strong, animal-like, bucking and charging. But little Laura inspired me to drive to new heights. Her hair was all over her face, it was running sweat, and I couldn't believe her strength. The crowd was shouting and stomping. A new favorite was being discovered; there was a wall of noise around us. I felt her weakening, she was lindying like a fighter out on her feet, and we stumbled off to the sidelines. The band was still blasting. I had to half-carry her; she was gasping for air. Some of the men in the band applauded. And even Duke Ellington half raised up from his piano stool and bowed.

If a showtime crowd liked your performance, when you came off you were mobbed, mauled, grasped, and pummeled like the team that's just taken the series. One bunch of the crowd swarmed Laura; they had her clear up off her feet. And I was being pounded on the back . . . when I caught this fine blonde's eyes. . . . This one I'd never seen among the white girls who came to the Roseland black dances. She was eyeing me levelly.

Now at that time, in Roxbury, in any black ghetto in

America, to have a white woman who wasn't a known, common whore was—for the average black man, at least— a status symbol of the first order. And this one, standing there, eyeing me, was almost too fine to believe. Shoulder-length hair, well built, and her clothes had cost somebody plenty.

It's shameful to admit, but I had just about forgotten Laura when she got loose from the mob and rushed up, big-eyed—and stopped. I guess she saw what there was to see in that girl's face—and mine—as we moved out to dance.

I'm going to call her Sophia.

She didn't dance well, at least not by Negro standards. But who cared? I could feel the staring eyes of other couples around us. We talked. I told her she was a good dancer, and asked her where she'd learned. I was trying to find out why she was there. Most white women came to the black dances for reasons I know, but you seldom saw her kind around there.

She had vague answers for everything. But in the space of that dance, we agreed that I would get Laura home early and rush back in a taxicab. And then she asked if I'd like to go for a drive later. I felt very lucky.

Laura was home and I was back at the Roseland in an hour flat. Sophia was waiting outside.

About five blocks down, she had a low convertible. She knew where she was going. Beyond Boston, she pulled off into a side road, and then off that into a deserted lane. And turned off everything but the radio.

For the next several months, Sophia would pick me up downtown, and I'd take her to dances, and to the bars around Roxbury. We drove all over. Sometimes it would be nearly daylight when she let me out in front of Ella's.

I paraded her. The Negro men loved her. And she just seemed to love all Negroes. Two or three nights a week, we would go out together. Sophia admitted that she also had dates with white fellows, "just for the looks of things," she said. She swore that a white man couldn't interest her.

I wondered for a long time, but I never did find out why she approached me so boldly that very first night. I always thought it was because of some earlier experience with another Negro, but I never asked, and she never said. Never ask a woman about other men. Either she'll tell you a lie, and you still won't know, or if she tells you the truth, you might not have wanted to hear it in the first place.

Anyway, she seemed entranced with me. I began to see less of Shorty. When I did see him and the gang, he would gibe, "Man, I had to comb the burrs out of my homeboy's head, and now he's got a Beacon Hill chick." But truly, because it was known that Shorty had "schooled" me, my having Sophia gave Shorty status. When I introduced her to him, she hugged him like a sister, and it just about finished Shorty off. His best had been white prostitutes and a few of those poor specimens that worked around in the mills and had "discovered" Negroes.

It was when I began to be seen around town with Sophia that I really began to mature into some real status in black downtown Roxbury. Up to then I had been just another among all of the conked and zooted youngsters. But now, with the best-looking white woman who ever walked in those bars and clubs, and with her giving me the money I spent, too, even the big, important black hustlers and "smart boys" —the club managers, name gamblers, numbers bankers, and others—were clapping me on the back, setting us up to drinks at special tables, and calling me "Red." Of course I knew their reason like I knew my own name: they wanted to steal my fine white woman away from me.

In the ghetto, as in suburbia, its the same status struggle to stand out in some envied way from the rest. At sixteen, I didn't have the money to buy a Cadillac, but she had her own fine "rubber," as we called a car in those days. And I had her, which was even better.

Laura never again came to the drugstore as long as I continued to work there. The next time I saw her, she was a wreck of a woman, notorious around black Roxbury, in and out of jail. She had finished high school, but by then she was already going the wrong way. Defying her grandmother, she had started going out late and drinking liquor. This led to dope, and that to selling herself to men. Learning to hate the men who bought her, she also became a Lesbian. One of the shames I have carried for years is that I blame myself for all of this. To have treated her as I did for a white woman made the blow doubly heavy. The only excuse I can offer is that like so many of my black brothers today, I was just deaf, dumb, and blind.

In any case, it wasn't long after I met Sophia that Ella found out about it, and watching from the windows one early morning, saw me getting out of Sophia's car. Not surprisingly, Ella began treating me like a viper.

About then, Shorty's cousin finally moved in with the woman he was so crazy about, and Sophia financed me to take over half of the apartment with Shorty—and I quit the drugstore and soon found a new job.

I became a bus boy at the Parker House in Boston. I wore a starched white jacket out in the dining room, where the waiters would put the customers' dirty plates and silver on big aluminum trays which I would take back to the kitchen's dishwashers.

A few weeks later, one Sunday morning, I ran in to work expecting to get fired, I was so late. But the whole kitchen crew was too excited and upset to notice: Japanese planes had just bombed a place called Pearl Harbor.

CHAPTER FIVE

HARLEMITE

"Get'cha goood haaaaam an' cheeeeese . . . sandwiches! Coffee! Candy! Cake! Ice Cream!" Rocking along the tracks every other day for four hours between Boston and New York in the coach aisles of the New York, New Haven & Hartford's "Yankee Clipper."

Old Man Rountree, an elderly Pullman porter and a friend of Ella's, had recommended the railroad job for me. He had told her the war was snatching away railroad men so fast that if I could pass for twenty-one, he could get me on.

Ella wanted to get me out of Boston and away from Sophia. She would have loved nothing better than to have seen me like one of those Negroes who were already thronging Roxbury in the Army's khaki and thick shoes—home on leave from boot camp. But my age of sixteen stopped that.

I went along with the railroad job for my own reasons. For a long time I'd wanted to visit New York City. Since I had been in Roxbury, I had heard a lot about "the Big Apple," as it was called by the well-traveled musicians, merchant mariners, salesmen, chauffeurs for white families, and various kinds of hustlers I ran into. Even as far back as Lansing, I had been hearing about how fabulous New York was, and especially Harlem. In fact, my father had described Harlem with pride, and showed us pictures of the huge parades by the Harlem followers of Marcus Garvey. And every time Joe Louis won a fight against a white opponent, big front-page pictures in the Negro newspapers such as the *Chicago Defender*, the *Pittsburgh Courier* and the *Afro-American* showed a sea of Harlem Negroes cheering and waving and the Brown Bomber waving back at them from the balcony of Harlem's Theresa Hotel. Everything I'd ever heard about New York City was exciting—things like Broadway's bright lights and the Savoy Ballroom and Apollo Theater in Harlem, where great bands played and famous songs and dance steps and Negro stars originated.

But you couldn't just pick up and go to visit New York from Lansing, or Boston, or anywhere else—not without money. So I'd never really given too much thought to getting to New York until the free way to travel there came in the form of Ella's talk with old man Rountree, who was a member of Ella's church.

What Ella didn't know, of course, was that I would continue to see Sophia. Sophia could get away only a few nights a week. She said, when I told her about the train job, that she'd get away every night I got back into Boston, and this would mean every other night, if I got the run I wanted. Sophia didn't want me to leave at all, but she believed I was draft age already, and thought the train job would keep me out of the Army.

Shorty thought it would be a great chance for me. He was worried sick himself about the draft call that he knew was soon to come. Like hundreds of the black ghetto's young men, he was taking some stuff that, it was said, would make your heart sound defective to the draft board's doctors.

Shorty felt about the war the same way I and most ghetto Negroes did: "Whitey owns everything. He wants us to go and bleed for him? Let him fight."

Anyway, at the railroad personnel hiring office down on Dover Street, a tired-acting old white clerk got down to the crucial point when I came to sign up. "Age, Little?" When I told him "Twenty-one," he never lifted his eyes from his pencil. I knew I had the job.

I was promised the first available Boston-to-New York fourth-cook job. But for a while, I worked there in the Dover Street Yard, helping to load food requisitions onto the trains. Fourth cook, I knew, was just a glorified name for dishwasher, but it wouldn't be my first time, and just as long as I traveled where I wanted, it didn't make any difference to me. Temporarily though, they put me on "The Colonial" that ran to Washington, D.C.

The kitchen crew, headed by a West Indian chef named Duke Vaughn, worked with almost unbelievable efficiency in the cramped quarters. Against the sound of the train clacking along, the waiters were jabbering the customers' orders, the cooks operated like machines, and five hundred miles of dirty pots and dishes and silverware rattled back to me. Then, on the overnight layover, I naturally went sightseeing in downtown Washington. I was astounded to find in the nation's capital, just a few blocks from Capitol Hill, thousands of Negroes living worse than any I'd ever seen in the poorest sections of Roxbury; in dirt-floor shacks along unspeakably filthy lanes with names like Pig Alley and Goat Alley. I had seen a lot, but never such a dense concentration of stumble-bums, pushers, hookers, public crap-shooters, even little kids running around at midnight begging for pennies, half-naked and barefooted. Some of the railroad cooks and waiters had told me to be very careful, because muggings, knifings and robberies went on every night among these Negroes . . . just a few blocks from the White House.

But I saw other Negroes better off; they lived in blocks of rundown red brick houses. The old "Colonial" railroaders had told me about Washington having a lot of "middle-class" Negroes with Howard University degrees, who were working as laborers, janitors, porters, guards, taxi-drivers, and the like. For the Negro in Washington, mail-carrying was a prestige job.

After a few of the Washington runs, I snatched the chance when one day personnel said I could temporarily replace a sandwich man on the "Yankee Clipper" to New York. I was into my zoot suit before the first passenger got off.

The cooks took me up to Harlem in a cab. White New York passed by like a movie set, then abruptly, when we left Central Park at the upper end, at 110th Street, the people's complexion began to change.

Busy Seventh Avenue ran along in front of a place called Small's Paradise. The crew had told me before we left Boston that it was their favorite night spot in Harlem, and not to miss it. No Negro place of business had ever impressed me so much. Around the big, luxurious-looking, circular bar were thirty or forty Negroes, mostly men, drinking and talking.

I was hit first, I think, by their conservative clothes and manners. Wherever I'd seen as many as ten Boston Negroes —let alone Lansing Negroes—drinking, there had been a big noise. But with all of these Harlemites drinking and talking, there was just a low murmur of sound. Customers came and went. The bartenders knew what most of them drank and automatically fixed it. A bottle was set on the bar before some.

Every Negro I'd ever known had made a point of flashing whatever money he had. But these Harlem Negroes quietly laid a bill on the bar. They drank. They nonchalantly nodded to the bartender to pour a drink, for some friend, while the bartenders, smooth as any of the customers, kept making change from the money on the bar.

Their manners seemed natural; they were not putting on any airs. I was awed. Within the first five minutes in Small's, I had left Boston and Roxbury forever.

I didn't yet know that these weren't what you might call everyday or average Harlem Negroes. Later on, even later that night, I would find out that Harlem contained hundreds of thousands of my people who were just as loud and gaudy as Negroes anywhere else. But these were the cream of the older, more mature operators in Harlem. The day's "numbers" business was done. The night's gambling and other forms of hustling hadn't yet begun. The usual night-life crowd, who worked on regular jobs all day, were at home eating their dinners. The hustlers at this time were in the daily six o'clock congregation, their favorite bars all over Harlem largely to themselves.

From Small's, I taxied over to the Apollo Theater. (I remember so well that Jay McShann's band was playing, because his vocalist was later my close friend, Walter Brown, the one who used to sing "Hooty Hooty Blues.") From there, on the other side of 125th Street, at Seventh Avenue, I saw the big, tall, gray Theresa Hotel. It was the finest in New York City where Negroes could then stay, years before the downtown hotels would accept the black man. (The Theresa is now best known as the place where Fidel Castro went during his U.N. visit, and achieved a psychological coup over the U.S. State Department when it confined him to Manhattan, never dreaming that he'd stay uptown in Harlem and make such an impression among the Negroes.)

The Braddock Hotel was just up 126th Street, near the Apollo's backstage entrance. I knew its bar was famous as a Negro celebrity hang-out. I walked in and saw, along that jam-packed bar, such famous stars as Dizzy Gillespie, Billy Eckstine, Billie Holiday, Ella Fitzgerald, and Dinah Washington.

As Dinah Washington was leaving with some friends, I overheard someone say she was on her way to the Savoy Ballroom where Lionel Hampton was appearing that night—

she was then Hamp's vocalist. The ballroom made the Roseland in Boston look small and shabby by comparison. And the lindy-hopping there matched the size and elegance of the place. Hampton's hard-driving outfit kept a red-hot pace with his greats such as Arnett Cobb, Illinois Jacquet, Dexter Gordon, Alvin Hayse, Joe Newman, and George Jenkins. I went a couple of rounds on the floor with girls from the sidelines.

Probably a third of the sideline booths were filled with white people, mostly just watching the Negroes dance; but some of them danced together, and, as in Boston, a few white women were with Negroes. The people kept shouting for Hamp's "Flyin' Home," and finally he did it. (I could believe the story I'd heard in Boston about this number—that once in the Apollo, Hamp's "Flyin' Home" had made some reefer-smoking Negro in the second balcony believe he could fly, so he tried—and jumped—and broke his leg, an event later immortalized in song when Earl Hines wrote a hit tune called "Second Balcony Jump.") I had never seen such fever-heat dancing. After a couple of slow numbers cooled the place off, they brought on Dinah Washington. When she did her "Salty Papa Blues," those people just about tore the Savoy roof off. (Poor Dinah's funeral was held not long ago in Chicago. I read that over 20,000 people viewed her body, and I should have been there myself. Poor Dinah! We became great friends, back in those days.)

But this night of my first visit was Kitchen Mechanics' Night at the Savoy, the traditional Thursday night off for domestics. I'd say there were twice as many women as men in there, not only kitchen workers and maids, but also war wives and defense-worker women, lonely and looking. Out in the street, when I left the ballroom, I heard a prostitute cursing bitterly that the professionals couldn't do any business because of the amateurs.

Up and down along and between Lenox and Seventh and Eighth Avenues, Harlem was like some technicolor bazaar. Hundreds of Negro soldiers and sailors, gawking and young like me, passed by. Harlem by now was officially off limits to white servicemen. There had already been some muggings and robberies, and several white servicemen had been found murdered. The police were also trying to discourage white civilians from coming uptown, but those who wanted to still did. Every man without a woman on his arm was being "worked" by the prostitutes. "Baby, wanna have some fun?"

The pimps would sidle up close, stage-whispering, "All kinds of women, Jack—want a white woman?" And the hustlers were merchandising: "Hundred dollar ring, man, diamond; ninety-dollar watch, too—look at 'em. Take 'em both for twenty-five."

In another two years, I could have given them all lessons. But that night, I was mesmerized. This world was where I belonged. On that night I had started on my way to becoming a Harlemite. I was going to become one of the most depraved parasitical hustlers among New York's eight million people—four million of whom work, and the other four million of whom live off them.

I couldn't quite believe all that I'd heard and seen that night as I lugged my shoulder-strap sandwich box and that heavy five-gallon aluminum coffee pot up and down the aisles of the "Yankee Clipper" back to Boston. I wished that Ella and I had been on better terms so that I could try to describe to her how I felt. But I did talk to Shorty, urging him to at least go to see the Big Apple music world. Sophia listened to me, too. She told me that I'd never be satisfied anywhere but New York. She was so right. In one night, New York—Harlem—had just about narcotized me.

That sandwich man I'd replaced had little chance of getting his job back. I went bellowing up and down those train aisles. I sold sandwiches, coffee, candy, cake, and ice cream as fast as the railroad's commissary department could supply them. It didn't take me a week to learn that all you had to do was give white people a show and they'd buy anything you offered them. It was like popping your shoeshine rag. The dining car waiters and Pullman porters knew it too, and they faked their Uncle Tomming to get bigger tips. We were in that world of Negroes who are both servants and psychologists, aware that white people are so obsessed with their own importance that they will pay liberally, even dearly, for the impression of being catered to and entertained.

Every layover night in Harlem, I ran and explored new places. I first got a room at the Harlem YMCA, because it was less than a block from Small's Paradise. Then, I got a cheaper room at Mrs. Fisher's rooming house which was close to the YMCA. Most of the railroad men stayed at Mrs. Fisher's. I combed not only the bright-light areas, but Harlem's residential areas from best to worst, from Sugar Hill up near the Polo Grounds, where many famous celebrities lived, down to the slum blocks of old rat-trap apartment houses, just crawling with everything you could mention that was illegal and immoral. Dirt, garbage cans overflowing or kicked over; drunks, dope addicts, beggars. Sleazy bars, storefront churches with gospels being shouted inside, "bargain" stores, hockshops, undertaking parlors. Greasy "home-cooking" restaurants, beauty shops smoky inside from Negro women's hair getting fried, barbershops advertising conk experts. Cadillacs, secondhand and new, conspicuous among the cars on the streets.

All of it was Lansing's West Side or Roxbury's South End magnified a thousand times. Little basement dance halls with "For Rent" signs on them. People offering you little cards advertising "rent-raising parties." I went to one of these— thirty or forty Negroes sweating, eating, drinking, dancing, and gambling in a jammed, beat-up apartment, the record player going full blast, the fried chicken or chitlins with potato salad and collard greens for a dollar a plate, and cans of beer or shots of liquor for fifty cents. Negro and white canvassers sidled up alongside you, talking fast as they tried to get you to buy a copy of the *Daily Worker:* "This paper's trying to keep your rent controlled . . . Make that greedy landlord kill them rats in your apartment . . . This paper represents the only political party that ever ran a black man for the Vice Presidency of the United States . . . Just want you to read, won't take but a little of your time . . . Who do you think fought the hardest to help free those Scottsboro boys?" Things I overheard among Negroes when the salesmen were around let me know that the paper somehow was tied in with the Russians, but to my sterile mind in those early days, it didn't mean much; the radio broadcasts and the newspapers were then full of our-ally-Russia, a strong, muscular people, peasants, with their backs to the wall helping America to fight Hitler and Mussolini.

But New York was heaven to me. And Harlem was Seventh Heaven! I hung around in Small's and the Braddock bar so much that the bartenders began to pour a shot of bourbon, my favorite brand of it, when they saw me walk in the door. And the steady customers in both places, the hustlers in Small's and the entertainers in the Braddock, began to call me "Red," a natural enough nickname in view of my bright red conk. I now had my conk done in Boston at the shop of Abbott and Fogey; it was the best conk shop on the East

Coast, according to the musical greats who had recommended it to me.

My friends now included musicians like Duke Ellington's great drummer, Sonny Greer, and that great personality with the violin, Ray Nance. He's the one who used to sing in that wild "scat" style: "blip-blip-de-blop-de-blam-blam—" And people like Cootie Williams, and Eddie "Cleanhead" Vinson, who'd kid me about his conk—he had nothing up there but skin. He was hitting the heights then with his song, "Hey, Pretty Mama, Chunk Me In Your Big Brass Bed." I also knew Sy Oliver; he was married to a red-complexioned girl, and they lived up on Sugar Hill; Sy did a lot of arranging for Tommy Dorsey in those days. His most famous tune, I believe, was "Yes, Indeed!"

The regular "Yankee Clipper" sandwich man, when he came back, was put on another train. He complained about seniority, but my sales record made them placate him some other way. The waiters and cooks had begun to call me "Sandwich Red."

By that time, they had a laughing bet going that I wasn't going to last, sales or not, because I had so rapidly become such an uncouth, wild young Negro. Profanity had become my language. I'd even curse customers, especially servicemen; I couldn't stand them. I remember that once, when some passenger complaints had gotten me a warning, and I wanted to be careful, I was working down the aisle and a big, beefy, red-faced cracker soldier got up in front of me, so drunk he was weaving, and announced loud enough that everybody in the car heard him, "I'm going to fight you, nigger." I remember the tension. I laughed and told him, "Sure, I'll fight, but you've got too many clothes on." He had on a big Army overcoat. He took that off, and I kept laughing and said he still had on too many. I was able to keep that cracker stripping off clothes until he stood there drunk with nothing on from his pants up, and the whole car was laughing at him, and some other soldiers got him out of the way. I went on. I never would forget that—that I couldn't have whipped that white man as badly with a club as I had with my mind.

Many of the New Haven Line's cooks and waiters still in railroad service today will remember old Pappy Cousins. He was the "Yankee Clipper" steward, a white man, of course, from Maine. (Negroes had been in dining car service as much as thirty and forty years, but in those days there were no Negro stewards on the New Haven Line.) Anyway, Pappy Cousins loved whisky, and he liked everybody, even me. A lot of passenger complaints about me, Pappy had let slide. He'd ask some of the old Negroes working with me to try and calm me down.

"Man, you can't tell him nothing!" they'd exclaim. And they couldn't. At home in Roxbury, they would see me parading with Sophia, dressed in my wild zoot suits. Then I'd come to work, loud and wild and half-high on liquor or reefers, and I'd stay that way, jamming sandwiches at people until we got to New York. Off the train, I'd go through that Grand Central Station afternoon rush-hour crowd, and many white people simply stopped in their tracks to watch me pass. The drape and the cut of a zoot suit showed to the best advantage if you were tall—and I was over six feet. My conk was fire-red. I was really a clown, but my ignorance made me think I was "sharp." My knob-toed, orange-colored "kick-up" shoes were nothing but Florsheims, the ghetto's Cadillac of shoes in those days. (Some shoe companies made these ridiculous styles for sale only in the black ghettoes where ignorant Negroes like me would pay the big-name price for something that we associated with being rich.) And then, between Small's Paradise, the Braddock Hotel, and other places—as much as my twenty- or twenty-five-dollar pay would allow, I drank liquor, smoked marijuana, painted the Big Apple red with increasing numbers of friends, and finally in Mrs. Fisher's rooming house I got a few hours of sleep before the "Yankee Clipper" rolled again.

It was inevitable that I was going to be fired sooner or later. What finally finished me was an angry letter from a passenger. The conductors added their bit, telling how many verbal complaints they'd had, and how many warnings I'd been given.

But I didn't care, because in those wartime days such jobs as I could aspire to were going begging. When the New Haven Line paid me off, I decided it would be nice to make a trip to visit my brothers and sisters in Lansing. I had accumulated some railroad free-travel privileges.

None of them back in Michigan could believe it was me. Only my oldest brother, Wilfred, wasn't there; he was away at Wilberforce University in Ohio studying a trade. But Philbert and Hilda were working in Lansing. Reginald, the one who had always looked up to me, had gotten big enough to fake his age, and he was planning soon to enter the merchant marine. Yvonne, Wesley and Robert were in school.

My conk and whole costume were so wild that I might have been taken as a man from Mars. I caused a minor automobile collision; one driver stopped to gape at me, and the driver behind bumped into him. My appearance staggered the older boys I had once envied; I'd stick out my hand, saying "Skin me, daddy-o!" My stories about the Big Apple, my reefers keeping me sky-high—wherever I went, I was the life of the party. "My man! . . . Gimme some skin!"

The only thing that brought me down to earth was the visit to the state hospital in Kalamazoo. My mother sort of half-sensed who I was.

And I looked up Shorty's mother. I knew he'd be touched by my doing that. She was an old lady, and she was glad to hear from Shorty through me. I told her that Shorty was doing fine and one day was going to be a great leader of his own band. She asked me to tell Shorty that she wished he'd write her, and send her something.

And I dropped over to Mason to see Mrs. Swerlin, the woman at the detention home who had kept me those couple of years. Her mouth flew open when she came to the door. My sharkskin gray "Cab Calloway" zoot suit, the long, narrow, knob-toed shoes, and the four-inch-brimmed pearl gray hat over my conked fire-red hair; it was just about too much for Mrs. Swerlin. She just managed to pull herself together enough to invite me in. Between the way I looked and my style of talk, I made her so nervous and uncomfortable that we were both glad when I left.

The night before I left, a dance was given in the Lincoln School gymnasium. (I've since learned that in a strange city, to find the Negroes without asking where, you just check in the phone book for a "Lincoln School." It's always located in the segregated black ghetto—at least it was, in those days.) I'd left Lansing unable to dance, but now I went around the gymnasium floor flinging little girls over my shoulders and hips, showing my most startling steps. Several times, the little band nearly stopped, and nearly everybody left the floor, watching with their eyes like saucers. That night, I even signed autographs—"Harlem Red"—and I left Lansing shocked and rocked.

Back in New York, stone broke and without any means

of support, I realized that the railroad was all that I actually knew anything about. So I went over to the Seaboard Line's hiring office. The railroads needed men so badly that all I had to do was tell them I had worked on the New Haven, and two days later I was on the "Silver Meteor" to St. Petersburg and Miami. Renting pillows and keeping the coaches clean and the white passengers happy, I made about as much as I had with sandwiches.

I soon ran afoul of the Florida cracker who was assistant conductor. Back in New York, they told me to find another job. But that afternoon, when I walked into Small's Paradise, one of the bartenders, knowing how much I loved New York, called me aside and said that if I were willing to quit the railroad, I might be able to replace a day waiter who was about to go into the Army.

The owner of the bar was Ed Small. He and his brother Charlie were inseparable, and I guess Harlem didn't have two more popular and respected people. They knew I was a railroad man, which, for a waiter, was the best kind of recommendation. Charlie Small was the one I actually talked with in their office. I was afraid he'd want to wait to ask some of his old-timer railroad friends for their opinion. Charlie wouldn't have gone for anybody he heard was wild. But he decided on the basis of his own impression, having seen me in his place so many times, sitting quietly, almost in awe, observing the hustling set. I told him, when he asked, that I'd never been in trouble with the police—and up to then, that was the truth. Charlie told me their rules for employees: no lateness, no laziness, no stealing, no kind of hustling off any customers, especially men in uniform. And I was hired.

This was in 1942. I had just turned seventeen.

With Small's practically in the center of everything, waiting tables there was Seventh Heaven seven times over. Charlie Small had no need to caution me against being late; I was so anxious to be there, I'd arrive an hour early. I relieved the morning waiter. As far as he was concerned, mine was the slowest, most no-tips time of day, and sometimes he'd stick around most of that hour teaching me things, for he didn't want to see me fired.

Thanks to him, I learned very quickly dozens of little things that could really ingratiate a new waiter with the cooks and bartenders. Both of these, depending on how they liked the waiter, could make his job miserable or pleasant—and I meant to become indispensable. Inside of a week, I had succeeded with both. And the customers who had seen me among them around the bar, recognizing me now in the waiter's jacket, were pleased and surprised; and they couldn't have been more friendly. And I couldn't have been more solicitous.

"Another drink? . . . Right away, sir . . . Would you like dinner? . . . It's very good . . . Could I get you a menu, sir? . . . Well, maybe a sandwich?"

Not only the bartenders and cooks, who knew everything about everything, it seemed to me, but even the customers, also began to school me, in little conversations by the bar when I wasn't busy. Sometimes a customer would talk to me as he ate. Sometimes I'd have long talks—absorbing everything—with the real old-timers, who had been around Harlem since Negroes first came there.

That, in fact, was one of my biggest surprises: that Harlem hadn't always been a community of Negroes.

It first had been a Dutch settlement, I learned. Then began the massive waves of poor and half-starved and ragged immigrants from Europe, arriving with everything they owned in the world in bags and sacks on their backs. The Germans came first; the Dutch edged away from them, and Harlem became all German.

Then came the Irish, running from the potato famine. The Germans ran, looking down their noses at the Irish, who took over Harlem. Next, the Italians; same thing—the Irish ran from them. The Italians had Harlem when the Jews came down the gangplanks—and then the Italians left.

Today, all these same immigrants' descendants are running as hard as they can to escape the descendants of the Negroes who helped to unload the immigrant ships.

I was staggered when old-timer Harlemites told me that while this immigrant musical chairs game had been going on, Negroes had been in New York City since 1683, before any of them came, and had been ghettoed all over the city. They had first been in the Wall Street area; then they were pushed into Greenwich Village. The next shove was up to the Pennsylvania Station area. And then, the last stop before Harlem, the black ghetto was concentrated around 52nd Street, which is how 52nd Street got the Swing Street name and reputation that lasted long after the Negroes were gone.

Then, in 1910, a Negro real estate man somehow got two or three Negro families into one Jewish Harlem apartment house. The Jews flew from that house, then from that block, and more Negroes came in to fill their apartments. Then whole blocks of Jews ran, and still more Negroes came uptown, until in a short time, Harlem was like it still is today—virtually all black.

Then, early in the 1920's music and entertainment sprang up as an industry in Harlem, supported by downtown whites who poured uptown every night. It all started about the time a tough young New Orleans cornet man named Louis "Satchmo" Armstrong climbed off a train in New York wearing clodhopper policemen's shoes, and started playing with Fletcher Henderson. In 1925, Small's Paradise had opened with crowds all across Seventh Avenue; in 1926, the great Cotton Club, where Duke Ellington's band would play for five years; also in 1926 the Savoy Ballroom opened, a whole block front on Lenox Avenue, with a two-hundred-foot dance floor under spotlights before two bandstands and a disappearing rear stage.

Harlem's famous image spread until it swarmed nightly with white people from all over the world. The tourist busses came there. The Cotton Club catered to whites only, and hundreds of other clubs ranging on down to cellar speakeasies catered to white people's money. Some of the best-known were Connie's Inn, the Lenox Club, Barron's, The Nest Club, Jimmy's Chicken Shack, and Minton's. The Savoy, the Golden Gate, and the Renaissance ballrooms battled for the crowds—the Savoy introduced such attractions as Thursday Kitchen Mechanics' Nights, bathing beauty contests, and a new car given away each Saturday night. They had bands from all across the country in the ballrooms and the Apollo and Lafayette theaters. They had colorful bandleaders like 'Fess Williams in his diamond-studded suit and top hat, and Cab Calloway in his white zoot suit to end all zoots, and his wide-brimmed white hat and string tie, setting Harlem afire with "Tiger Rag" and "hi-de-hi-de-ho" and "St. James Infirmary" and "Minnie the Moocher."

Blacktown crawled with white people, with pimps, prostitutes, bootleggers, with hustlers of all kinds, with colorful characters, and with police and prohibition agents. Negroes danced like they never have anywhere before or since. I guess I must have heard twenty-five of the old-timers in Small's swear to me that they had been the first to dance in the Savoy the "Lindy Hop," which was born there in 1927, named for Lindbergh, who had just made his flight to Paris.

Even the little cellar places with only piano space had fabulous keyboard artists such as James P. Johnson and Jelly Roll Morton, and singers such as Ethel Waters. And at four A.M., when all the legitimate clubs had to close, from all over town the white and Negro musicians would come to some prearranged Harlem after-hours spot and have thirty- and forty-piece jam sessions that would last into the next day.

When it all ended with the stock market crash in 1929, Harlem had a world reputation as America's Casbah. Small's had been a part of all that. There, I heard the old-timers reminisce about all those great times.

Every day I listened raptly to customers who felt like talking, and it all added to my education. My ears soaked it up like sponges when one of them, in a rare burst of confidence, or a little beyond his usual number of drinks, would tell me inside things about the particular form of hustling that he pursued as a way of life. I was thus schooled well, by experts in such hustles as the numbers, pimping, con games of many kinds, peddling dope, and thievery of all sorts, including armed robbery.

CHAPTER SIX

DETROIT RED

Every day, I would gamble all of my tips—as high as fifteen and twenty dollars—on the numbers, and dream of what I would do when I hit.

I saw people on their long, wild spending sprees, after big hits. I don't mean just hustlers who always had some money. I mean ordinary working people, the kind that we otherwise almost never saw in a bar like Small's, who, with a good enough hit, had quit their jobs working somewhere downtown for the white man. Often they had bought a Cadillac, and sometimes for three and four days, they were setting up drinks and buying steaks for all their friends. I would have to pull two tables together into one, and they would be throwing me two- and three-dollar tips each time I came with my tray.

Hundreds of thousands of New York City Negroes, every day but Sunday, would play from a penny on up to large sums on three-digit numbers. A hit meant duplicating the last three figures of the Stock Exchange's printed daily total of U.S. domestic and foreign sales.

With the odds at six hundred to one, a penny hit won $6, a dollar won $600, and so on. On $15, the hit would mean $9,000. Famous hits like that had bought controlling interests in lots of Harlem's bars and restaurants, or even bought some of them outright. The chances of hitting were a thousand to one. Many players practiced what was called "combinating." For example six cents would put one penny on each of the six possible combinations of three digits. The number 840, combinated, would include 840, 804, 048, 084, 408, and 480.

Practically everyone played every day in the poverty-ridden black ghetto of Harlem. Every day, someone you knew was likely to hit and of course it was neighborhood news; if big enough a hit, neighborhood excitement. Hits generally were small; a nickel, dime, or a quarter. Most people tried to play a dollar a day, but split it up among different numbers and combinated.

Harlem's numbers industry hummed every morning and into the early afternoon, with the runners jotting down people's bets on slips of paper in apartment house hallways, bars, barbershops, stores, on the sidewalks. The cops looked on; no runner lasted long who didn't, out of his pocket, put in a free "figger" for his working area's foot cops, and it was generally known that the numbers bankers paid off at higher levels of the police department.

The daily small army of runners each got ten percent of the money they turned in, along with the bet slips, to their controllers. (And if you hit, you gave the runner a ten percent tip.) A controller might have as many as fifty runners working for him, and the controller got five percent of what he turned over to the banker, who paid off the hit, paid off the police, and got rich off the balance.

Some people played one number all year. Many had lists of the daily hit numbers going back for years; they figured reappearance odds, and used other systems. Others played their hunches: addresses, license numbers of passing cars, any numbers on letters, telegrams, laundry slips, numbers from anywhere. Dream books that cost a dollar would say what number nearly any dream suggested. Evangelists who on Sundays peddled Jesus, and mystics, would pray a lucky number for you, for a fee.

Recently, the last three numbers of the post office's new Zip Code for a postal district of Harlem hit, and one banker almost went broke. Let this very book circulate widely in the black ghettoes of the country, and—although I'm no longer a gambling person—I'd lay a small wager for your favorite charity that millions of dollars would be bet by my poor, foolish black brothers and sisters upon, say, whatever happens to be the number of this page, or whatever is the total of the whole book's pages.

Every day in Small's Paradise Bar was fascinating to me. And from a Harlem point of view, I couldn't have been in a more educational situation. Some of the ablest of New

York's black hustlers took a liking to me, and knowing that I still was green by their terms, soon began in a paternal way to "straighten Red out."

Their methods would be indirect. A dark, businessman-looking West Indian often would sit at one of my tables. One day when I brought his beer, he said, "Red, hold still a minute." He went over me with one of those yellow tape measures, and jotted figures in his notebook. When I came to work the next afternoon, one of the bartenders handed me a package. In it was an expensive, dark blue suit, conservatively cut. The gift was thoughtful, and the message clear.

The bartenders let me know that this customer was one of the top executives of the fabulous Forty Thieves gang. That was the gang of organized boosters, who would deliver, to order, in one day, C.O.D., any kind of garment you desired. You would pay about one-third of the store's price.

I heard how they made mass hauls. A well-dressed member of the gang who wouldn't arouse suspicion by his manner would go into a selected store about closing time, hide somewhere, and get locked inside when the store closed. The police patrols would have been timed beforehand. After dark, he'd pack suits in bags, then turn off the burglar alarm, and use the telephone to call a waiting truck and crew. When the truck came, timed with the police patrols, it would be loaded and gone within a few minutes. I later got to know several members of the Forty Thieves.

Plainclothes detectives soon were quietly identified to me, by a nod, a wink. Knowing the law people in the area was elementary for the hustlers, and, like them, in time I would learn to sense the presence of any police types. In late 1942, each of the military services had their civilian-dress eyes and ears picking up anything of interest to them, such as hustles being used to avoid the draft, or who hadn't registered, or hustles that were being worked on servicemen.

Longshoremen, or fences for them, would come into the bars selling guns, cameras, perfumes, watches, and the like, stolen from the shipping docks. These Negroes got what white-longshoreman thievery left over. Merchant marine sailors often brought in foreign items, bargains, and the best marijuana cigarettes to be had were made of the *gunja* and *kisca* that merchant sailors smuggled in from Africa and Persia.

In the daytime, whites were given a guarded treatment.

Whites who came at night got a better reception; the several Harlem nightclubs they patronized were geared to entertain and jive the night white crowd to get their money.

And with so many law agencies guarding the "morals" of servicemen, any of them that came in, and a lot did, were given what they asked for, and were spoken to if they spoke, and that was all, unless someone knew them as natives of Harlem.

What I was learning was the hustling society's first rule; that you never trusted anyone outside of your own close-mouthed circle, and that you selected with time and care before you made any intimates even among these.

The bartenders would let me know which among the regular customers were mostly "fronts," and which really had something going; which were really in the underworld, with downtown police or political connections; which really handled some money, and which were making it from day to day; which were the real gamblers, and which had just hit a little luck; and which ones never to run afoul of in any way.

The latter were extremely well known about Harlem, and they were feared and respected. It was known that if upset, they would break open your head and think nothing of it. These were old-timers, not to be confused with the various hotheaded, wild, young hustlers out trying to make a name for themselves for being crazy with a pistol trigger or a knife. The old heads that I'm talking about were such as "Black Sammy," "Bub" Hulan, "King" Padmore and "West Indian Archie." Most of these tough ones had worked as strongarm men for Dutch Schultz back when he muscled into the Harlem numbers industry after white gangsters had awakened to the fortunes being made in what they had previously considered "nigger pennies"; and the numbers game was referred to by the white racketeers as "nigger pool."

Those tough Negroes' heyday had been before the big 1931 Seabury Investigation that started Dutch Schultz on the way out, until his career ended with his 1934 assassination. I heard stories of how they had "persuaded" people with lead pipes, wet cement, baseball bats, brass knuckles, fists, feet, and blackjacks. Nearly every one of them had done some time, and had come back on the scene, and since had worked as top runners for the biggest bankers who specialized in large bettors.

There seemed to be an understanding that these Negroes and the tough black cops never clashed; I guess both knew that someone would die. They had some bad black cops in Harlem, too. The Four Horsemen that worked Sugar Hill— I remember the worst one had freckles—there was a tough quartet. The biggest, blackest, worst cop of them all in Harlem was the West Indian, Brisbane. Negroes crossed the street to avoid him when he walked his 125th Street and Seventh Avenue beat. When I was in prison, someone brought me a story that Brisbane had been shot to death by a scared, nervous young kid who hadn't been up from the South long enough to realize how bad Brisbane was.

The world's mostly unlikely pimp was "Cadillac" Drake. He was shiny baldheaded, built like a football; he used to call his huge belly "the chippies' playground." Cadillac had a string of about a dozen of the stringiest, scrawniest, black and white street prostitutes in Harlem. Afternoons around the bar, the old-timers who knew Cadillac well enough would tease him about how women who looked like his made enough to feed themselves, let alone him. He'd roar with laughter right along with us; I can hear him now, "Bad-looking women work harder."

Just about the complete opposite of Cadillac was the young, smooth, independent-acting pimp, "Sammy the Pimp." He could, as I have mentioned, pick out potential prostitutes by watching their expressions in dance halls. Sammy and I became, in time, each other's closest friend. Sammy, who was from Kentucky, was a cool, collected expert in his business, and his business was women. Like Cadillac, he too had both black and white women out making his living, but Sammy's women—who would come into Small's sometimes, looking for him, to give him money, and have him buy them a drink —were about as beautiful as any prostitutes who operated anywhere, I'd imagine.

One of his white women, known as "Alabama Peach," a blonde, could put everybody in stitches with her drawl; even the several Negro women numbers controllers around Small's really liked her. What made a lot of Negroes around the bar laugh the hardest was the way she would take three syllables to say "nigger." But what she usually was saying was "Ah jes' lu-uv ni-uh-guhs—." Give her two drinks and she would tell her life story in a minute; how in whatever little Alabama town it was she came from, the first thing she remembered being conscious of was that she was supposed to "hate niggers." And then she started hearing older girls in grade school whispering the hush-hush that "niggers" were such sexual giants and athletes, and she started growing up secretly wanting to try one. Finally, right in her own house, with her family away, she threatened a Negro man who worked for her father that if he didn't take her she would swear he tried rape. He had no choice, except that he quit working for them. And from then until she finished high school, she managed it several times with other Negroes—and she somehow came to New York, and went straight to Harlem. Later on, Sammy told me how he had happened to spot her in the Savoy, not even dancing with anybody, just standing on the sidelines, watching, and he could tell. And once she really *went* for Negroes, the more the better, Sammy said, and wouldn't have a white man. I have wondered what ever became of her.

There was a big, fat pimp we called "Dollarbill." He loved to flash his "Kansas City roll," probably fifty one-dollar bills folded with a twenty on the inside and a one-hundred dollar bill on the outside. We always wondered what Dollarbill would do if someone ever stole his hundred-dollar "cover."

A man who, in his prime, could have stolen Dollarbill's whole roll, blindfolded, was threadbare, comic old "Fewclothes." Fewclothes had been one of the best pickpockets in Harlem, back when the white people swarmed up every night in the 1920's, but then during the Depression, he had contracted a bad case of arthritis in his hands. His finger joints were knotted and gnarled so that it made people uncomfortable to look at them. Rain, sleet, or snow, every afternoon, about six, Fewclothes would be at Small's, telling tall tales about the old days, and it was one of the day's rituals for one or another regular customer to ask the bartender to give him drinks, and me to feed him.

My heart goes out to all of us who in those afternoons at Small's enacted our scene with Fewclothes. I wish you could have seen him, pleasantly "high" with drinks, take his seat with dignity—no begging, not on anybody's Welfare —and open his napkin, and study the day's menu that I gave him, and place his order. I'd tell the cooks it was Fewclothes and he'd get the best in the house. I'd go back and serve it as though he were a millionaire.

Many times since, I have thought about it, and what it really meant. In one sense, we were huddled in there, bonded together in seeking security and warmth and comfort from each other, and we didn't know it. All of us—who might have probed space, or cured cancer, or built industries— were, instead, black victims of the white man's American social system. In another sense, the tragedy of the once master pickpocket made him, for those brother old-timer hustlers a "there but for the grace of God" symbol. To wolves who still were able to catch some rabbits, it had meaning that an old wolf who had lost his fangs was still eating.

Then there was the burglar, "Jumpsteady." In the ghettoes the white man has built for us, he has forced us not to aspire to greater things, but to view everyday living as *survival*— and in that kind of a community, survival is what is respected. In any average white neighborhood bar, you couldn't imagine a known cat-man thief regularly exposing himself, as one of the most popular people in there. But if Jumpsteady missed a few days running in Small's, we would begin inquiring for him.

Jumpsteady was called that because, it was said, when he worked in white residential areas downtown, he jumped from roof to roof and was so steady that he maneuvered along window ledges, leaning, balancing, edging with his toes. If he fell, he'd have been dead. He got into apartments through windows. It was said that he was so cool that he had stolen even with people in the next room. I later found out that Jumpsteady always keyed himself up high on dope when he worked. He taught me some things that I was to employ in later years when hard times would force me to have my own burglary ring.

I should stress that Small's wasn't any nest of criminals. I dwell upon the hustlers because it was their world that fascinated me. Actually, for the night life crowd, Small's was one of Harlem's two or three most decorous nightspots. In fact, the New York City police department recommended Small's to white people who would ask for a "safe" place in Harlem.

The first room I got after I left the railroad (half of Harlem roomed) was in the 800 block of St. Nicholas Avenue. You could walk into one or another room in this house and get a hot fur coat, a good camera, fine perfume, a gun, anything from hot women to hot cars, even hot ice. I was one of the very few males in this rooming house. This was during the war, when you couldn't turn on the radio and not hear about Guadalcanal or North Africa. In several of the apartments the women tenants were prostitutes. The minority were in some other racket or hustle—boosters, numbers runners, or dope-peddlers—and I'd guess that everyone who lived in the house used dope of some kind. This shouldn't reflect too badly on that particular building, because almost everyone in Harlem needed some kind of hustle to survive, and needed to stay high in some way to forget what they had to *do* to survive.

It was in this house that I learned more about women than I ever did in any other single place. It was these working prostitutes who schooled me to things that every wife and every husband should know. Later on, it was chiefly the women who weren't prostitutes who taught me to be very distrustful of most women; there seemed to be a higher code of ethics and sisterliness among those prostitutes than among numerous ladies of the church who have more men for kicks than the prostitutes have for pay. And I am talking about both black and white. Many of the black ones in those war-time days were right in step with the white ones in having husbands fighting overseas while they were laying up with other men, even giving them their husbands' money. And many women just faked as mothers and wives, while playing the field as hard as prostitutes—with their husbands and children right there in New York.

I got my first schooling about the cesspool morals of the white man from the best possible source, from his own women. And then as I got deeper into my own life of evil, I saw the white man's morals with my own eyes. I even made my living helping to guide him to the sick things he wanted.

I was young, working in the bar, not bothering with these women. Probably I touched their kid-brother instincts, something like that. Some would drop into my room when they weren't busy, and we would smoke reefers and talk. It generally would be after their morning rush—but let me tell you about that rush.

Seeing the hallways and stairs busy any hour of the night with white and black men coming and going was no more than one would expect when one lived in a building out of which prostitutes were working. But what astonished me was the full-house crowd that rushed in between, say, six and seven-thirty in the morning, then rushed away, and by about nine, I would be the only man in the house.

It was husbands—who had left home in time to stop by this St. Nicholas Avenue house before they went on to work. Of course not the same ones every day, but always enough of them to make up the rush. And it included white men who had come in cabs all the way up from downtown.

Domineering, complaining, demanding wives who had just about psychologically castrated their husbands were responsible for the early rush. These wives were so disagreeable and had made their men so tense that they were robbed of the satisfaction of being men. To escape this tension and the chance of being ridiculed by his own wife, each of these men had gotten up early and come to a prostitute.

The prostitutes had to make it their business to be students of men. They said that after most men passed their virile twenties, they went to bed mainly to satisfy their egos, and because a lot of women don't understand it that way, they damage and wreck a man's ego. No matter how little virility a man has to offer, prostitutes make him feel for a time that he is the greatest man in the world. That's why these prostitutes had that morning rush of business. More wives could keep their husbands if they realized their greatest urge is *to be men*.

Those women would tell me anything. Funny little stories about the bedroom differences they saw between white and black men. The perversities! I thought I had heard the whole range of perversities until I later became a steerer taking white men to what they wanted. Everyone in the house laughed about the little Italian fellow whom they called the "Ten Dollar A Minute Man." He came without fail every noontime, from his little basement restaurant up near the Polo Grounds; the joke was he never lasted more than two minutes . . . but he always left twenty dollars.

Most men, the prostitutes felt, were too easy to push around. Every day these prostitutes heard their customers complaining that they never heard anything but griping from women who were being taken care of and given everything. The prostitutes said that most men needed to know what the pimps knew. A woman should occasionally be babied enough to show her the man had affection, but beyond that she should be treated firmly. These tough women said that it worked with *them*. All women, by their nature, are fragile and weak: they are attracted to the male in whom they see strength.

From time to time, Sophia would come over to see me from Boston. Even among Harlem Negroes, her looks gave me status. They were just like the Negroes everywhere else. That was why the white prostitutes made so much money. It didn't make any difference if you were in Lansing, Boston, or New York—what the white racist said, and still says, was right in those days! All you had to do was put a white girl anywhere close to the average black man, and he would respond. The black woman also made the white man's eyes light up—but he was slick enough to hide it.

Sophia would come in on a late afternoon train. She would come to Small's and I'd introduce her around until I got off from work. She was bothered about me living among the prostitutes until I introduced her to some of them, and they talked, and she thought they were great. They would tell her they were keeping me straight for her. We would go to the Braddock Hotel bar, where we would meet some of the musicians who now would greet me like an old friend. "Hey, Red—who have we got here?" They would make a big deal over her; I couldn't even think about buying a drink. No Negroes in the world were more white-woman-crazy in those days than most of those musicians. People in show business, of course, were less inhibited by social and racial taboos.

The white racist won't tell you that it also works in reverse. When it got late, Sophia and I would go to some of the after-hours places and speakeasies. When the down-town nightclubs had closed, most of these Harlem places crawled with white people. These whites were just mad for Negro "atmosphere," especially some of the places which had what you might call Negro *soul*. Sometimes Negroes would talk about how a lot of whites seemed unable to have enough of being close around us, and among us—in groups. Both white men and women, it seemed, would get almost mesmerized by Negroes.

I remember one really peculiar case of this—a white girl who never missed a single night in the Savoy Ballroom. She fascinated my friend Sammy; he had watched her several times. Dancing only with Negroes, she seemed to go nearly into a trance. If a white man asked her to dance, she would refuse. Then when the place was ready to close, early in the morning, she would let a Negro take her as far as the subway entrance. And that was it. She never would tell anyone her name, let alone reveal where she lived.

Now, I'll tell you another peculiar case that worked out differently, and which taught me something I have since learned in a thousand other ways. This was my best early lesson in how most white men's hearts and guts will turn over inside of them, whatever they may have you otherwise believe, whenever they see a Negro man on close terms with a white woman.

A few of the white men around Harlem, younger ones whom we called "hippies," acted more Negro than Negroes. This particular one talked more "hip" talk than we did. He would have fought anyone who suggested he felt any race difference. Musicians around the Braddock could hardly move without falling over him. Every time I saw him, it was "Daddy! Come on, let's get our heads tight!" Sammy couldn't stand him; he was underfoot wherever you went. He even wore a wild zoot suit, used a heavy grease in his hair to make it look like a conk, and he wore the knob-toed shoes, the long, swinging chain—everything. And he not only wouldn't be seen with any woman but a black one, but in fact he lived with *two* of them in the same little apartment. I never was sure how they worked that one out, but I had my idea.

About three or four o'clock one morning, we ran into this white boy, in Creole Bill's speakeasy. He was high—in that marijuana glow where the world relaxes. I introduced Sophia; I went away to say hello to someone else. When I returned, Sophia looked peculiar—but she wouldn't tell me until we left. He had asked her, "Why is a white girl like you throwing yourself away with a spade?"

Creole Bill—naturally you know he was from New Orleans—became another good friend of mine. After Small's closed, I'd bring fast-spending white people who still wanted some drinking action to Creole Bill's speakeasy. That was my earliest experience at steering. The speakeasy was only Creole Bill's apartment. I think a partition had been knocked out to make the living room larger. But the atmosphere, plus the food, made the place one of Harlem's soul spots.

A record player maintained the right, soft music. There was any kind of drink. And Bill sold plates of his spicy, delicious Creole dishes—gumbo, jambalaya. Bill's girl friend —a beautiful black girl—served the customers. Bill called her "Brown Sugar," and finally everyone else did. If a good number of customers were to be served at one time, Creole Bill would bring out some pots, Brown Sugar would bring the plates, and Bill would serve everyone big platefuls; and he'd heap a plate for himself and eat with us. It was a treat to watch him eat; he loved his food so; it *was* good. Bill could cook rice like the Chinese—I mean rice that stood every grain on its own, but I never knew the Chinese to do what Bill could with seafood and beans.

Bill made money enough in that apartment speakeasy to open up a Creole restaurant famous in Harlem. He was a great baseball fan. All over the walls were framed, auto-graphed photographs of major league stars, and also some political and show business celebrities who would come there to eat, bringing friends. I wonder what's become of Creole Bill? His place is sold, and I haven't heard anything of him. I must remember to ask some of the Seventh Avenue old-timers, who would know.

Once, when I called Sophia in Boston, she said she couldn't get away until the following weekend. She had just married some well-to-do Boston white fellow. He was in the service, he had been home on leave, and he had just gone back. She didn't mean it to change a thing between us. I told her it made no difference. I had of course introduced Sophia to my friend Sammy, and we had gone out together some nights. And Sammy and I had thoroughly discussed the black man and white woman psychology. I had Sammy to thank that I was entirely prepared for Sophia's marriage.

Sammy said that white women were very practical; he had heard so many of them express how they felt. They knew that the black man had all the strikes against him, that the white man kept the black man down, under his heel, unable to get anywhere, really. The white woman wanted to be comfortable, she wanted to be looked upon with favor by her own kind, but also she wanted to have her pleasure. So some of them just married a white man for convenience and security, and kept right on going with a Negro. It wasn't that they were necessarily in love with the Negro, but they were in love with lust—particularly "taboo" lust.

A white man was not too unusual if he had a ten-, twenty-,

thirty-, forty-, or fifty-thousand-dollar-a-year job. A Negro man who made even five thousand in the white man's world was unusual. The white woman with a Negro man would be with him for one of two reasons: either extremely insane love, or to satisfy her lust.

When I had been around Harlem long enough to show signs of permanence, inevitably I got a nickname that would identify me beyond any confusion with two other red-conked and well-known "Reds" who were around. I had met them both; in fact, later on I'd work with them both. One, "St. Louis Red," was a professional armed robber. When I was sent to prison, he was serving time for trying to stick up a dining car steward on a train between New York and Philadelphia. He was finally freed; now, I hear, he is in prison for a New York City jewel robbery.

The other was "Chicago Red." We became good buddies in a speakeasy where later on I was a waiter; Chicago Red was the funniest dishwasher on this earth. Now he's making his living being funny as a nationally known stage and night-club comedian. I don't see any reason why old Chicago Red would mind me telling that he is Redd Foxx.

Anyway, before long, my nickname happened. Just when, I don't know—but people, knowing I was from Michigan, would ask me what city. Since most New Yorkers had never heard of Lansing, I would name Detroit. Gradually, I began to be called "Detroit Red"—and it stuck.

One afternoon in early 1943, before the regular six o'clock crowd had gathered, a black soldier sat drinking by himself at one of my tables. He must have been there an hour or more. He looked dumb and pitiful and just up from the Deep South. The fourth or fifth drink I served this soldier, wiping the table I bent over close and asked him if he wanted a woman.

I knew better. It wasn't only Small's Paradise law, it was the law of every tavern that wanted to stay in business—never get involved with anything that could be interpreted as "impairing the morals" of servicemen, or any kind of hust-ling off them. This had caused trouble for dozens of places: some had been put off limits by the military; some had lost their state or city licenses.

I played right into the hands of a military spy. He sure would like a woman. He acted so grateful. He even put on an extreme Southern accent. And I gave him the phone number of one of my best friends among the prostitutes where I lived.

But something felt wrong. I gave the fellow a half-hour to get there, and then I telephoned. I expected the answer I got—that no soldier had been there.

I didn't even bother to go back out to the bar. I just went straight to Charlie Small's office.

"I just did something, Charlie," I said. "I don't know why I did it—" and I told him.

Charlie looked at me. "I wish you hadn't done that, Red." We both knew what he meant.

When the West Indian plainclothes detective, Joe Baker, came in, I was waiting. I didn't even ask him any questions. When we got to the 135th Street precinct, it was busy with police in uniform, and MP's with soldiers in tow. I was recognized by some other detectives who, like Joe Baker, sometimes dropped in at Small's.

Two things were in my favor. I'd never given the police any trouble, and when that black spy soldier had tried to tip me, I had waved it away, telling him I was just doing him a favor. They must have agreed that Joe Baker should just scare me.

I didn't know enough to be aware that I wasn't taken to the desk and booked. Joe Baker took me back inside of the precinct building, into a small room. In the next room, we could hear somebody getting whipped. *Whop! Whop!* He'd cry out, "Please! Please don't beat my face, that's how I make my living!" I knew from that it was some pimp. *Whop! Whop!* "Please! Please!"

(Not much later, I heard that Joe Baker had gotten trapped over in New Jersey, shaking down a Negro pimp and his white prostitute. He was dischaged from the New York City police force, the State of New Jersey convicted him, and he went off to do some time.)

More bitter than getting fired, I was barred from Small's. I could understand. Even if I wasn't actually what was called "hot," I was now going to be under surveillance— and the Small brothers had to protect their business.

Sammy proved to be my friend in need. He put word on the wire for me to come over to his place. I had never been there. His place seemed to me a small palace; his women really kept him in style. While we talked about what

kind of a hustle I should get into, Sammy gave me some
of the best marijuana I'd ever used.

Various numbers controllers, Small's regulars, had offered
me jobs as a runner. But that meant I would earn very
little until I could build up a clientele. Pimping, as Sammy
did, was out. I felt I had no abilities in that direction, and
that I'd certainly starve to death trying to recruit prostitutes.

Peddling reefers, Sammy and I pretty soon agreed, was
the best thing. It was a relatively uninvolved lone-wolf type
of operation, and one in which I could make money immediately. For anyone with even a little brains, no experience was
needed, especially if one had any knack at all with people.

Both Sammy and I knew some merchant seamen and
others who could supply me with loose marijuana. And
musicians, among whom I had so many good contacts, were
the heaviest consistent market for reefers. And then, musicians also used the heavier narcotics, if I later wanted to
graduate to them. That would be more risky, but also more
money. Handling heroin and cocaine could earn one hundreds of dollars a day, but it required a lot of experience
with the narcotics squad for one to be able to last long
enough to make anything.

I had been around long enough either to know or to spot
instinctively most regular detectives and cops, though not
the narcotics people. And among the Small's veteran hustler
regulars, I had a variety of potentially helpful contacts.
This was important because just as Sammy could get me
supplied with marijuana, a large facet of any hustler's success was knowing where he could get help when he needed
it. The help could involve police and detectives—as well as
higher ups. But I hadn't yet reached that stage. So Sammy
staked me, about twenty dollars, I think it was.

Later that same night, I knocked at his door and gave
him back his money and asked him if I could lend him
some. I had gone straight from Sammy's to a supplier he
had mentioned. I got just a small amount of marijuana, and
I got some of the paper to roll up my own sticks. As they
were only about the size of stick matches, I was able to
make enough of them so that, after selling them to musicians
I knew at the Braddock Hotel, I could pay back Sammy
and have enough profit to be in business. And those
musicians when they saw their buddy, and their fan, in
business: "My man!" "Crazy, Red!"

In every band, at least half of the musicians smoked reefers. I'm not going to list names; I'd have to include some of those most prominent then in popular music, even a number of them around today. In one case, every man in one of the bands which is still famous was on marijuana. Or again, any number of musicians could tell you who I mean when I say that one of the most famous singers smoked his reefers though a chicken thighbone. He had smoked so many through the bone that he could just light a match before the empty bone, draw the heat through, and get what he called a "contact" high.

I kept turning over my profit, increasing my supplies, and I sold reefers like a wild man. I scarcely slept; I was wherever musicians congregated. A roll of money was in my pocket. Every day, I cleared at least fifty or sixty dollars. In those days (or for that matter these days), this was a fortune to a seventeen-year-old Negro. I felt, for the first time in my life, that great feeling of *free!* Suddenly, now, I was the peer of the other young hustlers I had admired.

It was at this time that I discovered the movies. Sometimes I made as many as five in one day, both downtown and in Harlem. I loved the tough guys, the action, Humphrey Bogart in "Casablanca," and I loved all of that dancing and carrying on in such films as "Stormy Weather" and "Cabin in the Sky." After leaving the movies, I'd make my connections for supplies, then roll my sticks, and, about dark, I'd start my rounds. I'd give a couple of extra sticks when someone bought ten, which was five dollars' worth. And I didn't sell and run, because my customers were my friends. Often I'd smoke along with them. None of them stayed any more high than I did.

Free now to do what I pleased, upon an impulse I went to Boston. Of course, I saw Ella. I gave her some money: it was just a token of appreciation, I told her, for helping me when I had come from Lansing. She wasn't the same old Ella; she still hadn't forgiven me for Laura. She never mentioned her, nor did I. But, even so, Ella acted better than she had when I had left for New York. We reviewed the family changes. Wilfred had proved so good at his trade they had asked him to stay on at Wilberforce as an instructor. And Ella had gotten a card from Reginald who had managed to get into the merchant marine.

From Shorty's apartment, I called Sophia. She met me

at the apartment just about as Shorty went off to work. I would have liked to take her out to some of the Roxbury clubs, but Shorty had told us that, as in New York, the Boston cops used the war as an excuse to harass interracial couples, stopping them and grilling the Negro about his draft status. Of course Sophia's now being married made us more cautious, too.

When Sophia caught a cab home, I went to hear Shorty's band. Yes, he had a band now. He had succeeded in getting a 4-F classification, and I was pleased for him and happy to go. His band was—well, fair. But Shorty was making out well in Boston, playing in small clubs. Back in the apartment, we talked into the next day. "Homeboy, you're something else!" Shorty kept saying. I told him some of the wild things I'd done in Harlem, and about the friends I had. I told him the story of Sammy the Pimp.

In Sammy's native Paducah, Kentucky, he had gotten a girl pregnant. Her parents made it so hot that Sammy had come to Harlem, where he got a job as a restaurant waiter. When a woman came in to eat alone, and he found she really was alone, not married, or living with somebody, it generally was not hard for smooth Sammy to get invited to her apartment. He'd insist on going out to a nearby restaurant to bring back some dinner, and while he was out he would have her key duplicated. Then, when he knew she was away, Sammy would go in and clean out all her valuables. Sammy was then able to offer some little stake, to help her back on her feet. This could be the beginning of an emotional and financial dependency, which Sammy knew how to develop until she was his virtual slave.

Around Harlem, the narcotics squad detectives didn't take long to find out I was selling reefers, and occasionally one of them would follow me. Many a peddler was in jail because he had been caught with the evidence on his person; I figured a way to avoid that. The law specified that if the evidence wasn't actually in your possession, you couldn't be arrested. Hollowed-out shoe heels, fake hat-linings, these things were old stuff to the detectives.

I carried about fifty sticks in a small package inside my coat, under my armpit, keeping my arm flat against my side. Moving about, I kept my eyes open. If anybody looked suspicious, I'd quickly cross the street, or go through a door, or turn a corner, loosening my arm enough to let the package drop. At night, when I usually did my selling, any suspicious person wouldn't be likely to see the trick. If I decided I had been mistaken, I'd go back and get my sticks.

However, I lost many a stick this way. Sometimes, I knew I had frustrated a detective. And I kept out of the courts.

One morning, though, I came in and found signs that my room had been entered. I knew it had been detectives. I'd heard too many times how if they couldn't find any evidence, they would plant some, where you would never find it, then they'd come back in and "find" it. I didn't even have to think twice what to do. I packed my few belongings and never looked back. When I went to sleep again, it was in another room.

It was then that I began carrying a little .25 automatic. I got it, for some reefers, from an addict who I knew had stolen it somewhere. I carried it pressed under my belt right down the center of my back. Someone had told me that the cops never hit there in any routine patting-down. And unless I knew who I was with, I never allowed myself to get caught in any crush of people. The narcotics cops had been known to rush up and get their hands on you and plant evidence while "searching." I felt that as long as I kept on the go, and in the open, I had a good chance. I don't know now what my real thoughts were about carrying the pistol. But I imagine I felt that I wasn't going to get put away if somebody tried framing me in any situation that I could help.

I sold less than before because having to be so careful consumed so much time. Every now and then, on a hunch, I'd move to another room. I told nobody but Sammy where I slept.

Finally, it was on the wire that the Harlem narcotics squad had me on its special list.

Now, every other day or so, usually in some public place, they would flash the badge to search me. But I'd tell them at once, loud enough for others standing about to hear me, that I had nothing on me, and I didn't want to get anything planted on me. Then they wouldn't, because Harlem already thought little enough of the law, and they did have to be careful that some crowd of Negroes would not intervene roughly. Negroes were starting to get very tense in Harlem. One could almost smell trouble ready to break out—as it did very soon.

But it was really tough on me then. I was having to hide my sticks in various places near where I was selling. I'd put five sticks in an empty cigarette pack, and drop the empty-looking pack by a lamppost, or behind a garbage can, or a box. And I'd first tell customers to pay me, and then where to pick up.

But my regular customers didn't go for that. You couldn't expect a well-known musician to go grubbing behind a garbage can. So I began to pick up some of the street trade, the people you could see looked high. I collected a number of empty Red Cross bandage boxes and used them for drops. That worked pretty good.

But the middle-Harlem narcotics force found so many ways to harass me that I had to change my area. I moved down to lower Harlem, around 110th Street. There were many more reefer smokers around there, but these were a cheaper type, this was the worst of the ghetto, the poorest people, the ones who in every ghetto keep themselves narcotized to keep from having to face their miserable existence. I didn't last long down there, either. I lost too much of my product. After I sold to some of those reefer smokers who had the instincts of animals, they followed me and learned my pattern. They would dart out of a doorway, I'd drop my stuff, and they would be on it like a chicken on corn. When you become an animal, a vulture, in the ghetto, as I had become, you enter a world of animals and vultures. It becomes truly the survival of only the fittest.

Soon I found myself borrowing little stakes, from Sammy, from some of the musicians. Enough to buy supplies, enough to keep high myself, enough sometimes to just eat.

Then Sammy gave me an idea.

"Red, you still got your old railroad identification?" I did have it. They hadn't taken it back. "Well, why don't you use it to make a few runs, until the heat cools?"

He was right.

I found that if you walked up and showed a railroad line's employee identification card, the conductor—even a real cracker, if you approached him right, not begging—would just wave you aboard. And when he came around he would punch you one of those little coach seat slips to ride wherever the train went.

The idea came to me that, this way, I could travel all over the East Coast selling reefers among my friends who were on tour with their bands.

I had the New Haven identification. I worked a couple of weeks for other railroads, to get their identification, and then I was set.

In New York, I rolled and packed a great quantity of sticks, and sealed them into jars. The identification card worked perfectly. If you persuaded the conductor you were a fellow employee who had to go home on some family business, he just did the favor for you without a second thought. Most whites don't give a Negro credit for having sense enough to fool them—or nerve enough.

I'd turn up in towns where my friends were playing. "Red!" I was an old friend from home. In the sticks, I was somebody from the Braddock Hotel. *"My man! Daddy-o!"* And I had Big Apple reefers. Nobody had ever heard of a traveling reefer peddler.

I followed no particular band. Each band's musicians knew the other bands' one-nighter touring schedules. When I ran out of supplies, I'd return to New York, and load up, then hit the road again. Auditoriums or gymnasiums all lighted up, the band's chartered bus outside, the dressed-up, excited, local dancers pouring in. At the door, I'd announce that I was some bandman's brother; in most cases they thought I was one of the musicians. Throughout the dance, I'd show the country folks some plain and fancy lindy-hopping. Sometimes, I'd stay overnight in a town. Sometimes I'd ride the band's bus to their next stop. Sometimes, back in New York, I would stay awhile. Things had cooled down. Word was around that I had left town, and the narcotics squad was satisfied with that. In some of the small towns, people thinking I was with the band even mobbed me for autographs. Once, in Buffalo, my suit was nearly torn off.

My brother Reginald was waiting for me one day when I pulled into New York. The day before, his merchant ship had put into port over in New Jersey. Thinking I still worked at Small's, Reginald had gone there, and the bartenders had directed him to Sammy, who put him up.

It felt good to see my brother. It was hard to believe that he was once the little kid who tagged after me. Reginald now was almost six feet tall, but still a few inches shorter than me. His complexion was darker than mine, but he had greenish eyes, and a white streak in his hair, which was otherwise dark reddish, something like mine.

I took Reginald everywhere, introducing him. Studying my brother, I liked him. He was a lot more self-possessed than I had been at sixteen.

I didn't have a room right at the time, but I had some money, so did Reginald, and we checked into the St. Nicholas Hotel on Sugar Hill. It has since been torn down.

Reginald and I talked all night about the Lansing years, about our family. I told him things about our father and mother that he couldn't remember. Then Reginald filled me in on our brothers and sisters. Wilfred was still a trade instructor at Wilberforce University. Hilda, still in Lansing, was talking of getting married; so was Philbert.

Reginald and I were the next two in line. And Yvonne, Wesley, and Robert were still in Lansing, in school.

Reginald and I laughed about Philbert, who, the last time I had seen him, had gotten deeply religious; he wore one of those round straw hats.

Reginald's ship was in for about a week getting some kind of repairs on its engines. I was pleased to see that Reginald, though he said little about it, admired my living by my wits. Reginald dressed a little too loudly, I thought. I got a reefer customer of mine to get him a more conservative overcoat and suit. I told Reginald what I had learned: that in order to get something you had to look as though you already had something.

Before Reginald left, I urged him to leave the merchant marine and I would help him get started in Harlem. I must have felt that having my kid brother around me would be a good thing. Then there would be two people I could trust —Sammy was the other.

Reginald was cool. At his age, I would have been willing to run behind the train, to get to New York and to Harlem. But Reginald, when he left, said, "I'll think about it."

Not long after Reginald left, I dragged out the wildest zoot suit in New York. This was 1943. The Boston draft board had written me at Ella's, and when they had no results there, had notified the New York draft board, and, in care of Sammy, I received Uncle Sam's Greetings.

In those days only three things in the world scared me: jail, a job, and the Army. I had about ten days before I was to show up at the induction center. I went right to work. The Army Intelligence soldiers, those black spies in civilian clothes, hung around in Harlem with their ears open for the white man downtown. I knew exactly where to start dropping the word. I started noising around that I was frantic to join . . . the Japanese Army.

When I sensed that I had the ears of the spies, I would talk and act high and crazy. A lot of Harlem hustlers actually had reached that state—as I would later. It was inevitable when one had gone long enough on heavier and heavier narcotics, and under the steadily tightening vise of the hustling life. I'd snatch out and read my Greetings aloud, to make certain they heard who I was, and when I'd report downtown. (This was probably the only time my real name was ever heard in Harlem in those days.)

The day I went down there, I costumed like an actor. With my wild zoot suit I wore the yellow knob-toe shoes, and I frizzled my hair up into a reddish bush of conk.

I went in, skipping and tipping, and I thrust my tattered Greetings at that reception desk's white soldier—"Crazy-o, daddy-o, get me moving. I can't wait to get in that brown—," very likely that soldier hasn't recovered from me yet.

They had their wire on me from uptown, all right. But they still put me through the line. In that big starting room were forty or fifty other prospective inductees. The room had fallen vacuum-quiet, with me running my mouth a mile a minute, talking nothing but slang. I was going to fight on all fronts: I was going to be a general, man, before I got done—such talk as that.

Most of them were white, of course. The tender-looking ones appeared ready to run from me. Some others had that vinegary "worst kind of nigger" look. And a few were amused, seeing me as the "Harlem jigaboo" archetype.

Also amused were some of the room's ten or twelve Negroes. But the stony-faced rest of them looked as if they were ready to sign up to go off killing somebody—they would have liked to start with me.

The line moved along. Pretty soon, stripped to my shorts, I was making my eager-to-join comments in the medical examination rooms—and everybody in the white coats that I saw had 4-F in his eyes.

I stayed in the line longer than I expected, before they siphoned me off. One of the white coats accompanied me around a turning hallway: I knew we were on the way to a headshrinker—the Army psychiatrist.

The receptionist there was a Negro nurse. I remember she was in her early twenties, and not bad to look at. She was one of those Negro "firsts."

Negroes know what I'm talking about. Back then, the white man during the war was so pressed for personnel that he began letting some Negroes put down their buckets and mops and dust rags and use a pencil, or sit at some desk, or hold some twenty-five-cent title. You couldn't read the Negro press for the big pictures of smug black "firsts."

Somebody was inside with the psychiatrist. I didn't even have to put on any act for this black girl; she was already sick of me.

When, finally, a buzz came at her desk, she didn't send me, *she* went in. I knew what she was doing, she was going to make clear, in advance, what she thought of me. This is still one of the black man's big troubles today. So many of those so-called "upper class" Negroes are so busy trying to impress on the white man that they are "different from those others" that they can't see they are only helping the white man to keep his low opinion of *all* Negroes.

And then, with her prestige in the clear, she came out and nodded to me to go in.

I must say this for that psychiatrist. He tried to be objective and professional in his manner. He sat there and doodled with his blue pencil on a tablet, listening to me spiel to him for three or four minutes before he got a word in.

His tack was quiet questions, to get at why I was so anxious. I didn't rush him; I circled and hedged, watching him closely, to let him think he was pulling what he wanted out of me. I kept jerking around, backward, as though somebody might be listening. I knew I was going to send him back to the books to figure what kind of a case I was.

Suddenly, I sprang up and peeped under both doors, the one I'd entered and another that probably was a closet. And then I bent and whispered fast in his ear. "Daddy-o, now you and me, we're from up North here, so don't you tell nobody. . . . I want to get sent down South. Organize them nigger soldiers, you dig? Steal us some guns, and kill up crackers!"

That psychiatrist's blue pencil dropped, and his professional manner fell off in all directions. He stared at me as if I were a snake's egg hatching, fumbling for his red pencil. I knew I had him. I was going back out past Miss First when he said, "That will be all."

A 4-F card came to me in the mail, and I never heard from the Army any more, and never bothered to ask why I was rejected.

CHAPTER SEVEN

HUSTLER

I can't remember all the hustles I had during the next two years in Harlem, after the abrupt end of my riding the trains and peddling reefers to the touring bands.

Negro railroad men waited for their trains in their big locker room on the lower level of Grand Central Station. Big blackjack and poker games went on in there around the clock. Sometimes five hundred dollars would be on the table. One day, in a blackjack game, an old cook who was dealing the cards tried to be slick, and I had to drop my pistol in his face.

The next time I went into one of those games, intuition told me to stick my gun under my belt right down the middle of my back. Sure enough, someone had squealed. Two big, beefy-faced Irish cops came in. They frisked me —and they missed my gun where they hadn't expected one.

The cops told me never again to be caught in Grand Central Station unless I had a ticket to ride somewhere. And I knew that by the next day, every railroad's personnel office would have a blackball on me, so I never tried to get another railroad job.

There I was back in Harlem's streets among all the rest of the hustlers. I couldn't sell reefers; the dope squad detectives were too familiar with me. I was a true hustler— uneducated, unskilled at anything honorable, and I considered myself nervy and cunning enough to live by my wits, exploiting any prey that presented itself. I would risk just about anything.

Right now, in every big city ghetto, tens of thousands of yesterday's and today's school drop-outs are keeping body and soul together by some form of hustling in the same way

I did. And they inevitably move into more and more, worse and worse, illegality and immorality. Full-time hustlers never can relax to appraise what they are doing and where they are bound. As is the case in any jungle, the hustler's every waking hour is lived with both the practical and the subconscious knowledge that if he ever relaxes, if he ever slows down, the other hungry, restless foxes, ferrets, wolves, and vultures out there with him won't hesitate to make him their prey.

During the next six to eight months, I pulled my first robberies and stick-ups. Only small ones. Always in other, nearby cities. And I got away. As the pros did, I too would key myself to pull these jobs by my first use of hard dope. I began with Sammy's recommendation—sniffing cocaine.

Normally now, for street wear, I might call it, I carried a hardly noticeable little flat, blue-steel .25 automatic. But for working, I carried a .32, a .38 or a .45. I saw how when the eyes stared at the big black hole, the faces fell slack and the mouths sagged open. And when I spoke, the people seemed to hear as though they were far away, and they would do whatever I asked.

Between jobs, staying high on narcotics kept me from getting nervous. Still, upon sudden impulses, just to play safe, I would abruptly move from one to another fifteen- to twenty-dollar-a-week room, always in my favorite 147th-150th Street area, just flanking Sugar Hill.

Once on a job with Sammy, we had a pretty close call. Someone must have seen us. We were making our getaway, running, when we heard the sirens. Instantly, we slowed to walking. As a police car screeched to a stop, we stepped out into the street, meeting it, hailing it to ask for directions. They must have thought we were about to give them some information. They just cursed us and raced on. Again, it didn't cross the white men's minds that a trick like that might be pulled on them by Negroes.

The suits that I wore, the finest, I bought hot for about thirty-five to fifty dollars. I made it my rule never to go after more than I needed to live on. Any experienced hustler will tell you that getting greedy is the quickest road to prison. I kept "cased" in my head vulnerable places and situations and I would perform the next job only when my bankroll in my pocket began to get too low.

Some weeks, I bet large amounts on the numbers. I still

played with the same runner with whom I'd started in Small's Paradise. Playing my hunches, many a day I'd have up to forty dollars on two numbers, hoping for that fabulous six hundred-to-one payoff. But I never did hit a big number full force. There's no telling what I would have done if ever I'd landed $10,000 or $12,000 at one time. Of course, once in a while I'd hit a small combination figure. Sometimes, flush like that, I'd telephone Sophia to come over from Boston for a couple of days.

I went to the movies a lot again. And I never missed my musician friends wherever they were playing, either in Harlem, downtown at the big theaters, or on 52nd Street.

Reginald and I got very close the next time his ship came back into New York. We discussed our family, and what a shame it was that our book-loving oldest brother Wilfred had never had the chance to go to some of those big universities where he would have gone far. And we exchanged thoughts we had never shared with anyone.

Reginald, in his quiet way, was a mad fan of musicians and music. When his ship sailed one morning without him, a principal reason was that I had thoroughly exposed him to the exciting musical world. We had wild times backstage with the musicians when they were playing the Roxy, or the Paramount. After selling reefers with the bands as they traveled, I was known to almost every popular Negro musician around New York in 1944-1945.

Reginald and I went to the Savoy Ballroom, the Apollo Theater, the Braddock Hotel bar, the nightclubs and speakeasies, wherever Negroes played music. The great Lady Day, Billie Holiday, hugged him and called him "baby brother." Reginald shared tens of thousands of Negroes' feelings that the living end of the big bands was Lionel Hampton's. I was very close to many of the men in Hamp's band; I introduced Reginald to them, and also to Hamp himself, and Hamp's wife and business manager, Gladys Hampton. One of this world's sweetest people is Hamp. Anyone who knows him will tell you that he'd often do the most generous things for people he barely knew. As much money as Hamp has made, and still makes, he would be broke today if his money and his business weren't handled by Gladys, who is one of the brainiest women I ever met. The Apollo Theater's owner, Frank Schiffman, could tell you. He generally signed bands to play for a set weekly amount, but I know that once during those days Gladys Hampton instead arranged a deal for Hamp's band to play for a cut of the gate. Then the usual number of shows was doubled up—if I'm not mistaken, eight shows a day, instead of the usual four—and Hamp's pulling power cleaned up. Gladys Hampton used to talk to me a lot, and she tried to give me good advice: "Calm down, Red." Gladys saw how wild I was. She saw me headed toward a bad end.

One of the things I liked about Reginald was that when I left him to go away "working," Reginald asked me no questions. After he came to Harlem, I went on more jobs than usual. I guess that what influenced me to get my first actual apartment was my not wanting Reginald to be knocking around Harlem without anywhere to call "home." That first apartment was three rooms, for a hundred dollars a month, I think, in the front basement of a house on 147th Street between Convent and St. Nicholas Avenues. Living in the rear basement apartment, right behind Reginald and me, was one of Harlem's most successful narcotics dealers.

With the apartment as our headquarters, I gradually got Reginald introduced around to Creole Bill's, and other Harlem after-hours spots. About two o'clock every morning, as the downtown white nightclubs closed, Reginald and I would stand around in front of this or that Harlem after-hours place, and I'd school him to what was happening.

Especially after the nightclubs downtown closed, the taxis and black limousines would be driving uptown, bringing those white people who never could get enough of Negro *soul*. The places popular with these whites ranged all the way from the big locally famous ones such as Jimmy's Chicken Shack, and Dickie Wells', to the little here-tonight-gone-tomorrow-night private clubs, so-called, where a dollar was collected at the door for "membership."

Inside every after-hours spot, the smoke would hurt your eyes. Four white people to every Negro would be in there drinking whisky from coffee cups and eating fried chicken. The generally flush-faced white men and their makeup-masked, glittery-eyed women would be pounding each other's backs and uproariously laughing and applauding the music. A lot of the whites, drunk, would go staggering up to Negroes, the waiters, the owners, or Negroes at tables, wringing their hands, even trying to hug them, "You're just as good as I am—I want you to know that!" The most famous places drew both Negro and white celebrities who enjoyed each other. A jam-packed four-thirty A.M. crowd at Jimmie's Chicken Shack or Dickie Wells' might have such jam-session entertainment as Hazel Scott playing the piano for Billie Holiday singing the blues. Jimmy's Chicken Shack, incidentally, was where once, later on, I worked briefly as a waiter. That's where Redd Foxx was the dishwasher who kept the kitchen crew in stitches.

After a while, my brother Reginald had to have a hustle, and I gave much thought to what would be, for him, a good, safe hustle. After he'd learned his own way around, it would be up to him to take risks for himself—if he wanted to make more and quicker money.

The hustle I got Reginald into really was very simple. It utilized the psychology of the ghetto jungle. Downtown, he paid the two dollars, or whatever it was, for a regular city peddler's license. Then I took him to a manufacturers' outlet where we bought a supply of cheap imperfect "seconds"—shirts, underwear, cheap rings, watches, all kinds of quick-sale items.

Watching me work this hustle back in Harlem, Reginald quickly caught on to how to go into barbershops, beauty parlors, and bars acting very nervous as he let the customers peep into his small valise of "loot." With so many thieves around anxious to get rid of stolen good-quality merchandise cheaply, many Harlemites, purely because of this conditioning, jumped to pay hot prices for inferior goods whose sale was perfectly legitimate. It never took long to get rid of a valiseful for at least twice what it had cost. And if any cop stopped Reginald, he had in his pocket both the peddler's license and the manufacturers' outlet bills of sale. Reginald only had to be certain that none of the customers to whom he sold ever saw that he was legitimate.

I assumed that Reginald, like most of the Negroes I knew, would go for a white woman. I'd point out Negro-happy white women to him, and explain that a Negro with any brains could wrap these women around his fingers. But I have to say this for Reginald: he never liked white women. I remember the one time he met Sophia; he was so cool it upset Sophia, and it tickled me.

Reginald got himself a black woman. I'd guess she was

pushing thirty; an "old settler," as we called them back in
those days. She was a waitress in an exclusive restaurant
downtown. She lavished on Reginald everything she had,
she was so happy to get a young man. I mean she bought
him clothes, cooked and washed for him, and everything, as
though he were a baby.

That was just another example of why my respect for my
younger brother kept increasing. Reginald showed, in often
surprising ways, more sense than a lot of working hustlers
twice his age. Reginald then was only sixteen, but, a six-
footer, he looked and acted much older than his years.

All through the war, the Harlem racial picture never was
too bright. Tension built to a pretty high pitch. Old-timers
told me that Harlem had never been the same since the
1935 riot, when millions of dollars worth of damage was
done by thousands of Negroes, infuriated chiefly by the white
merchants in Harlem refusing to hire a Negro even as their
stores raked in Harlem's money.

During World War II, Mayor LaGuardia officially closed
the Savoy Ballroom. Harlem said the real reason was to
stop Negroes from dancing with white women. Harlem said
that no one dragged the white women in there. Adam Clayton Powell made it a big fight. He had successfully fought
Consolidated Edison and the New York Telephone Company
until they had hired Negroes. Then he had helped to battle
the U. S. Navy and the U. S. Army about their segregating
of uniformed Negroes. But Powell couldn't win this battle.
City Hall kept the Savoy closed for a long time. It was just
another one of the "liberal North" actions that didn't help
Harlem to love the white man any.

Finally, rumor flashed that in the Braddock Hotel, white
cops had shot a Negro soldier. I was walking down St.
Nicholas Avenue; I saw all of these Negroes hollering and
running north from 125th Street. Some of them were loaded
down with armfuls of stuff. I remember it was the band-
leader Fletcher Henderson's nephew "Shorty" Henderson
who told me what had happened. Negroes were smashing
store windows, and taking everything they could grab and
carry—furniture, food, jewelry, clothes, whisky. Within an
hour, every New York City cop seemed to be in Harlem.
Mayor LaGuardia and the NAACP's then Secretary, the

famed late Walter White, were in a red firecar, riding around pleading over a loudspeaker to all of those shouting, milling, angry Negroes to please go home and stay inside.

Just recently I ran into Shorty Henderson on Seventh Avenue. We were laughing about a fellow whom the riot had left with the nickname of "Left Feet." In a scramble in a women's shoe store, somehow he'd grabbed five shoes, all of them for left feet! And we laughed about the scared little Chinese whose restaurant didn't have a hand laid on it, because the rioters just about convulsed laughing when they saw the sign the Chinese had hastily stuck on his front door: "Me Colored Too."

After the riot, things got very tight in Harlem. It was terrible for the night-life people, and for those hustlers whose main income had been the white man's money. The 1935 riot had left only a relative trickle of the money which had poured into Harlem during the 1920's. And now this new riot ended even that trickle.

Today the white people who visit Harlem, and this mostly on weekend nights, are hardly more than a few dozen who do the twist, the frug, the Watusi, and all the rest of the current dance crazes in Small's Paradise, owned now by the great basketball champion "Wilt the Stilt" Chamberlain, who draws crowds with his big, clean, All-American-athlete image. Most white people today are physically afraid to come to Harlem—and it's for good reasons, too. Even for Negroes, Harlem night life is about finished. Most of the Negroes who have money to spend are spending it downtown somewhere in this hypocritical "integration," in places where previously the police would have been called to haul off any Negro insane enough to try and get in. The already Croesus-rich white man can't get another skyscraper hotel finished and opened before all these integration-mad Negroes, who themselves don't own a tool shed, are booking the swanky new hotel for "cotillions" and "conventions." Those rich whites could afford it when they used to throw away their money in Harlem. But Negroes can't afford to be taking their money downtown to the white man.

Sammy and I, on a robbery job, got a bad scare, a very close call.

Things had grown so tight in Harlem that some hustlers had been forced to go to work. Even some prostitutes had gotten jobs as domestics, and cleaning office buildings at night. The pimping was so poor, Sammy had gone on the job with me. We had selected one of those situations considered "impossible." But wherever people think that, the guards will unconsciously grow gradually more relaxed, until sometimes those can be the easiest jobs of all.

But right in the middle of the act, we had some bad luck. A bullet grazed Sammy. We just barely escaped.

Sammy fortunately wasn't really hurt. We split up, which was always wise to do.

Just before daybreak, I went to Sammy's apartment. His newest woman, one of those beautiful but hot-headed Spanish Negroes, was in there crying and carrying on over Sammy. She went for me, screaming and clawing; she knew I'd been in on it with him. I fended her off. Not able to figure out why Sammy didn't shut her up, I did . . . and from the corner of my eye, I saw Sammy going for his gun.

Sammy's reaction that way to my hitting his woman—close as he and I were—was the only weak spot I'd ever glimpsed. The woman screamed and dove for him. She knew as I did that when your best friend draws a gun on you, he usually has lost all control of his emotions, and he intends to shoot. She distracted Sammy long enough for me to bolt through the door. Sammy chased me, about a block.

We soon made up—on the surface. But things never are fully right again with anyone you have seen trying to kill you.

Intuition told us that we had better lay low for a good while. The worst thing was that we'd been seen. The police in that nearby town had surely circulated our general descriptions.

I just couldn't forget that incident over Sammy's woman. I came to rely more and more upon my brother Reginald as the only one in my world I could completely trust.

Reginald was lazy, I'd discovered that. He had quit his hustle altogether. But I didn't mind that, really, because one could be as lazy as he wanted, if he would only use his head, as Reginald was doing. He had left my apartment by now. He was living off his "old settler" woman—when he was in town. I had also taught Reginald how he could work a little while for a railroad, then use his identification card to travel for nothing—and Reginald loved to travel. Several times, he had gone visiting all around, among our brothers and sisters. They had now begun to scatter to different cities. In Boston, Reginald was closer to our sister Mary than to Ella, who had been my favorite. Both Reginald and Mary were quiet types, and Ella and I were extroverts. And Shorty in Boston had given my brother a royal time.

Because of my reputation, it was easy for me to get into the numbers racket. That was probably Harlem's only hustle which hadn't slumped in business. In return for a favor to some white mobster, my new boss and his wife had just been given a six-months numbers banking privilege for the Bronx railroad area called Motthaven Yards. The white mobsters had the numbers racket split into specific areas. A designated area would be assigned to someone for a specified period of time. My boss' wife had been Dutch Schultz's secretary in the 1930's, during the time when Schultz had strong-armed his way into control of the Harlem numbers business.

My job now was to ride a bus across the George Washington Bridge where a fellow was waiting for me to hand him a bag of numbers betting slips. We never spoke. I'd cross the street and catch the next bus back to Harlem. I never knew who that fellow was. I never knew who picked up the betting money for the slips that I handled. You didn't ask questions in the rackets.

My boss' wife and Gladys Hampton were the only two women I ever met in Harlem whose business ability I really respected. My boss' wife, when she had the time and the inclination to talk, would tell me many interesting things. She would talk to me about the Dutch Schultz days—about deals that she had known, about graft paid to officials—rookie cops and shyster lawyers right on up into the top levels of police and politics. She knew from personal experience how crime existed only to the degree that the law cooperated with it. She showed me how, in the country's entire social, political and economic structure, the criminal, the law, and the politicians were actually inseparable partners.

It was at this time that I changed from my old numbers man, the one I'd used since I first worked in Small's Paradise. He hated to lose a heavy player, but he readily understood why I would now want to play with a runner of my own outfit. That was how I began placing my bets with West Indian Archie. I've mentioned him before—one of Harlem's really *bad* Negroes; one of those former Dutch Schultz strong-arm men around Harlem.

West Indian Archie had finished time in Sing Sing not long before I came to Harlem. But my boss' wife had hired him not just because she knew him from the old days. West Indian Archie had the kind of photographic memory that put him among the elite of numbers runners. He never wrote down your number; even in the case of combination plays, he would just nod. He was able to file all the numbers in his head, and write them down for the banker only when he turned in his money. This made him the ideal runner because cops could never catch him with any betting slips.

I've often reflected upon such black veteran numbers men as West Indian Archie. If they had lived in another kind of society, their exceptional mathematical talents might have been better used. But they were black.

Anyway, it was status just to be known as a client of West Indian Archie's, because he handled only sizable bettors. He also required integrity and sound credit: it wasn't necessary that you pay as you played; you could pay West Indian Archie by the week. He always carried a couple of thousand dollars on him, his own money. If a client came up to him and said he'd hit for some moderate amount, say a fifty-cent or one dollar combination, West Indian Archie would peel off the three or six hundred dollars, and later get his money back from the banker.

Every weekend, I'd pay my bill—anywhere from fifty to even one hundred dollars, if I had really plunged on some hunch. And when, once or twice, I did hit, always just some combination, as I've described, West Indian Archie paid me off from his own roll.

The six months finally ended for my boss and his wife. They had done well. Their runners got nice tips, and promptly were snatched up by other bankers. I continued working for my boss and his wife in a gambling house they opened.

A Harlem madam I'd come to know—through having done a friend of hers a favor—introduced me to a special facet of the Harlem night world, something which the riot had only interrupted. It was the world where, behind locked doors, Negroes catered to monied white people's weird sexual tastes.

The whites I'd known loved to rub shoulders publicly

with black folks in the after-hours clubs and speakeasies. These, on the other hand, were whites who did not want it known that they had been anywhere near Harlem. The riot had made these exclusive white customers nervous. Their slipping into and about Harlem hadn't been so noticeable when other whites were also around. But now they would be conspicuous; they also feared the recently aroused anger of Harlem Negroes. So the madam was safeguarding her growing operation by offering me a steerer's job.

During the war, it was extremely difficult to get a telephone. One day the madam told me to stay at my apartment the next morning. She talked to somebody. I don't know who it was, but before that next noon, I dialed the madam from my own telephone—unlisted.

This madam was a specialist in her field. If her own girls could not—or would not—accommodate a customer, she would send me to another place, usually an apartment somewhere else in Harlem, where the requested "specialty" was done.

My post for picking up the customers was right outside the Astor Hotel, that always-busy northwest corner of 45th Street and Broadway. Watching the moving traffic, I was soon able to spot the taxi, car, or limousine—even before it slowed down—with the anxious white faces peering out for the tall, reddish-brown-complexioned Negro wearing a dark suit, or raincoat, with a white flower in his lapel.

If they were in a private car, unless it was chauffeured I would take the wheel and drive where we were going. But if they were in a taxi, I would always tell the cabbie, "The Apollo Theater in Harlem, please," since among New York City taxis a certain percentage are driven by cops. We would get another cab—driven by a black man—and I'd give him the right address.

As soon as I got that party settled, I'd telephone the madam. She would generally have me rush by taxi right back downtown to be on the 45th Street and Broadway corner at a specified time. Appointments were strictly punctual; rarely was I on the corner as much as five minutes. And I knew how to keep moving about so as not to attract the attention of any vice squad plainclothes men or uniformed cops.

With tips, which were often heavy, sometimes I would make over a hundred dollars a night steering up to ten customers in a party—to see anything, to do anything, to have anything done to them, that they wanted. I hardly ever knew the identities of my customers, but the few I did recognize, or whose names I happened to hear, remind me now of the Profumo case in England. The English are not far ahead of rich and influential Americans when it comes to seeking rarities and oddities.

Rich men, middle-aged and beyond, men well past their prime: these weren't college boys, these were their Ivy League fathers. Even grandfathers, I guess. Society leaders. Big politicians. Tycoons. Important friends from out of town. City government big shots. All kinds of professional people. Star performing artists. Theatrical and Hollywood celebrities. And, of course, racketeers.

Harlem was their sin-den, their fleshpot. They stole off among taboo black people, and took off whatever antiseptic, important, dignified masks they wore in their white world. These were men who could afford to spend large amounts of money for two, three, or four hours indulging their strange appetites.

But in this black-white nether world, nobody judged the customers. Anything they could name, anything they could imagine, anything they could describe, they could do, or could have done to them, just as long as they paid.

In the Profumo case in England, Christine Keeler's friend testified that some of her customers wanted to be whipped. One of my main steers to one specialty address away from the madam's house was the apartment of a big, coal-black girl, strong as an ox, with muscles like a dockworker's. A funny thing, it generally was the oldest of these white men—in their sixties, I know, some maybe in their seventies—they couldn't seem to recover quickly enough from their last whipping so they could have me meet them again at 45th and Broadway to take them back to that apartment, to cringe on their knees and beg and cry out for mercy under that black girl's whip. Some of them would pay me extra to come and watch them being beaten. That girl greased her big Amazon body all over to look shinier and blacker. She used small, plaited whips, she would draw blood, and she was making herself a small fortune off those old white men.

I wouldn't tell all the things I've seen. I used to wonder, later on, when I was in prison, what a psychiatrist would make of it all. And so many of these men held responsible positions; they exercised guidance, influence, and authority over others.

In prison later, I'd think, too, about another thing. Just about all of those whites specifically expressed as their preference black, *black*, "the blacker the better!" The madam, having long since learned this, had in her house nothing but the blackest accommodating women she could find.

In all of my time in Harlem, I never saw a white prostitute touched by a white man. White girls were in some of the various Harlem specialty places. They would participate in customers' most frequent exhibition requests—a sleek, black Negro male having a white woman. Was this the white man wanting to witness his deepest sexual fear? A few times, I even had parties that included white women whom the men had brought with them to watch this. I never steered any white women other than in these instances, brought by their own men, or who had been put into contact with me by a white Lesbian whom I knew, who was another variety of specialty madam.

This Lesbian, a beautiful white woman, had a male Negro stable. Her vocabulary was all profanity. She supplied Negro males, on order, to well-to-do white women.

I'd seen this Lesbian and her blonde girl friend around Harlem, drinking and talking at bars, always with young Negroes. No one who didn't know would ever guess that the Lesbian was recruiting. But one night I gave her and her girl friend some reefers which they said were the best they'd ever smoked. They lived in a hotel downtown, and after that, now and then, they would call me, and I would bring them some reefers, and we'd talk.

She told me how she had accidentally gotten started in her specialty. As a Harlem habitué, she had known Harlem Negroes who liked white women. Her role developed from a pattern of talk she often heard from bored, well-to-do white women where she worked, in an East Side beauty salon. Hearing the women complain about sexually inadequate mates, she would tell what she'd "heard" about Negro men. Observing how excited some of the women seemed to become, she finally arranged some dates with some of the Harlem Negroes she knew at her own apartment.

Eventually, she rented three midtown apartments where a woman customer could meet a Negro by appointment. Her customers recommended her service to their friends. She quit the beauty salon, set up a messenger service as an operating front, and ran all of her business by telephone.

She had also noticed the color preference. I never could substitute in an emergency, she would tell me with a laugh, because I was too light. She told me that nearly every white woman in her clientele would specify "a black one"; sometimes they would say "a *real* one," meaning black, no brown Negroes, no red Negroes.

The Lesbian thought up her messenger service idea because some of her trade wanted the Negroes to come to their homes, at times carefully arranged by telephone. These women lived in neighborhoods of swank brownstones and exclusive apartment houses, with doormen dressed like admirals. But white society never thinks about challenging any Negro in a servant role. Doormen would telephone up and hear "Oh, yes, send him right up, James"; service elevators would speed those neatly dressed Negro messenger boys right up—so that they could "deliver" what had been ordered by some of the most privileged white women in Manhattan.

The irony is that those white women had no more respect for those Negroes than white men have had for the Negro women they have been "using" since slavery times. And, in turn, Negroes have no respect for the whites they get into bed with. I know the way I felt about Sophia, who still came to New York whenever I called her.

The West Indian boy friend of the Profumo scandal's Christine Keeler, Lucky Gordon, and his friends must have felt the same way. After England's leaders had been with those white girls, those girls, for their satisfaction, went to Negroes, to smoke reefers and make fun of some of England's greatest peers as cuckolds and fools. I don't doubt that Lucky Gordon knows the identity of "the man in the mask" and much more. If Gordon told everything those white girls told him, he would give England a new scandal.

It's no different from what happens in some of America's topmost white circles. Twenty years ago, I saw them nightly, with my own eyes, I heard them with my own ears.

The hypocritical white man will talk about the Negro's "low morals." But who has the world's lowest morals if not whites? And not only that, but the "upper-class" whites! Recently, details were published about a group of suburban

New York City white housewives and mothers operating as a professional call-girl ring. In some cases, these wives were out prostituting with the agreement, even the cooperation, of husbands, some of whom even waited at home, attending the children. And the customers—to quote a major New York City morning newspaper: "Some 16 ledgers and books with names of 200 Johns, many important social, financial and political figures, were seized in the raid Friday night."

I have also read recently about groups of young white couples who get together, the husbands throw their house keys into a hat, then, blindfolded, the husbands draw out a key and spend the night with the wife that the house key matches. I have never heard of anything like that being done by Negroes, even Negroes who live in the worst ghettoes and alleys and gutters.

Early one morning in Harlem, a tall, light Negro wearing a hat and with a woman's stocking drawn down over his face held up a Negro bartender and manager who were counting up the night's receipts. Like most bars in Harlem, Negroes fronted, and a Jew really owned the place. To get a license, one had to know somebody in the State Liquor Authority, and Jews working with Jews seemed to have the best S.L.A. contacts. The black manager hired some Negro hoodlums to go hunting for the hold-up man. And the man's description caused them to include me among their suspects. About daybreak that same morning, they kicked in the door of my apartment.

I told them I didn't know a thing about it, that I hadn't had a thing to do with whatever they were talking about. I told them I had been out on my hustle, steering, until maybe four in the morning, and then I had come straight to my apartment and gone to bed.

The strong-arm thugs were bluffing. They were trying to flush out the man who had done it. They still had other suspects to check out—that's all that saved me.

I put on my clothes and took a taxi and I woke up two people, the madam, then Sammy. I had some money, but the madam gave me some more, and I told Sammy I was going to see my brother Philbert in Michigan. I gave Sammy the address, so that he could let me know when things got straightened out.

This was the trip to Michigan in the wintertime when I

put congolene on my head, then discovered that the bathroom sink's pipes were frozen. To keep the lye from burning up my scalp, I had to stick my head into the stool and flush and flush to rinse out the stuff.

A week passed in frigid Michigan before Sammy's telegram came. Another red Negro had confessed, which enabled me to live in Harlem again.

But I didn't go back into steering. I can't remember why I didn't. I imagine I must have felt like staying away from hustling for a while, going to some of the clubs at night, and narcotizing with my friends. Anyway, I just never went back to the madam's job.

It was at about this time, too, I remember, that I began to be sick. I had colds all the time. It got to be a steady irritation, always sniffling and wiping my nose, all day, all night. I stayed so high that I was in a dream world. Now, sometimes, I smoked opium with some white friends, actors who lived downtown. And I smoked more reefers than ever before. I didn't smoke the usual wooden-match-sized sticks of marijuana. I was so far gone by now that I smoked it almost by the ounce.

After awhile, I worked downtown for a Jew. He liked me because of something I had managed to do for him. He bought rundown restaurants and bars. Hymie was his name. He would remodel these places, then stage a big, gala reopening, with banners and a spotlight outside. The jam-packed, busy place with the big "Under New Management" sign in the window would attract speculators, usually other Jews who were around looking for something to invest money in. Sometimes even in the week of the new opening, Hymie would re-sell, at a good profit.

Hymie really liked me, and I liked him. He loved to talk. I loved to listen. Half his talk was about Jews and Negroes. Jews who had anglicized their names were Hymie's favorite hate. Spitting and curling his mouth in scorn, he would reel off names of people he said had done this. Some of them were famous names whom most people never thought of as Jews.

"Red, I'm a Jew and you're black," he would say. "These Gentiles don't like either one of us. If the Jew wasn't smarter than the Gentile, he'd get treated worse than your people."

Hymie paid me good money while I was with him, sometimes two hundred and three hundred dollars a week. I would have done anything for Hymie. I did do all kinds of things. But my main job was transporting bootleg liquor that Hymie supplied, usually to those spruced-up bars which he had sold to someone.

Another fellow and I would drive out to Long Island where a big bootleg whisky outfit operated. We'd take with us cartons of empty bonded whisky bottles that were saved illegally by bars we supplied. We would buy five-gallon containers of bootleg, funnel it into the bottles, then deliver, according to Hymie's instructions, this or that many crates back to the bars.

Many people claiming they drank only such-and-such a brand couldn't tell their only brand from pure week-old Long Island bootleg. Most ordinary whisky drinkers are "brand" chumps like this. On the side, with Hymie's approval, I was myself at that time supplying some lesser quantities of bootleg to reputable Harlem bars, as well as to some of the few speakeasies still in Harlem.

But one weekend on Long Island, something happened involving the State Liquor Authority. One of New York State's biggest recent scandals has been the exposure of wholesale S.L.A. graft and corruption. In the bootleg racket I was involved in, someone high up must have been taken for a real pile. A rumor about some "inside" tipster spread among Hymie and the others. One day Hymie didn't show up where he had told me to meet him. I never heard from him again . . . but I did hear that he was put in the ocean, and I knew he couldn't swim.

Up in the Bronx, a Negro held up some Italian racketeers in a floating crap game. I heard about it on the wire. Whoever did it, aside from being a fool, was said to be a "tall, light-skinned" Negro, masked with a woman's stocking. It has always made me wonder if that bar stickup had really been solved, or if the wrong man had confessed under beatings. But, anyway, the past suspicion of me helped to revive suspicion of me again.

Up in Fat Man's Bar on the hill overlooking the Polo Grounds, I had just gone into a telephone booth. Everyone in the bar—all over Harlem, in fact—was drinking up, excited about the news that Branch Rickey, the Brooklyn Dodgers' owner, had just signed Jackie Robinson to play in major league baseball, with the Dodgers' farm team in

Montreal—which would place the time in the fall of 1945.

Earlier in the afternoon, I had collected from West Indian Archie for a fifty-cent combination bet; he had paid me three hundred dollars right out of his pocket. I was telephoning Jean Parks. Jean was one of the most beautiful women who ever lived in Harlem. She once sang with Sarah Vaughan in the Bluebonnets, a quartet that sang with Earl Hines. For a long time, Jean and I had enjoyed a standing, friendly deal that we'd go out and celebrate when either of us hit the numbers. Since my last hit, Jean had treated me twice, and we laughed on the phone, glad that now I'd treat her to a night out. We arranged to go to a 52nd Street night club to hear Billie Holiday, who had been on the road and was just back in New York.

As I hung up, I spotted the two lean, tough-looking *paisanos* gazing in at me cooped up in the booth.

I didn't need any intuition. And I had no gun. A cigarette case was the only thing in my pocket. I started easing my hand down into my pocket, to try bluffing . . . and one of them snatched open the door. They were dark-olive, swarthy-featured Italians. I had my hand down into my pocket.

"Come on outside, we'll hold court," one said.

At that moment, a cop walked through the front door. The two thugs slipped out. I never in my life have been so glad to see a cop.

I was still shaking when I got to the apartment of my friend, Sammy the Pimp. He told me that not long before, West Indian Archie had been there looking for me.

Sometimes, recalling all of this, I don't know, to tell the truth, how I am alive to tell it today. They say God takes care of fools and babies. I've so often thought that Allah was watching over me. Through all of this time of my life, I really *was* dead—mentally dead. I just didn't know that I was.

Anyway, to kill time, Sammy and I sniffed some of his cocaine, until the time came to pick up Jean Parks, to go down and hear Lady Day. Sammy's having told me about West Indian Archie looking for me didn't mean a thing . . . not right then.

CHAPTER EIGHT

TRAPPED

There was the knocking at the door. Sammy, lying on his bed in pajamas and a bathrobe, called "Who?"

When West Indian Archie answered, Sammy slid the round, two-sided shaving mirror under the bed, with what little of the cocaine powder—or crystals, actually—was left, and I opened the door.

"Red—I want my money!"

A .32-20 is a funny kind of gun. It's bigger than a .32. But it's not as big as a .38. I had faced down some dangerous Negroes. But no one who wasn't ready to die messed with West Indian Archie.

I couldn't believe it. He truly scared me. I was so incredulous at what was happening that it was hard to form words with my brain and my mouth.

"Man—what's the beef?"

West Indian Archie said he'd thought I was trying something when I'd told him I'd hit, but he'd paid me the three hundred dollars until he could double-check his written betting slips; and, as he'd thought, I hadn't combinated the number I'd claimed, but another.

"Man, you're crazy!" I talked fast; I'd seen out of the corner of my eye Sammy's hand easing under his pillow where he kept his Army .45. "Archie, smart a man as you're supposed to be, you'd pay somebody who hadn't hit?"

The .32-20 moved, and Sammy froze. West Indian Archie told him, "I ought to shoot you through the ear." And he looked back at me. "You don't have my money?"

I must have shaken my head.

"I'll give you until twelve o'clock tomorrow."

And he put his hand behind him and pulled open the door. He backed out, and slammed it.

It was a classic hustler-code impasse. The money wasn't the problem. I still had about two hundred dollars of it. Had money been the issue, Sammy could have made up the difference; if it wasn't in his pocket, his women could quickly have raised it. West Indian Archie himself, for that matter, would have loaned me three hundred dollars if I'd ever asked him, as many thousands of dollars of mine as he'd gotten ten percent of. Once, in fact, when he'd heard I was broke, he had looked me up and handed me some money and grunted, "Stick this in your pocket."

The issue was the position which his action had put us both into. For a hustler in our sidewalk jungle world, "face" and "honor" were important. No hustler could have it known that he'd been "hyped," meaning outsmarted or made a fool of. And worse, a hustler could never afford to have it demonstrated that he could be bluffed, that he could be frightened by a threat, that he lacked nerve.

West Indian Archie knew that some young hustlers rose in stature in our world when they somehow hoodwinked older hustlers, then put it on the wire for everyone to hear. He believed I was trying that.

In turn, I knew he would be protecting his stature by broadcasting all over the wire his threat to me.

Because of this code, in my time in Harlem I'd personally known a dozen hustlers who, threatened, left town, disgraced.

Once the wire had it, any retreat by either of us was unthinkable. The wire would be awaiting the report of the showdown.

I'd also known of at least another dozen showdowns in which one took the Dead On Arrival ride to the morgue, and the other went to prison for manslaughter or the electric chair for murder.

Sammy let me hold his .32. My guns were at my apartment. I put the .32 in my pocket, with my hand on it, and walked out.

I couldn't stay out of sight. I had to show up at all of my usual haunts. I was glad that Reginald was out of town. He might have tried protecting me, and I didn't want him shot in the head by West Indian Archie.

I stood a while on the corner, with my mind confused—the muddled thinking that's characteristic of the addict. Was West Indian Archie, I began to wonder, bluffing a hype on me? To make fun of me? Some old hustlers did love to hype younger ones. I knew he wouldn't do it as some would, just to pick up three hundred dollars. But everyone was so slick. In this Harlem jungle people would hype their brothers. Numbers runners often had hyped addicts who had hit, who were so drugged that, when challenged, they really couldn't be sure if they had played a certain number.

I began to wonder whether West Indian Archie might not be right. Had I really gotten my combination confused? I certainly knew the two numbers I'd played; I knew I'd told him to combinate only one of them. Had I gotten mixed up about which number?

Have you ever been so sure you did something that you never would have thought of it again—unless it was brought up again? Then you start trying to mentally confirm—and you're only about half-sure?

It was just about time for me to go and pick up Jean Parks, to go downtown to see Billie at the Oynx Club. So much was swirling in my head. I thought about telephoning her and calling it off, making some excuse. But I knew that running now was the worst thing I could do. So I went on and picked up Jean at her place. We took a taxi on down to 52nd Street. *"Billie Holiday"* and those big photo blow-ups of her were under the lights outside. Inside, the tables were jammed against the wall, tables about big enough to get two drinks and four elbows on; the Onyx was one of those very little places.

Billie, at the microphone, had just finished a number when she saw Jean and me. Her white gown glittered under the spotlight, her face had that coppery, Indianish look, and her hair was in that trademark ponytail. For her next number she did the one she knew I always liked so: "You Don't Know What Love Is"—"until you face each dawn with sleepless eyes . . . until you've lost a love you hate to lose—"

When her set was done, Billie came over to our table. She and Jean, who hadn't seen each other in a long time, hugged each other. Billie sensed something wrong with me. She knew that I was always high, but she knew me well enough to see that something else was wrong, and asked in her customary profane language what was the matter with me. And in my own foul vocabulary of those days, I pretended to be without a care, so she let it drop.

We had a picture taken by the club photographer that night. The three of us were sitting close together. That was the last time I ever saw Lady Day. She's dead; dope and heartbreak stopped that heart as big as a barn and that sound and style that no one successfully copies. Lady Day sang with the *soul* of Negroes from the centuries of sorrow and oppression. What a shame that proud, fine, black woman never lived where the true greatness of the black race was appreciated!

In the Onyx Club men's room, I sniffed the little packet of cocaine I had gotten from Sammy. Jean and I, riding back up to Harlem in a cab, decided to have another drink. She had no idea what was happening when she suggested one of my main hang-outs, the bar of the La Marr-Cheri on the corner of 147th Street and St. Nicholas Avenue. I had my gun, and the cocaine courage, and I said okay. And by the time we'd had the drink, I was so high that I asked Jean to take a cab on home, and she did. I never have seen Jean again, either.

Like a fool, I didn't leave the bar. I stayed there, sitting, like a bigger fool, with my back to the door, thinking about West Indian Archie. Since that day, I have never sat with my back to a door—and I never will again. But it's a good thing I was then. I'm positive if I'd seen West Indian Archie come in, I'd have shot to kill.

The next thing I knew West Indian Archie was standing before me, cursing me, loud, his gun on me. He was really making his public point, floor-showing for the people. He called me foul names, threatened me.

Everyone, bartenders and customers, sat or stood as though carved, drinks in mid-air. The juke box, in the rear, was going. I had never seen West Indian Archie high before. Not a whisky high, I could tell it was something else. I knew the hustlers' characteristic of keying up on dope to do a job.

I was thinking, "I'm going to kill Archie . . . I'm just going to wait until he turns around—to get the drop on him." I could feel my own .32 resting against my ribs where it was tucked under my belt, beneath my coat.

West Indian Archie, seeming to read my mind, quit cursing. And his words jarred me.

"You're thinking you're going to kill me first, Red. But

I'm going to give you something to think about. I'm sixty. I'm an old man. I've been to Sing Sing. My life is over. You're a young man. Kill me, you're lost anyway. All you can do is go to prison."

I've since thought that West Indian Archie may have been trying to scare me into running, to save both his face and his life. It may be that's why he was high. No one knew that I hadn't killed anyone, but no one who knew me, including myself, would doubt that I'd kill.

I can't guess what might have happened. But under the code, if West Indian Archie had gone out of the door, after having humiliated me as he had, I'd have had to follow him out. We'd have shot it out in the street.

But some friends of West Indian Archie moved up alongside him, quietly calling his name, "Archie . . . Archie."

And he let them put their hands on him—and they drew him aside. I watched them move him past where I was sitting, glaring at me. They were working him back toward the rear.

Then, taking my time, I got down off the stool. I dropped a bill on the bar for the bartender. Without looking back, I went out.

I stood outside, in full view of the bar, with my hand in my pocket, for perhaps five minutes. When West Indian Archie didn't come out, I left.

It must have been five in the morning when, downtown, I woke up a white actor I knew who lived in the Howard Hotel on 45th Street, off Sixth Avenue.

I knew I had to stay high.

The amount of dope I put into myself within the next several hours sounds inconceivable. I got some opium from that fellow. I took a cab back up to my apartment and I smoked it. My gun was ready if I heard a mosquito cough.

My telephone rang. It was the white Lesbian who lived downtown. She wanted me to bring her and her girl friend fifty dollars worth of reefers.

I felt that if I had always done it, I had to do it now. Opium had me drowsy. I had a bottle of benzedrine tablets in my bathroom; I swallowed some of them to perk up. The two drugs working in me had my head going in opposite directions at the same time.

I knocked at the apartment right behind mine. The dealer let me have loose marijuana on credit. He saw I was so high that he even helped me roll it—a hundred sticks. And while we were rolling it, we both smoked some.

Now opium, benzedrine, reefers.

I stopped by Sammy's on the way downtown. His flashing-eyed Spanish Negro woman opened the door. Sammy had gotten weak for that woman. He had never let any other of his women hang around so much; now she was even answering his doorbell. Sammy was by this time very badly addicted. He seemed hardly to recognize me. Lying in bed, he reached under and again brought out that inevitable shaving mirror on which, for some reason, he always kept his cocaine crystals. He motioned for me to sniff some. I didn't refuse.

Going downtown to deliver the reefers, I felt sensations I cannot describe, in all those different grooves at the same time. The only word to describe it was a *timelessness*. A day might have seemed to me five minutes. Or a half-hour might have seemed a week.

I can't imagine how I looked when I got to the hotel. When the Lesbian and her girl friend saw me, they helped me to a bed; I fell across it and passed out.

That night, when they woke me up, it was half a day beyond West Indian Archie's deadline. Late, I went back uptown. It was on the wire. I could see people who knew me finding business elsewhere. I knew nobody wanted to be caught in a crossfire.

But nothing happened. The next day, either. I just stayed high.

Some raw kid hustler in a bar, I had to bust in his mouth. He came back, pulling a blade; I would have shot him, but somebody grabbed him. They put him out, cursing that he was going to kill me.

Intuition told me to get rid of my gun. I gave a hustler the eye across the bar. I'd no more than slipped him the gun from my belt when a cop I'd seen about came in the other door. He had his hand on his gun butt. He knew what was all over the wire; he was certain I'd be armed. He came slowly over toward me, and I knew if I sneezed, he'd blast me down.

He said, "Take your hand out of your pocket, Red—*real* carefully."

I did. Once he saw me empty handed, we both could relax a little. He motioned for me to walk outside, ahead of him, and I did. His partner was waiting on the sidewalk, opposite their patrol car, double-parked with its radio going. With people stopping, looking, they patted me down there on the sidewalk.

"What are you looking for?" I asked them when they didn't find anything.

"Red, there's a report you're carrying a gun."

"I had one," I said. "But I threw it in the river."

The one who had come into the bar said, "I think I'd leave town if I were you, Red."

I went back into the bar. Saying that I had thrown my gun away had kept them from taking me to my apartment. Things I had there could have gotten me more time than ten guns, and could have gotten them a promotion.

Everything was building up, closing in on me. I was trapped in so many cross turns. West Indian Archie gunning for me. The Italians who thought I'd stuck up their crap game after me. The scared kid hustler I'd hit. The cops.

For four years, up to that point, I'd been lucky enough, or slick enough, to escape jail, or even getting arrested. Or any *serious* trouble. But I knew that any minute now something had to give.

Sammy had done something that I've often wished I could have thanked him for.

When I heard the car's horn, I was walking on St. Nicholas Avenue. But my ears were hearing a gun. I didn't dream the horn could possibly be for me.

"Homeboy!"

I jerked around; I came close to shooting.

Shorty—from Boston!

I'd scared him nearly to death.

"Daddy-o!"

I couldn't have been happier.

Inside the car, he told me Sammy had telephoned about how I was jammed up tight and told him he'd better come and get me. And Shorty did his band's date, then borrowed his piano man's car, and burned up the miles to New York.

I didn't put up any objections to leaving. Shorty stood watch outside my apartment. I brought out and stuffed into the car's trunk what little stuff I cared to hang onto. Then we hit the highway. Shorty had been without sleep for about thirty-six hours. He told me afterward that through just about the whole ride back, I talked out of my head.

CHAPTER NINE

CAUGHT

Ella couldn't believe how atheist, how uncouth I had become. I believed that a man should do anything that he was slick enough, or bad and bold enough, to do and that a woman was nothing but another commodity. Every word I spoke was hip or profane. I would bet that my working vocabulary wasn't two hundred words.

Even Shorty, whose apartment I now again shared, wasn't prepared for how I lived and thought—like a predatory animal. Sometimes I would catch him watching me.

At first, I slept a lot—even at night. I had slept mostly in the daytime during the preceding two years. When awake, I smoked reefers. Shorty had originally introduced me to marijuana, and my consumption of it now astounded him.

I didn't want to talk much, at first. When awake, I'd play records continuously. The reefers gave me a feeling of contentment. I would enjoy hours of floating, day dreaming, imaginary conversations with my New York musician friends.

Within two weeks, I'd had more sleep than during any two months when I had been in Harlem hustling day and night. When I finally went out in the Roxbury streets, it took me only a little while to locate a peddler of "snow"—cocaine. It was when I got back into that familiar snow feeling that I began to want to talk.

Cocaine produces, for those who sniff its powdery white crystals, an illusion of supreme well-being, and a soaring overconfidence in both physical and mental ability. You think you could whip the heavyweight champion, and that you are smarter than everybody. There was also that feeling of timelessness. And there were intervals of ability to recall and review things that had happened years back with an astonishing clarity.

Shorty's band played at spots around Boston three or four nights a week. After he left for work, Sophia would come over and I'd talk about my plans. She would be gone back to her husband by the time Shorty returned from work, and I'd bend his ear until daybreak.

Sophia's husband had gotten out of the military, and he was some sort of salesman. He was supposed to have a big deal going which soon would require his traveling a lot to the West Coast. I didn't ask questions, but Sophia often indicated they weren't doing too well. I know *I* had nothing to do with that. He never dreamed I existed. A white woman might blow up at her husband and scream and yell and call him every name she can think of, and say the most vicious things in an effort to hurt him, and talk about his mother and his grandmother, too, but one thing she never will tell him herself is that she is going with a black man. That's one automatic red murder flag to the white man, and his woman knows it.

Sophia always had given me money. Even when I had hundreds of dollars in my pocket, when she came to Harlem I would take everything she had short of her train fare back to Boston. It seems that some women love to be exploited. When they are not exploited, they exploit the man. Anyway, it was his money that she gave me, I guess, because she never had worked. But now my demands on her increased, and she came up with more; again, I don't know where she got it. Always, every now and then, I had given her a hard time, just to keep her in line. Every once in a while a woman seems to need, in fact *wants* this, too. But now, I would feel evil and slap her around worse than ever, some of the nights when Shorty was away. She would cry, curse me, and swear that she would never be back. But I knew she wasn't even thinking about not coming back.

Sophia's being around was one of Shorty's greatest pleasures about my homecoming. I have said it before, I never in my life have seen a black man that desired white women as sincerely as Shorty did. Since I had known him, he had had several. He had never been able to keep a white woman any length of time, though, because he was too good to them, and, as I have said, any woman, white or black, seems to get bored with that.

It happened that Shorty was between white women when one night Sophia brought to the house her seventeen-year-old sister. I never saw anything like the way that she and Shorty nearly jumped for each other. For him, she wasn't only a white girl, but a *young* white girl. For her, he wasn't only a Negro, but a Negro *musician*. In looks, she was a younger version of Sophia, who still turned heads. Sometimes I'd take the two girls to Negro places where Shorty played. Negroes showed thirty-two teeth apiece as soon as they saw the white girls. They would come over to your booth, or your table; they would stand there and drool. And Shorty was no better. He'd stand up there playing and watching that young girl waiting for him, and waving at him, and winking. As soon as the set was over, he'd practically run over people getting down to our table.

I didn't lindy-hop any more now, I wouldn't even have thought of it now, just as I wouldn't have been caught in a zoot suit now. All of my suits were conservative. A banker might have worn my shoes.

I met Laura again. We were really glad to see each other. She was a lot more like me now, a good-time girl. We talked and laughed. She looked a lot older than she really was. She had no one man, she free-lanced around. She had long since moved away from her grandmother. Laura told me she had finished school, but then she gave up the college idea. Laura was high whenever I saw her, now, too; we smoked some reefers together.

After about a month of "laying dead," as inactivity was called, I knew I had to get some kind of hustle going.

A hustler, broke, needs a stake. Some nights when Shorty was playing, I would take whatever Sophia had been able to get for me, and I'd try to run it up into something, playing stud poker at John Hughes' gambling house.

When I had lived in Roxbury before, John Hughes had been a big gambler who wouldn't have spoken to me. But during the war the Roxbury "wire" had carried a lot about things I was doing in Harlem, and now the New York name magic was on me. That was the feeling that hustlers everywhere else had: if you could hustle and make it in New York, they were well off to know you; it gave them prestige. Anyway, through the same flush war years, John Hughes had hustled profitably enough to be able to open a pretty good gambling house.

John, one night, was playing in a game I was in. After the first two cards were dealt around the table, I had an ace showing. I looked beneath it at my hole card; another ace—a pair, back-to-back.

My ace showing made it my turn to bet.

But I didn't rush. I sat there and studied.

Finally, I knocked my knuckles on the table, passing, leaving the betting to the next man. My action implied that beneath my ace was some "nothing" card that I didn't care to risk my money on.

The player sitting next to me took the bait. He bet pretty heavily. And the next man raised him. Possibly each of them had small pairs. Maybe they just wanted to scare me out before I drew another ace. Finally, the bet reached John, who had a queen showing; he raised everybody.

Now, there was no telling what John had. John truly was a clever gambler. He could gamble as well as anybody I had gambled with in New York.

So the bet came back to me. It was going to cost me a lot of money to call all the raises. Some of them obviously had good cards but I knew I had every one of them beat. But again I studied, and studied; I pretended perplexity. And finally I put in my money, calling the bets.

The same betting pattern went on, with each new card, right around to the last card. And when that last card went around, I hit another ace in sight. Three aces. And John hit another queen in sight.

He bet a pile. Now, everyone else studied a long time— and, one by one, all folded their hands. Except me. All I could do was put what I had left on the table.

If I'd had the money, I could have raised five hundred dollars or more, and he'd have had to call me. John couldn't have gone the rest of his life wondering if I had bluffed him out of a pot that big.

I showed my hole card ace; John had three queens. As I hauled in the pot, something over five hundred dollars—my first real stake in Boston—John got up from the table. He'd quit. He told his house man, "Anytime Red comes in here and wants anything, let him have it." He said, "I've never seen a young man play his hole card like he played."

John said "young man," being himself about fifty, I guess, although you can never be certain about a Negro's age. He thought, as most people would have, that I was about thirty. No one in Roxbury except my sisters Ella and Mary suspected my real age.

The story of that poker game helped my on-scene reputation among the other gamblers and hustlers around Roxbury. Another thing that happened in John's gambling house contributed: the incident that made it known that I carried not a gun, but some guns.

John had a standing rule that anyone who came into the place to gamble had to check his guns if he had any. I always checked two guns. Then, one night, when a gambler tried to pull something slick, I drew a third gun, from its shoulder holster. This added to the rest of my reputation the word that I was "trigger-happy" and "crazy."

Looking back, I think I really was at least slightly out of my mind. I viewed narcotics as most people regard food. I wore my guns as today I wear my neckties. Deep down, I actually believed that after living as fully as humanly possible, one should then die violently. I expected then, as I still expect today, to die at any time. But then, I think I deliberately invited death in many, sometimes insane ways.

For instance, a merchant marine sailor who knew me and my reputation came into a bar carrying a package. He motioned me to follow him downstairs into the men's room. He unwrapped a stolen machine gun; he wanted to sell it. I said, "How do I know it works?" He loaded it with a cartridge clip, and told me that all I would have to do then was squeeze the trigger release. I took the gun, examined it, and the first thing he knew I had it jammed right up in his belly. I told him I would blow him wide open. He went backwards out of the restroom and up the stairs the way Bill "Bojangles" Robinson used to dance going backwards. He knew I was crazy enough to kill him. I was insane enough not to consider that he might just wait his chance to kill me. For perhaps a month I kept the machine gun at Shorty's before I was broke and sold it.

When Reginald came to Roxbury visiting, he was shocked at what he'd found out upon returning to Harlem. I spent some time with him. He still was the kid brother whom I still felt more "family" toward than I felt now even for our sister Ella. Ella still liked me. I would go to see her once in a while. But Ella had never been able to reconcile herself to the way I had changed. She has since told me that she had a steady foreboding that I was on my way into big trouble. But I always had the feeling that Ella somehow admired my rebellion against the world, because she, who had so much more drive and guts than most men, often felt stymied by having been born female.

Had I been thinking only in terms of myself, maybe I would have chosen steady gambling as a hustle. There were enough chump gamblers that hung around John Hughes' for a good gambler to make a living off them; chumps that worked, usually. One would just have to never miss the games on their paydays. Besides, John Hughes had offered me a job dealing for games; I didn't want that.

But I had come around to thinking not only of myself. I wanted to get something going that could help Shorty, too. We had been talking; I really felt sorry for Shorty. The same old musician story. The so-called glamor of being a musician, earning just about enough money so that after he paid rent and bought his reefers and food and other routine things, he had nothing left. Plus debts. How could Shorty have anything? I'd spent years in Harlem and on the road around the most popular musicians, the "names," even, who really were making big money for musicians—and they had nothing.

For that matter, all the thousands of dollars I'd handled, and *I* had nothing. Just satisfying my cocaine habit alone cost me about twenty dollars a day. I guess another five dollars a day could have been added for reefers and plain tobacco cigarettes that I smoked; besides getting high on drugs, I chain-smoked as many as four packs a day. And, if you ask me today, I'll tell you that tobacco, in all its forms, is just as much an addiction as any narcotic.

When I opened the subject of a hustle with Shorty, I started by first bringing him to agree with my concept—of which he was a living proof—that only squares kept on believing they could ever get anything by slaving.

And when I mentioned what I had in mind—house burglary—Shorty, who always had been so relatively conservative, really surprised me by how quickly he agreed. He didn't even know anything about burglarizing.

When I began to explain how it was done, Shorty wanted to bring in this friend of his, whom I had met, and liked, called Rudy.

Rudy's mother was Italian, his father was a Negro. He was born right there in Boston, a short, light fellow, a pretty boy type. Rudy worked regularly for an employment agency that sent him to wait on tables at exclusive parties. He had a side deal going, a hustle that took me right back to the old steering days in Harlem. Once a week, Rudy went to the home of this old, rich Boston blueblood, pillar-of-society aristocrat. He paid Rudy to undress them both, then pick up the old man like a baby, lay him on his bed, then stand over him and sprinkle him all over with *talcum powder*.

Rudy said the old man would actually reach his climax from that.

I told him and Shorty about some of the things I'd seen. Rudy said that as far as he knew, Boston had no organized specialty sex houses, just individual rich whites who had their private specialty desires catered to by Negroes who came to their homes camouflaged as chauffeurs, maids, waiters, or some other accepted image. Just as in New York, these were the rich, the highest society—the predominantly old men, past the age of ability to conduct any kind of ordinary sex, always hunting for new ways to be "sensitive."

Rudy, I remember, spoke of one old white man who paid a black couple to let him watch them have intercourse on his bed. Another was so "sensitive" that he paid to sit on a chair outside a room where a couple was—he got his satisfaction just from imagining what was going on inside.

A good burglary team includes, I knew, what is called a "finder." A finder is one who locates lucrative places to rob. Another principal need is someone able to "case" these places' physical layouts—to determine means of entry, the best getaway routes, and so forth. Rudy qualified on both counts. Being sent to work in rich homes, he wouldn't be suspected when he sized up their loot and cased the joint, just running around looking busy with a white coat on.

Rudy's reaction, when he was told what we had in mind, was something, I remember, like "Man, when do we start?"

But I wasn't rushing off half-cocked. I had learned from some of the pros, and from my own experience, how important it was to be careful and plan. Burglary, properly executed, though it had its dangers, offered the maximum chances of success with the minimum risk. If you did your job so that you never met any of your victims, it first lessened your chances of having to attack or perhaps kill someone. And if through some slip-up you were caught, later, by the police, there was never a positive eyewitness.

It is also important to select an area of burglary and stick to that. There are specific specialties among burglars. Some work apartments only, others houses only, others stores only, or warehouses; still others will go after only safes or strongboxes.

Within the residence burglary category, there are further specialty distinctions. There are the day burglars, the dinner and theater-time burglars, the night burglars. I think that any city's police will tell you that very rarely do they find one type who will work at another time. For instance Jumpsteady, in Harlem, was a nighttime apartment specialist. It would have been hard to persuade Jumpsteady to work in the daytime if a millionaire had gone out for lunch and left his front door wide open.

I had one very practical reason never to work in the daytime, aside from my inclinations. With my high visibility, I'd have been sunk in the daytime. I could just hear people: "A reddish-brown Negro over six feet tall." One glance would be enough.

Setting up what I wanted to be the perfect operation, I thought about pulling the white girls into it for two reasons. One was that I realized we'd be too limited relying only upon places where Rudy worked as a waiter. He didn't get to work in too many places; it wouldn't be very long before we ran out of sources. And when other places had to be found and cased in the rich, white residential areas, Negroes hanging around would stick out like sore thumbs, but these white girls could get invited into the right places.

I disliked the idea of having too many people involved, all at the same time. But with Shorty and Sophia's sister so close now, and Sophia and me as though we had been together for fifty years, and Rudy as eager and cool as he was, nobody would be apt to spill, everybody would be under the same risk; we would be like a family unit.

I never doubted that Sophia would go along. Sophia would do anything I said. And her sister would do anything that Sophia said. They both went for it. Sophia's husband was away on one of his trips to the coast when I told her and her sister.

Most burglars, I knew, were caught not on the job, but trying to dispose of the loot. Finding the fence we used was a rare piece of luck. We agreed upon the plan for operations.

The fence didn't work with us directly. He had a representative, an ex-con, who dealt with me, and no one else in my gang. Aside from his regular business, he owned around Boston several garages and small warehouses. The arrangement was that before a job, I would alert the representative, and give him a general idea of what we expected to get, and he'd tell me at which garage or warehouse we should make the drop. After we had made our drop, the representative would examine the stolen articles. He would remove all identifying marks from everything. Then he would call the fence, who would come and make a personal appraisal. The next day the representative would meet me at a pre-arranged place and would make the payment for what we had stolen—in cash.

One thing I remember. This fence always sent your money in crisp, brand-new bills. He was smart. Somehow that had a very definite psychological effect upon all of us, after we had pulled a job, walking around with that crisp green money in our pockets. He may have had other reasons.

We needed a base of operations—not in Roxbury. The girls rented an apartment in Harvard Square. Unlike Negroes, these white girls could go shopping for the locale and physical situation we wanted. It was on the ground floor, where, moving late at night, all of us could come and go without attracting notice.

In any organization, someone must be the boss. If it's even just one person, you've got to be the boss of yourself.

At our gang's first meeting in the apartment, we discussed how we were going to work. The girls would get into houses to case them by ringing bells and saying they were saleswomen, poll-takers, college girls making a survey, or anything else suitable. Once in the houses, they would get around as much as they could without attracting attention. Then, back, they would report what special valuables they had seen, and where. They would draw the layout for Shorty, Rudy, and me. We agreed that the girls would actually burglarize only in special cases where there would be some advantage. But generally the three men would go, two of us to do the job while the third kept watch in the getaway car, with the motor running.

Talking to them, laying down the plans, I had deliberately sat on a bed away from them. All of a sudden, I pulled out my gun, shook out all five bullets, and then let them see me put back only one bullet. I twirled the cylinder, and put the muzzle to my head.

"Now, I'm going to see how much guts all of you have," I said.

I grinned at them. All of their mouths had flapped open. I pulled the trigger—we all heard it *click*.

"I'm going to do it again, now."

They begged me to stop. I could see in Shorty's and Rudy's eyes some idea of rushing me.

We all heard the hammer *click* on another empty cylinder.

The women were in hysterics. Rudy and Shorty were begging, *"Man . . . Red . . . cut it out, man! . . . Freeze!"* I pulled the trigger once more.

"I'm doing this, showing you I'm not afraid to die," I told them. "Never cross a man not afraid to die . . . now, let's get to work!"

I never had one moment's trouble with any of them after that. Sophia acted awed, her sister all but called me "Mr. Red." Shorty and Rudy were never again quite the same with me. Neither of them ever mentioned it. They thought I was crazy. They were afraid of me.

We pulled the first job that night—the place of the old man who hired Rudy to sprinkle him with talcum powder. A cleaner job couldn't have been asked for. Everything went like clockwork. The fence was full of praise; he proved he meant it with his crisp, new money. The old man later told Rudy how a small army of detectives had been there— and they decided that the job had the earmarks of some gang which had been operating around Boston for about a year.

We quickly got it down to a science. The girls would scout and case in wealthy neighborhoods. The burglary would be pulled; sometimes it took no more than ten minutes. Shorty and I did most of the actual burglary. Rudy generally had the getaway car.

If the people weren't at home, we'd use a passkey on a common door lock. On a patent lock, we'd use a jimmy, as it's called, or a lockpick. Or, sometimes, we would enter by windows from a fire-escape, or a roof. Gullible women often took the girls all over their houses, just to hear them exclaiming over the finery. With the help of the girls' drawings and a finger-beam searchlight, we went straight to the things we wanted.

Sometimes the victims were in their beds asleep. That may sound very daring. Actually, it was almost easy. The first thing we had to do when people were in the house was to wait, very still, and pick up the sounds of breathing. Snorers we loved; they made it real easy. In stockinged feet, we'd go right into the bedrooms. Moving swiftly, like shadows, we would lift clothes, watches, wallets, handbags, and jewelry boxes.

The Christmas season was Santa Claus for us; people had expensive presents lying all over their houses. And they had taken more cash than usual out of their banks. Sometimes, working earlier than we usually did, we even worked houses that we hadn't cased. If the shades were drawn full, and no lights were on, and there was no answer when one of the girls rang the bell, we would take the chance and go in.

I can give you a very good tip if you want to keep burglars out of your house. A light on for the burglar to see is the very best single means of protection. One of the ideal things is to leave a bathroom light on all night. The bathroom is one place where somebody could be, for any length of time, at any time of the night, and he would be likely to hear the slightest strange sound. The burglar, knowing this, won't try to enter. It's also the cheapest possible protection. The kilowatts are a lot cheaper than your valuables.

We became efficient. The fence sometimes relayed tips as to where we could find good loot. It was in this way that for one period, one of our best periods, I remember, we specialized in Oriental rugs. I have always suspected that the fence himself sold the rugs to the people we stole them from. But, anyway, you wouldn't imagine the value of those things. I remember one small one that brought us a thousand dollars. There's no telling what the fence got for it. Every burglar knew that fences robbed the burglars worse than the burglars had robbed the victims.

Our only close brush with the law came once when we were making our getaway, three of us in the front seat of the car, and the back seat loaded with stuff. Suddenly we saw a police car round the corner, coming toward us, and it went on past us. They were just cruising. But then in the rear-view mirror, we saw them make a U-turn, and we knew they were going to flash us to stop. They had spotted us, in passing, as Negroes, and they knew that Negroes had no business in the area at that hour.

It was a close situation. There was a lot of robbery going on; we weren't the only gang working, we knew, not by any means. But I knew that the white man is rare who will ever consider that a Negro can outsmart him. Before their light began flashing, I told Rudy to stop. I did what I'd done once before—got out and flagged them, walking toward them. When they stopped, I was at their car. I asked them, bumbling my words like a confused Negro, if they could tell me how to get to a Roxbury address. They told me, and we, and they, went on about our respective businesses.

We were going along fine. We'd make a good pile and then lay low awhile, living it up. Shorty still played with his band, Rudy never missed attending his sensitive old man, or the table-waiting at his exclusive parties, and the girls maintained their routine home schedules.

Sometimes, I still took the girls out to places where Shorty played, and to other places, spending money as though it were going out of style, the girls dressed in jewelry and furs they had selected from our hauls. No one knew our hustle, but it was clear that we were doing fine. And sometimes, the girls would come over and we'd meet them either at Shorty's in Roxbury or in our Harvard Square place, and just smoke reefers, and play music. It's a shame to tell on a man, but Shorty was so obsessed with the white girl that even if the lights were out, he would pull up the shade to be able to see that white flesh by the street lamp from outside.

Early evenings when we were laying low between jobs, I often went to a Massachusetts Avenue night club called the Savoy. And Sophia would telephone me there punctually. Even when we pulled jobs, I would leave from this club, then rush back there after the job. The reason was so that if it was ever necessary, people could testify that they had seen me at just about the time the job was pulled. Negroes being questioned by policemen would be very hard to pin down on any exact time.

Boston at this time had two Negro detectives. Ever since I had come back on the Roxbury scene, one of these detectives, a dark brown fellow named Turner, had never been able to stand me, and it was mutual. He talked about what he would do to me, and I had promptly put an answer back on the wire. I knew from the way he began to act that he had heard it. Everyone knew that I carried guns. And he did have sense enough to know that I wouldn't hesitate to use them—and on him, detective or not.

This early evening I was in this place when at the usual time, the phone in the booth rang. It rang just as this detective Turner happened to walk in through the front door. He saw me start to get up, he knew the call was for me, but stepped inside the booth, and answered.

I heard him saying, looking straight at me, "Hello, hello, hello—" And I knew that Sophia, taking no chances with the strange voice, had hung up.

"Wasn't that call for me?" I asked Turner.

He said that it was.

I said, "Well, why didn't you say so?"

He gave me a rude answer. I knew he wanted me to make a move, first. We both were being cagey. We both knew that we wanted to kill each other. Neither wanted to say the wrong thing. Turner didn't want to say anything that, repeated, would make him sound bad. I didn't want to say anything that could be interpreted as a threat to a cop.

But I remember exactly what I said to him anyway, purposely loud enough for some people at the bar to hear me. I said, "You know, Turner—you're trying to make history. Don't you know that if you play with me, you certainly will go down in history because you've got to kill me?"

Turner looked at me. Then he backed down. He walked on by me. I guess he wasn't ready to make history.

I had gotten to the point where I was walking on my own coffin.

It's a law of the rackets that every criminal expects to get caught. He tries to stave off the inevitable for as long as he can.

Drugs helped me push the thought to the back of my mind. They were the center of my life. I had gotten to the stage where every day I used enough drugs—reefers, cocaine, or both—so that I felt above any worries, any strains. If any worries did manage to push their way through to the surface of my consciousness, I could float them back where they came from until tomorrow, and then until the next day.

But where, always before, I had been able to smoke the reefers and to sniff the snow and rarely show it very much, by now it was not that easy.

One week when we weren't working—after a big haul—I was just staying high, and I was out nightclubbing. I came into this club, and from the bartender's face when he spoke, "Hello, Red," I knew that something was wrong. But I didn't ask him anything. I've always had this rule—never ask anybody in that kind of situation; they will tell you what they want you to know. But the bartender didn't get a chance to tell me, if he had meant to. When I sat down on a stool and ordered a drink, I saw them.

Sophia and her sister sat at a table inside, near the dance floor, with a white man.

I don't know how I ever made such a mistake as I next did. I could have talked to her later. I didn't know, or care, who the white fellow was. My cocaine told me to get up.

It wasn't Sophia's husband. It was his closest friend. They had served in the war together. With her husband out of town, he had asked Sophia and her sister out to dinner, and they went. But then, later, after dinner, driving around, he had suddenly suggested going over to the black ghetto.

Every Negro that lives in a city has seen the type a thousand times, the Northern cracker who will go to visit "niggertown," to be amused at "the coons."

The girls, so well known in the Negro places in Roxbury, had tried to change his mind, but he had insisted. So they had just held their breaths coming into this club where they had been a hundred times. They walked in stiff-eyeing the bartenders and waiters who caught their message and acted as though they never had seen them before. And they were sitting there with drinks before them, praying that no Negro who knew them would barge up to their table.

Then up I came. I know I called them "Baby." They were chalky-white, he was beet-red.

That same night, back at the Harvard Square place, I really got sick. It was less of a physical sickness than it was all of the last five years catching up. I was in my pajamas in bed, half asleep, when I heard someone knock.

I knew that something was wrong. We all had keys. No one ever knocked at the door. I rolled off and under the bed; I was so groggy it didn't cross my mind to grab for my gun on the dresser.

Under the bed, I heard the key turn, and I saw the

shoes and pants cuffs walk in. I watched them walk around. I saw them stop. Every time they stopped, I knew what the eyes were looking at. And I knew, before he did, that he was going to get down and look under the bed. He did. It was Sophia's husband's friend. His face was about two feet from mine. It looked congealed.

"Ha, ha, ha, I fooled you, didn't I?" I said. It wasn't at all funny. I got out from under the bed, still fake-laughing. He didn't run, I'll say that for him. He stood back; he watched me as though I were a snake.

I didn't try to hide what he already knew. The girls had some things in the closets, and around; he had seen all of that. We even talked some. I told him the girls weren't there, and he left. What shook me the most was realizing that I had trapped myself under the bed without a gun. I really was slipping.

I had put a stolen watch into a jewelry shop to replace a broken crystal. It was about two days later, when I went to pick up the watch, that things fell apart.

As I have said, a gun was as much a part of my dress as a necktie. I had my gun in a shoulder holster, under my coat.

The loser of the watch, the person from whom it had been stolen by us, I later found, had described the repair that it needed. It was a very expensive watch, that's why I had kept it for myself. And all of the jewelers in Boston had been alerted.

The Jew waited until I had paid him before he laid the watch on the counter. He gave his signal—and this other fellow suddenly appeared, from the back, walking toward me.

One hand was in his pocket. I knew he was a cop.

He said, quietly, "Step into the back."

Just as I started back there, an innocent Negro walked into the shop. I remember later hearing that he had just that day gotten out of the military. The detective, thinking he was with me, turned to him.

There I was, wearing my gun, and the detective talking to that Negro with his back to me. Today I believe that Allah was with me even then. I didn't try to shoot him. And that saved my life.

I remember that his name was Detective Slack.

I raised my arm, and motioned to him, "Here, take my gun."

I saw his face when he took it. He was shocked. Because of the sudden appearance of the other Negro, he had never thought about a gun. It really moved him that I hadn't tried to kill him.

Then, holding my gun in his hand, he signaled. And out from where they had been concealed walked two other detectives. They'd had me covered. One false move, I'd have been dead.

I was going to have a long time in prison to think about that.

If I hadn't been arrested right when I was, I could have been dead another way. Sophia's husband's friend had told her husband about me. And the husband had arrived that morning, and had gone to the apartment with a gun, looking for me. He was at the apartment just about when they took me to the precinct.

The detectives grilled me. They didn't beat me. They didn't even put a finger on me. And I knew it was because I hadn't tried to kill the detective.

They got my address from some papers they found on me. The girls soon were picked up. Shorty was pulled right off the bandstand that night. The girls also had implicated Rudy. To this day, I have always marveled at how Rudy, somehow, got the word, and I know he must have caught the first thing smoking out of Boston, and he got away. They never got him.

I have thought a thousand times, I guess, about how I so narrowly escaped death twice that day. That's why I believe that everything is written.

The cops found the apartment loaded with evidence— fur coats, some jewelry, other small stuff—plus the tools of our trade. A jimmy, a lockpick, glass cutters, screwdrivers, pencil-beam flashlights, false keys . . . and my small arsenal of guns.

The girls got low bail. They were still white—burglars or not. Their worst crime was their involvement with Negroes. But Shorty and I had bail set at $10,000 each, which they knew we were nowhere near able to raise.

The social workers worked on us. White women in league with Negroes was their main obsession. The girls weren't so-called "tramps," or "trash," they were well-to-do upper-middle-class whites. That bothered the social workers and the forces of the law more than anything else.

How, where, when, had I met them? Did we sleep together? Nobody wanted to know anything at all about the robberies. All they could see was that we had taken the white man's women.

I just looked at the social workers: "Now, what do *you* think?"

Even the court clerks and the bailiffs: "Nice white girls . . . goddam niggers—" It was the same even from our court-appointed lawyers as we sat down, under guard, at a table, as our hearing assembled. Before the judge entered, I said to one lawyer, "We seem to be getting sentenced because of those girls." He got red from the neck up and shuffled his papers: "You had no business with white girls!"

Later, when I had learned the full truth about the white man, I reflected many times that the average burglary sentence for a first offender, as we all were, was about two years. But we weren't going to get the average—not for *our* crime.

I want to say before I go on that I have never previously told anyone my sordid past in detail. I haven't done it now to sound as though I might be proud of how bad, how evil, I was.

But people are always speculating—why am I as I am? To understand that of any person, his whole life, from birth, must be reviewed. All of our experiences fuse into our personality. Everything that ever happened to us is an ingredient.

Today, when everything that I do has an urgency, I would not spend one hour in the preparation of a book which had the ambition to perhaps titillate some readers. But I am spending many hours because the full story is the best way that I know to have it seen, and understood, that I had sunk to the very bottom of the American white man's society when—soon now, in prison—I found Allah and the religion of Islam and it completely transformed my life.

CHAPTER TEN

SATAN

Shorty didn't know what the word "concurrently" meant.

Somehow, Lansing-to-Boston bus fare had been scraped up by Shorty's old mother. "Son, read the Book of Revelations and pray to God!" she had kept telling Shorty, visiting him, and once me, while we awaited our sentencing. Shorty had read the Bible's Revelation pages; he had actually gotten down on his knees, praying like some Negro Baptist deacon.

Then we were looking up at the judge in Middlesex County Court. (Our, I think, fourteen counts of crime were committed in that county.) Shorty's mother was sitting, sobbing with her head bowing up and down to her Jesus, over near Ella and Reginald. Shorty was the first of us called to stand up.

"Count one, eight to ten years—

"Count two, eight to ten years—

"Count three . . ."

And, finally, "The sentences to run concurrently."

Shorty, sweating so hard that his black face looked as though it had been greased, and not understanding the word "concurrently," had counted in his head to probably over a hundred years; he cried out, he began slumping. The bailiffs had to catch and support him.

In eight to ten seconds, Shorty had turned as atheist as I had been to start with.

I got ten years.

The girls got one to five years, in the Women's Reformatory at Framingham, Massachusetts.

This was in February, 1946. I wasn't quite twenty-one. I had not even started shaving.

They took Shorty and me, handcuffed together, to the Charlestown State Prison.

I can't remember any of my prison numbers. That seems surprising, even after the dozen years since I have been out of prison. Because your number in prison became part of you. You never heard your name, only your number. On all of your clothing, every item, was your number, stenciled. It grew stenciled on your brain.

Any person who claims to have deep feeling for other human beings should think a long, long time before he votes to have other men kept behind bars—caged. I am not saying there shouldn't be prisons, but there shouldn't be bars. Behind bars, a man never reforms. He will never forget. He never will get completely over the memory of the bars.

After he gets out, his mind tries to erase the experience, but he can't. I've talked with numerous former convicts. It has been very interesting to me to find that all of our minds had blotted away many details of years in prison. But in every case, he will tell you that he can't forget those bars.

As a "fish" (prison slang for a new inmate) at Charlestown, I was physically miserable and as evil-tempered as a snake, being suddenly without drugs. The cells didn't have running water. The prison had been built in 1805—in Napoleon's day—and was even styled after the Bastille. In the dirty, cramped cell, I could lie on my cot and touch both walls. The toilet was a covered pail; I don't care how strong you are, you can't stand having to smell a whole cell row of defecation.

The prison psychologist interviewed me and he got called every filthy name I could think of, and the prison chaplain got called worse. My first letter, I remember, was from my religious brother Philbert in Detroit, telling me his "holiness" church was going to pray for me. I scrawled him a reply I'm ashamed to think of today.

Ella was my first visitor. I remember seeing her catch herself, then try to smile at me, now in the faded dungarees stenciled with my number. Neither of us could find much to say, until I wished she hadn't come at all. The guards with guns watched about fifty convicts and visitors. I have heard scores of new prisoners swearing back in their cells that when free their first act would be to waylay those visiting-room guards. Hatred often focused on them.

I first got high in Charlestown on nutmeg. My cellmate was among at least a hundred nutmeg men who, for money or cigarettes, bought from kitchen-worker inmates penny matchboxes full of stolen nutmeg. I grabbed a box as though it were a pound of heavy drugs. Stirred into a glass of cold water, a penny matchbox full of nutmeg had the kick of three or four reefers.

With some money sent by Ella, I was finally able to buy stuff for better highs from guards in the prison. I got reefers, Nembutal, and benzedrine. Smuggling to prisoners was the guards' sideline; every prison's inmates know that's how guards make most of their living.

I served a total of seven years in prison. Now, when I try to separate that first year-plus that I spent at Charlestown, it runs all together in a memory of nutmeg and the other semi-drugs, of cursing guards, throwing things out of my cell, balking in the lines, dropping my tray in the dining hall, refusing to answer my number—claiming I forgot it—and things like that.

I preferred the solitary that this behavior brought me. I would pace for hours like a caged leopard, viciously cursing aloud to myself. And my favorite targets were the Bible and God. But there was a legal limit to how much time one could be kept in solitary. Eventually, the men in the cellblock had a name for me: "Satan." Because of my antireligious attitude.

The first man I met in prison who made any positive impression on me whatever was a fellow inmate, "Bimbi." I met him in 1947, at Charlestown. He was a light, kind of red-complexioned Negro, as I was; about my height, and he had freckles. Bimbi, an old-time burglar, had been in many prisons. In the license plate shop where our gang worked, he operated the machine that stamped out the numbers. I was along the conveyor belt where the numbers were painted.

Bimbi was the first Negro convict I'd known who didn't respond to "What'cha know, Daddy?" Often, after we had done our day's license plate quota, we would sit around, perhaps fifteen of us, and listen to Bimbi. Normally, white prisoners wouldn't think of listening to Negro prisoners' opinions on anything, but guards, even, would wander over close to hear Bimbi on any subject.

He would have a cluster of people riveted, often on odd subjects you never would think of. He would prove to us, dipping into the science of human behavior, that the only difference between us and outside people was that we had been caught. He liked to talk about historical events and figures. When he talked about the history of Concord, where I was to be transferred later, you would have thought he was hired by the Chamber of Commerce, and I wasn't the first inmate who had never heard of Thoreau until Bimbi expounded upon him. Bimbi was known as the library's best customer. What fascinated me with him most of all was that he was the first man I had ever seen command total respect . . . with his words.

Bimbi seldom said much to me; he was gruff to individuals, but I sensed he liked me. What made me seek his friendship was when I heard him discuss religion. I considered myself beyond atheism—I was Satan. But Bimbi put the atheist philosophy in a framework, so to speak. That ended my vicious cursing attacks. My approach sounded so weak alongside his, and he never used a foul word.

Out of the blue one day, Bimbi told me flatly, as was his way, that I had some brains, if I'd use them. I had wanted his friendship, not that kind of advice. I might have cursed another convict, but nobody cursed Bimbi. He told me I should take advantage of the prison correspondence courses and the library.

When I had finished the eighth grade back in Mason, Michigan, that was the last time I'd thought of studying anything that didn't have some hustle purpose. And the streets had erased everything I'd ever learned in school; I didn't know a verb from a house. My sister Hilda had written a suggestion that, if possible in prison, I should study English and penmanship; she had barely been able to read a couple of picture post cards I had sent her when I was selling reefers on the road.

So, feeling I had time on my hands, I did begin a correspondence course in English. When the mimeographed listings of available books passed from cell to cell, I would put my number next to titles that appealed to me which weren't already taken.

Through the correspondence exercises and lessons, some of the mechanics of grammar gradually began to come back to me.

After about a year, I guess, I could write a decent and

legible letter. About then, too, influenced by having heard Bimbi often explain word derivations, I quietly started another correspondence course—in Latin.

Under Bimbi's tutelage, too, I had gotten myself some little cellblock swindles going. For packs of cigarettes, I beat just about anyone at dominoes. I always had several cartons of cigarettes in my cell; they were, in prison, nearly as valuable a medium of exchange as money. I booked cigarette and money bets on fights and ball games. I'll never forget the prison sensation created that day in April, 1947, when Jackie Robinson was brought up to play with the Brooklyn Dodgers. Jackie Robinson had, then, his most fanatic fan in me. When he played, my ear was glued to the radio, and no game ended without my refiguring his average up through his last turn at bat.

One day in 1948, after I had been transferred to Concord Prison, my brother Philbert, who was forever joining something, wrote me this time that he had discovered the "natural religion for the black man." He belonged now, he said, to something called "the Nation of Islam." He said I should "pray to Allah for deliverance." I wrote Philbert a letter which, although in improved English, was worse than my earlier reply to his news that I was being prayed for by his "holiness" church.

When a letter from Reginald arrived, I never dreamed of associating the two letters, although I knew that Reginald had been spending a lot of time with Wilfred, Hilda, and Philbert in Detroit. Reginald's letter was newsy, and also it contained this instruction: "Malcolm, don't eat any more pork, and don't smoke any more cigarettes. I'll show you how to get out of prison."

My automatic response was to think he had come upon some way I could work a hype on the penal authorities. I went to sleep—and woke up—trying to figure what kind of a hype it could be. Something psychological, such as my act with the New York draft board? Could I, after going without pork and smoking no cigarettes for a while, claim some physical trouble that could bring about my release?

"Get out of prison." The words hung in the air around me, I wanted out so badly.

I wanted, in the worst way, to consult with Bimbi about

it. But something big, instinct said, you spilled to nobody.

Quitting cigarettes wasn't going to be too difficult. I had been conditioned by days in solitary without cigarettes. Whatever this chance was, I wasn't going to fluff it. After I read that letter, I finished the pack I then had open. I haven't smoked another cigarette to this day, since 1948.

It was about three or four days later when pork was served for the noon meal.

I wasn't even thinking about pork when I took my seat at the long table. Sit-grab-gobble-stand-file out; that was the Emily Post in prison eating. When the meat platter was passed to me, I didn't even know what the meat was; usually, you couldn't tell, anyway—but it was suddenly as though *don't eat any more pork* flashed on a screen before me.

I hesitated, with the platter in mid-air; then I passed it along to the inmate waiting next to me. He began serving himself; abruptly, he stopped. I remember him turning, looking surprised at me.

I said to him, "I don't eat pork."

The platter then kept on down the table.

It was the funniest thing, the reaction, and the way that it spread. In prison, where so little breaks the monotonous routine, the smallest thing causes a commotion of talk. It was being mentioned all over the cell block by night that Satan didn't eat pork.

It made me very proud, in some odd way. One of the universal images of the Negro, in prison and out, was that he couldn't do without pork. It made me feel good to see that my not eating it had especially startled the white convicts.

Later I would learn, when I had read and studied Islam a good deal, that, unconsciously, my first pre-Islamic submission had been manifested. I had experienced, for the first time, the Muslim teaching, "If you will take one step toward Allah—Allah will take two steps toward you."

My brothers and sisters in Detroit and Chicago had all become converted to what they were being taught was the "natural religion for the black man" of which Philbert had written to me. They all prayed for me to become converted while I was in prison. But after Philbert reported my vicious reply, they discussed what was the best thing to do. They had decided that Reginald, the latest convert, the one to whom I felt closest, would best know how to approach me, since he knew me so well in the street life.

Independently of all this, my sister Ella had been steadily working to get me transferred to the Norfolk, Massachusetts, Prison Colony, which was an experimental rehabilitation jail. In other prisons, convicts often said that if you had the right money, or connections, you could get transferred to this Colony whose penal policies sounded almost too good to be true. Somehow, Ella's efforts in my behalf were successful in late 1948, and I was transferred to Norfolk.

The Colony was, comparatively, a heaven, in many respects. It had flushing toilets; there were no bars, only walls —and within the walls, you had far more freedom. There was plenty of fresh air to breathe; it was not in a city.

There were twenty-four "house" units, fifty men living in each unit, if memory serves me correctly. This would mean that the Colony had a total of around 1200 inmates. Each "house" had three floors and, greatest blessing of all, each inmate had his own room.

About fifteen per cent of the inmates were Negroes, distributed about five to nine Negroes in each house.

Norfolk Prison Colony represented the most enlightened form of prison that I have ever head of. In place of the atmosphere of malicious gossip, perversion, grafting, hateful guards, there was more relative "culture," as "culture" is interpreted in prisons. A high percentage of the Norfolk Prison Colony inmates went in for "intellectual" things, group discussions, debates, and such. Instructors for the educational rehabilitation programs came from Harvard, Boston University, and other educational institutions in the area. The visting rules, far more lenient than other prisons', permitted visitors almost every day, and allowed them to stay two hours. You had your choice of sitting alongside your visitor, or facing each other.

Norfolk Prison Colony's library was one of its outstanding features. A millionaire named Parkhurst had willed his library there; he had probably been interested in the rehabilitation program. History and religions were his special interests. Thousands of his books were on the shelves, and in the back were boxes and crates full, for which there wasn't space on the shelves. At Norfolk, we could actually go into the library, with permission—walk up and down the shelves, pick books. There were hundreds of old volumes, some of them probably quite rare. I read aimlessly, until I learned to read selectively, with a purpose.

I hadn't heard from Reginald in a good while after I got to Norfolk Prison Colony. But I had come in there not smoking cigarettes, or eating pork when it was served. That caused a bit of eyebrow-raising. Then a letter from Reginald telling me when he was coming to see me. By the time he came, I was really keyed up to hear the hype he was going to explain.

Reginald knew how my street-hustler mind operated. That's why his approach was so effective.

He had always dressed well, and now, when he came to visit, was carefully groomed. I was aching with wanting the "no pork and cigarettes" riddle answered. But he talked about the family, what was happening in Detroit, Harlem the last time he was there. I have never pushed anyone to tell me anything before he is ready. The offhand way Reginald talked and acted made me know that something big was coming.

He said, finally, as though it had just happened to come into his mind, "Malcolm, if a man knew every imaginable thing that there is to know, who would he be?"

Back in Harlem, he had often liked to get at something through this kind of indirection. It had often irritated me, because my way had always been direct. I looked at him. "Well, he would have to be some kind of a god—"

Reginald said, "There's a *man* who knows everything."

I asked, "Who is that?"

"God is a man," Reginald said. "His real name is Allah."

Allah. That word came back to me from Philbert's letter; it was my first hint of any connection. But Reginald went on. He said that God had 360 degrees of knowledge. He said that 360 degrees represented "the sum total of knowledge."

To say I was confused is an understatement. I don't have to remind you of the background against which I sat hearing my brother Reginald talk like this. I just listened, knowing he was taking his time in putting me onto something. And if somebody is trying to put you onto something, you need to listen.

"The devil has only thirty-three degrees of knowledge— known as Masonry," Reginald said. I can so specifically remember the exact phrases since, later, I was gong to teach them so many times to others. "The devil uses his Masonry to rule other people."

He told me that this God had come to America, and that he had made himself known to a man named Elijah—"a black man, just like us." This God had let Elijah know, Reginald said, that the devil's "time was up."

I didn't know what to think. I just listened.

"The devil is also a man," Reginald said.

"What do you mean?"

With a slight movement of his head, Reginald indicated some white inmates and their visitors talking, as we were, across the room.

"Them," he said. "The white man is the devil."

He told me that all whites knew they were devils—"especially Masons."

I never will forget: my mind was involuntarily flashing across the entire spectrum of white people I had ever known; and for some reason it stopped upon Hymie, the Jew, who had been so good to me.

Reginald, a couple of times, had gone out with me to that Long Island bootlegging operation to buy and bottle up the bootleg liquor for Hymie.

I said, "Without any exception?"

"Without any exception."

"What about Hymie?"

"What is it if I let you make five hundred dollars to let me make ten thousand?"

After Reginald left, I thought. I thought. Thought.

I couldn't make of it head, or tail, or middle.

The white people I had known marched before my mind's eye. From the start of my life. The state white people always in our house after the other whites I didn't know had killed my father . . . the white people who kept calling my mother "crazy" to her face and before me and my brothers and sisters, until she finally was taken off by white people to the Kalamazoo asylum . . . the white judge and others who had split up the children . . . the Swerlins, the other whites around Mason . . . white youngsters I was in school there with, and the teachers—the one who told me in the eighth grade to "be a carpenter" because thinking of being a lawyer was foolish for a Negro. . . .

My head swam with the parading faces of white people.

The ones in Boston, in the white-only dances at the Rose-land Ballroom where I shined their shoes . . . at the Parker House where I took their dirty plates back to the kitchen . . . the railroad crewmen and passengers . . . Sophia. . . .

The whites in New York City—the cops, the white crimi-nals I'd dealt with . . . the whites who piled into the Negro speakeasies for a taste of Negro *soul* . . . the white women who wanted Negro men . . . the men I'd steered to the black "specialty sex" they wanted. . . .

The fence back in Boston, and his ex-con representative . . . Boston cops . . . Sophia's husband's friend, and her husband, whom I'd never seen, but knew so much about . . . Sophia's sister . . . the Jew jeweler who'd helped trap me . . . the social workers . . . the Middlesex County Court people . . . the judge who gave me ten years . . . the prisoners I'd known, the guards and the officials. . . .

A celebrity among the Norfolk Prison Colony inmates was a rich, older fellow, a paralytic, called John. He had killed his baby, one of those "mercy" killings. He was a proud, big-shot type, always reminding everyone that he was a 33rd-degree Mason, and what powers Masons had—that only Masons ever had been U. S. Presidents, that Masons in distress could secretly signal to judges and other Masons in powerful positions.

I kept thinking about what Reginald had said. I wanted to test it with John. He worked in a soft job in the prison's school. I went over there.

"John," I said, "how many degrees in a circle?"

He said, "Three hundred and sixty."

I drew a square. "How many degrees in that?" He said three hundred and sixty.

I asked him was three hundred and sixty degrees, then, the maximum of degrees in anything?

He said "Yes."

I said, "Well, why is it that Masons go only to thirty-three degrees?"

He had no satisfactory answer. But for me, the answer was that Masonry, actually, is only thirty-three degrees of the religion of Islam, which is the full projection, forever denied to Masons, although they know it exists.

Reginald, when he came to visit me again in a few days, could gauge from my attitude the effect that his talking had had upon me. He seemed very pleased. Then, very seriously, he talked for two solid hours about "the devil white man" and "the brainwashed black man."

When Reginald left, he left me rocking with some of the first serious thoughts I had ever had in my life: that the white man was fast losing his power to oppress and exploit the dark world; that the dark world was starting to rise to rule the world again, as it had before; that the white man's world was on the way down, it was on the way out.

"You don't even know who you are," Reginald had said. "You don't even know, the white devil has hidden it from you, that you are of a race of people of ancient civilizations, and riches in gold and kings. You don't even know your true family name, you wouldn't recognize your true language if you heard it. You have been cut off by the devil white man from all true knowledge of your own kind. You have been a victim of the evil of the devil white man ever since he murdered and raped and stole you from your native land in the seeds of your forefathers. . . ."

I began to receive at least two letters every day from my brothers and sisters in Detroit. My oldest brother, Wilfred, wrote, and his first wife, Bertha, the mother of his two children (since her death, Wilfred has met and married his present wife, Ruth). Philbert wrote, and my sister Hilda. And Reginald visited, staying in Boston awhile before he went back to Detroit, where he had been the most recent of them to be converted. They were all Muslims, followers of a man they described to me as "The Honorable Elijah Muhammad," a small, gentle man, whom they sometimes referred to as "The Messenger of Allah." He was, they said, "a black man, like us." He had been born in America on a farm in Georgia. He had moved with his family to Detroit, and there had met a Mr. Wallace D. Fard who he claimed was "God in person." Mr. Wallace D. Fard had given to Elijah Muhammad Allah's message for the black people who were "the Lost-Found Nation of Islam here in this wilderness of North America."

All of them urged me to "accept the teachings of The Honorable Elijah Muhammad." Reginald explained that pork was not eaten by those who worshiped in the religion of Islam, and not smoking cigarettes was a rule of the followers of The Honorable Elijah Muhammad, because they did not take injurious things such as narcotics, tobacco, or liquor into their bodies. Over and over, I read, and heard, "The key to a Muslim is submission, the attunement of one toward Allah."

And what they termed "the true knowledge of the black man" that was possessed by the followers of The Honorable Elijah Muhammad was given shape for me in their lengthy letters, sometimes containing printed literature.

"The true knowledge," reconstructed much more briefly than I received it, was that history had been "whitened" in the white man's history books, and that the black man had been "brainwashed for hundreds of years." Original Man was black, in the continent called Africa where the human race had emerged on the planet Earth.

The black man, original man, built great empires and civilizations and cultures while the white man was still living on all fours in caves. "The devil white man," down through history, out of his devilish nature, had pillaged, murdered, raped, and exploited every race of man not white.

Human history's greatest crime was the traffic in black flesh when the devil white man went into Africa and murdered and kidnapped to bring to the West in chains, in slave ships, millions of black men, women, and children, who were worked and beaten and tortured as slaves.

The devil white man cut these black people off from all knowledge of their own kind, and cut them off from any knowledge of their own language, religion, and past culture, until the black man in America was the earth's only race of people who had absolutely no knowledge of his true identity.

In one generation, the black slave women in America had been raped by the slavemaster white man until there had begun to emerge a homemade, handmade, brainwashed race that was no longer even of its true color, that no longer even knew its true family names. The slavemaster forced his family name upon this rape-mixed race, which the slavemaster began to call "the Negro."

This "Negro" was taught of his native Africa that it was peopled by heathen, black savages, swinging like monkeys from trees. This "Negro" accepted this along with every other teaching of the slavemaster that was designed to make him accept and obey and worship the white man.

And where the religion of every other people on earth

taught its believers of a God with whom they could identify, a God who at least looked like one of their own kind, the slavemaster injected his Christian religion into this "Negro." This "Negro" was taught to worship an alien God having the same blond hair, pale skin, and blue eyes as the slavemaster.

This religion taught the "Negro" that black was a curse. It taught him to hate everything black, including himself. It taught him that everything white was good, to be admired, respected, and loved. It brainwashed this "Negro" to think he was superior if his complexion showed more of the white pollution of the slavemaster. This white man's Christian religion further deceived and brainwashed this "Negro" to always turn the other cheek, and grin, and scrape, and bow, and be humble, and to sing, and to pray, and to take whatever was dished out by the devilish white man; and to look for his pie in the sky, and for his heaven in the hereafter, while right here on earth the slavemaster white man enjoyed *his* heaven.

Many a time, I have looked back, trying to assess, just for myself, my first reactions to all this. Every instinct of the ghetto jungle streets, every hustling fox and criminal wolf instinct in me, which would have scoffed at and rejected anything else, was struck numb. It was as though all of that life merely was back there, without any remaining effect, or influence. I remember how, some time later, reading the Bible in the Norfolk Prison Colony library, I came upon, then I read, over and over, how Paul on the road to Damascus, upon hearing the voice of Christ, was so smitten that he was knocked off his horse, in a daze. I do not now, and I did not then, liken myself to Paul. But I do understand his experience.

I have since learned—helping me to understand what then began to happen within me—that the truth can be quickly received, or received at all, only by the sinner who knows and admits that he is guilty of having sinned much. Stated another way: only guilt admitted accepts truth. The Bible again: the one people whom Jesus could not help were the Pharisees; they didn't feel they needed any help.

The very enormity of my previous life's guilt prepared me to accept the truth.

Not for weeks yet would I deal with the direct, personal application to myself, as a black man, of the truth. It still was like a blinding light.

Reginald left Boston and went back to Detroit. I would sit in my room and stare. At the dining-room table, I would hardly eat, only drink the water. I nearly starved. Fellow inmates, concerned, and guards, apprehensive, asked what was wrong with me. It was suggested that I visit the doctor, and I didn't. The doctor, advised, visited me. I don't know what his diagnosis was, probably that I was working on some act.

I was going through the hardest thing, also the greatest thing, for any human being to do; to accept that which is already within you, and around you.

I learned later that my brothers and sisters in Detroit put together the money for my sister Hilda to come and visit me. She told me that when The Honorable Elijah Muhammad was in Detroit, he would stay as a guest at my brother Wilfred's home, which was on McKay Street. Hilda kept urging me to write to Mr. Muhammad. He understood what it was to be in the white man's prison, she said, because he, himself, had not long before gotten out of the federal prison at Milan, Michigan, where he had served five years for evading the draft.

Hilda said that The Honorable Elijah Muhammad came to Detroit to reorganize his Temple Number One, which had become disorganized during his prison time; but he lived in Chicago, where he was organizing and building his Temple Number Two.

It was Hilda who said to me, "Would you like to hear how the white man came to this planet Earth?"

And she told me that key lesson of Mr. Elijah Muhammad's teachings, which I later learned was the demonology that every religion has, called "Yacub's History." Elijah Muhammad teaches his followers that, first, the moon separated from the earth. Then, the first humans, Original Man, were a black people. They founded the Holy City Mecca.

Among this black race were twenty-four wise scientists. One of the scientists, at odds with the rest, created the especially strong black tribe of Shabazz, from which America's Negroes, so-called, descend.

About sixty-six hundred years ago, when seventy per cent

of the people were satisfied, and thirty per cent were dissatisfied, among the dissatisfied was born a "Mr. Yacub."
He was born to create trouble, to break the peace, and to
kill. His head was unusually large. When he was four years
old, he began school. At the age of eighteen, Yacub had
finished all of his nation's colleges and universities. He was
known as "the big-head scientist." Among many other things,
he had learned how to breed races scientifically.

This big-head scientist, Mr. Yacub, began preaching in
the streets of Mecca, making such hosts of converts that
the authorities, increasingly concerned, finally exiled him
with 59,999 followers to the island of Patmos—described
in the Bible as the island where John received the message
contained in Revelations in the New Testament.

Though he was a black man, Mr. Yacub, embittered
toward Allah now, decided, as revenge, to create upon the
earth a devil race—a bleached-out, white race of people.

From his studies, the big-head scientist knew that black
men contained two germs, black and brown. He knew that
the brown germ stayed dormant as, being the lighter of the
two germs, it was the weaker. Mr. Yacub, to upset the law
of nature, conceived the idea of employing what we today
know as the recessive genes structure, to separate from
each other the two germs, black and brown, and then grafting the brown germ to progressively lighter, weaker stages.
The humans resulting, he knew, would be, as they became
lighter, and weaker, progressively also more susceptible to
wickedness and evil. And in this way finally he would
achieve the intended bleached-out white race of devils.

He knew that it would take him several total color-
change stages to get from black to white. Mr. Yacub began
his work by setting up a eugenics law on the island of
Patmos.

Among Mr. Yacub's 59,999 all-black followers, every
third or so child that was born would show some trace of
brown. As these became adult, only brown and brown, or
black and brown, were permitted to marry. As their children were born, Mr. Yacub's law dictated that, if a black
child, the attending nurse, or midwife, should stick a needle
into its brain and give the body to cremators. The mothers
were told it had been an "angel baby," which had gone to
heaven, to prepare a place for her.

But a brown child's mother was told to take very good care of it.

Others, assistants, were trained by Mr. Yacub to continue his objective. Mr. Yacub, when he died on the island at the age of one hundred and fifty-two, had left laws, and rules, for them to follow. According to the teachings of Mr. Elijah Muhammad, Mr. Yacub, except in his mind, never saw the bleached-out devil race that his procedures and laws and rules created.

A two-hundred-year span was needed to eliminate on the island of Patmos all of the black people—until only brown people remained.

The next two hundred years were needed to create from the brown race the red race—with no more browns left on the island.

In another two hundred years, from the red race was created the yellow race.

Two hundred years later—the white race had at last been created.

On the island of Patmos was nothing but these blond, pale-skinned, cold-blue-eyed devils—savages, nude and shameless; hairy, like animals, they walked on all fours and they lived in trees.

Six hundred more years passed before this race of people returned to the mainland, among the natural black people.

Mr. Elijah Muhammad teaches his followers that within six months time, through telling lies that set the black men fighting among each other, this devil race had turned what had beeen a peaceful heaven on earth into a hell torn by quarreling and fighting.

But finally the original black people recognized that their sudden troubles stemmed from this devil white race that Mr. Yacub had made. They rounded them up, put them in chains. With little aprons to cover their nakedness, this devil race was marched off across the Arabian desert to the caves of Europe.

The lambskin and the cable-tow used in Masonry today are symbolic of how the nakedness of the white man was covered when he was chained and driven across the hot sand.

Mr. Elijah Muhammad further teaches that the white devil race in Europe's caves was savage. The animals tried to kill him. He climbed trees outside his cave, made clubs, trying to protect his family from the wild beasts outside trying to get in.

When this devil race had spent two thousand years in the caves, Allah raised up Moses to civilize them, and bring them out of the caves. It was written that this devil white race would rule the world for six thousand years.

The Books of Moses are missing. That's why it is not known that he was in the caves.

When Moses arrived, the first of these devils to accept his teachings, the first he led out, were those we call today the Jews.

According to the teachings of this "Yacub's History," when the Bible says "Moses lifted up the serpent in the wilderness," that serpent is symbolic of the devil white race Moses lifted up out of the caves of Europe, teaching them civilization.

It was written that after Yacub's bleached white race had ruled the world for six thousand years—down to our time— the black original race would give birth to one whose wisdom, knowledge, and power would be infinite.

It was written that some of the original black people should be brought as slaves to North America—to learn to better understand, at first hand, the white devil's true nature, in modern times.

Elijah Muhammad teaches that the greatest and mightiest God who appeared on the earth was Master W. D. Fard. He came from the East to the West, appearing in North America at a time when the history and the prophecy that is written was coming to realization, as the non-white people all over the world began to rise, and as the devil white civilization, condemned by Allah, was, through its devilish nature, destroying itself.

Master W. D. Fard was half black and half white. He was made in this way to enable him to be accepted by the black people in America, and to lead them, while at the same time he was enabled to move undiscovered among the white people, so that he could understand and judge the enemy of the blacks.

Master W. D. Fard, in 1931, posing as a seller of silks, met, in Detroit, Michigan, Elijah Muhammad. Master W. D. Fard gave to Elijah Muhammad Allah's message, and Allah's divine guidance, to save the Lost-Found Nation of Islam, the so-called Negroes, here in "this wilderness of North America."

When my sister, Hilda, had finished telling me this "Yacub's History," she left. I don't know if I was able to open my mouth and say good-bye.

I was to learn later that Elijah Muhammad's tales, like this one of "Yacub," infuriated the Muslims of the East. While at Mecca, I reminded them that it was their fault, since they themselves hadn't done enough to make real Islam known in the West. Their silence left a vacuum into which any religious faker could step and mislead our people.

CHAPTER ELEVEN

SAVED

I did write to Elijah Muhammad. He lived in Chicago at that time, at 6116 South Michigan Avenue. At least twenty-five times I must have written that first one-page letter to him, over and over. I was trying to make it both legible and understandable. I practically couldn't read my handwriting myself; it shames even to remember it. My spelling and my grammar were as bad, if not worse. Anyway, as well as I could express it, I said I had been told about him by my brothers and sisters, and I apologized for my poor letter.

Mr. Muhammad sent me a typed reply. It had an all but electrical effect upon me to see the signature of the "Messenger of Allah." After he welcomed me into the "true knowledge," he gave me something to think about. The black prisoner, he said, symbolized white society's crime of keeping black men oppressed and deprived and ignorant, and unable to get decent jobs, turning them into criminals.

He told me to have courage. He even enclosed some money for me, a five-dollar bill. Mr. Muhammad sends money all over the country to prison inmates who write to him, probably to this day.

Regularly my family wrote to me, "Turn to Allah . . . pray to the East."

The hardest test I ever faced in my life was praying. You understand. My comprehending, my believing the teachings of Mr. Muhammad had only required my mind's saying to me, "That's right!" or "I never thought of that."

But bending my knees to pray—that *act*—well, that took me a week.

You know what my life had been. Picking a lock to rob someone's house was the only way my knees had ever been bent before.

I had to force myself to bend my knees. And waves of shame and embarrassment would force me back up.

For evil to bend its knees, admitting its guilt, to implore the forgiveness of God, is the hardest thing in the world. It's easy for me to see and to say that now. But then, when I was the personification of evil, I was going through it. Again, again, I would force myself back down into the praying-to-Allah posture. When finally I was able to make myself stay down—I didn't know what to say to Allah.

For the next years, I was the nearest thing to a hermit in the Norfolk Prison Colony. I never have been more busy in my life. I still marvel at how swiftly my previous life's thinking pattern slid away from me, like snow off a roof. It is as though someone else I knew of had lived by hustling and crime. I would be startled to catch myself thinking in a remote way of my earlier self as another person.

The things I felt, I was pitifully unable to express in the one-page letter that went every day to Mr. Elijah Muhammad. And I wrote at least one more daily letter, replying to one of my brothers and sisters. Every letter I received from them added something to my knowledge of the teachings of Mr. Muhammad. I would sit for long periods and study his photographs.

I've never been one for inaction. Everything I've ever felt strongly about, I've done something about. I guess that's why, unable to do anything else, I soon began writing to people I had known in the hustling world, such as Sammy the Pimp, John Hughes, the gambling house owner, the thief Jumpsteady, and several dope peddlers. I wrote them all about Allah and Islam and Mr. Elijah Muhammad. I had no idea where most of them lived. I addressed their letters in care of the Harlem or Roxbury bars and clubs where I'd known them.

I never got a single reply. The average hustler and criminal was too uneducated to write a letter. I have known many slick, sharp-looking hustlers, who would have you think they had an interest in Wall Street; privately, they would get someone else to read a letter if they received one. Besides, neither would I have replied to anyone writing me something as wild as "the white man is the devil."

What certainly went on the Harlem and Roxbury wires was that Detroit Red was going crazy in stir, or else he was trying some hype to shake up the warden's office.

During the years that I stayed in the Norfolk Prison Colony, never did any official directly say anything to me about those letters, although, of course, they all passed through the prison censorship. I'm sure, however, they monitored what I wrote to add to the files which every state and federal prison keeps on the conversion of Negro inmates by the teachings of Mr. Elijah Muhammad.

But at that time, I felt that the real reason was that the white man knew that he was the devil.

Later on, I even wrote to the Mayor of Boston, to the Governor of Massachusetts, and to Harry S. Truman. They never answered; they probably never even saw my letters. I handscratched to them how the white man's society was responsible for the black man's condition in this wilderness of North America.

It was because of my letters that I happened to stumble upon starting to acquire some kind of a homemade education.

I became increasingly frustrated at not being able to express what I wanted to convey in letters that I wrote, especially those to Mr. Elijah Muhammad. In the street, I had been the most articulate hustler out there—I had commanded attention when I said something. But now, trying to write simple English, I not only wasn't articulate, I wasn't even functional. How would I sound writing in slang, the way I would *say* it, something such as, "Look, daddy, let me pull your coat about a cat, Elijah Muhammad—"

Many who today hear me somewhere in person, or on television, or those who read something I've said, will think I went to school far beyond the eighth grade. This impression is due entirely to my prison studies.

It had really begun back in the Charlestown Prison, when Bimbi first made me feel envy of his stock of knowledge. Bimbi had always taken charge of any conversation he was in, and I had tried to emulate him. But every book I picked up had few sentences which didn't contain anywhere from one to nearly all of the words that might as well have been in Chinese. When I just skipped those words, of course, I really ended up with little idea of what the book said. So I had come to the Norfolk Prison Colony still going through only book-reading motions. Pretty soon, I would have quit even these motions, unless I had received the motivation that I did.

I saw that the best thing I could do was get hold of a dictionary—to study, to learn some words. I was lucky enough to reason also that I should try to improve my penmanship. It was sad. I couldn't even write in a straight line. It was both ideas together that moved me to request a dictionary along with some tablets and pencils from the Norfolk Prison Colony school.

I spent two days just riffling uncertainly through the dictionary's pages. I'd never realized so many words existed! I didn't know *which* words I needed to learn. Finally, just to start some kind of action, I began copying.

In my slow, painstaking, ragged handwriting, I copied into my tablet everything printed on that first page, down to the punctuation marks.

I believe it took me a day. Then, aloud, I read back, to myself, everything I'd written on the tablet. Over and over, aloud, to myself, I read my own handwriting.

I woke up the next morning, thinking about those words —immensely proud to realize that not only had I written so much at one time, but I'd written words that I never knew were in the world. Moreover, with a little effort, I also could remember what many of these words meant. I reviewed the words whose meanings I didn't remember. Funny thing, from the dictionary first page right now, that "aardvark" springs to my mind. The dictionary had a picture of it, a long-tailed, long-eared, burrowing African mammal, which lives off termites caught by sticking out its tongue as an anteater does for ants.

I was so fascinated that I went on—I copied the dictionary's next page. And the same experience came when I studied that. With every succeeding page, I also learned of people and places and events from history. Actually the dictionary is like a miniature encyclopedia. Finally the dictionary's A section had filled a whole tablet—and I went on into the B's. That was the way I started copying what eventually became the entire dictionary. It went a lot faster after so much practice helped me to pick up handwriting speed. Between what I wrote in my tablet, and writing letters, during the rest of my time in prison I would guess I wrote a million words.

I suppose it was inevitable that as my word-base broadened, I could for the first time pick up a book and read and now begin to understand what the book was saying. Anyone who has read a great deal can imagine the new world that opened. Let me tell you something: from then until I left that prison, in every free moment I had, if I was not reading in the library, I was reading on my bunk. You couldn't have gotten me out of books with a wedge. Between Mr. Muhammad's teachings, my correspondence, my visitors—usually Ella and Reginald—and my reading of books, months passed without my even thinking about being imprisoned. In fact, up to then, I never had been so truly free in my life.

The Norfolk Prison Colony's library was in the school building. A variety of classes was taught there by instructors who came from such places as Harvard and Boston universities. The weekly debates between inmate teams were also held in the school building. You would be astonished to know how worked up convict debaters and audiences would get over subjects like "Should Babies Be Fed Milk?"

Available on the prison library's shelves were books on just about every general subject. Much of the big private collection that Parkhurst had willed to the prison was still in crates and boxes in the back of the library—thousands of old books. Some of them looked ancient: covers faded, old-time parchment-looking binding. Parkhurst, I've mentioned, seemed to have been principally interested in history and religion. He had the money and the special interest to have a lot of books that you wouldn't have in general circulation. Any college library would have been lucky to get that collection.

As you can imagine, especially in a prison where there was heavy emphasis on rehabilitation, an inmate was smiled upon if he demonstrated an unusually intense interest in books. There was a sizable number of well-read inmates, especially the popular debaters. Some were said by many to be practically walking encyclopedias. They were almost celebrities. No university would ask any student to devour literature as I did when this new world opened to me, of being able to read and *understand*.

I read more in my room than in the library itself. An inmate who was known to read a lot could check out more than the permitted maximum number of books. I preferred reading in the total isolation of my own room.

When I had progressed to really serious reading, every night at about ten P.M. I would be outraged with the "lights out." It always seemed to catch me right in the middle of something engrossing.

Fortunately, right outside my door was a corridor light that cast a glow into my room. The glow was enough to read by, once my eyes adjusted to it. So when "lights out" came, I would sit on the floor where I could continue reading in that glow.

At one-hour intervals the night guards paced past every room. Each time I heard the approaching footsteps, I jumped into bed and feigned sleep. And as soon as the guard passed, I got back out of bed onto the floor area of that light-glow, where I would read for another fifty-eight minutes—until the guard approached again. That went on until three or four every morning. Three or four hours of sleep a night was enough for me. Often in the years in the streets I had slept less than that.

The teachings of Mr. Muhammad stressed how history had been "whitened"—when white men had written history books, the black man simply had been left out. Mr. Muhammad couldn't have said anything that would have struck me much harder. I had never forgotten how when my class, me and all of those whites, had studied seventh-grade United States history back in Mason, the history of the Negro had been covered in one paragraph, and the teacher had gotten a big laugh with his joke, "Negroes' feet are so big that when they walk, they leave a hole in the ground."

This is one reason why Mr. Muhammad's teachings spread so swiftly all over the United States, among *all* Negroes, whether or not they became followers of Mr. Muhammad. The teachings ring true—to every Negro. You can hardly show me a black adult in America—or a white one, for that matter—who knows from the history books anything like the truth about the black man's role. In my own case, once I heard of the "glorious history of the black man," I took special pains to hunt in the library for books that would inform me on details about black history.

I can remember accurately the very first set of books that really impressed me. I have since bought that set of books and have it at home for my children to read as they grow up. It's called *Wonders of the World*. It's full of pictures of archeological finds, statues that depict, usually, non-European people.

I found books like Will Durant's *Story of Civilization.* I read H. G. Wells' *Outline of History. Souls Of Black Folk* by W. E. B. Du Bois gave me a glimpse into the black people's history before they came to this country. Carter G. Woodson's *Negro History* opened my eyes about black empires before the black slave was brought to the United States, and the early Negro struggles for freedom.

J. A. Rogers' three volumes of *Sex and Race* told about race-mixing before Christ's time; about Aesop being a black man who told fables; about Egypt's Pharaohs; about the great Coptic Christian Empires; about Ethiopia, the earth's oldest continuous black civilization, as China is the oldest continuous civilization.

Mr. Muhammad's teaching about how the white man had been created led me to *Findings In Genetics* by Gregor Mendel. (The dictionary's G section was where I had learned what "genetics" meant.) I really studied this book by the Austrian monk. Reading it over and over, especially certain sections, helped me to understand that if you started with a black man, a white man could be produced; but starting with a white man, you never could produce a black man—because the white chromosome is recessive. And since no one disputes that there was but one Original Man, the conclusion is clear.

During the last year or so, in the *New York Times,* Arnold Toynbee used the word "bleached" in describing the white man. (His words were: "White (i.e. bleached) human beings of North European origin. . . .") Toynbee also referred to the European geographic area as only a peninsula of Asia. He said there is no such thing as Europe. And if you look at the globe, you will see for yourself that America is only an extension of Asia. (But at the same time Toynbee is among those who have helped to bleach history. He has written that Africa was the only continent that produced no history. He won't write that again. Every day now, the truth is coming to light.)

I never will forget how shocked I was when I began reading about slavery's total horror. It made such an impact upon me that it later became one of my favorite subjects when I became a minister of Mr. Muhammad's. The world's most monstrous crime, the sin and the blood on the white man's hands, are almost impossible to believe. Books like the one by Frederick Olmstead opened my eyes to the horrors suffered when the slave was landed in the United States. The

European woman, Fannie Kimball, who had married a Southern white slaveowner, described how human beings were degraded. Of course I read *Uncle Tom's Cabin*. In fact, I believe that's the only novel I have ever read since I started serious reading.

Parkhurst's collection also contained some bound pamphlets of the Abolitionist Anti-Slavery Society of New England. I read descriptions of atrocities, saw those illustrations of black slave women tied up and flogged with whips; of black mothers watching their babies being dragged off, never to be seen by their mothers again; of dogs after slaves, and of the fugitive slave catchers, evil white men with whips and clubs and chains and guns. I read about the slave preacher Nat Turner, who put the fear of God into the white slavemaster. Nat Turner wasn't going around preaching pie-in-the-sky and "non-violent" freedom for the black man. There in Virginia one night in 1831, Nat and seven other slaves started out at his master's home and through the night they went from one plantation "big house" to the next, killing, until by the next morning 57 white people were dead and Nat had about 70 slaves following him. White people, terrified for their lives, fled from their homes, locked themselves up in public buildings, hid in the woods, and some even left the state. A small army of soldiers took two months to catch and hang Nat Turner. Somewhere I have read where Nat Turner's example is said to have inspired John Brown to invade Virginia and attack Harper's Ferry nearly thirty years later, with thirteen white men and five Negroes.

I read Herodotus, "the father of History," or, rather, I read about him. And I read the histories of various nations, which opened my eyes gradually, then wider and wider, to how the whole world's white men had indeed acted like devils, pillaging and raping and bleeding and draining the whole world's non-white people. I remember, for instance, books such as Will Durant's story of Oriental civilization, and Mahatma Gandhi's accounts of the struggle to drive the British out of India.

Book after book showed me how the white man had brought upon the world's black, brown, red, and yellow peoples every variety of the sufferings of exploitation. I saw how since the sixteenth century, the so-called "Christian trader" white man began to ply the seas in his lust for Asian and African empires, and plunder, and power. I read, I saw, how the white man never has gone among the non-white peoples bearing the Cross in the true manner and spirit of Christ's teachings—meek, humble, and Christ-like.

I perceived, as I read, how the collective white man had been actually nothing but a piratical opportunist who used Faustian machinations to make his own Christianity his initial wedge in criminal conquests. First, always "religiously," he branded "heathen" and "pagan" labels upon ancient non-white cultures and civilizations. The stage thus set, he then turned upon his non-white victims his weapons of war.

I read how, entering India—half a *billion* deeply religious brown people—the British white man, by 1759, through promises, trickery and manipulations, controlled much of India through Great Britain's East India Company. The parasitical British administration kept tentacling out to half of the sub-continent. In 1857, some of the desperate people of India finally mutinied—and, excepting the African slave trade, nowhere has history recorded any more unnecessary bestial and ruthless human carnage than the British suppression of the non-white Indian people.

Over 115 million African blacks—close to the 1930's population of the United States—were murdered or enslaved during the slave trade. And I read how when the slave market was glutted, the cannibalistic white powers of Europe next carved up, as their colonies, the richest areas of the black continent. And Europe's chancelleries for the next century played a chess game of naked exploitation and power from Cape Horn to Cairo.

Ten guards and the warden couldn't have torn me out of those books. Not even Elijah Muhammad could have been more eloquent than those books were in providing indisputable proof that the collective white man had acted like a devil in virtually every contact he had with the world's collective non-white man. I listen today to the radio, and watch television, and read the headlines about the collective white man's fear and tension concerning China. When the white man professes ignorance about why the Chinese hate him so, my mind can't help flashing back to what I read, there in prison, about how the blood forebears of this same white man raped China at a time when China was trusting and helpless. Those original white "Christian traders" sent into China millions of pounds of opium. By 1839, so many of the Chinese were addicts that China's desperate government destroyed twenty thousand chests of opium. The first Opium War was promptly declared by the white man. Imagine! Declaring *war* upon someone who objects to being narcotized! The Chinese were severely beaten, with Chinese-invented gunpowder.

The Treaty of Nanking made China pay the British white man for the destroyed opium; forced open China's major ports to British trade; forced China to abandon Hong Kong; fixed China's import tariffs so low that cheap British articles soon flooded in, maiming China's industrial development.

After a second Opium War, the Tientsin Treaties legalized the ravaging opium trade, legalized a British-French-American control of China's customs. China tried delaying that Treaty's ratification; Peking was looted and burned.

"Kill the foreign white devils!" was the 1901 Chinese war cry in the Boxer Rebellion. Losing again, this time the Chinese were driven from Peking's choicest areas. The vicious, arrogant white man put up the famous signs, "Chinese and dogs not allowed."

Red China after World War II closed its doors to the Western white world. Massive Chinese agricultural, scientific, and industrial efforts are described in a book that *Life* magazine recently published. Some observers inside Red China have reported that the world never has known such a hate-white campaign as is now going on in this non-white country where, present birth-rates continuing, in fifty more years Chinese will be half the earth's population. And it seems that some Chinese chickens will soon come home to roost, with China's recent successful nuclear tests.

Let us face reality. We can see in the United Nations a new world order being shaped, along color lines—an alliance among the non-white nations. America's U.N. Ambassador Adlai Stevenson complained not long ago that in the United Nations "a skin game" was being played. He was right He was facing reality. A "skin game" *is* being played. But Ambassador Stevenson sounded like Jesse James accusing the marshal of carrying a gun. Because who in the world's history ever has played a worse "skin game" than the white man?

Mr. Muhammad, to whom I was writing daily, had no idea of what a new world had opened up to me through my efforts to document his teachings in books.

When I discovered philosophy, I tried to touch all the landmarks of philosophical development. Gradually, I read most of the old philosophers, Occidental and Oriental. The Oriental philosophers were the ones I came to prefer; finally, my impression was that most Occidental philosophy had largely been borrowed from the Oriental thinkers. Socrates, for instance, traveled in Egypt. Some sources even say that Socrates was initiated into some of the Egyptian mysteries. Obviously Socrates got some of his wisdom among the East's wise men.

I have often reflected upon the new vistas that reading opened to me. I knew right there in prison that reading had changed forever the course of my life. As I see it today, the ability to read awoke inside me some long dormant craving to be mentally alive. I certainly wasn't seeking any degree, the way a college confers a status symbol upon its students. My homemade education gave me, with every additional book that I read, a little bit more sensitivity to the deafness, dumbness, and blindness that was afflicting the black race in America. Not long ago, an English writer telephoned me from London, asking questions. One was, "What's your alma mater?" I told him, "Books." You will never catch me with a free fifteen minutes in which I'm not studying something I feel might be able to help the black man.

Yesterday I spoke in London, and both ways on the plane across the Atlantic I was studying a document about how the United Nations proposes to insure the human rights of the oppressed minorities of the world. The American black man is the world's most shameful case of minority oppression. What makes the black man think of himself as only an internal United States issue is just a catch-phrase, two words, "civil rights." How is the black man going to get "civil rights" before first he wins his *human* rights? If the American black man will start thinking about his *human* rights, and then start thinking of himself as part of one of the world's great peoples, he will see he has a case for the United Nations.

I can't think of a better case! Four hundred years of black blood and sweat invested here in America, and the white man still has the black man begging for what every immigrant fresh off the ship can take for granted the minute he walks down the gangplank.

But I'm digressing. I told the Englishman that my alma mater was books, a good library. Every time I catch a plane,

I have with me a book that I want to read—and that's a lot of books these days. If I weren't out here every day battling the white man, I could spend the rest of my life reading, just satisfying my curiosity—because you can hardly mention anything I'm not curious about. I don't think anybody ever got more out of going to prison than I did. In fact, prison enabled me to study far more intensively than I would have if my life had gone differently and I had attended some college. I imagine that one of the biggest troubles with colleges is there are too many distractions, too much panty-raiding, fraternities, and boola-boola and all of that. Where else but in a prison could I have attacked my ignorance by being able to study intensely sometimes as much as fifteen hours a day?

Schopenhauer, Kant, Nietzsche, naturally, I read all of those. I don't respect them; I am just trying to remember some of those whose theories I soaked up in those years. These three, it's said, laid the groundwork on which the Facist and Nazi philosophy was built. I don't respect them because it seems to me that most of their time was spent arguing about things that are not really important. They remind me of so many of the Negro "intellectuals," so-called, with whom I have come in contact—they are always arguing about something useless.

Spinoza impressed me for a while when I found out that he was black. A black Spanish Jew. The Jews excommunicated him because he advocated a pantheistic doctrine, something like the "allness of God," or "God in everything." The Jews read their bural services for Spinoza, meaning that he was dead as far as they were concerned; his family was run out of Spain, they ended up in Holland, I think.

I'll tell you something. The whole stream of Western philosophy has now wound up in a cul-de-sac. The white man has perpetrated upon himself, as well as upon the black man, so gigantic a fraud that he has put himself into a crack. He did it through his elaborate, neurotic necessity to hide the black man's true role in history.

And today the white man is faced head on with what is happening on the Black Continent, Africa. Look at the artifacts being discovered there, that are proving over and over again, how the black man had great, fine, sensitive civilizations before the white man was out of the caves. Below the Sahara, in the places where most of America's Negroes' foreparents were kidnapped, there is being unearthed some of the finest craftsmanship, sculpture and other objects, that has ever been seen by modern man. Some of these things now are on view in such places as New York City's Museum of Modern Art. Gold work of such fine tolerance and workmanship that it has no rival. Ancient objects produced by black hands . . . refined by those black hands with results that no human hand today can equal.

History has been so "whitened" by the white man that even the black professors have known little more than the most ignorant black man about the talents and rich civilizations and cultures of the black man of millenniums ago. I have lectured in Negro colleges and some of these brainwashed black Ph.D.'s, with their suspenders dragging the ground with degrees, have run to the white man's newspapers calling me a "black fanatic." Why, a lot of them are fifty years behind the times. If I were president of one of these black colleges, I'd hock the campus if I had to, to send a bunch of black students off digging in Africa for more, more and more proof of the black race's historical greatness. The white man now is in Africa digging and searching. An African elephant can't stumble without falling on some white man with a shovel. Practically every week, we read about some great new find from Africa's lost civilizations. All that's new is white science's attitude. The ancient civilizations of the black man have been buried on the Black Continent all the time.

Here is an example: a British anthropologist named Dr. Louis S. B. Leakey is displaying some fossil bones—a foot, part of a hand, some jaws, and skull fragments. On the basis of these, Dr. Leakey has said it's time to rewrite completely the history of man's origin.

This species of man lived 1,818,036 years before Christ. And these bones were found in Tanganyika. In the Black Continent.

It's a crime, the lie that has been told to generations of black men and white men both. Little innocent black children, born of parents who believed that their race had no history. Little black children seeing, before they could talk, that their parents considered themselves inferior. Innocent black children growing up, living out their lives, dying of old age—and all of their lives ashamed of being black. But the truth is pouring out of the bag now.

Two other areas of experience which have been extremely formative in my life since prison were first opened to me in the Norfolk Prison Colony. For one thing, I had my first experiences in opening the eyes of my brainwashed black brethren to some truths about the black race. And, the other: when I had read enough to know something, I began to enter the Prison Colony's weekly debating program—my baptism into public speaking.

I have to admit a sad, shameful fact. I had so loved being around the white man that in prison I really disliked how Negro convicts stuck together so much. But when Mr. Muhammad's teachings reversed my attitude toward my black brothers, in my guilt and shame I began to catch every chance I could to recruit for Mr. Muhammad.

You have to be careful, very careful, introducing the truth to the black man who has never previously heard the truth about himself, his own kind, and the white man. My brother Reginald had told me that all Muslims experienced this in their recruiting for Mr. Muhammad. The black brother is so brainwashed that he may even be repelled when he first hears the truth. Reginald advised that the truth had to be dropped only a little bit at a time. And you had to wait a while to let it sink in before advancing the next step.

I began first telling my black brother inmates about the glorious history of the black man—things they never had dreamed. I told them the horrible slavery-trade truths that they never knew. I would watch their faces when I told them about that, because the white man had completely erased the slaves' past, a Negro in America can never know his true family name, or even what tribe he was descended from: the Mandingos, the Wolof, the Serer, the Fula, the Fanti, the Ashanti, or others. I told them that some slaves brought from Africa spoke Arabic, and were Islamic in their religion. A lot of these black convicts still wouldn't believe it unless they could see that a white man had said it. So, often, I would read to these brothers selected passages from white men's books. I'd explain to them that the real truth was known to some white men, the scholars; but there had been a conspiracy down through the generations to keep the truth from black men.

I would keep close watch on how each one reacted. I always had to be careful. I never knew when some brainwashed black imp, some dyed-in-the-wool Uncle Tom, would nod at me and then go running to tell the white man. When one was ripe—and I could tell—then away from the rest, I'd drop it on him, what Mr. Muhammad taught: "The white man is the devil."

That would shock many of them—until they started thinking about it.

This is probably as big a single worry as the American prison system has today—the way the Muslim teachings, circulated among all Negroes in the country, are converting new Muslims among black men in prison, and black men are in prison in far greater numbers than their proportion in the population.

The reason is that among all Negroes the black convict is the most perfectly preconditioned to hear the words, "the white man is the devil."

You tell that to any Negro. Except for those relatively few "integration"-mad so-called "intellectuals," and those black men who are otherwise fat, happy, and deaf, dumb, and blinded, with their crumbs from the white man's rich table, you have struck a nerve center in the American black man. He may take a day to react, a month, a year; he may never respond, openly; but of one thing you can be sure—when he thinks about his own life, he is going to see where, to him, personally, the white man sure has acted like a devil.

And, as I say, above all Negroes, the black prisoner. Here is a black man caged behind bars, probably for years, put there by the white man. Usually the convict comes from among those bottom-of-the-pile Negroes, the Negroes who through their entire lives have been kicked about, treated like children—Negroes who never have met one white man who didn't either take something from them or do something to them.

You let this caged-up black man start thinking, the same way I did when I first heard Elijah Muhammad's teachings: let him start thinking how, with better breaks when he was young and ambitious he might have been a lawyer, a doctor, a scientist, anything. You let this caged-up black man start realizing, as I did, how from the first landing of the first slave ship, the millions of black men in America have been like sheep in a den of wolves. That's why black prisoners become Muslims so fast when Elijah Muhammad's teachings filter into their cages by way of other Muslim convicts. "The white man is the devil" is a perfect echo of that black convict's lifelong experience.

I've told how debating was a weekly event there at the Norfolk Prison Colony. My reading had my mind like steam under pressure. Some way, I had to start telling the white man about himself to his face. I decided I could do this by putting my name down to debate.

Standing up and speaking before an audience was a thing that throughout my previous life never would have crossed my mind. Out there in the streets, hustling, pushing dope, and robbing, I could have had the dreams from a pound of hashish and I'd never have dreamed anything so wild as that one day I would speak in coliseums and arenas, at the greatest American universities, and on radio and television programs, not to mention speaking all over Egypt and Africa and in England.

But I will tell you that, right there, in the prison, debating, speaking to a crowd, was as exhilarating to me as the discovery of knowledge through reading had been. Standing up there, the faces looking up at me, the things in my head coming out of my mouth, while my brain searched for the next best thing to follow what I was saying, and if I could sway them to my side by handling it right, then I had won the debate—once my feet got wet, I was gone on debating. Whichever side of the selected subject was assigned to me, I'd track down and study everything I could find on it. I'd put myself in my opponent's place and decide how I'd try to win if I had the other side; and then I'd figure a way to knock down those points. And if there was any way in the world, I'd work into my speech the devilishness of the white man.

"Compulsory Military Training—Or None?" That's one good chance I got unexpectedly, I remember. My opponent flailed the air about the Ethiopians throwing rocks and spears at Italian airplanes, "proving" that compulsory military training was needed. I said the Ethiopians' black flesh had been spattered against trees by bombs the Pope in Rome had blessed, and the Ethiopians would have thrown even their bare bodies at the airplanes because they had seen that they were fighting the devil incarnate.

They yelled "foul," that I'd made the subject a race issue. I said it wasn't race, it was a historical fact, that they ought to go and read Pierre van Paassen's *Days of Our Years*, and something not surprising to me, that book, right after the debate, disappeared from the prison library. It was right there in prison that I made up my mind to devote the rest of my life to telling the white man about himself—or die. In a debate about whether or not Homer had ever existed, I threw into those white faces the theory that Homer only symbolized how white Europeans kidnapped black Africans, then blinded them so that they could never get back to their own people. (Homer and Omar and *Moor*, you see, are related terms; it's like saying Peter, Pedro, and *petra*, all three of which mean rock.) These blinded Moors the Europeans taught to sing about the Europeans' glorious accomplishments. I made it clear that was the devilish white man's idea of kicks. Aesop's *Fables*—another case in point. "Aesop" was only the Greek name for an Ethiopian.

Another hot debate I remember I was in had to do with the identity of Shakespeare. No color was involved there; I just got intrigued over the Shakespearean dilemma. The King James translation of the Bible is considered the greatest piece of literature in English. Its language supposedly represents the ultimate in using the King's English. Well, Shakespeare's language and the Bible's language are one and the same. They say that from 1604 to 1611, King James got poets to translate, to write the Bible. Well, if Shakespeare existed, he was then the top poet around. But Shakespeare is nowhere reported connected with the Bible. If he existed, why didn't King James use him? And if he did use him, why is it one of the world's best kept secrets?

I know that many say that Francis Bacon was Shakespeare. If that is true, why would Bacon have kept it secret? Bacon wasn't royalty, when royalty sometimes used the *nom de plume* because it was "improper" for royalty to be artistic or theatrical. What would Bacon have had to lose? Bacon, in fact, would have had everything to gain.

In the prison debates I argued for the theory that King James himself was the real poet who used the *nom de plume* Shakespeare. King James was brilliant. He was the greatest king who ever sat on the British throne. Who else among royalty, in his time, would have had the giant talent to write Shakespeare's works? It was he who poetically "fixed" the Bible—which in itself and its present King James version has enslaved the world.

When my brother Reginald visited, I would talk to him about new evidence I found to document the Muslim teachings. In either volume 43 or 44 of The Harvard Classics, I read Milton's *Paradise Lost*. The devil, kicked out of Paradise, was trying to regain possession. He was using the forces of Europe, personified by the Popes, Charlemagne, Richard the Lionhearted, and other knights. I interpreted this to show that the Europeans were motivated and led by the devil, or the personification of the devil. So Milton and Mr. Elijah Muhammad were actually saying the same thing.

I couldn't believe it when Reginald began to speak ill of Elijah Muhammad. I can't specify the exact things he said. They were more in the nature of implications against Mr. Muhammad—the pitch of Reginald's voice, or the way that Reginald looked, rather than what he said.

It caught me totally unprepared. It threw me into a state of confusion. My blood brother, Reginald, in whom I had so much confidence, for whom I had so much respect, the one who had introduced me to the Nation of Islam. I couldn't believe it! And now Islam meant more to me than anything I ever had known in my life. Islam and Mr. Elijah Muhammad had changed my whole world.

Reginald, I learned, had been suspended from the Nation of Islam by Elijah Muhammad. He had not practiced moral restraint. After he had learned the truth, and had accepted the truth, and the Muslim laws, Reginald was still carrying on improper relations with the then secretary of the New York Temple. Some other Muslim who learned of it had made charges against Reginald to Mr. Muhammad in Chicago, and Mr. Muhammad had suspended Reginald.

When Reginald left, I was in torment. That night, finally, I wrote to Mr. Muhammad, trying to defend my brother, appealing for him. I told him what Reginald was to me, what my brother meant to me.

I put the letter into the box for the prison censor. Then all the rest of that night, I prayed to Allah. I don't think anyone ever prayed more sincerely to Allah. I prayed for some kind of relief from my confusion.

It was the next night, as I lay on my bed, I suddenly, with a start, became aware of a man sitting beside me in my chair. He had on a dark suit. I remember. I could see him as plainly as I see anyone I look at. He wasn't black, and he wasn't white. He was light-brown-skinned, an Asiatic cast of countenance, and he had oily black hair.

I looked right into his face.

I didn't get frightened. I knew I wasn't dreaming. I couldn't move, I didn't speak, and he didn't. I couldn't place him racially—other than that I knew he was a non-European. I had no idea whatsoever who he was. He just sat there. Then, suddenly as he had come, he was gone.

Soon, Mr. Muhammad sent me a reply about Reginald. He wrote, "If you once believed in the truth, and now you are beginning to doubt the truth, you didn't believe the truth in the first place. What could make you doubt the truth other than your own weak self?"

That struck me. Reginald was not leading the disciplined life of a Muslim. And I knew that Elijah Muhammad was right, and my blood brother was wrong. Because right is right, and wrong is wrong. Little did I then realize the day would come when Elijah Muhammad would be accused by his own sons as being guilty of the same acts of immorality that he judged Reginald and so many others for.

But at that time, all of the doubt and confusion in my mind was removed. All of the influence that my brother had wielded over me was broken. From that day on, as far as I am concerned, everything that my brother Reginald has done is wrong.

But Reginald kept visiting me. When he had been a Muslim, he had been immaculate in his attire. But now, he wore things like a T-shirt, shabby-looking trousers, and sneakers. I could see him on the way down. When he spoke, I heard him coldly. But I would listen. He was my blood brother.

Gradually, I saw the chastisement of Allah—what Christians would call "the curse"—come upon Reginald. Elijah Muhammad said that Allah was chastising Reginald—and that anyone who challenged Elijah Muhammad would be chastened by Allah. In Islam we were taught that as long as one didn't know the truth, he lived in darkness. But once the truth was accepted, and recognized, he lived in light, and whoever would then go against it would be punished by Allah.

Mr. Muhammad taught that the five-pointed star stands for justice, and also for the five senses of man. We were taught that Allah executes justice by working upon the five senses of those who rebel against His Messenger, or against His truth. We were taught that this was Allah's way of letting Muslims know His sufficiency to defend His Messenger against any and all opposition, as long as the Messenger himself didn't deviate from the path of truth. We were taught that Allah turned the minds of any defectors into a turmoil. I thought truly that it was Allah doing this to my brother.

One letter, I think from my brother Philbert, told me that Reginald was with them in Detroit. I heard no more about Reginald until one day, weeks later, Ella visited me; she told me that Reginald was at her home in Roxbury, sleeping. Ella said she had heard a knock, she had gone to the door, and there was Reginald, looking terrible. Ella said she had asked, "Where did you come from?" And Reginald had told her he came from Detroit. She said she asked him, "How did you get here?" And he had told her, "I walked."

I believed he *had* walked. I believed in Elijah Muhammad, and he had convinced us that Allah's chastisement upon Reginald's mind had taken away Reginald's ability to gauge distance and time. There is a dimension of time with which we are not familiar here in the West. Elijah Muhammad said that under Allah's chastisement, the five senses of a man can be so deranged by those whose mental powers are greater than his that in five minutes his hair can turn snow white. Or he will walk nine hundred miles as he might walk five blocks.

In prison, since I had become a Muslim, I had grown a beard. When Reginald visited me, he nervously moved about in his chair; he told me that each hair on my beard was a snake. Everywhere, he saw snakes.

He next began to believe that he was the "Messenger of Allah." Reginald went around in the streets of Roxbury, Ella reported to me, telling people that he had some divine power. He graduated from this to saying that he was Allah.

He finally began saying he was *greater* than Allah.

Authorities picked up Reginald, and he was put into an institution. They couldn't find what was wrong. They had no way to understand Allah's chastisement. Reginald was released. Then he was picked up again, and was put into another institution.

Reginald is in an institution now. I know where, but I won't say. I would not want to cause him any more trouble than he has already had.

I believe, today, that it was written, it was meant, for Reginald to be used for one purpose only: as a bait, as a minnow to reach into the ocean of blackness where I was, to save me.

I cannot understand it any other way.

After Elijah Muhammad himself was later accused as a very immoral man, I came to believe that it wasn't a divine chastisement upon Reginald, but the pain he felt when his own family totally rejected him for Elijah Muhammad, and this hurt made Reginald turn insanely upon Elijah Muhammad.

It's impossible to dream, or to see, or to have a vision of someone whom you never have seen before—and to see him exactly as he is. To see someone, and to see him exactly as he looks, is to have a pre-vision.

I would later come to believe that my pre-vision was of Master W. D. Fard, the Messiah, the one whom Elijah Muhammad said had appointed him—Elijah Muhammad—as His Last Messenger to the black people of North America.

My last year in prison was spent back in the Charlestown Prison. Even among the white inmates, the word had filtered around. Some of those brainwashed black convicts talked too much. And I know that the censors had reported on my mail. The Norfolk Prison Colony officials had become upset. They used as a reason for my transfer that I refused to take some kind of shots, an inoculation or something.

The only thing that worried me was that I hadn't much time left before I would be eligible for parole-board consideration. But I reasoned that they might look at my representing and spreading Islam in another way: instead of keeping me in they might want to get me out.

I had come to prison with 20/20 vision. But when I got sent back to Charlestown, I had read so much by the lights-out glow in my room at the Norfolk Prison Colony that I had astigmatism and the first pair of the eyeglasses that I have worn ever since.

I had less maneuverability back in the much stricter Charlestown Prison. But I found that a lot of Negroes attended a Bible class, and I went there.

Conducting the class was a tall, blond, blue-eyed (a perfect "devil") Harvard Seminary student. He lectured, and then he started in a question-and-answer session. I don't know which of us had read the Bible more, he or I, but I had to give him credit; he really was heavy on his religion. I puzzled and puzzled for a way to upset him, and to give those Negroes present something to think and talk about and circulate.

Finally, I put up my hand; he nodded. He had talked about Paul.

I stood up and asked, "What color was Paul?" And I kept talking, with pauses, "He had to be black . . . because he was a Hebrew . . . and the original Hebrews were black . . . weren't they?"

He had started flushing red. You know the way white people do. He said "Yes."

I wasn't through yet. "What color was Jesus . . . he was Hebrew, too . . . wasn't he?"

Both the Negro and the white convicts had sat bolt upright. I don't care how tough the convict, be he brainwashed black Christian, or a "devil" white Christian, neither of them is ready to hear anybody saying Jesus wasn't white. The instructor walked around. He shouldn't have felt bad. In all of the years since, I never have met any intelligent white man who would try to insist that Jesus was white. How could they? He said, "Jesus was brown."

I let him get away with that compromise.

Exactly as I had known it would, almost overnight the Charlestown convicts, black and white, began buzzing with the story. Wherever I went, I could feel the nodding. And anytime I got a chance to exchange words with a black brother in stripes, I'd say, "My man! You ever heard about somebody named Mr. Elijah Muhammad?"

CHAPTER TWELVE

SAVIOR

During the spring of nineteen fifty-two I joyously wrote Elijah Muhammad and my family that the Massachusetts State Parole Board had voted that I should be released. But still a few months were taken up with the red tape delay of paper work that went back and forth, arranging for my parole release in the custody of my oldest brother, Wilfred, in Detroit, who now managed a furniture store. Wilfred got the Jew who owned the store to sign a promise that upon release I would be given immediate employment.

By the prison system wire, I heard that Shorty also was up for parole. But Shorty was having trouble getting some reputable person to sign for him. (Later, I found out that in prison Shorty had studied musical composition. He had even progressed to writing some pieces; one of them I know he named "The Bastille Concerto.")

My going to Detroit instead of back to Harlem or Boston was influenced by my family's feeling expressed in their letters. Especially my sister Hilda had stressed to me that although I felt I understood Elijah Muhammad's teachings, I had much to learn, and I ought to come to Detroit and become a member of a temple of practicing Muslims.

It was in August when they gave me a lecture, a cheap L'il Abner suit, and a small amount of money, and I walked out of the gate. I never looked back, but that doesn't make me any different from a million inmates who have left a prison behind them.

The first stop I made was at a Turkish bath. I got some of that physical feeling of prison-taint steamed off me. Ella, with whom I stayed only overnight, had also agreed that it would be best for me to start again in Detroit. The police in a new city wouldn't have it in for me; that was Ella's consideration—not the Muslims, for whom Ella had no use. Both Hilda and Reginald had tried to work on Ella. But Ella, with her strong will, didn't go for it at all. She told me that she felt anyone could be whatever he wanted to be, Holy Roller, Seventh Day Adventist, or whatever it was, but she wasn't going to become any Muslim.

Hilda, the next morning, gave me some money to put in my pocket. Before I left, I went out and bought three things I remember well. I bought a better-looking pair of eyeglasses than the pair the prison had issued to me; and I bought a suitcase and a wrist watch.

I have thought, since, that without fully knowing it, I was preparing for what my life was about to become. Because those are three things I've used more than anything else. My eyeglasses correct the astigmatism that I got from all the reading in prison. I travel so much now that my wife keeps alternate suitcases packed so that, when necessary, I can just grab one. And you won't find anybody more time-conscious than I am. I live by my watch, keeping appointments. Even when I'm using my car, I drive by my watch, not my speedometer. Time is more important to me than distance.

I caught a bus to Detroit. The furniture store that my brother Wilfred managed was right in the black ghetto of Detroit; I'd better not name the store, if I'm going to tell the way they robbed Negroes. Wilfred introduced me to the Jews who owned the store. And, as agreed, I was put to work, as a salesman.

"Nothing Down" advertisements drew poor Negroes into that store like flypaper. It was a shame, the way they paid three and four times what the furniture had cost, because they could get credit from those Jews. It was the same kind of cheap, gaudy-looking junk that you can see in any of the black ghetto furniture stores today. Fabrics were stapled on the sofas. Imitation "leopard skin" bedspreads, "tiger skin" rugs, such stuff as that. I would see clumsy, work-hardened, calloused hands scrawling and scratching signatures on the contract, agreeing to highway-robbery interest rates in the fine print that never was read.

I was seeing in real life the same point made in a joke that during the 1964 Presidential campaign *Jet* magazine reported that Senator Barry Goldwater had told somewhere. It was that a white man, a Negro, and a Jew were given one wish each. The white man asked for securities; the Negro asked for a lot of money; the Jew asked for some imitation jewelry "and that colored boy's address."

In all my years in the streets, I'd been looking at the exploitation that for the first time I really saw and understood. Now I watched brothers entwining themselves in the economic clutches of the white man who went home every night with another bag of the money drained out of the ghetto. I saw that the money, instead of helping the black man, was going to help enrich these white merchants, who usually lived in an "exclusive" area where a black man had better not get caught unless he worked there for somebody white.

Wilfred invited me to share his home, and gratefully I accepted. The warmth of a home and a family was a healing change from the prison cage for me. It would deeply move almost any newly freed convict, I think. But especially this Muslim home's atmosphere sent me often to my knees to praise Allah. My family's letters while I was in prison had included a description of the Muslim home routine, but to truly appreciate it, one had to be a part of the routine. Each act, and the significance of that act, was gently, patiently explained to me by my brother Wilfred.

There was none of the morning confusion that exists in most homes. Wilfred, the father, the family protector and provider, was the first to rise. "The father prepares the way for his family," he said. He, then I, performed the morning ablutions. Next came Wilfred's wife, Ruth, and then their children, so that orderliness prevailed in the use of the bathroom.

"In the name of Allah, I perform the ablution," the Muslim said aloud before washing first the right hand, then the left hand. The teeth were thoroughly brushed, followed by three rinsings out of the mouth. The nostrils also were rinsed out thrice. A shower then completed the whole body's purification in readiness for prayer.

Each family member, even children upon meeting each other for that new day's first time, greeted softly and pleasantly, "As-Salaam-Alaikum" (the Arabic for "Peace be unto you"). "Wa-Alaikum-Salaam" ("and unto you be peace") was the other's reply. Over and over again, the Muslim said in his own mind, "Allahu-Akbar, Allahu-Akbar" ("Allah is the greatest").

The prayer rug was spread by Wilfred while the rest of the

family purified themselves. It was explained to me that a Muslim family prayed with the sun near the horizon. If that time was missed, the prayer had to be deferred until the sun was beyond the horizon. "Muslims are not sun-worshipers. We pray facing the East to be in unity with the rest of our 725 million brothers and sisters in the entire Muslim world."

All the family, in robes, lined up facing East. In unison, we stepped from our slippers to stand on the prayer rug.

Today, I say with my family in the Arabic tongue the prayer which I first learned in English: "I perform the morning prayer to Allah, the Most High, Allah is the greatest. Glory to Thee Oh Allah, Thine is the praise, Blessed is Thy Name, and Exalted is Thy Majesty. I bear witness that nothing deserves to be served or worshiped besides Thee."

No solid food, only juice and coffee, was taken for our breakfasts. Wilfred and I went off to work. There, at noon and again at around three in the afternoon, unnoticed by others in the furniture store, we would rinse our hands, faces and mouths, and softly meditate.

Muslim children did likewise at school, and Muslim wives and mothers interrupted their chores to join the world's 725 million Muslims in communicating with God.

Wednesdays, Fridays, and Sundays were the meeting days of the relatively small Detroit Temple Number One. Near the temple, which actually was a storefront, were three hog-slaughtering pens. The squealing of hogs being slaughtered filtered into our Wednesday and Friday meetings. I'm describing the condition that we Muslims were in back in the early 1950's.

The address of Temple Number One was 1470 Frederick Street, I think. The first Temple to be formed, back in 1931, by Master W. D. Fard, was formed in Detroit, Michigan. I never had seen any Christian-believing Negroes conduct themselves like the Muslims, the individuals and the families alike. The men were quietly, tastefully dressed. The women wore ankle-length gowns, no makeup, and scarves covered their heads. The neat children were mannerly not only to adults but to other children as well.

I had never dreamed of anything like that atmosphere among black people who had learned to be proud they were black, who had learned to love other black people instead of being jealous and suspicious. I thrilled to how we Muslim men used both hands to grasp a black brother's both hands, voicing and smiling our happiness to meet him again. The Muslim sisters, both married and single, were given an honor and respect that I'd never seen black men give to their women, and it felt wonderful to me. The salutations which we all exchanged were warm, filled with mutual respect and dignity: "Brother" . . . "Sister" . . . "Ma'am" . . . "Sir." Even children speaking to other children used these terms. Beautiful!

Lemuel Hassan then was the Minister at Temple Number One. "As-Salaikum," he greeted us. "Wa-Salaikum," we returned. Minister Lemuel stood before us, near a blackboard. The blackboard had fixed upon it in permanent paint, on one side, the United States flag and under it the words "Slavery, Suffering and Death," then the word "Christianity" alongside the sign of the Cross. Beneath the Cross was a painting of a black man hanged from a tree. On the other side was painted what we were taught was the Muslim flag, the crescent and star on a red background with the words "Islam: Freedom, Justice, Equality," and beneath that "Which One Will Survive the War of Armageddon?"

For more than an hour, Minister Lemuel lectured about Elijah Muhammad's teachings. I sat raptly absorbing Minister Lemuel's every syllable and gesture. Frequently, he graphically illustrated points by chalking key words or phrases on the blackboard.

I thought it was outrageous that our small temple still had some empty seats. I complained to my brother Wilfred that there should be no empty seats, with the surrounding streets full of our brainwashed black brothers and sisters, drinking, cursing, fighting, dancing, carousing, and using dope—the very things that Mr. Muhammad taught were helping the black man to stay under the heel of the white man here in America.

From what I could gather, the recruitment attitude at the temple seemed to me to amount to a self-defeating waiting view . . . an assumption that Allah would bring us more Muslims. I felt that Allah would be more inclined to help those who helped themselves. I had lived for years in ghetto streets; I knew the Negroes in those streets. Harlem or Detroit were no different. I said I disagreed, that I thought we should go out into the streets and get more Muslims into the fold. All of my life, as you know, I had been an activist, I had been impatient. My brother Wilfred counseled me to keep patience. And for me to be patient was made easier by the fact that I could anticipate soon seeing and perhaps meeting the man who was called "The Messenger," Elijah Muhammad himself.

Today, I have appointments with world-famous personages, including some heads of nations. But I looked forward to the Sunday before Labor Day in 1952 with an eagerness never since duplicated. Detroit Temple Number One Muslims were going in a motor caravan—I think about ten automobiles—to visit Chicago Temple Number Two, to hear Elijah Muhammad.

Not since childhood had I been so excited as when we drove in Wilfred's car. At great Muslim rallies since then I have seen, and heard, and felt ten thousand black people applauding and cheering. But on that Sunday afternoon when our two little temples assembled, perhaps only two hundred Muslims, the Chicagoans welcoming and greeting us Detroiters, I experienced tinglings up my spine as I've never had since.

I was totally unprepared for the Messenger Elijah Muhammad's physical impact upon my emotions. From the rear of Temple Number Two, he came toward the platform. The small, sensitive, gentle, brown face that I had studied on photographs, until I had dreamed about it, was fixed straight ahead as the Messenger strode, encircled by the marching, strapping Fruit of Islam guards. The Messenger, compared to them, seemed fragile, almost tiny. He and the Fruit of Islam were dressed in dark suits, white shirts, and bow ties. The Messenger wore a gold-embroidered fez.

I stared at the great man who had taken the time to write to me when I was a convict whom he knew nothing about. He was the man whom I had been told had spent years of his life in suffering and sacrifice to lead us, the black people, because he loved us so much. And then, hearing his voice, I sat leaning forward, riveted upon his words. (I try to reconstruct what Elijah Muhammad said from having since heard him speak hundreds of times.)

"I have not stopped one day for the past twenty-one years. I have been standing, preaching to you throughout those past twenty-one years, while I was free, and even while I was in bondage. I spent three and one-half years in the federal penitentiary, and also over a year in the city jail for teaching this truth. I was also deprived of a father's love for his family for seven long years while I was running from hypocrites and other enemies of this word and revelation of God—which will give life to you, and put you on the same level with all other civilized and independent nations and peoples of this planet earth. . . ."

Elijah Muhammad spoke of how in this wilderness of North America, for centuries the "blue-eyed devil white man" had brainwashed the "so-called Negro." He told us how, as one result, the black man in America was "mentally, morally and spiritually dead." Elijah Muhammad spoke of how the black man was Original Man, who had been kidnapped from his homeland and stripped of his language, his culture, his family structure, his family name, until the black man in America did not even realize who he was.

He told us, and showed us, how his teachings of the true knowledge of ourselves would lift up the black man from the bottom of the white man's society and place the black man where he had begun, at the top of civilization.

Concluding, pausing for breath, he called my name.

It was like an electrical shock. Not looking at me directly, he asked me to stand.

He told them that I was just out of prison. He said how "strong" I had been while in prison. "Every day," he said, "for years, Brother Malcolm has written a letter from prison to me. And I have written to him as often as I could."

Standing there, feeling the eyes of the two hundred Muslims upon me, I heard him make a parable about me.

When God bragged about how faithful Job was, said Elijah Muhammad, the devil said only God's hedge around Job kept Job so faithful. "Remove that protective hedge," the devil told God, "and I will make Job curse you to your face."

The devil could claim that, hedged in prison, I had just used Islam, Mr. Muhammad said. But the devil would say that now, out of prison, I would return to my drinking, smoking, dope, and life of crime.

"Well, now, our good brother Malcolm's hedge is removed and we will see how he does," Mr. Muhammad said. "I believe that he is going to remain faithful."

And Allah blessed me to remain true, firm and strong in my faith in Islam, despite many severe trials to my faith. And even when events produced a crisis between Elijah

Muhammad and me, I told him at the beginning of the crisis, with all the sincerity I had in me, that I still believed in him more strongly than he believed in himself.

Mr. Muhammad and I are not together today only because of envy and jealousy. I had more faith in Elijah Muhammad than I could ever have in any other man upon this earth.

You will remember my having said that, when I was in prison, Mr. Muhammad would be my brother Wilfred's house guest whenever he visited Detroit Temple Number One. Every Muslim said that never could you do as much for Mr. Muhammad as he would do for you in return. That Sunday, after the meeting, he invited our entire family group and Minister Lemuel Hassan to be his guests for dinner that evening, at his new home.

Mr. Muhammad said that his children and his followers had insisted that he move into this larger, better eighteen-room house in Chicago at 4847 Woodlawn Avenue. They had just moved in that week, I believe. When we arrived, Mr. Muhammad showed us where he had just been painting. I had to restrain my impulse to run and bring a chair for the Messenger of Allah. Instead, as I had heard he would do, he was worrying about my comfort.

We had hoped to hear his wisdom during the dinner, but instead he encouraged us to talk. I sat thinking of how our Detroit Temple more or less just sat and awaited Allah to bring converts—and, beyond that, of the millions of black people all over America, who never had heard of the teachings that could stir and wake and resurrect the black man . . . and there at Mr. Muhammad's table, I found my tongue. I have always been one to speak my mind.

During a conversational lull, I asked Mr. Muhammad how many Muslims were supposed to be in our Temple Number One in Detroit.

He said, "There are supposed to be thousands."

"Yes, sir," I said. "Sir, what is your opinion of the best way of getting thousands there?"

"Go after the young people," he said. "Once you get them, the older ones will follow through shame."

I made up my mind that we were going to follow that advice.

Back in Detroit, I talked with my brother Wilfred. I offered my services to our Temple's Minister, Lemuel Hassan. He shared my determination that we should apply Mr. Muhammad's formula in a recruitment drive. Beginning that day, every evening, straight from work at the furniture store, I went doing what we Muslims later came to call "fishing." I knew the thinking and the language of ghetto streets: "My man, let me pull your coat to something—"

My application had, of course, been made and during this time I received from Chicago my "X." The Muslim's "X" symbolized the true African family name that he never could know. For me, my "X" replaced the white slave-master name of "Little" which some blue-eyed devil named Little had imposed upon my paternal forebears. The receipt of my "X" meant that forever after in the nation of Islam, I would be known as Malcolm X. Mr. Muhammad taught that we would keep this "X" until God Himself returned and gave us a Holy Name from His own mouth.

Recruit as I would in the Detroit ghetto bars, in the pool-rooms, and on the corners, I found my poor, ignorant, brain-washed black brothers mostly too deaf, dumb, and blind, mentally, morally, and spiritually, to respond. It angered me that only now and then would one display even a little curiosity about the teachings that would resurrect the black man.

These few I would almost beg to visit Temple Number One at our next meeting. But then not half of those who agreed to come would actually show up.

Gradually, enough were made interested, though, that each month, a few more automobiles lengthened our cara-vans to Temple Two in Chicago. But even after seeing and hearing Elijah Muhammad in person, only a few of the interested visitors would apply by formal letter to Mr. Muhammad to be accepted for Nation of Islam membership.

With a few months of plugging away, however, our storefront Temple One about tripled its membership. And that so deeply pleased Mr. Muhammad that he paid us the honor of a personal visit.

Mr. Muhammad gave me warm praise when Minister Lemuel Hassan told how hard I had labored in the cause of Islam.

Our caravans grew. I remember with what pride we led twenty-five automobiles to Chicago. And each time we went, we were honored with dinner at the home of Elijah Muham-mad. He was interested in my potential, I could tell from things he would say.

And I worshiped him.

In early 1953, I left the furniture store. I earned a little better weekly pay check working at the Gar Wood factory in Detroit. Where big garbage truck bodies were made, I cleaned up behind the welders each time they finished another truck body.

Mr. Muhammad was saying at his dining table by this time that one of his worst needs was more young men willing to work as hard as they would have to in order to bear the responsibilities of his ministers. He was saying that the teachings should be spreading further than they had, and temples needed to be established in other cities.

It simply had never occurred to me that *I* might be a minister. I had never felt remotely qualified to directly represent Mr. Muhammad. If someone had asked me about becoming a minister, I would have been astonished, and told them I was happy and willing to serve Mr. Muhammad in the lowliest capacity.

I don't know if Mr. Muhammad suggested it or if our Temple One Minister Lemuel Hassan on his own decision encouraged me to address our assembled brothers and sisters. I know that I testified to what Mr. Muhammad's teachings had done for me: "If I told you the life I have lived, you would find it hard to believe me. . . . When I say something about the white man, I am not talking about someone I don't know. . . ."

Soon after that, Minister Lemuel Hassan urged me to address the brothers and sisters with an extemporaneous lecture. I was uncertain, and hesitant—but at least I had debated in prison, and I tried my best. (Of course, I can't remember exactly what I said, but I do know that in my beginning efforts my favorite subject was Christianity and the horrors of slavery, where I felt well-equipped from so much reading in prison.)

"My brothers and sisters, our white slavemaster's Christian religion has taught us black people here in the wilderness of North America that we will sprout wings when we die and fly up into the sky where God will have for us a special place called heaven. This is white man's Christian religion used to *brainwash* us black people! We have *accepted* it! We have *embraced* it! We have *believed* it! We have *practiced* it! And while we are doing all of that, for himself, this blue-eyed devil has *twisted* his Christianity, to keep his *foot* on our backs . . . to keep our eyes fixed on the pie in the sky and heaven in the hereafter . . . while *he* enjoys *his* heaven right *here* . . . on *this earth* . . . in *this life*."

Today when thousands of Muslims and others have been audiences out before me, when audiences of millions have been beyond radio and television microphones, I'm sure I rarely feel as much electricity as was then generated in me by the upturned faces of those seventy-five or a hundred Muslims, plus other curious visitors, sitting there in our storefront temple with the squealing of pigs filtering in from the slaughterhouse just outside.

In the summer of 1953—all praise is due to Allah—I was named Detroit Temple Number One's Assistant Minister.

Every day after work, I walked, "fishing" for potential converts in the Detroit black ghetto. I saw the African features of my black brothers and sisters whom the devilish white man had brainwashed. I saw the hair as mine had been for years, conked by cooking it with lye until it lay limp, looking straight like the white man's hair. Time and again Mr. Muhammad's teachings were rebuffed and even ridiculed. . . . "Aw, man, get out of my face, you niggers are crazy!" My head would reel sometimes, with mingled anger and pity for my poor blind black brothers. I couldn't wait for the next time our Minister Lemuel Hassan would let me speak:

"We didn't land on Plymouth Rock, my brothers and sisters—Plymouth Rock landed on *us!*" . . . "Give *all* you can to help Messenger Elijah Muhammad's independence program for the black man! . . . This white man always has controlled us black people by keeping us running to him begging, 'Please, lawdy, please, Mr. White Man, boss, would you push me off another crumb down from your table that's sagging with riches. . . .'

". . . my *beautiful*, black brothers and sisters! And when we say 'black,' we mean everything not white, brothers and sisters! Because *look* at your skins! We're all black to the white man, but we're a thousand and one different colors. Turn around, *look* at each other! What shade of black African polluted by devil white man are you? You see me —well, in the streets they used to call me Detroit Red. Yes! Yes, that raping, red-headed devil was my *grandfather!* That close, yes! My *mother's* father! She didn't like to speak of it, can you blame her? She said she never laid eyes on him! She was *glad* for that! I'm *glad* for her! If I could drain away *his* blood that pollutes *my* body, and pollutes *my* complexion, I'd do it! Because I hate every drop of the rapist's blood that's in me!

"And it's not just me, it's *all* of us! During slavery, *think* of it, it was a *rare* one of our black grandmothers, our great-grandmothers and our great-great-grandmothers who escaped the white rapist slavemaster. That rapist slavemaster who emasculated the black man . . . with threats, with fear . . . until even today the black man lives with fear of the white man in his heart! Lives even today still under the heel of the white man!

"*Think* of it—think of that black slave man filled with fear and dread, hearing the screams of his wife, his mother, his daughter being *taken*—in the barn, the kitchen, in the bushes! *Think* of it, my dear brothers and sisters! *Think* of hearing wives, mothers, daughters, being *raped!* And you were too filled with *fear* of the rapist to do anything about it! And his vicious, animal attacks' offspring, this white man named things like 'mulatto' and 'quadroon' and 'octoroon' and all those other things that he has called us—you and me—when he is not calling us *'nigger'!*

"Turn around and look at each other, brothers and sisters, and *think* of this! You and me, polluted all these colors— and this devil has the arrogance and the gall to think we, his victims, should *love* him!"

I would become so choked up that sometimes I would walk in the streets until late into the night. Sometimes I would speak to no one for hours, thinking to myself about what the white man had done to our poor people here in America.

At the Gar Wood factory where I worked, one day the supervisor came, looking nervous. He said that a man in the office was waiting to see me.

The white man standing in there said, "I'm from the F.B.I." He flipped open—that way they do, to shock you— his little folded black leather case containing his identification. He told me to come with him. He didn't say for what, or why.

I went with him. They wanted to know, at their office, why hadn't I registered for the Korean War draft?

"I just got out of prison," I said. "I didn't know you took anybody with prison records."

They really believed I thought ex-convicts weren't supposed to register. They asked a lot of questions. I was glad they didn't ask if I intended to put on the white man's uniform, because I didn't. They just took it for granted that I would. They told me they weren't going to send me to jail for failing to register, that they were going to give me a break, but that I would have to register immediately.

So I went straight from there to the draft board. When they gave me a form to fill out, I wrote in the appropriate places that I was a Muslim, and that I was a conscientious objector.

I turned in the form. This middle-aged, bored-acting devil who scanned it looked out from under his eyes at me. He got up and went into another office, obviously to consult someone over him. After a while, he came out and motioned for me to go in there.

These three—I believe there were three, as I remember—older devils sat behind desks. They all wore that "troublesome nigger" expression. And I looked "white devil" right back into their eyes. They asked me on what basis did I claim to be a Muslim in my religion. I told them that the Messenger of Allah was Mr. Elijah Muhammad, and that all who followed Mr. Muhammad here in America were Muslims. I knew they had heard this before from some Temple One young brothers who had been there before me.

They asked if I knew what "conscientious objector" meant. I told them that when the white man asked me to go off somewhere and fight and maybe die to preserve the way the white man treated the black man in America, then my conscience made me object.

They told me that my case would be "pending." But I was put through the physical anyway, and they sent me a card with some kind of a classification. That was 1953, then I heard no more for seven years, when I received another classification card in the mail. In fact, I carry it in my wallet right now. Here: it's card number 20 219 25 1377, it's dated November 21, 1960. It says "Class 5-A," whatever that means, and stamped on the card's back is "Michigan Local Board No. 19, Wayne County, 3604 South Wayne Road, Wayne, Michigan."

Every time I spoke at our Temple One, my voice would still be hoarse from the last time. My throat took a long time to get into condition.

"Do you know *why* the white man really hates you? It's because every time he sees your face, he sees a mirror of his crime—and his guilty conscience can't bear to face it!

"Every white man in America, when he looks into a black man's eyes, should fall to his knees and say 'I'm sorry, I'm sorry—my kind has committed history's greatest crime against your kind; will you give me the chance to atone?' But do you brothers and sisters expect any white man to do that? *No,* you *know* better! And why won't he do it? Because he *can't* do it. The white man was *created* a devil, to bring chaos upon this earth. . . ."

Somewhere about this time, I left the Gar Wood factory and I went to work for the Ford Motor Company, one of the Lincoln-Mercury Division assembly lines.

As a young minister, I would go to Chicago and see Mr. Elijah Muhammad every time I could get off. He encouraged me to come when I could. I was treated as if I had been one of the sons of Mr. Muhammad and his dark, good wife Sister Clara Muhammad. I saw their children only occasionally. Most of them in those years worked around Chicago in various jobs, laborers, driving taxis, and things such as that. Also living in the home was Mr. Muhammad's dear Mother Marie.

I would spend almost as much time with Mother Marie as I did with Mr. Muhammad. I loved to hear her reminiscences about her son Elijah's early life when they lived in Sandersville, Georgia, where he was born in 1897.

Mr. Muhammad would talk with me for hours. After eating good, healthful Muslim food, we would stay at the dinner table and talk. Or I would ride with him as he drove on his daily rounds between the few grocery stores that the Muslims then owned in Chicago. The stores were examples to help black people see what they could do for themselves by hiring their own kind and trading with their own kind and thus quit being exploited by the white man.

In the Muslim-owned combination grocery-drug store on Wentworth and 31st Street, Mr. Muhammad would sweep the floor or something like that. He would do such work himself as an example to his followers whom he taught that idleness and laziness were among the black man's greatest sins against himself. I would want to snatch the broom from Mr. Muhammad's hand, because I thought he was too valuable to be sweeping a floor. But he wouldn't let me do anything but stay with him and listen while he advised me on the best ways to spread his message.

The way we were with each other, it would make me think of Socrates on the steps of the Athens market place, spreading his wisdom to his students. Or how one of those students, Aristotle, had his students following behind him, walking through the Lyceum.

One day, I remember, a dirty glass of water was on a counter and Mr. Muhammad put a clean glass of water beside it. "You want to know how to spread my teachings?" he said, and he pointed to the glasses of water. Don't condemn if you see a person has a dirty glass of water," he said, "just show them the clean glass of water that you have. When they inspect it, you won't have to say that yours is better."

Of all the things that Mr. Muhammad ever was to teach me, I don't know why, that still stands out in my mind. Although I haven't always practiced it. I love too much to battle. I'm inclined to tell somebody if his glass of water is dirty.

Mother Marie, when Mr. Muhammad was busy, would tell me about her son's boyhood and of his growing up in Georgia to young manhood.

Mother Marie's account of her son began when she was herself but seven years old. She told me that then she had a vision that one day she would be the mother of a very great man. She married a Baptist minister, Reverend Poole, who worked around Sandersville on the farms, and in the sawmills. Among their thirteen children, said Mother Marie, little Elijah was very different, almost from when he could walk and talk.

The small, frail boy usually settled his older brothers' and sisters' disputes, Mother Marie said. And young as he was, he became regarded by them as their leader. And Elijah, about the time he entered school, began displaying a strong race consciousness. After the fourth grade, because the family was so poor, Elijah had to quit school and begin full-time working. An older sister taught Elijah as much as she was able at night.

Mother Marie said that Elijah spent hours poring through the Bible, with tears shining in his eyes. (Mr. Muhammad told me himself later that as a boy he felt that the Bible's words were a locked door, that could be unlocked, if only he knew how, and he cried because of his frustrated anxiety to receive understanding.) Elijah grew up into a still-frail teen-ager who displayed a most uncommonly strong love for his race, and, Mother Marie said, instead of condemning Negroes' faults, young Elijah always would speak of reasons for those faults.

Mother Marie has since died. I believe that she had as large a funeral as Chicago has seen. Not only Muslims, but others knew of the deep bond that Messenger Elijah had with his mother.

"I am not ashamed to say how little learning I have had," Mr. Muhammad told me. "My going to school no further than the fourth grade proves that I can know nothing except the truth I have been taught by Allah. Allah taught me mathematics. He found me with a sluggish tongue, and taught me how to pronounce words."

Mr. Muhammad said that somehow, he never could stand how the Sandersville white farmers, the sawmill foremen, or other white employers would habitually and often curse Negro workers. He said he would politely ask any for whom he worked never to curse him. "I would ask them to just fire me if they didn't like my work, but just don't curse me." (Mr. Muhammad's ordinary conversation was the manner he used when making speeches. He was not "eloquent," as eloquence is usually meant, but whatever he uttered had an impact on me that trained orators did not begin to have.) He said that on the jobs he got, he worked so honestly that generally he was put in charge of the other Negroes.

After Mr. Muhammad and Sister Clara met and married and their first two children had been born, a white employer early in 1923 did curse Mr. Muhammad, then Elijah Poole. Elijah Poole, determined to avoid trouble, took his family to Detroit, arriving when he was twenty-five. Five more children would be born there in Detroit, and, finally, the last one in Chicago.

In Detroit in 1931, Mr. Muhammad met Master W. D. Fard.

The effects of the depression were bad everywhere, but in the black ghetto they were horrible, Mr. Muhammad told me. A small, light brown-skinned man knocked from door to door at the apartments of the poverty-stricken Negroes. The man offered for sale silks and other yard goods, and he identified himself as "a brother from the East."

This man began to tell Negroes how they came from a distant land, in the seeds of their forefathers.

He warned them against eating the "filthy pig" and other "wrong foods" that it was habitual for Negroes to eat.

Among the Negroes whom he found most receptive, he began holding little meetings in their poor homes. The man taught both the Quran and the Bible, and his students included Elijah Poole.

This man said his name was W. D. Fard. He said that he was born in the *Koreish* tribe of Muhammad ibn Abdullah, the Arabian prophet Himself. This peddler of silks and yard goods, Mr. W. D. Fard, knew the Bible better than any of the Christian-bred Negroes.

In the essence, Mr. W. D. Fard taught that God's true name was Allah, that His true religion was Islam, that the true name for that religion's people was Muslims.

Mr. W. D. Fard taught that the Negroes in America were directly descended from Muslims. He taught that Negroes in America were Lost Sheep, lost for four hundred years from the Nation of Islam, and that he, Mr. Fard, had come to redeem and return the Negro to his true religion.

No heaven was in the sky, Mr. Fard taught, and no hell was in the ground. Instead, both heaven and hell were conditions in which people lived right here on this planet Earth. Mr. Fard taught that the Negro in America had been for four hundred years in hell, and he, Mr. Fard, had come to return them to where heaven for them was—back home, among their own kind.

Master Fard taught that as hell was on earth, also on earth was the devil—the white race which was bred from black Original Man six thousand years before, purposely to create a hell on earth for the next six thousand years.

The black people, God's children, were Gods themselves, Master Fard taught. And he taught that among them was one, also a human being like the others, who was the God of Gods: The Most, Most High, The Supreme Being, supreme in wisdom and power—and His proper name was Allah.

Among his handful of first converts in 1931 in Detroit, Master W. D. Fard taught that every religion says that near the Last Day, or near the End of Time, God would come, to resurrect the Lost Sheep, to separate them from their enemies, and restore them to their own people. Master Fard taught that Prophecy referred to this Finder and Savior of the Lost Sheep as The Son of Man, or God in Person, or The Life-giver, The Redeemer, or The Messiah, who would come as lightning from the East and appear in the West.

He was the One to whom the Jews referred as The Messiah, the Christians as The Christ, and the Muslims as The Mahdi.

I would sit, galvanized, hearing what I then accepted from Mr. Muhammad's own mouth as being the true history of our religion, the true religion for the black man. Mr. Muhammad told me that one evening he had a revelation that Master W. D. Fard represented the fulfillment of the prophecy.

"I asked Him," said Mr. Muhammad, "Who are you, and what is your real name?" And He said, 'I am The One the world has been looking for to come for the past two thousand years.'

"I said to Him again," said Mr. Muhammad, "What is your *true* name?' And then He said, 'My name is Mahdi. I came to guide you into the right path.'"

Mr. Elijah Muhammad says that he sat listening with an open heart and an open mind—the way I was sitting listening to Mr. Muhammad. And Mr. Muhammad said he never doubted any word that the "Savior" taught him.

Starting to organize, Master W. D. Fard set up a class for training ministers to carry the teachings to America's black people. In giving names to these first ministers, Master Fard named Elijah Poole "Elijah Karriem."

Next, Master W. D. Fard established in 1931 in Detroit a University of Islam. It had adult classes which taught, among other things, mathematics, to help the poor Negroes quit being duped and deceived by the "tricknology" of "the blue-eyed devil white man."

Starting a school in the rough meant that it lacked quali-fied teachers, but a start had to be made somewhere. Mr. Elijah Karriem removed his own children from Detroit public schools, to start a nucleus of children in the University of Islam.

Mr. Muhammad told me that his older children's lack of formal education reflected their sacrifice to form the back-bone for today's Universities of Islam in Detroit and Chicago which have better-qualified faculties.

Master W. D. Fard selected Elijah Karriem to be the Supreme Minister, over all other ministers, and among all of those others sprang up a bitter jealousy. All of them had better education than Elijah Karriem, and also they were more articulate than he was. They raged, even in his presence, "Why should we bow down to someone who appears less qualified?"

But Mr. Elijah Karriem was then in some way re-named "Elijah Muhammad," who as the Supreme Minister began to receive from Master W. D. Fard for the next three and a half years private teachings, during which time he says he "heard things never revealed to others."

During this period, Mr. Elijah Muhammad and Master W. D. Fard went to Chicago and established Temple Number Two. They also established in Milwaukee the beginnings of a Temple Number Three.

In 1934, Master W. D. Fard disappeared, without a trace.

Elijah Muhammad says that attempts were made upon his life, because the others ministers' jealousy had reached such a pitch. He says that these "hypocrites" forced him to flee to Chicago. Temple Number Two became his head-quarters until the "hypocrites" pursued him there, forcing him to flee again. In Washington, D.C., he began Temple Number Four. Also while there, in the Congressional Library, he studied books which he says Master W. D. Fard had told him contained different pieces of the truth that devil white man had recorded, but which were not in books generally available to the public.

Saying that he was still pursued by the "hypocrites," Mr. Muhammad fled from city to city, never staying long in any. Whenever able, now and then, he slipped home to see his wife and his eight young children, who were fed by other poor Muslims who shared what little they had. Even Mr. Muhammad's original Chicago followers wouldn't know he was at home, for he says the "hypocrites" made serious efforts to kill him.

In 1942, Mr. Muhammad was arrested. He says Uncle Tom Negroes had tipped off the devil white man to his teachings, and he was charged by this devil white man with draft-dodging, although he was too old for military service. He was sentenced to five years in prison. In the Milan, Michigan, federal prison, Mr. Muhammad served three and a half years, then he was paroled. He had returned to his work in 1946, to remove the blinders from the eyes of the black man in the wilderness of North America.

I can hear myself now, at the lectern in our little Muslim Temple, passionately addressing my black brothers and sisters:

"This little, gentle, sweet man! The Honorable Elijah Muhammad who is at this very hour teaching our brothers and sisters over there in Chicago! Allah's Messenger—which makes him the most powerful black man in America! For you and me, he has sacrificed seven years on the run from filthy hypocrites, he spent another three and a half years in a prison cage! He was put there by the devil white man! That devil white man does not want the Honorable Elijah Muhammad stirring awake the sleeping giant of you and me, and all of our ignorant, brainwashed kind here in the white man's heaven and the black man's hell here in the wilderness of North America!

"I have sat at our Messenger's feet, hearing the truth from his own mouth! I have pledged on my knees to Allah to tell the white man about his crimes and the black man the true teachings of our Honorable Elijah Muhammad. I don't care if it costs my life. . . ."

This was my attitude. These were my uncompromising words, uttered anywhere, without hesitation or fear. I was his most faithful servant, and I know today that I did believe in him more firmly than he believed in himself.

In the years to come, I was going to have to face a psychological and spiritual crisis.

CHAPTER THIRTEEN

MINISTER MALCOLM X

I quit the Ford Motor Company's Lincoln-Mercury Division. It had become clear to me that Mr. Muhammad needed ministers to spread his teachings, to establish more temples among the twenty-two million black brothers who were brainwashed and sleeping in the cities of North America.

My decision came relatively quickly. I have always been an activist, and my personal chemistry perhaps made me reach more quickly than most ministers in the Nation of Islam that stage of dedication. But every minister in the Nation, in his own time, in his own way, in the privacy of his own soul, came to the conviction that it was written that all of his "before" life had been only conditioning and preparation to become a disciple of Mr. Muhammad's.

Everything that happens—Islam teaches—is written.

Mr. Muhammad invited me to visit his home in Chicago, as often as possible, while he trained me, for months.

Never in prison had I studied and absorbed so intensely as I did now under Mr. Muhammad's guidance. I was immersed in the worship rituals; in what he taught us were the true natures of men and women; the organizational and administrative procedures; the real meanings, and the interrelated meanings, and uses, of the Bible and the Quran.

I went to bed every night ever more awed. If not Allah, who else could have put such wisdom into that little humble lamb of a man from the Georgia fourth grade and sawmills and cotton patches. The "lamb of a man" analogy I drew for myself from the prophecy in the Book of Revelations of a symbolic lamb with a two-edged sword in its mouth. Mr. Muhammad's two-edged sword was his teachings, which cut back and forth to free the black man's mind from the white man.

My adoration of Mr. Muhammad grew, in the sense of the Latin root word *adorare*. It means much more than our "adoration" or "adore." It means that my worship of him was so awesome that he was the first man whom I had ever feared—not fear such as of a man with a gun, but the fear such as one has of the power of the sun.

Mr. Muhammad, when he felt me able, permitted me to go to Boston. Brother Lloyd X lived there. He invited people whom he had gotten interested in Islam to hear me in his living room.

I quote what I said when I was just starting out, and then later on in other places, as I can best remember the general pattern that I used, in successive phases, in those days. I know that then I always liked to start off with my favorite analogy of Mr. Muhammad.

"God has given Mr. Muhammad some sharp truth," I told them. "It is like a two-edged sword. It cuts into you. It causes you great pain, but if you can take the truth, it will cure you and save you from what otherwise would be certain death."

Then I wouldn't waste any time to start opening their eyes about the devil white man. "I know you don't realize the enormity, the horrors, of the so-called *Christian* white man's crime. . . .

"Not even in the *Bible* is there such a crime! God in His wrath struck down with *fire* the perpetrators of *lesser* crimes! *One hundred million* of us black people! Your grandparents! Mine! *Murdered* by this white man. To get fifteen million of us here to make us his slaves, on the way he murdered one hundred million! I wish it was possible for me to show you the sea bottom in those days—the black bodies, the blood, the bones broken by boots and clubs! The pregnant black women who were thrown overboard if they got too sick! Thrown overboard to the sharks that had learned that following these slave ships was the way to grow fat!

"Why, the white man's raping of the black race's woman began right on those slave ships! The blue-eyed devil could not even wait until he got them here! Why, brothers and sisters, civilized mankind has never known such an orgy of greed and lust and murder. . . ."

The dramatization of slavery never failed intensely to arouse Negroes hearing its horrors spelled out for the first time. It's unbelievable how many black men and women have let the white man fool them into holding an almost romantic idea of what slave days were like. And once I had them fired up with slavery, I would shift the scene to themselves.

"I want you, when you leave this room, to start to *see* all this whenever you see this devil white man. Oh, yes, he's a devil! I just want you to start watching him, in his places where he doesn't want you around; watch him reveling in his preciousness, and his exclusiveness, and his vanity, while he continues to subjugate you and me.

"Every time you see a white man, think about the devil you're seeing! Think of how it was on *your* slave foreparents' bloody, sweaty backs that he *built* this empire that's today the richest of all nations—where his evil and his greed cause him to be hated around the world!"

Every meeting, the people who had been there before returned, bringing friends. None of them ever had heard the wraps taken off the white man. I can't remember any black man ever in those living-room audiences in Brother Lloyd X's home at 5 Wellington Street who didn't stand up immediately when I asked after each lecture, "Will all stand who *believe* what you have heard?" And each Sunday night, some of them stood, while I could see others not quite ready, when I asked, "How many of you want to *follow* The Honorable Elijah Muhammad?"

Enough had stood up after about three months that we were able to open a little temple. I remember with what pleasure we rented some folding chairs. I was beside myself with joy when I could report to Mr. Muhammad a new temple address.

It was when we got this little mosque that my sister Ella first began to come to hear me. She sat, staring, as though she couldn't believe it was me. Ella never moved, even when I had only asked all who believed what they had heard to stand up. She contributed when our collection was held. It didn't bother or challenge me at all about Ella. I never even thought about converting her, as toughminded and cautious about joining anything as I personally knew her to be. I wouldn't have expected anyone short of Allah Himself to have been able to convert Ella.

I would close the meeting as Mr. Muhammad had taught me: "In the name of Allah, the beneficent, the merciful, all praise is due to Allah, the Lord of all the worlds, the beneficent, merciful master of the day of judgment in which we now live—Thee alone do we serve, and Thee alone do we beseech for Thine aid. Guide us on the right path, the path of those upon whom Thou has bestowed favors—not of those upon whom Thy wrath is brought down, nor the path of those who go astray after they have heard Thy teaching. I bear witness that there is no God but Thee and The Honorable Elijah Muhammad is Thy Servant and Apostle." I believed he had been divinely sent to our people by Allah Himself.

I would raise my hand, for them to be dismissed: "Do nothing unto anyone that you would not like to have done unto yourself. Seek peace, and never be the aggressor—but if anyone attacks you, we do not teach you to turn the other cheek. May Allah bless you to be successful and victorious in all that you do."

Except for that one day when I had stayed with Ella on the way to Detroit after prison, I had not been in the old Roxbury streets for seven years. I went to have a reunion with Shorty.

Shorty, when I found him, acted uncertain. The wire had told him I was in town, and on some "religious kick." He didn't know if I was serious, or if I was another of the hustling preacher-pimps to be found in every black ghetto, the ones with some little storefront churches of mostly hardworking, older women, who kept their "pretty boy" young preacher dressed in "sharp" clothes and driving a fancy car. I quickly let Shorty know how serious I was with Islam, but then, talking the old street talk, I quickly put him at his ease, and we had a great reunion. We laughed until we cried at Shorty's dramatization of his reactions when he heard that judge keep saying "Count one, ten years . . . count two, ten years—" We talked about how having those white girls with us had gotten us ten years where we had seen in prison plenty of worse offenders with far less time to serve.

Shorty still had a little band, and he was doing fairly well. He was rightfully very proud that in prison he had studied music. I told him enough about Islam to see from his reactions that he didn't really want to hear it. In prison, he had misheard about our religion. He got me off the subject by making a joke. He said that he hadn't had enough pork chops and white women. I don't know if he has yet, or not. I know that he's married to a white woman now . . . and he's fat as a hog from eating hog.

I also saw John Hughes, the gambling-house owner, and some others I had known who were still around Roxbury. The wire about me had made them all uncomfortable, but my "What you know, Daddy?" approach at least enabled us to have some conversations. I never mentioned Islam to most of them. I knew, from what I had been when I was with them, how brainwashed they were.

As Temple Eleven's minister, I served only briefly, because as soon as I got it organized, by March 1954, I left it in charge of Minister Ulysses X, and the Messenger moved me on to Philadelphia.

The City of Brotherly Love black people reacted even faster to the truth about the white man than the Bostonians had. And Philadelphia's Temple Twelve was established by the end of May. It had taken a little under three months.

The next month, because of those Boston and Philadelphia successes, Mr. Muhammad appointed me to be the minister of Temple Seven—in vital New York City.

I can't start to describe for you my welter of emotions. For Mr. Muhammad's teachings really to resurrect American black people, Islam obviously had to grow, to grow very big. And nowhere in America was such a single temple potential available as in New York's five boroughs.

They contained over a million black people.

It was nine years since West Indian Archie and I had been stalking the streets, momentarily expecting to try and shoot each other down like dogs.

"Red!" . . . "My man!" . . . "Red, this can't be you—"

With my natural kinky red hair now close-cropped, in place of the old long-haired, lye-cooked conk they had always known on my head, I know I looked much different.

"Gim'me some skin, man! A drink here, bartender—what? You quit! Aw, man, come off it!"

It was so good seeing so many whom I had known so well. You can understand how that was. But it was West Indian Archie and Sammy the Pimp for whom I was primarily looking. And the first nasty shock came quickly, about Sammy. He had quit pimping, he had gotten pretty high up in the numbers business, and was doing well. Sammy even had married. Some fast young girl. But then shortly after his wedding one morning he was found lying dead across his bed—they said with twenty-five thousand dollars in his pockets. (People don't want to believe the sums that even the minor underworld handles. Why, listen: in March 1964, a Chicago nickel-and-dime bets Wheel of Fortune man, Lawrence Wakefield, died, and over $760,000 in cash was in his apartment, in sacks and bags . . . all taken from poor Negroes . . . and we wonder why we stay so poor.)

Sick about Sammy, I queried from bar to bar among old-timers for West Indian Archie. The wire hadn't reported him dead, or living somewhere else, but none seemed to know where he was. I heard the usual hustler fates of so many others. Bullets, knives, prison, dope, diseases, insanity, alcoholism. I imagine it was about in that order. And so many of the survivors whom I knew as tough hyenas and wolves of the streets in the old days now were so pitiful. They had known all the angles, but beneath that surface they were poor, ignorant, untrained black men; life had eased up on them and hyped them. I ran across close to twenty-five of these old-timers I had known pretty well, who in the space of nine years had been reduced to the ghetto's minor, scavenger hustles to scratch up room rent and food money. Some now worked downtown, messengers, janitors, things like that. I was thankful to Allah that I had become a Muslim and escaped their fate.

There was Cadillac Drake. He was a big jolly, cigar-smoking, fat, black, gaudy-dressing pimp, a regular afternoon character when I was waiting on tables in Small's Paradise. Well, I recognized him shuffling toward me on the street. He had gotten hooked on heroin; I'd heard that. He was the dirtiest, sloppiest bum you ever laid eyes on. I hurried past because we would both have been embarrassed if he recognized me, the kid he used to toss a dollar tip.

The wire worked to locate West Indian Archie for me. The wire of the streets, when it wants to, is something like Western Union with the F.B.I. for messengers. At one of my early services at Temple Seven, an old scavenger hustler, to whom I gave a few dollars, came up when services were dismissed. He told me that West Indian Archie was sick, living up in a rented room in the Bronx.

I took a taxi to the address. West Indian Archie opened the door. He stood there in rumpled pajamas and barefooted, squinting at me.

Have you ever seen someone who seemed a ghost of the person you remembered? It took him a few seconds to fix me in his memory. He exclaimed, hoarsely, "Red! I'm so glad to see you!"

I all but hugged the old man. He was sick in that weak way. I helped him back. He sat down on the edge of his bed. I sat in his one chair, and I told him how his forcing me out of Harlem had saved my life by turning me in the direction of Islam.

He said, "I always liked you, Red," and he said that he had never really wanted to kill me. I told him it had made me shudder many times to think how close we had come to killing each other. I told him I had sincerely thought I had hit that combinated six-way number for the three hundred dollars he had paid me. Archie said that he had later wondered if he had made some mistake, since I was so ready to die about it. And then we agreed that it wasn't worth even talking about, it didn't mean anything anymore. He kept saying, over and over, in between other things, that he was so glad to see me.

I went into a little of Mr. Muhammad's teaching with Archie. I told him how I had found out that all of us who had been in the streets were victims of the white man's society. I told Archie what I had thought in prison about him; that his brain, which could tape-record hundreds of number combinations a day, should have been put at the service of mathematics or science. "Red, that sure is something to think about," I can remember him saying.

But neither of us would say that it was not too late. I have the feeling that he knew, as I could see, that the end was closing in on Archie. I became too moved about what he had been and what he had now become to be able to stay much longer. I didn't have much money, and he didn't want to accept what little I was able to press on him. But I made him take it.

I keep having to remind myself that then, in June, 1954, Temple Seven in New York City was a little storefront. Why, it's almost unbelievable that one bus couldn't have been filled with the Muslims in New York City! Even among our own black people in the Harlem ghetto, you could have said "Muslim" to a thousand, and maybe only one would not have asked you "What's that?" As for white people, except for that relative handful privy to certain police or prison files, not five hundred white people in all of America knew we existed.

I began firing Mr. Muhammad's teaching at the New York members and the few friends they managed to bring in. And with each meeting, my discomfort grew that in Harlem, choked with poor, ignorant black men suffering all of the evils that Islam could cure, every time I lectured my heart out and then asked those who wanted to follow Mr. Muhammad to stand, only two or three would. And, I have to admit, sometimes not that many.

I think I was all the angrier with my own ineffectiveness because I *knew* the streets. I had to get myself together and think out the problem. And the big trouble, obviously, was that we were only one among the many voices of black discontent on every busy Harlem corner. The different Nationalist groups, the "Buy Black!" forces, and others like that; dozens of their step-ladder orators were trying to increase their followings. I had nothing against anyone trying to promote independence and unity among black men, but they still were making it tough for Mr. Muhammad's voice to be heard.

In my first effort to get over this hurdle, I had some little leaflets printed. There wasn't a much-traveled Harlem street corner that five or six good Muslim brothers and I missed. We would step up right in front of a walking black man or woman so that they had to accept our leaflet, and if they hesitated one second, they had to hear us saying some catch thing such as "Hear how the white man kidnapped and robbed and raped our black race—"

Next, we went to work "fishing" on those Harlem corners— on the fringes of the Nationalist meetings. The method today has many refinements, but then it consisted of working the always shifting edges of the audiences that others had managed to draw. At a Nationalist meeting, everyone who was listening was interested in the revolution of the black race. We began to get visible results almost immediately after we began thrusting handbills in people's hands, "Come to hear us, too, brother. The Honorable Elijah Muhammad teaches us how to cure the black man's spiritual, mental, moral, economic, and political sicknesses—"

I saw the new faces of our Temple Seven meetings. And then we discovered the best "fishing" audience of all, by far the best-conditioned audience for Mr. Muhammad's teachings: the Christian churches.

Our Sunday services were held at two P.M. All over Harlem

during the hour or so before that, Christian church services were dismissing. We by-passed the larger churches with their higher ratio of so-called "middle class" Negroes who were so full of pretense and "status" that they wouldn't be caught in our little storefront.

We went "fishing" fast and furiously when those little evangelical storefront churches each let out their thirty to fifty people on the sidewalk. "Come to hear us, brother, sister—" "You haven't heard anything until you have heard the teachings of The Honorable Elijah Muhammad—" These congregations were usually Southern migrant people, usually older, who would go anywhere to hear what they called "good preaching." These were the church congregations who were always putting out little signs announcing that inside they were selling fried chicken and chitlin dinners to raise some money. And three or four nights a week, they were in their storefront rehearsing for the next Sunday, I guess, shaking and rattling and rolling the gospels with their guitars and tambourines.

I don't know if you know it, but there's a whole circuit of commercial gospel entertainers who have come out of these little churches in the city ghettoes or from down South. People such as Sister Rosetta Tharpe, The Clara Ward Singers are examples, and there must be five hundred lesser lights on the same general order. Mahalia Jackson, the greatest of them all—she was a preacher's daughter in Louisiana. She came up there to Chicago where she worked cooking and scrubbing for white people and then in a factory while she sang in the Negro churches the gospel style that, when it caught on, made her the first Negro that Negroes ever made famous. She was selling hundreds of thousands of records among Negroes before white people ever knew who Mahalia Jackson was. Anyway, I know that somewhere I once read that Mahalia said that every time she can, she will slip unannounced into some little ghetto storefront church and sing with her people. She calls that "my filling station."

The black Christians we "fished" to our Temple were conditioned, I found, by the very shock I could give them about what had been happening to them while they worshiped a blond, blue-eyed God. I knew the temple that I could build if I could really get to those Christians. I tailored the teachings for them. I would start to speak and sometimes be so emotionally charged I had to explain myself:

"You see my tears, brothers and sisters. . . . Tears haven't been in my eyes since I was a young boy. But I cannot help this when I feel the responsibility I have to help you comprehend for the first time what this white man's religion that we call Christianity has *done* to us. . . .

"Brothers and sisters here for the first time, please don't let that shock you. I know you didn't expect this. Because almost none of us black people have thought that maybe we were making a mistake not wondering if there wasn't a special religion somewhere for us—a special religion for the black man.

"Well, there *is* such a religion. It's called Islam. Let me spell it for you, I-s-l-a-m! *Islam!* But I'm going to tell you about Islam a little later. First, we need to understand some things about this Christianity before we can understand why the *answer* for us is Islam.

"Brothers and sisters, the white man has brainwashed us black people to fasten our gaze upon a blond-haired, blue-eyed Jesus! We're worshiping a Jesus that doesn't even *look* like us! Oh, yes! Now just bear with me, listen to the teachings of the Messenger of Allah, The Honorable Elijah Muhammad. Now, just think of this. The blond-haired, blue-eyed white man has taught you and me to worship a *white* Jesus, and to shout and sing and pray to this God that's *his* God, the white man's God. The white man has taught us to shout and sing and pray until we *die*, to wait until *death*, for some dreamy heaven-in-the-hereafter, when we're *dead*, while this white man has his milk and honey in the streets paved with golden dollars right here on *this* earth!

"You don't want to believe what I am telling you, brothers and sisters? Well, I'll tell you what you do. You go out of here, you just take a good look around where you live. Look at not only how *you* live, but look at how anybody that you *know* lives—that way, you'll be sure that you're not just a bad-luck accident. And when you get through looking at where *you* live, then you take you a walk down across Central Park, and start to look at what this white God has brought to the white man. I mean, take yourself a look down there at how the white man is living!

"And don't stop there. In fact, you won't be able to stop for long—his doormen are going to tell you 'Move on!' But catch a subway and keep on downtown. Anywhere you may want to get off, *look* at the white man's apartments, businesses! Go right on down to the tip of Manhattan Island that this devilish white man stole from the trusting Indians for twenty-four dollars! Look at his City Hall, down there; look at his Wall Street! Look at yourself! Look at *his* God!"

I had learned early one important thing, and that was to always teach in terms that the people could understand. Also, where the Nationalists whom we had "fished" were almost all men, among the storefront Christians, a heavy preponderance were women, and I had the sense to offer something special for them. "*Beautiful* black woman! The Honorable Elijah Muhammad teaches us that the black man is going around saying he wants respect; well, the black man never will get anybody's respect until he first learns to respect his own women! The black man needs *today* to stand up and throw off the weaknesses imposed upon him by the slavemaster white man! The black man needs to start today to shelter and protect and *respect* his black women!"

One hundred percent would stand up without hesitation when I said, "How many *believe* what they have heard?" But still never more than an agonizing few would stand up when I invited, "Will those stand who want to *follow* The Honorable Elijah Muhammad?"

I knew that our strict moral code and discipline was what repelled them most. I fired at this point, at the reason for our code. "The white man *wants* black men to stay immoral, unclean and ignorant. As long as we stay in these conditions we will keep on begging him and he will control us. We never can win freedom and justice and equality until we are doing something for ourselves!"

The code, of course, had to be explained to any who were tentatively interested in becoming Muslims. And the word got around in their little storefronts quickly, which is why they would come to hear me, yet wouldn't join Mr. Muhammad. Any fornication was absolutely forbidden in the Nation of Islam. Any eating of the filthy pork, or other injurious or unhealthful foods; any use of tobacco, alcohol, or narcotics. No Muslim who followed Elijah Muhammad could dance, gamble, date, attend movies, or sports, or take long vacations from work. Muslims slept no more than health required. Any domestic quarreling, any discourtesy, especially to women, was not allowed. No lying or stealing, and no insubordination to civil authority, except on the grounds of religious obligation.

Our moral laws were policed by our Fruit of Islam—able, dedicated, and trained Muslim men. Infractions resulted in suspension by Mr. Muhammad, or isolation for various periods, or even expulsion for the worst offenses "from the only group that really cares about you."

Temple Seven grew somewhat with each meeting. It just grew too slowly to suit me. During the weekdays, I traveled by bus and train. I taught each Wednesday at Philadelphia's Temple Twelve. I went to Springfield, Massachusetts, to try to start a new temple. A temple which Mr. Muhammad numbered Thirteen was established there with the help of Brother Osborne, who had first heard of Islam from me in prison. A lady visiting a Springfield meeting asked if I'd come to Hartford, where she lived; she specified the next Thursday and said she would assemble some friends. And I was right there.

Thursday is traditionally domestic servants' day off. This sister had in her housing project apartment about fifteen of the maids, cooks, chauffeurs and house men who worked for the Hartford-area white people. You've heard that saying, "No man is a hero to his valet." Well, those Negroes who waited on wealthy whites hand and foot opened their eyes quicker than most Negroes. And when they went "fishing" enough among more servants, and other black people in and around Hartford, Mr. Muhammad before long was able to assign to a Hartford temple the number Fourteen. And every Thursday I scheduled my teaching there.

Mr. Muhammad, when I went to see him in Chicago, had to chastise me on some point during nearly every visit. I just couldn't keep from showing in some manner that with his ministers equipped with the power of his message, I felt the Nation should go much faster. His patience and his wisdom in chastising me would always humble me from head to foot. He said, one time, that no true leader burdened his followers with a greater load than they could carry, and no true leader sets too fast a pace for his followers to keep up.

"Most people seeing a man in an old touring car going real slow think the man doesn't want to go fast," Mr. Muhammad said, "but the man knows that to drive any faster would destroy the old car. When he gets a fast car, then he will drive at a fast speed." And I remember him telling me another time, when I complained about an inefficient minister at one of his mosques, "I would rather have a mule I can depend upon than a race horse that I can't depend upon."

I knew that Mr. Muhammad *wanted* that fast car to drive. And I don't think you could pick the same number of faithful brothers and sisters from the Nation of Islam today and find "fishing" teams to beat the efforts of those who helped to bring growth to the Boston, Philadelphia, Springfield, Hartford, and New York temples. I'm, of course, just mentioning those that I knew most about because I was directly involved. This was through 1955. And 1955 was the year I made my first trip of any distance. It was to help open the temple that today is Number Fifteen—in Atlanta, Georgia.

Any Muslim who ever moved for personal reasons from one city to another was of course exhorted to plant seeds for Mr. Muhammad. Brother James X, one of our top Temple Twelve brothers, had interested enough black people in Atlanta so that when Mr. Muhammad was advised, he told me to go to Atlanta and hold a first meeting. I think I have had a hand in most of Mr. Muhammad's temples, but I'll never forget that opening in Atlanta.

A funeral parlor was the only place large enough that Brother James X could afford to rent. Everything that the Nation of Islam did in those days, from Mr. Muhammad on down, was strictly on a shoestring. When we all arrived, though, a Christian Negro's funeral was just dismissing, so we had to wait awhile, and we watched the mourners out.

"You saw them all crying over their physical dead," I told our group when we got inside. "But the Nation of Islam is rejoicing over you, our mentally dead. That may shock you, but, oh, yes, you just don't realize how our whole black race in America is mentally dead. We are here today with Mr. Elijah Muhammad's teachings which resurrect the black man from the dead. . . ."

And, speaking of funerals, I should mention that we never failed to get some new Muslims when non-Muslims, family and friends of a Muslim deceased, attended our short, moving ceremony that illustrated Mr. Muhammad's teaching, "Christians have their funerals for the living, ours are for our departed."

As the minister of several temples, conducting the Muslim ceremony had occasionally fallen to my lot. As Mr. Muhammad had taught me, I would start by reading over the casket of the departed brother or sister a prayer to Allah. Next I read a simple obituary record of his or her life. Then I usually read from Job; two passages, in the seventh and fourteenth chapters, where Job speaks of no life after death. Then another passage where David, when his son died, spoke also of no life after death.

To the audience before me, I explained why no tears were to be shed, and why we had no flowers, or singing, or organ-playing. "We shed tears for our brother, and gave him our music and our tears while he was alive. If he wasn't wept for and given our music and flowers then, well, now there is no need, because he is no longer aware. We now will give his family any money we might have spent."

Appointed Muslim Sisters quickly passed small trays from which everyone took a thin, round patty of peppermint candy. At my signal, the candy was put into mouths. "We will file by now for a last look at our brother. We won't cry—just as we don't cry over candy. Just as this sweet candy will dissolve, so will our brother's sweetness that we have enjoyed when he lived now dissolve into a sweetness in our memories."

I have had probably a couple of hundred Muslims tell me that it was attending one of our funerals for a departed brother or sister that first turned them toward Allah. But I was to learn later that Mr. Muhammad's teaching about death and the Muslim funeral service was in drastic contradiction to what Islam taught in the East.

We had grown, by 1956—well, sizable. Every temple had "fished" with enough success that there were far more Muslims, especially in the major cities of Detroit, Chicago, and New York than anyone would have guessed from the outside. In fact, as you know, in the really big cities, you can have a very big organization and, if it makes no public show, or noise, no one will necessarily be aware that it is around.

But more than just increase in numbers, Mr. Muhammad's version of Islam now had been getting in some other types of black people. We began now getting those with some education, both academic, and vocations and trades, and even some with "positions" in the white world, and all of this was starting to bring us closer to the desired fast car for Mr. Muhammad to drive. We had, for instance, some civil servants, some nurses, clerical workers, salesmen from the department stores. And one of the best things was that some brothers of this type were developing into smart, fine, aggressive young ministers for Mr. Muhammad.

I went without a lot of sleep trying to merit his increasing evidences of trust and confidence in my efforts to help build our Nation of Islam. It was in 1956 that Mr. Muhammad was able to authorize Temple Seven to buy and assign for my use a new Chevrolet. (The car was the Nation's, not mine. I had nothing that was mine but my clothes, wrist watch, and suitcase. As in the case of all of the Nation's ministers, my living expenses were paid and I had some pocket money. Where once you couldn't have named anything I wouldn't have done for money, now money was the last thing to cross my mind.) Anyway, in letting me know about the car, Mr. Muhammad told me he knew how I loved to roam, planting seeds for new Muslims, or more temples, so he didn't want me to be tied down.

In five months, I put about 30,000 miles of "fishing" on that car before I had an accident. Late one night a brother and I were coming through Weathersfield, Connecticut, when I stopped for a red light and a car smashed into me from behind. I was just shook up, not hurt. That excited devil had a woman with him, hiding her face, so I knew she wasn't his wife. We were exchanging our identification (he lived in Meriden, Connecticut) when the police arrived, and their actions told me he was somebody important. I later found out he was one of Connecticut's most prominent politicians; I won't call his name. Anyway, Temple Seven settled on a lawyer's advice, and that money went down on an Oldsmobile, the make of car I've been driving ever since.

I had always been very careful to stay completely clear of any personal closeness with any of the Muslim sisters. My total commitment to Islam demanded having no other interests, especially, I felt, no women. In almost every temple at least one single sister had let out some broad hint that she thought I needed a wife. So I always made it clear that marriage had no interest for me whatsoever; I was too busy.

Every month, when I went to Chicago, I would find that some sister had written complaining to Mr. Muhammad that I talked so hard against women when I taught our special classes about the different natures of the two sexes. Now,

Islam has very strict laws and teachings about women, the core of them being that the true nature of a man is to be strong, and a woman's true nature is to be weak, and while a man must at all times respect his woman, at the same time he needs to understand that he must control her if he expects to get her respect.

But in those days I had my own personal reasons. I wouldn't have considered it possible for me to love any woman. I'd had too much experience that women were only tricky, deceitful, untrustworthy flesh. I had seen too many men ruined, or at least tied down, or in some other way messed up by women. Women talked too much. To tell a woman not to talk too much was like telling Jesse James not to carry a gun, or telling a hen not to cackle. Can you imagine Jesse James without a gun, or a hen that didn't cackle? And for anyone in any kind of a leadership position, such as I was, the worst thing in the world that he could have was the wrong woman. Even Samson, the world's strongest man, was destroyed by the woman who slept in his arms. She was the one whose words hurt him.

I mean, I'd had *so* much experience. I had talked to too many prostitutes and mistresses. They knew more about a whole lot of husbands than the wives of those husbands did. The wives always filled their husbands' ears so full of wife complaints that it wasn't the wives, it was the prostitutes and mistresses who heard the husbands' innermost problems and secrets. They thought of him, and comforted him, and that included listening to him, and so he would tell them everything.

Anyway, it had been ten years since I thought anything about any mistress, I guess, and as a minister now, I was thinking even less about getting any wife. And Mr. Muhammad himself encouraged me to stay single.

Temple Seven sisters used to tell brothers, "You're just staying single because Brother Minister Malcolm never looks at anybody." No, I didn't make it any secret to any of those sisters, how I felt. And, yes, I did tell the brothers to be very, very careful.

This sister—well, in 1956, she joined Temple Seven. I just noticed her, not with the slightest interest, you understand. For about the next year, I just noticed her. You know, she never would have dreamed I was even thinking about her. In fact, probably you couldn't have convinced her I even knew

her name. It was Sister Betty X. She was tall, brown-skinned
—darker than I was. And she had brown eyes.

I knew she was a native of Detroit, and that she had been
a student at Tuskegee Institute down in Alabama—an education major. She was in New York at one of the big hospitals'
school of nursing. She lectured to the Muslim girls' and
women's classes on hygiene and medical facts.

I ought to explain that each week night a different Muslim
class, or event, is scheduled. Monday night, every temple's
Fruit of Islam trains. People think this is just military drill,
judo, karate, things like that—which *is* part of the F.O.I.
training, but only one part. The F.O.I. spends a lot more
time in lectures and discussions on men learning to be men.
They deal with the responsibilities of a husband and father;
what to expect of women; the rights of women which are
not to be abrogated by the husband; the importance of the
father-male image in the strong household; current events;
why honesty, and chastity, are vital in a person, a home, a
community, a nation, and a civilization; why one should
bathe at least once each twenty-four hours; business princi-
ples; and things of that nature.

Then, Tuesday night in every Muslim temple is Unity
Night, where the brothers and sisters enjoy each other's conversational company and refreshments, such as cookies and
sweet and sour fruit punches. Wednesday nights, at eight P.M.,
is what is called Student Enrollment, where Islam's basic
issues are discussed; it is about the equivalent of catechism
class in the Catholic religion.

Thursday nights there are the M.G.T. (Muslim Girls'
Training) and the G.C.C. (General Civilization Class), where
the women and girls of Islam are taught how to keep homes,
how to rear children, how to care for husbands, how to
cook, sew, how to act at home and abroad, and other things
that are important to being a good Muslim sister and mother
and wife.

Fridays are devoted to Civilization Night, when classes
are held for brothers and sisters in the area of the domestic
relations, emphasizing how both husbands and wives must
understand and respect each other's true natures. Then Saturday night is for all Muslims a free night, when, usually, they
visit at each other's homes. And, of course, on Sundays, every
Muslim temple holds its services.

On the Thursday M.G.T. and G.C.C. nights, sometimes I

would drop in on the classes, and maybe at Sister Betty X's classes—just as on other nights I might drop in on the different brothers' classes. At first I would just ask her things like how were the sisters learning—things like that, and she would say "Fine, Brother Minister." I'd say, "Thank you, Sister." Like that. And that would be all there was to it. And after a while, I would have very short conversations with her, just to be friendly.

One day I thought it would help the women's classes if I took her—just because she happened to be an instructor, to the Museum of Natural History. I wanted to show her some Museum displays having to do with the tree of evolution, that would help her in her lectures. I could show her proofs of Mr. Muhammad's teachings of such things as that the filthy pig is only a large rodent. The pig is a graft between a rat, a cat and a dog, Mr. Muhammad taught us. When I mentioned my idea to Sister Betty X, I made it very clear that it was just to help her lectures to the sisters. I had even convinced myself that this was the only reason.

Then by the time of the afternoon I said we would go, well, I telephoned her; I told her I had to cancel the trip, that something important had come up. She said, "Well, you sure waited long enough to tell me, Brother Minister, I was just ready to walk out of the door." So I told her, well, all right, come on then, I'd make it somehow. But I wasn't going to have much time.

While we were down there, offhandedly I asked her all kinds of things. I just wanted some idea of her thinking; you understand, I mean *how* she thought. I was halfway impressed by her intelligence and also her education. In those days she was one of the few whom we had attracted who had attended college.

Then, right after that, one of the older sisters confided to me a personal problem that Sister Betty X was having. I was really surprised that when she had had the chance, Sister Betty X had not mentioned anything to me about it. Every Muslim minister is always hearing the problems of young people whose parents have ostracized them for becoming Muslims. Well, when Sister Betty X told her foster parents, who were financing her education, that she was a Muslim, they gave her a choice: leave the Muslims, or they'd cut off her nursing school.

It was right near the end of her term—but she was hanging on to Islam. She began taking baby-sitting jobs for some of the doctors who lived on the grounds of the hospital where she was training.

In my position, I would never have made any move without thinking how it would affect the Nation of Islam organization as a whole.

I got to turning it over in my mind. What would happen if I just *should* happen, sometime, to think about getting married to somebody? For instance Sister Betty X—although it could be any sister in any temple, but Sister Betty X, for instance, would just happen to be the right height for somebody my height, and also the right age.

Mr. Elijah Muhammad taught us that a tall man married to a too-short woman, or vice-versa, they looked odd, not matched. And he taught that a wife's ideal age was half the man's age, plus seven. He taught that women are physiologically ahead of men. Mr. Muhammad taught that no marriage could succeed where the woman did not look up with respect to the man. And that the man had to have something above and beyond the wife in order for her to be able to look to him for psychological security.

I was so shocked at myself, when I realized *what* I was thinking, I quit going anywhere near Sister Betty X, or anywhere I knew she would be. If she came into our restaurant and I was there, I went out somewhere. I was glad I knew that she had no idea what I had been thinking about. My not talking to her wouldn't give her any reason to think anything, since there had never been one *personal* word spoken between us—even if she had *thought* anything.

I studied about if I just *should* happen to say something to her—what would her position be? Because she wasn't going to get any chance to embarrass me. I had heard too many women bragging, "I told that chump 'Get lost!'" I'd had too much experience of the kind to make a man very cautious.

I knew one good thing; she had few relatives. My feeling about in-laws was that they were outlaws. Right among the Temple Seven Muslims, I had seen more marriages destroyed by in-laws, usually anti-Muslim, than any other single thing I knew of.

I wasn't about to say any of that romance stuff that Hollywood and television had filled women's heads with. If I was going to do something, I was going to do it directly. And anything I was going to do, I was going to do *my* way. And because *I* wanted to do it. Not because I saw somebody do it. Or read about it in a book. Or saw it in a moving picture somewhere.

I told Mr. Muhammad, when I visited him in Chicago that month, that I was thinking about a very serious step. He smiled when he heard what it was.

I told him I was just thinking about it, that was all. Mr. Muhammad said that he'd like to meet this sister.

The Nation by this time was financially able to bear the expenses so that instructor sisters from different temples could be sent to Chicago to attend the Headquarters Temple Two women's classes, and, while there, to meet The Honorable Elijah Muhammad in person. Sister Betty X, of course, knew all about this, so there was no reason for her to think anything of it when it was arranged for her to go to Chicago. And like all visiting instructor sisters, she was the house guest of the Messenger and Sister Clara Muhammad.

Mr. Muhammad told me that he thought that Sister Betty X was a fine sister.

If you are thinking about doing a thing, you ought to make up your mind if you are going to do it, or not do it. One Sunday night, after the Temple Seven meeting, I drove my car out on the Garden State Parkway. I was on my way to visit my brother Wilfred, in Detroit. Wilfred, the year before, in 1957, had been made the minister of Detroit's Temple One. I hadn't seen him, or any of my family, in a good while.

It was about ten in the morning when I got inside Detroit. Getting gas at a filling station, I just went to their pay phone on a wall; I telephoned Sister Betty X. I had to get Information to get the number of the nurses' residence at this hospital. Most numbers I memorized, but I had always made it some point never to memorize her number. Somebody got her to the phone finally. She said, "Oh, hello, Brother Minister—" I just said it to her direct: "Look, do you want to get married?"

Naturally, she acted all surprised and shocked.

The more I have thought about it, to this day I believe she was only putting on an act. Because women know. They know.

She said, just like I knew she would, "Yes." Then I said,

well, I didn't have a whole lot of time, she'd better catch a plane to Detroit.

So she grabbed a plane. I met her foster parents who lived in Detroit. They had made up by this time. They were very friendly, and happily surprised. At least, they acted that way.

Then I introduced Sister Betty X at my oldest brother Wilfred's house. I had already asked him where people could get married without a whole lot of mess and waiting. He told me in Indiana.

Early the next morning, I picked up Betty at her parents' home. We drove to the first town in Indiana. We found out that only a few days before, the state law had been changed, and now Indiana had a long waiting period.

This was the fourteenth of January, 1958; a Tuesday. We weren't far from Lansing, where my brother Philbert lived. I drove there. Philbert was at work when we stopped at his house and I introduced Betty X. She and Philbert's wife were talking when I found out on the phone that we could get married in one day, if we rushed.

We got the necessary blood tests, then the license. Where the certificate said "Religion," I wrote "Muslim." Then we went to the Justice of the Peace.

An old hunchbacked white man performed the wedding. And all of the witnesses were white. Where you are supposed to say all those "I do's," we did. They were all standing there, smiling and watching every move. The old devil said, "I pronounce you man and wife," and then, "Kiss your bride."

I got her out of there. All of that Hollywood stuff! Like these women wanting men to pick them up and carry them across thresholds and some of them weigh more than you do. I don't know how many marriage breakups are caused by these movie- and television-addicted women expecting some bouquets and kissing and hugging and being swept out like Cinderella for dinner and dancing—then getting mad when a poor, scraggly husband comes in tired and sweaty from working like a dog all day, looking for some food.

We had dinner there at Philbert's home in Lansing. "I've got a surprise for you," I told him when we came in. "You haven't got any surprise for me," he said. When he got home from work and heard I'd been there introducing a Muslim sister, he knew I was either married, or on the way to get married.

Betty's nursing school schedule called for her to fly right back to New York, and she could return in four days. She claims she didn't tell anybody in Temple Seven that we had married.

That Sunday, Mr. Muhammad was going to teach at Detroit's Temple One. I had an Assistant Minister in New York now; I telephoned him to take over for me. Saturday, Betty came back. The Messenger, after his teaching on Sunday, made the announcement. Even in Michigan, my steering clear of all sisters was so well known, they just couldn't believe it.

We drove right back to New York together. The news really shook everybody in Temple Seven. Some young brothers looked at me as though I had betrayed them. But everybody else was grinning like Cheshire cats. The sisters just about ate up Betty. I never will forget hearing one exclaim, "You got him!" That's like I was telling you, the *nature* of women. She'd *got* me. That's part of why I never have been able to shake it out of my mind that she knew something—all the time. Maybe she did get me!

Anyway, we lived for the next two and a half years in Queens, sharing a house of two small apartments with Brother John Ali and his wife of that time. He's now the National Secretary in Chicago.

Attilah, our oldest daughter, was born in November 1958. She's named for Attilah the Hun (he sacked Rome). Shortly after Attilah came, we moved to our present seven-room house in an all-black section of Queens, Long Island.

Another girl, Qubilah (named after Qubilah Khan) was born on Christmas Day of 1960. Then, Ilyasah ("Ilyas" is Arabic for "Elijah") was born in July 1962. And in 1964 our fourth daughter, Amilah, arrived.

I guess by now I will say I love Betty. She's the only woman I ever even thought about loving. And she's one of the very few—four women—whom I have ever trusted. The thing is, Betty's a good Muslim woman and wife. You see, Islam is the only religion that gives both husband and wife a true understanding of what love is. The Western "love" concept, you take it apart, it really is lust. But love transcends just the physical. Love is disposition, behavior, attitude, thoughts, likes, dislikes—these things make a beautiful woman, a beautiful wife. This is the beauty that never fades. You find in your Western civilization that when a man's wife's physical beauty fails, she loses her attraction. But Islam teaches us to look into the woman, and teaches her to look into us.

Betty does this, so she understands me. I would even say I don't imagine many other women might put up with the way I am. Awakening this brainwashed black man and telling this arrogant, devilish white man the truth about himself, Betty understands, is a full-time job. If I have work to do when I am home, the little time I am at home, she lets me have the quiet I need to work in. I'm rarely at home more than half of any week; I have been away as much as five months. I never get much chance to take her anywhere, and I know she likes to be with her husband. She is used to my calling her from airports anywhere from Boston to San Francisco, or Miami to Seattle, or, here lately, cabling her from Cairo, Accra, or the Holy City of Mecca. Once on the long-distance telephone, Betty told me in beautiful phrasing the way she thinks. She said, "You are present when you are away."

Later that year, after Betty and I were married, I exhausted myself trying to be everywhere at once, trying to help the Nation to keep growing. Guest-teaching at the Temple in Boston, I ended, as always, "Who among you wish to *follow* The Honorable Elijah Muhammad?" And then I saw, in utter astonishment, that among those who were standing was my sister—*Ella!* We have a saying that those who are the hardest to convince make the best Muslims. And for Ella it had taken five years.

I mentioned, you will remember, how in a big city, a sizable organization can remain practically unknown, unless something happens that brings it to the general public's attention. Well, certainly no one in the Nation of Islam had any anticipation of the kind of thing that would happen in Harlem one night.

Two white policemen, breaking up a street scuffle between some Negroes, ordered other Negro passers-by to "Move on!" Of these bystanders, two happened to be Muslim brother Johnson Hinton and another brother of Temple Seven. They didn't scatter and run the way the white cops wanted. Brother Hinton was attacked with nightsticks. His scalp was split open, and a police car came and he was taken to a nearby precinct.

The second brother telephoned our restaurant. And with some telephone calls, in less than half an hour about fifty of Temple Seven's men of the Fruit of Islam were standing in ranks-formation outside the police precinct house.

Other Negroes, curious, came running, and gathered in

excitement behind the Muslims. The police, coming to the station house front door, and looking out of the windows, couldn't believe what they saw. I went in, as the minister of Temple Seven, and demanded to see our brother. The police first said he wasn't there. Then they admitted he was, but said I couldn't see him. I said that until he was seen, and we were sure he received proper medical attention, the Muslims would remain where they were.

They were nervous and scared of the gathering crowd outside. When I saw our Brother Hinton, it was all I could do to contain myself. He was only semi-conscious. Blood had bathed his head and face and shoulders. I hope I never again have to withstand seeing another case of sheer police brutality like that.

I told the lieutenant in charge, "That man belongs in the hospital." They called an ambulance. When it came and Brother Hinton was taken to Harlem Hospital, we Muslims followed, in loose formations, for about fifteen blocks along Lenox Avenue, probably the busiest thoroughfare in Harlem. Negroes who never had seen anything like this were coming out of stores and restaurants and bars and enlarging the crowd following us.

The crowd was big, and angry, behind the Muslims in front of Harlem Hospital. Harlem's black people were long since sick and tired of police brutality. And they never had seen any organization of black men take a firm stand as we were.

A high police official came up to me, saying "Get those people out of there." I told him that our brothers were standing peacefully, disciplined perfectly, and harming no one. He told me those others, behind them, weren't disciplined. I politely told him those others were his problem.

When doctors assured us that Brother Hinton was receiving the best of care, I gave the order and the Muslims slipped away. The other Negroes' mood was ugly, but they dispersed also, when we left. We wouldn't learn until later that a steel plate would have to be put into Brother Hinton's skull. (After that operation, the Nation of Islam helped him to sue; a jury awarded him over $70,000, the largest police brutality judgment that New York City has ever paid.)

For New York City's millions of readers of the downtown papers, it was, at that time, another one of the periodic "Racial Unrest in Harlem" stories. It was not played up, because of what had happened. But the police department, to be sure, pulled out and carefully studied the files on the Nation of Islam, and appraised us with new eyes. Most important, in Harlem, the world's most heavily populated black ghetto, the *Amsterdam News* made the whole story headline news, and for the first time the black man, woman, and child in the streets was discussing "those Muslims."

CHAPTER FOURTEEN

BLACK MUSLIMS

In the spring of nineteen fifty-nine—some months before Brother Johnson Hinton's case had awakened the Harlem black ghetto to us—a Negro journalist, Louis Lomax, then living in New York, asked me one morning whether our Nation of Islam would cooperate in being filmed as a television documentary program for the Mike Wallace Show, which featured controversial subjects. I told Lomax that, naturally, anything like that would have to be referred to The Honorable Elijah Muhammad. And Lomax did fly to Chicago to consult Mr. Muhammad. After questioning Lomax, then cautioning him against some things he did not desire, Mr. Muhammad gave his consent.

Cameramen began filming Nation of Islam scenes around our mosques in New York, Chicago, and Washington, D.C. Sound recordings were made of Mr. Muhammad and some ministers, including me, teaching black audiences the truths about the brainwashed black man and the devil white man.

At Boston University around the same time, C. Eric Lincoln, a Negro scholar then working for his doctorate, had selected for his thesis subject the Nation of Islam. Lincoln's interest had been aroused the previous year when, teaching at Clark College in Atlanta, Georgia, he received from one of his Religion students a term paper whose introduction I can now quote from Lincoln's book. It was the plainspoken convictions of one of Atlanta's numerous young black collegians who often visited our local Temple Fifteen.

"The Christian religion is incompatible with the Negro's aspirations for dignity and equality in America," the student had written. "It has hindered where it might have helped; it has been evasive when it was morally bound to be forthright;

it has separated believers on the basis of color, although it has declared its mission to be a universal brotherhood under Jesus Christ. Christian love is the white man's love for himself and for his race. For the man who is not white, Islam is the hope for justice and equality in the world we must build tomorrow."

After some preliminary research showed Professor Lincoln what a subject he had hold of, he had been able to obtain several grants, and a publisher's encouragement to expand his thesis into a book.

On the wire of our relatively small Nation, these two big developments—a television show, and a book about us—naturally were big news. Every Muslim happily anticipated that now, through the white man's powerful communications media, our brainwashed black brothers and sisters across the United States, and devils, too, were going to see, hear, and read Mr. Muhammad's teachings which cut back and forth like a two-edged sword.

We had made our own very limited efforts to employ the power of print. First, some time back, I had made an appointment to see editor James Hicks of the *Amsterdam News,* published in Harlem. Editor Hicks said he felt every voice in the community deserved to be heard. Soon, each week's *Amsterdam News* carried a little column that I wrote. Then, Mr. Muhammad agreed to write a column for that valuable *Amsterdam News* space, and my column was transferred to another black newspaper, the Los Angeles *Herald Dispatch.*

But I kept wanting to start, somehow, our own newspaper, that would be filled with Nation of Islam news.

Mr. Muhammad in 1957 sent me to organize a Temple in Los Angeles. When I had done that, being in that city where the *Herald Dispatch* was, I went visiting and I worked in their office; they let me observe how a newspaper was put together. I've always been blessed in that if I can once watch something being done, generally I can catch onto how to do it myself. Quick "picking up" was probably the number one survival rule when I'd been out there in the streets as a hustler.

Back in New York, I bought a second-hand camera. I don't know how many rolls of film I shot until I could take usable pictures. Every chance I had, I wrote some little news about interesting Nation of Islam happenings. One day every month, I'd lock up in a room and assemble my material and pictures for a printer that I found. I named the newspaper *Muhammad Speaks* and Muslim brothers sold it on the ghetto sidewalks. Little did I dream that later on, when jealousy set in among the hierarchy, nothing about me would be printed in the paper I had founded.

Anyway, national publicity was in the offing for the Nation of Islam when Mr. Muhammad sent me on a three-week trip to Africa. Even as small as we then were, some of the African and Asian personages had sent Mr. Muhammad private word that they liked his efforts to awaken and lift up the American black people. Sometimes, the messages had been sent through me. As Mr. Muhammad's emissary, I went to Egypt, Arabia, to the Sudan, to Nigeria, and Ghana.

You will often hear today a lot of the Negro leaders complaining that what thrust the Muslims into international prominence was the white man's press, radio, television, and other media. I have no shred of argument with that. They are absolutely correct. Why, none of us in the Nation of Islam remotely anticipated what was about to happen.

In late 1959, the television program was aired. "The Hate That Hate Produced"—the title—was edited tightly into a kaleidoscope of "shocker" images . . . Mr. Muhammad, me, and others speaking . . . strong-looking, set-faced black men, our Fruit of Islam . . . white-scarved, white-gowned Muslim sisters of all ages . . . Muslims in our restaurants, and other businesses . . . Muslims and other black people entering and leaving our mosques. . . .

Every phrase was edited to increase the shock mood. As the producers intended, I think people sat just about limp when the program went off.

In a way, the public reaction was like what happened back in the 1930's when Orson Welles frightened America with a radio program describing, as though it was actually happening, an invasion by "men from Mars."

No one now jumped from any windows, but in New York City there was an instant avalanche of public reaction. It's my personal opinion that the "Hate . . . Hate . . ." title was primarily responsible for the reaction. Hundreds of thousands of New Yorkers, black and white, were exclaiming "Did you hear it? Did you see it? Preaching *hate* of white people!"

Here was one of the white man's most characteristic behavior patterns—where black men are concerned. He loves himself so much that he is startled if he discovers that his victims don't share his vainglorious self-opinion. In America for centuries it had been just fine as long as the victimized, brutalized and exploited black people had been grinning and begging and "Yessa, Massa" and Uncle Tomming. But now, things were different. First came the white newspapers—feature writers and columnists: "Alarming" . . . "hate-messengers" . . . "threat to the good relations between the races" . . . "black segregationists" . . . "black supremacists," and the like.

And the newspapers' ink wasn't dry before the big national weekly news magazines started: "Hate-teachers" . . . "violence-seekers" . . . "black racists" . . . "black fascists" . . . "anti-Christian" . . . "possibly Communist-inspired. . . ."

It rolled out of the presses of the biggest devil in the history of mankind. And then the aroused white man made his next move.

Since slavery, the American white man has always kept some handpicked Negroes who fared much better than the black masses suffering and slaving out in the hot fields. The white man had these "house" and "yard" Negroes for his special servants. He threw them more crumbs from his rich table, he even let them eat in his kitchen. He knew that he could always count on them to keep "good massa" happy in his self-image of being so "good" and "righteous." "Good massa" always heard just what he wanted to hear from these "house" and "yard" blacks. "You're such a good, *fine* massa!" Or, "Oh, massa, those old black nigger fieldhands out there, they're happy just like they are; why, massa, they're not intelligent enough for you to try and do any better for them, massa—"

Well, slavery time's "house" and "yard" Negroes had become more sophisticated, that was all. When now the white man picked up his telephone and dialed his "house" and "yard" Negroes—why, he didn't even need to instruct the trained black puppets. They had seen the television program; had read the newspapers. They were already composing their lines. They knew what to do.

I'm not going to call any names. But if you make a list of the biggest Negro "leaders," so-called, in 1960, then you've named the ones who began to attack us "field" Negroes who were sounding *insane,* talking that way about "good massa."

"By no means do these Muslims represent the Negro

masses—" That was the first worry, to reassure "good massa" that he had no reason to be concerned about his fieldhands in the ghettoes. "An irresponsible hate cult" . . . "an unfortunate Negro image, just when the racial picture is improving—"

They were stumbling over each other to get quoted. "A deplorable reverse-racism" . . . "Ridiculous pretenders to the ancient Islamic doctrine" . . . "Heretic anti-Christianity—"

The telephone in our then small Temple Seven restaurant nearly jumped off the wall. I had a receiver against my ear five hours a day. I was listening, and jotting in my notebook, as press, radio, and television people called, all of them wanting the Muslim reaction to the quoted attacks of these black "leaders." Or I was on long-distance to Mr. Muhammad in Chicago, reading from my notebook and asking for Mr. Muhammad's instructions.

I couldn't understand how Mr. Muhammad could maintain his calm and patience, hearing the things I told him. I could scarcely contain myself.

My unlisted home telephone number somehow got out. My wife Betty put down the phone after taking one message, and it was ringing again. It seemed that wherever I went, telephones were ringing.

The calls naturally were directed to me, New York City being the major news-media headquarters, and I was the New York minister of Mr. Muhammad. Calls came, long-distance from San Francisco to Maine . . . from even London, Stockholm, Paris. I would see a Muslim brother at our restaurant, or Betty at home, trying to keep cool; they'd hand me the receiver, and I couldn't believe it, either. One funny thing— in all that hectic period, something quickly struck my notice: the Europeans never pressed the "hate" question. Only the American white man was so plagued and obsessed with being "hated." He was so guilty, it was clear to me, of hating Negroes.

"Mr. Malcolm X, why do you teach black supremacy, and hate?" A red flag waved for me, something chemical happened inside me, every time I heard that. When we Muslims had talked about "the devil white man" he had been relatively abstract, someone we Muslims rarely actually came into contact with, but now here was that devil-in-the-flesh on the phone —with all of his calculating, cold-eyed, self-righteous tricks and nerve and gall. The voices questioning me became to me as breathing, living devils.

And I tried to pour on pure fire in return. "The white man so guilty of white supremacy can't hide *his* guilt by trying to accuse The Honorable Elijah Muhammad of teaching black supremacy and hate! All Mr. Muhammad is doing is trying to uplift the black man's mentality and the black man's social and economic condition in this country.

"The guilty, two-faced white man can't decide *what* he wants. Our slave foreparents would have been put to death for advocating so-called 'integration' with the white man. Now when Mr. Muhammad speaks of 'separation,' the white man calls us 'hate-teachers' and 'fascists'!

"The white man doesn't *want* the blacks! He doesn't *want* the blacks that are a parasite upon him! He doesn't *want* this black man whose presence and condition in this country expose the white man to the world for what he is! So why do you attack Mr. Muhammad?"

I'd have *scathing* in my voice; I *felt* it.

"For the white man to ask the black man if he hates him is just like the rapist asking the *raped*, or the wolf asking the *sheep*, 'Do you hate me?' The white man is in no moral *position* to accuse anyone else of hate!

"Why, when all of my ancestors are snake-bitten, and I'm snake-bitten, and I warn my children to avoid snakes, what does that *snake* sound like accusing *me* of hate-teaching?"

"Mr. Malcolm X," those devils would ask, "why is your Fruit of Islam being trained in judo and karate?" An image of black men learning anything suggesting self-defense seemed to terrify the white man. I'd turn their question around: "Why does judo or karate suddenly get so ominous because black men study it? Across America, the Boy Scouts, the YMCA, even the YWCA, the CYP, PAL—they *all* teach judo! It's all right, it's fine—until *black men* teach it! Even little grammar school classes, little girls, are taught to defend themselves—"

"How many of you are in your organization, Mr. Malcolm X? Right Reverend Bishop T. Chickenwing says you have only a handful of members—"

"Whoever tells you how many Muslims there are doesn't know, and whoever does know will never tell you—"

The Bishop Chickenwings were also often quoted about our "anti-Christianity." I'd fire right back on that:

"Christianity is the white man's religion. The Holy Bible in the white man's hands and his interpretations of it have been the greatest single ideological weapon for enslaving millions of non-white human beings. Every country the white man has conquered with his guns, he has always paved the way, and salved his conscience, by carrying the Bible and interpreting it to call the people 'heathens' and 'pagans'; then he sends his guns, then his missionaries behind the guns to mop up—"

White reporters, anger in their voices, would call us "demagogues," and I would try to be ready after I had been asked the same question two or three times.

"Well, let's go back to the Greek, and maybe you will learn the first thing you need to know about the word 'demagogue.' 'Demagogue' means, actually, 'teacher of the people.' And let's examine some demagogues. The greatest of all Greeks, Socrates, was killed as a 'demagogue.' Jesus Christ died on the cross because the Pharisees of His day were upholding their law, not the spirit. The modern Pharisees are trying to heap destruction upon Mr. Muhammad, calling him a demagogue, a crackpot, and fanatic. What about Gandhi? The man that Churchill called 'a naked little fakir,' refusing food in a British jail? But then a quarter of a billion people, a whole subcontinent, rallied behind Gandhi—and they twisted the British Lion's tail! What about Galileo, standing before his inquisitors, saying 'The earth *does* move!' What about Martin Luther, nailing on a door his thesis against the all-powerful Catholic chuch which called him 'heretic'? We, the followers of The Honorable Elijah Muhammad, are today in the ghettoes as once the sect of Christianity's followers were like termites in the catacombs and the grottoes—and they were preparing the grave of the mighty Roman Empire!"

I can remember those hot telephone sessions with those reporters as if it were yesterday. The reporters were angry. I was angry. When I'd reach into history, they'd try to pull me back to the present. They would quit interviewing, quit their work, trying to defend their personal white devil selves. They would unearth Lincoln and his freeing of the slaves. I'd tell them things Lincoln said in speeches, *against* the blacks. They would drag up the 1954 Supreme Court decision on school integration.

"That was one of the greatest magical feats ever performed in America," I'd tell them. "Do you mean to tell me that nine Supreme Court judges, who are past masters of legal phraseology, couldn't have worked their decision to make it stick as *law?* No! It was trickery and magic that told Negroes they were desegregated—Hooray! Hooray!—and at the same time it told whites 'Here are your loopholes.' "

The reporters would try their utmost to raise some "good" white man whom I couldn't refute as such. I'll never forget how one practically lost his voice. He asked me did I feel *any* white men had ever done anything for the black man in America. I told him, "Yes, I can think of two. Hitler, and Stalin. The black man in America couldn't get a decent factory job until Hitler put so much pressure on the white man. And then Stalin kept up the pressure—"

But I don't care what points I made in the interviews, it practically never got printed the way I said it. I was learning under fire how the press, when it wants to, can twist and slant. If I had said "Mary had a little lamb," what probably would have appeared was "Malcom X Lampoons Mary."

Even so, my bitterness was less against the white press than it was against those Negro "leaders" who kept attacking us. Mr. Muhammad said he wanted us to try our best not to publicly counterattack the black "leaders" because one of the white man's tricks was keeping the black race divided and fighting against each other. Mr. Muhammad said that this had traditionally kept the black people from achieving the unity which was the worst need of the black race in America.

But instead of abating, the black puppets continued ripping and tearing at Mr. Muhammad and the Nation of Islam—until it began to appear as though we were afraid to speak out against these "important" Negroes. That's when Mr. Muhammad's patience wore thin. And with his nod, I began returning their fire.

"Today's Uncle Tom doesn't wear a handkerchief on his head. This modern, twentieth-century Uncle Thomas now often wears a top hat. He's usually well-dressed and well-educated. He's often the personification of culture and refinement. The twentieth-century Uncle Thomas sometimes speaks with a Yale or Harvard accent. Sometimes he is known as Professor, Doctor, Judge, and Reverend, even Right Reverend Doctor. This twentieth-century Uncle Thomas is a *professional* Negro . . . by that I mean his profession is being a Negro for the white man."

Never before in America had these hand-picked so-called "leaders" been publicly blasted in this way. They reacted to the truth about themselves even more hotly than the devilish white man. Now their "institutional" indictments of us began. Instead of "leaders" speaking as themselves, for themselves, now their weighty name organizations attacked Mr. Muhammad.

"Black bodies with white heads!" I called them what they were. Every one of those "Negro progress" organizations had the same composition. Black "leaders" were out in the public eye—to be seen by the Negroes for whom they were supposed to be fighting the white man. But obscurely, behind the scenes, was a white boss—a president, or board chairman, or some other title, pulling the real strings.

It was hot, hot copy, both in the white and the black press. *Life, Look, Newsweek* and *Time* reported us. Some newspaper chains began to run not one story, but a series of three, four, or five "exposures" of the Nation of Islam. The *Reader's Digest* with its worldwide circulation of twenty-four million copies in thirteen languages carried an article titled "Mr. Muhammad Speaks," by the writer to whom I am telling this book; and that led off other major monthly magazines' coverage of us.

Before very long, radio and television people began asking me to defend our Nation of Islam in panel discussions and debates. I was to be confronted by handpicked scholars, both whites and some of those Ph.D. "house" and "yard" Negroes who had been attacking us. Every day, I was more incensed with the general misrepresentation and distortion of Mr. Muhammad's teachings; I truly think that not once did it cross my mind that previously I never had been *inside* a radio or television station—let alone faced a microphone to audiences of millions of people. Prison debating had been my only experience speaking to anyone but Muslims.

From the old hustling days I knew that there were tricks to everything. In the prison debating, I had learned tricks to upset my opponents, to catch them where they didn't expect to be caught. I knew there were bound to be tricks I didn't know anything about in arguing on the air.

I knew that if I closely studied what the others did, I could learn things in a hurry to help me to defend Mr. Muhammad and his teachings.

I'd walk into those studios. The devils and black Ph.D. puppets would be acting so friendly and "integrated" with each other—laughing and calling each other by first names, and all that; it was such a big lie it made me sick in my stomach. They would even be trying to act friendly toward me—we all knowing they had asked me there to try and beat out my brains. They would offer me coffee. I would tell them "No, thanks," to please just tell me where was I supposed to sit. Sometimes the microphone sat on the table before you, at other times a smaller, cylindrical microphone was hung on a cord around your neck. From the start, I liked those microphones better; I didn't have to keep constantly aware of my distance from a microphone on the table.

The program hosts would start with some kind of dice-loading, non-religious introduction for me. It would be something like "—and we have with us today the fiery, angry chief Malcolm X of the New York Muslims. . . ." I made up my own introduction. At home, or driving my car, I practiced until I could interrupt a radio or television host and introduce myself.

"I represent Mr. Elijah Muhammad, the spiritual head of the fastest-growing group of Muslims in the Western Hemisphere. We who follow him know that he has been divinely taught and sent to us by God Himself. We believe that the miserable plight of America's twenty million black people is the fulfillment of divine prophecy. We also believe the presence today in America of The Honorable Elijah Muhammad, his teachings among the so-called Negroes, and his naked warning to America concerning her treatment of these so-called Negroes, is all the fulfillment of divine prophecy. I am privileged to be the minister of our Temple Number Seven here in New York City which is a part of the Nation of Islam, under the divine leadership of The Honorable Elijah Muhammad—"

I would look around at those devils and their trained black parrots staring at me, while I was catching my breath—and I had set my tone.

They would outdo each other, leaping in on me, hammering at Mr. Muhammad, at me, and at the Nation of Islam. Those "integration"-mad Negroes—you know what they jumped on. *Why* couldn't Muslims *see* that "integration" was the answer to American Negroes' problems? I'd try to rip that to pieces.

"No *sane* black man really wants integration! No *sane* white man really wants integration! No sane black man really believes that the white man ever will give the black man anything more than token integration. No! The Honorable Elijah Muhammad teaches that for the black man in America the only solution is complete *separation* from the white man!"

Anyone who has ever head me on radio or television programs knows that my technique is non-stop, until what I want to get said is said. I was developing the technique then.

"The Honorable Elijah Muhammad teaches us that since Western society is deteriorating, it has become overrun with immorality, and God is going to judge it, and destroy it. And the only way the black people caught up in this society can be saved is not to *integrate* into this corrupt society, but to *separate* from it, to a land of our *own*, where we can reform ourselves, lift up our moral standards, and try to be godly. The Western world's most learned diplomats have failed to solve this grave race problem. Her learned legal experts have failed. Her sociologists have failed. Her civil leaders have failed. Her fraternal leaders have failed. Since all of these have *failed* to solve this race problem, it is time for us to sit down and *reason!* I am certain that we will be forced to agree that it takes *God Himself* to solve this grave racial dilemma."

Every time I mentioned "separation," some of them would cry that we Muslims were standing for the same thing that white racists and demagogues stood for. I would explain the difference. "No! We reject *segregation* even more militantly than you say you do! We want *separation,* which is not the same! The Honorable Elijah Muhammad teaches us that *segregation* is when your life and liberty are controlled, regulated, *by someone else.* To *segregate* means to control. Segregation is that which is forced upon inferiors by superiors. But *separation* is that which is done voluntarily, by two equals— for the good of both! The Honorable Elijah Muhammad teaches us that as long as our people here in America are dependent upon the white man, we will always be begging him for jobs, food, clothing, and housing. And he will always control our lives, regulate our lives, and have the power to segregate us. The Negro here in America has been treated like a child. A child stays within the mother until the time of birth! When the time of birth arrives, the child must be separated, or it will *destroy* its mother and itself. The mother can't carry that child after its time. The child cries for and needs its own world!"

Anyone who has listened to me will have to agree that I believed in Elijah Muhammad and represented him one hundred per cent. I never tried to take any credit for myself.

I was never in one of those panel discussions without some of them just waiting their chance to accuse me of "inciting Negroes to violence." I didn't even have to do any special studying to prepare for that one.

"The greatest miracle Christianity has achieved in America is that the black man in white Christian hands has not grown violent. It *is* a miracle that 22 million black people have not *risen up* against their oppressors—in which they would have been justified by all moral criteria, and even by the democratic tradition! It is a miracle that a nation of black people has so fervently continued to believe in a turn-the-other-cheek and heaven-for-you-after-you-die philosophy! It *is a miracle* that the American black people have remained a peaceful people, while catching all the centuries of hell that they have caught, here in white man's heaven! The *miracle* is that the white man's puppet Negro 'leaders,' his preachers and the educated Negroes laden with degrees, and others who have been allowed to wax fat off their black poor brothers, have been able to hold the black masses quiet until now."

I guarantee you one thing—every time I was mixed up in those studios with those brainwashed, "integration"-mad black puppets, and those tricky devils trying to rip and tear me down, as long as the little red light glowed "on the air," I tried to represent Elijah Muhammad and the Nation of Islam to the utmost.

Dr. C. Eric Lincoln's book was published amid widening controversy about us Muslims, at just about the time we were starting to put on our first big mass rallies.

Just as the television "Hate That Hate Produced" title had projected that "hate-teaching" image of us, now Dr. Lincoln's book was titled *The Black Muslims in America*. The press snatched at that name. "Black Muslims" was in all the book reviews, which quoted from the book only what was critical of us, and generally praised Dr. Lincoln's writing.

The public mind fixed on "Black Muslims." From Mr. Muhammad on down, the name "Black Muslims" distressed everyone in the Nation of Islam. I tried for at least two years to kill off that *"Black* Muslims." Every newspaper and magazine writer and microphone I got close to: *"No!* We are black *people* here in America. Our *religion* is Islam. We are properly called 'Muslims'!" But that "Black Muslims" name never got dislodged.

Our mass rallies, from their very beginning, were astounding successes. Where once Detroit's struggling little Temple

One proudly sent a ten-automobile caravan to Chicago to hear Mr. Muhammad, now, from East Coast Temples—the older Temples as well as the new ones that all of the massive publicity had helped to bring into being—as many as 150, 200 and even as many as 300 big, chartered buses rolled the highways to wherever Mr. Muhammad was going to speak. On each bus, two Fruit of Islam men were in charge. Big three-by-nine-foot painted canvas banners hung on the buses' sides, to be read by the highway traffic and thousands of people at home and on the sidewalks of the towns the buses passed through.

Hundreds more Muslims and curious Negroes drove their own cars. And Mr. Muhammad with his personal jet plane from Chicago. From the airport to the rally hall, Mr. Muhammad's motorcade had a siren-screaming police escort. Law agencies once had scoffed at our Nation as "black crackpots"; now they took special pains to safeguard against some "white crackpots" causing any "incidents" or "accidents."

America had never seen such fantastic all-black meetings! To hear Elijah Muhammad, up to ten thousand and more black people poured from public and private transportation to overflow the big halls we rented, such as the St. Nicholas Arena in New York City, Chicago's Coliseum, and Washington, D.C.'s Uline Arena.

The white man was barred from attendance—the first time the American black man had ever dreamed of such a thing. And that brought us new attacks from the white man and his black puppets. "Black segregationists . . . racists!" Accusing *us* of segregation! Across America, whites barring blacks was standard.

Many hundreds arrived too late for us to seat them. We always had to wire up outside loudspeakers. An electric atmosphere excited the great, shifting masses of black people. The long lines, three and four abreast, funneling to the meeting hall, were kept in strict order by Fruit of Islam men communicating by walkie-talkie. In anterooms just inside the halls, more Fruit of Islam men and white-gowned, veiled mature Muslim sisters thoroughly searched every man, woman, and child seeking to enter. Any alcohol and tobacco had to be checked, and any objects which could possibly be used to attempt to harm Mr. Muhammad. He always seemed deathly afraid that some one would harm him, and he insisted that everyone be searched to forestall this. Today I understand better, why.

The hundreds of Fruit of Islam men represented contingents which had arrived early that morning, from their Temples in the nearest cities. Some were detailed as ushers, who seated the people by designated sections. The balconies and the rear half of the main floor were filled with black people of the general public. Ahead of them were the all-Muslim seating sections—the white-garbed beautiful black sisters, and the dark-suited, white-shirted brothers. A special section near the front was for black so-called "dignitaries." Many of these had been invited. Among them were our black puppet and parrot attackers, the intellectuals and professional Negroes over whom Mr. Muhammad grieved so much, for these were the educated ones who should have been foremost in leading their poor black brothers out of the maze of misery and want. We wanted them to miss not a single syllable of the truths from Mr. Muhammad in person.

The front two or three press rows were filled with the black reporters and cameramen representing the Negro press, or those who had been hired by the white man's newspapers, magazines, radio, and television. America's black writers should hold a banquet for Mr. Muhammad. Writing about the Nation of Islam was the path to success for most of the black writers who now are recognized.

Up on the speaker's platform, we ministers and other officials of the Nation, entering from backstage, found ourselves chairs in the five or six rows behind the big chair reserved for Mr. Muhammad. Some of the ministers had come hundreds of miles to be present. We would be turning about in our chairs, beaming with smiles, wringing each other's hands, and exchanging "As-Salaam-Alaikum" and "Wa-Alaikum-Salaam" in our genuine deep rejoicing to see each other again.

Always, meeting us older hands in Mr. Muhammad's service for the first time, there were several new ministers of small new Temples. My brothers Wilfred and Philbert were respectively now the ministers of the Detroit and Lansing Temples. Minister Jeremiah X headed Atlanta's Temple. Minister John X had Los Angeles' Temple. The Messenger's son, Minister Wallace Muhammad, had the Philadelphia Temple. Minister Woodrow X had the Atlantic City Temple. Some of our ministers had unusual backgrounds. The Washington, D.C., Temple Minister Lucius X was previously a Seventh Day Adventist and a 32nd degree Mason. Minister George X of the Camden, New Jersey, Temple was a pathologist. Minister

David X was previously the minister of a Richmond, Virginia, Christian church; he and enough of his congregation had become Muslims so that the congregation split and the majority turned the church into our Richmond Temple. The Boston Temple's outstanding young Minister Louis X, previously a well-known and rising popular singer called "The Charmer," had written our Nation's popular first song, titled "White Man's Heaven Is Black Man's Hell." Minister Louis X had also authored our first play, "Orgena" ("A Negro" spelled backwards); its theme was the all-black trial of a symbolic white man for his world crimes against non-whites; found guilty, sentenced to death, he was dragged off shouting about all he had done "for the nigra people."

Younger even than our talented Louis X were some newer ministers, Minister Thomas J. X of the Hartford Temple being one example, and another the Buffalo Temple's Minister Robert J. X.

I had either originally established or organized for Mr. Muhammad most of the represented temples. Greeting each of these Temples' brother ministers would bring back into my mind images of "fishing" for converts along the streets and from door-to-door wherever the black people were congregated. I remembered the countless meetings in living rooms where maybe seven would be a crowd; the gradually building, building—on up to renting folding chairs for dingy little storefronts which Muslims scrubbed to spotlessness.

We together on a huge hall's speaking platform, and that vast audience before us, miraculously manifested, as far as I was concerned, the incomprehensible power of Allah. For the first time, I truly understood something Mr. Muhammad had told me: he claimed that when he was going through the sacrificial trials of fleeing the black hypocrites from city to city, Allah had often sent him visions of great audiences who would one day hear the teachings; and Mr. Muhammad said the visions also buoyed him when he was locked up for years in the white man's prison.

The great audience's restless whisperings would cease. . . .

At the microphone would be the Nation's National Secretary John Ali, or the Boston Temple Minister Louis X. They enlivened the all-black atmosphere, speaking of the new world open to the black man through the Nation of Islam. Sister Tynetta Dynear would speak beautifully of the Muslim women's powerful, vital contributions, of the Muslim women's roles in our Nation's efforts to raise the physical, mental, moral, social, and political condition of America's black people.

Next, I would come to the microphone, specifically to condition the audience to hear Mr. Muhammad who had flown from Chicago to teach us all in person.

I would raise up my hand, *"As-Salaikum-Salaam—"*

"Wa-Alaikum-Salaam!" It was a roared response from the great audience's Muslim seating section.

There was a general pattern that I would follow on these occasions:

"My black brothers and sisters—of all religious beliefs, or of no religious beliefs—we all have in common the greatest binding tie we could have . . . we all are *black* people!

"I'm not going to take all day telling you some of the greatnesses of The Honorable Elijah Muhammad. I'm just going to tell you now his *greatest* greatness! He is the *first,* the *only* black leader to identify, to you and me, *who* is our enemy!

"The Honorable Elijah Muhammad is the first black leader among us with the *courage* to tell us—out here in public— something which when you begin to think of it back in your homes, you will realize we black people have been *living* with, we have been *seeing,* we have been *suffering,* all of our lives!

"Our *enemy* is the *white man!*

"And why is Mr. Muhammad's teaching us this such a great thing? Because when you know *who* your enemy is, he can no longer keep you divided, and fighting, one brother against the other! Because when you *recognize* who your enemy is, he can no longer use trickery, promises, lies, hypocrisy, and his evil acts to keep you deaf, dumb, and blinded!

"When you recognize *who* your enemy is, he can no longer brainwash you, he can no longer pull wool over your eyes so that you never stop to see that you are living in pure *hell* on this earth, while *he* lives in pure *heaven* right on this same earth!—This enemy who tells you that you are both supposed to be worshiping the same white Christian God that—you are told—stands for the *same* things for *all* men!

"Oh, *yes,* that devil is our enemy. I'll *prove* it! Pick up any daily newspaper! Read the false charges leveled against our beloved religious leader. It only points up the fact that the Caucasian race never wants any black man who is not their puppet or parrot to speak for our people. This Caucasian devil slavemaster does not want or trust us to leave him—yet when we stay here among him, he continues to keep us at the very *lowest level* of his society!

"The white man has always *loved* it when he could keep us black men tucked away somewhere, always out of sight, around the corner! The white man has always *loved* the kind of black leaders whom he could ask, 'Well, how's things with your people up there?' But because Mr. Elijah Muhammad takes an uncompromising stand with the white man, the white man *hates* him! When you hear the *white man* hate him, you, too, because you don't understand Biblical prophecy, wrongly label Mr. Muhammad—as a racist, a hate-teacher, or of being anti-white and teaching black supremacy—"

The audience suddenly would begin a rustling of turning. . . .

Mr. Muhammad would be rapidly moving along up a center aisle from the rear—as once he had entered our humble little mosques—this man whom we regarded as Islam's gentle, meek, brown-skinned Lamb. Stalwart, striding, close-cropped, handpicked Fruit of Islam guards were a circle surrounding him. He carried his Holy Bible, his holy Quran. The small, dark pillbox atop his head was gold-embroidered with Islam's flag, the sun, moon, and stars. The Muslims were crying out their adoration and their welcome. "Little Lamb!" "As-Salai-kum-Salaam!" "Praise be to Allah!"

Tears would be in more eyes than mine. He had rescued me when I was a convict; Mr. Muhammad had trained me in his home, as if I was his son. I think that my life's peaks of emotion, until recently, at least, were when, suddenly, the Fruit of Islam guards would stop stiffly at attention, and the platform's several steps would be mounted alone by Mr. Muhammad, and his ministers, including me, sprang around him, embracing him, wringing both his hands. . . .

I would turn right back to the microphone, not to keep waiting those world's biggest black audiences who had come to hear him.

"My black brothers and sisters—*no* one will know *who* we are . . . until *we* know who we are! We never will be able to *go* anywhere until we know *where* we are! The Honorable Elijah Muhammad is giving us a true identity, and a true position—the first time they have ever been *known* to the American black man!

"You can be around this man and never *dream* from his actions the power and the authority he has—" (Behind me, believe me when I tell you, I could *feel* Mr. Muhammad's *power*.)

"He does not *display*, and *parade*, his *power*! But no other black leader in America has followers who will lay down their lives if he says so! And I don't mean all of this non-violent, begging-the-white-man kind of dying . . . all of this sitting-in, sliding-in, wading-in, eating-in, diving-in, and all the rest—

"My black brothers and sisters, you have come from your homes to hear—now you are *going* to hear—America's *wisest* black man! America's *boldest* black man! America's most *fearless* black man! This wilderness of North America's most *powerful* black man!"

Mr. Muhammad would come quickly to the stand, looking out over the vacuum-quiet audience, his gentle-looking face set, for just a fleeting moment. Then, "As-Salaikum-Salaam—"

"WA-ALAIKUM-SALAAM!"

The Muslims roared it, as they settled to listen. From experience, they knew that for the next two hours Mr. Muhammad would wield his two-edged sword of truth. In fact, every Muslim worried that he overtaxed himself in the length of his speeches, considering his bronchial asthmatic condition.

"I don't have a degree like many of you out there before me have. But history don't care anything about your degrees.

"The white man, he has filled you with a fear of him from ever since you were little black babies. So over you is the greatest enemy a man can have—and that is fear. I know some of you are afraid to listen to the truth—you have been raised on fear and lies. But I am going to preach to you the truth until you are free of that fear. . . .

"Your slavemaster, he brought you over here, and of your past everything was destroyed. Today, you do not know your true language. What tribe are you from? You would not recognize your tribe's name if you heard it. You don't know nothing about your true culture. You don't even know your family's real name. You are wearing a *white man's* name! The white slavemaster, who *hates* you!

"You are a people who think you know all about the Bible, and all about Christianity. You even are foolish enough to believe that nothing is *right* but Christianity!

"You are the planet Earth's only group of people ignorant of yourself, ignorant of your own kind, of your true history, ignorant of your enemy! You know nothing at *all* but what your white slavemaster has chosen to tell you. And he has told you only that which will benefit himself, and his own kind. He has taught you, for *his* benefit, that you are a neutral, shiftless, helpless so-called 'Negro.'

"I say 'so-called' because you are *not* a '*Negro*.' There is no such thing as a race of '*Negroes*.' You are members of the Asiatic nation, from the tribe of *Shabazz*! 'Negro' is a false label forced on you by your slavemaster! He has been pushing things onto you and me and our kind ever since he brought the first slave shipload of us black people here—"

When Mr. Muhammad paused, the Muslims before him cried out, "Little Lamb!" . . . "All praise is due to Allah!" . . . "*Teach*, Messenger!" He would continue.

"The *ignorance* we of the black race here in America have, and the *self-hatred* we have, they are fine examples of what the white slavemaster has seen fit to teach to us. Do we show the plain common sense, like every other people on this planet Earth, to unite among ourselves? No! We are humbling ourselves, sitting-in, and begging-in, trying to *unite* with the slavemaster! I don't seem able to imagine any more ridiculous sight. A thousand ways every day, the white man is telling you 'You can't live here, you can't enter here, you can't eat here, drink here, walk here, work here, you can't ride here, you can't play here, you can't study here.' Haven't we yet seen enough to see that he has no plan to *unite* with you?

"You have tilled his fields! Cooked his food! Washed his clothes! You have cared for his wife and children when he was away. In many cases, you have even suckled him at your *breast*! You have been far and away better Christians than this slavemaster who *taught* you his Christianity!

"You have sweated blood to help him build a country so rich that he can today afford to give away millions—even to his *enemies*! And when those enemies have gotten enough from him to then be able to attack him, you have been his brave soldiers, *dying* for him. And you have been always his most faithful servant during the so-called 'peaceful' times—

"And, *still*, this Christian American white man has not got it in him to find the human *decency*, and enough sense of *justice*, to recognize us, and accept us, the black people who have done so much for him, as fellow human beings!"

"YAH, Man!" . . . "*Um-huh!*" "*Teach*, Messenger!" . . . "*Yah!*" . . . "*Tell 'em!*" . . . "*You right!*" . . . "Take your *time* up there, little Messenger!" . . . "Oh, *yes!*"

Others besides the Muslims would be shouting now. We Muslims were less extroverted than Christian Negroes. It would sound now like an old-fashioned camp meeting.

"So let us, the black people, *separate* ourselves from this white man slavemaster, who despises us so much! You are out here begging him for some so-called *'integration!'* But what is this slavemaster white, *rapist*, going about saying! He is saying *he* won't integrate because black blood will *mongrelize* his race! *He* says that—and look at *us!* Turn around in your seats and look at each other! This slavemaster white man already has *'integrated'* us until you can hardly find among us today any more than a very few who are the black color of our foreparents!"

"God-a-mighty, the man's right!" . . . "*Teach*, Messenger—" "*Hear* him! *Hear* him!"

"He has left such a little black in us," Mr. Muhammad would go on, "that now he despises us so bad—meaning he despises *himself*, for what he has *done* to us—that he tells us that *legally* if we have got *one drop* of black blood in us, that means you are all-black as far as his laws are concerned! Well, if that's all we've got left, we want to *reclaim* that one drop!"

Mr. Muhammad's frail strength could be seen to be waning. But he would teach on:

"So let us *separate* from this white man, and for the same reason *he* says—in time to save ourselves from any more *'integration!'*

"Why *shouldn't* this white man who likes to think and call himself so good, and so generous, this white man who finances even his enemies—why *shouldn't* he subsidize a separate state, a separate territory, for we black people who have been such faithful slaves and servants? A separate territory on which we can lift *ourselves* out of these white man's *slums* for us, and his *breadlines* for us. And even for *those* he is complaining that we cost him too much! We can do something for *ourselves!* We never have done what we *could*—because we have been brainwashed so well by the slavemaster white man that we must come to him, begging him, for everything we want, and need—"

After perhaps ninety minutes, behind Mr. Muhammad, every minister would have to restrain himself from bolting up to his side, to urge him that it was enough. He would be pressing his hands tightly against the edges of the speaker's stand, to support himself.

"We black people don't *know* what we can do. You never can know what *anything* can do—until it is set *free*, to act by itself! If you have a cat in your house that you pamper and pet, you have to free that cat, set it on its *own*, in the woods, before you can see that the cat had it *in* him to shelter and feed itself!

"We, the black people here in America, we never have been *free* to find *out* what we really can *do!* We have knowledge and experience to pool to do for ourselves! All of our lives we have farmed—we can grow our own food. We can set up factories to manufacture our own necessities! We can build other kinds of businesses, to establish trade, and commerce— and become independent, as other civilized people are—

"We can *throw off* our brainwashing, and our self-hate, and live as *brothers* together . . .

". . . some land of our *own!* . . . Something for *ourselves!* . . . leave this white slavemaster to *himself.* . . . "

Mr. Muhammad always stopped abruptly when he was unable to speak any longer.

The standing ovation, a solid wall of sound, would go on unabating.

Standing up there, flailing my arms, finally I could quiet the audiences as Fruit of Islam ushers began to pass along the seating rows the large, waxed paper buckets we used to take up the collection. I would speak.

"You *know*, from what you have just heard, that no white money finances The Honorable Elijah Muhammad and his program—to 'advise' him and 'contain' him! Mr. Muhammad's program, and his followers, are not 'integrated.' Mr. Muhammad's program and organization are *all*-black!

"We are the *only* black organization that *only* black people support! These so-called 'Negro progress' organizations—Why, they insult your intelligence, claiming they are fighting in your behalf, to get you the equal rights you are asking for . . . claiming they are *fighting* the white man who refuses to give you your rights. Why, the white man *supports* those organizations! If you belong, you pay your two, or three, or five dollars a year—but *who* gives those organizations those two, and three, and five *thousand* dollar donations? The *white* man! He *feeds* those organizations! So he controls those organizations! He *advises* them—so he *contains* them! Use your common sense—aren't you going to advise and control and contain anyone that you support, like your child?

"The white man would love to support Mr. Elijah Muhammad. Because if Mr. Muhammad had to rely on his support, he could *advise* Mr. Muhammad. My black brothers and sisters, it is *only* because *your* money, *black* money, supports Mr. Muhammad, that he can hold these all-black meetings from city to city, telling us black men the *truth!* That's why we are asking for your all-black *support!*"

Nearly all bills—and far from all one-dollar bills, either, filled the waxed buckets. The buckets were swiftly emptied, then refilled, as the Fruit of Islam ushers covered the entire audience.

The audience atmosphere was almost as if the people had gone limp. The collections always covered the rally expenses, and anything beyond that helped to continue building the Nation of Islam.

After several big rallies, Mr. Muhammad directed that we would admit the white press. Fruit of Islam men thoroughly searched them, as everyone else was searched—their notebooks, their cameras, camera cases, and whatever else they carried. Later, Mr. Muhammad said that *any* whites who wanted to hear the truth could attend our public rallies, until a small separate section for whites was filled.

Most whites who came were students and scholars. I would watch their congealed and reddened faces staring up at Mr. Muhammad. "The white man *knows* that his acts have been those of a devil!" I would watch also the faces of the professional black men, the so-called intellectuals who attacked us. They possessed the academic know-how, they possessed the technical and the scientific skills that could help to lead their mass of poor, black brothers out of our condition. But all these intellectual and professional black men could seem to think of was humbling themselves, and begging, trying to "integrate" with the so-called "liberal" white man who was telling them, "In time . . . everything's going to work out one day . . . just wait and have patience." These intellectual and professional Negroes couldn't use what they knew for the benefit of their own black kind simply because even among themselves they were disunited. United among themselves, united with their own kind, they could have benefited black people all over the world!

I would watch the faces of those intellectual and professional Negroes growing grave, and set—as the truth hit home to them.

We were watched. Our telephones were tapped. Still right today, on my home telephone, if I said, "I'm going to bomb the Empire State Building," I guarantee you in five minutes it would be surrounded. When I was speaking publicly sometimes I'd guess which were F.B.I. faces in the audience, or other types of agents. Both the police and the F.B.I. intently and persistently visited and questioned us. "I do not fear them," Mr. Muhammad said. "I have all that I need—the truth."

Many a night, I drifted off to sleep, filled with wonder at how the two-edged-sword teachings so hurt, confused, concerned, and upset the government full of men trained highly in all of the modern sciences. I felt that it never could have been unless The Most Learned One, Allah Himself, had given the little fourth-grade-trained Messenger something.

Black agents were sent to infiltrate us. But the white man's "secret" spy often proved, first of all, a black man. I can't say *all* of them, of course, there's no way to know—but some of them, after joining us, and hearing, seeing and *feeling* the truth for every black man, revealed their roles to us. Some resigned from the white man's agencies and came to work in the Nation of Islam. A few kept their jobs to counterspy, telling us the white man's statements and plans about our Nation. This was how we learned that after wanting to know what happened within our Temples, the white law agencies' second major concern was the thing that I believe still ranks today as a big worry among America's penologists: the steadily increasing rate at which black convicts embrace Islam.

Generally, while still in prison, our convict-converts preconditioned themselves to met our Nation's moral laws. As it had happened with me, when they left prison, they entered a Temple fully qualified to become registered Muslims. In fact, convict-converts usually were better prepared than were numerous prospective Muslims who never had been inside a prison.

We were not nearly so easy to enter as a Christian church. One did not merely declare himself a follower of Mr. Muhammad, then continue leading the same old, sinful, immoral life. The Muslim first had to change his physical and moral self to meet our strict rules. To remain a Muslim he had to maintain those rules.

Few temple meetings were held, for instance, without the minister looking down upon some freshly shaved bald domes of new Muslim brothers in the audience. They had just banished from their lives forever that phony, lye-conked, metallic-looking hair, or "the process," as some call it these days. It grieves me that I don't care where you go, you see this symbol of ignorance and self-hate on so many Negroes' heads. I know it's bound to hurt the feelings of some of my good conked non-Muslim friends—but if you study closely any conked or "processed" Negro, you usually find he is an ignorant Negro. Whatever "show" or "front" he affects, his hair lye-cooked to be "white-looking" fairly shouts to everyone who looks at his head, "I'm ashamed to be a Negro." He will discover, just as I did, that he will be much-improved mentally whenever he discovers enough black self-pride to have that mess clipped off, and then wear the natural hair that God gives black men to wear.

No Muslim smokes—that was another of our rules. Some prospective Muslims found it more difficult to quit tobacco than others found quitting the dope habit. But black men and women quit more easily when we got them to consider seriously how the white man's government cared less about the public's health than about continuing the tobacco industry's *billions* in tax revenue. "What does a serviceman pay for a carton of cigarettes?" a prospective Muslim convert would be asked. It helped him to see that every regularly priced carton he bought meant that the white man's government took around two dollars of a black man's hard-earned money for taxes, not for tobacco.

You may have read somewhere—a lot has been written concerning it—about the Nation of Islam's phenomenal record of dope-addiction cures of longtime junkies. In fact, the *New York Times* carried a story about how some of the social agencies have asked representatives of the Muslim program for clinical suggestions.

The Muslim program began with recognizing that color and addiction have a distinct connection. It is no accident that in the entire Western Hemisphere, the greatest localized concentration of addicts is in *Harlem*.

Our cure program's first major ingredient was the painfully patient work of Muslims who previously were junkies themselves.

In the ghetto's dope jungle, the Muslim ex-junkies would fish out addicts who knew them back in those days. Then with an agonizing patience that might span anywhere from a few months to a year, our ex-junky Muslims would conduct the addicts through the Muslim six-point therapeutic process.

The addict first was brought to admit to himself that he was an addict. Secondly, he was taught *why* he used narcotics. Third, he was shown that there was a *way* to stop addiction. Fourth, the addict's shattered self-image, and ego, were built up until the addict realized that he had, *within*, the self-power to end his addiction. Fifth, the addict voluntarily underwent a cold turkey break with drugs. Sixth, finally cured, now an ex-addict completes the cycle by "fishing" up other addicts whom he knows, and supervising their salvaging.

This sixth stage always instantly eliminated what so often defeats the average social agencies—the characteristic addict's hostility and suspicion. The addict who is "fished" up knew personally that the Muslim approaching him very recently had the same fifteen to thirty dollar a day habit. The Muslim may be this addict's buddy; they had plied the same dope jungle. They even may have been thieves together. The addict had *seen* the Muslim drifting off to sleep leaning against a building, or stepping as high over a matchstick as if it were a dog. And the Muslim, approaching the addict, uses the same old junkie jungle language.

Like the alcoholic, the junkie can never start to cure himself until he recognizes and accepts his true condition. The Muslim sticks like a leech, drumming at his old junkie buddy, "You're hooked, man!" It might take months before the addict comes to grips with this. The curative program is never really underway until this happens.

The next cure-phase is the addict's realization of *why* he takes dope. Still working on his man, right in the old jungle locale, in dives that you wouldn't believe existed, the Muslim often collects audiences of a dozen junkies. They listen only because they know the clean-cut proud Muslim had earlier been like them.

Every addict takes junk to escape something, the Muslim explains. He explains that most black junkies really are trying to narcotize themselves against being a black man in the white man's America. But, actually, the Muslim says, the black man taking dope is only helping the white man to "prove" that the black man is nothing.

The Muslim talks confidentially, and straight. "Daddy, you know I know how you feel. Wasn't I right out here with you? Scratching like a monkey, smelling all bad, living mad, hungry, stealing and running and hiding from Whitey. Man, what's a black man buying Whitey's dope for but to make Whitey richer—killing yourself!"

The Muslim can tell when his quarry is ready to be shown that the way for him to quit dope is through joining the Nation of Islam. The addict is brought into the local Muslim restaurant, he may occasionally be exposed to some other social situations—among proud, clean Muslims who show each other mutual affection and respect instead of the familiar hostility of the ghetto streets. For the first time in years, the addict hears himself called, genuinely, "Brother," "Sir" and "Mr." No one cares about his past. His addiction may casually be mentioned, but if so, it is spoken of as merely an especially tough challenge that he must face. Everyone whom this addict meets is confident that he will kick his habit.

As the addict's new image of himself builds, inevitably he begins thinking that he can break the habit. For the first time he is feeling the effects of black self-pride.

That's a powerful combination for a man who has been existing in the mud of society. In fact, once he is motivated no one can change more completely than the man who has been at the bottom. I call myself the best example of that.

Finally, vitally, this addict will decide for himself that he wants to go on cold turkey. This means to endure the physical agonies of abruptly quitting dope.

When this time comes, ex-addict Muslims will arrange to spend the necessary days in around-the-clock shifts, attending the addict who intends to purge himself, on the way to becoming a Muslim.

When the addict's withdrawal sets in, and he is screaming, cursing, and begging, "Just one shot, man!" the Muslims are right there talking junkie jargon to him. "Baby, knock that monkey off your back! Kick that habit! Kick Whitey off your back!" The addict, writhing in pain, his nose and eyes running, is pouring sweat from head to foot. He's trying to knock his head against the wall, flailing his arms, trying to fight his attendants, he is vomiting, suffering diarrhea. "Don't hold nothing back! Let Whitey go, baby! You're going to stand tall, man! I can see you now in the Fruit of Islam!"

When the awful ordeal is ended, when the grip of dope is broken, the Muslims comfort the weak ex-addict, feeding him soups and broths, to get him on his feet again. He will never forget these brothers who stood by him during this time. He will never forget that it was the Nation of Islam's program which rescued him from the special hell of dope. And that black brother (or the sister, whom Muslim sisters attend) rarely ever will return to the use of narcotics. Instead, the ex-addict when he is proud, clean, renewed, can scarcely wait to hit the same junkie jungle he was in, to "fish" out some buddy and salvage *him!*

If some white man, or "approved" black man, created a narcotics cure program as successful as the one conducted under the aegis of the Muslims, why, there would be government subsidy, and praise and spotlights, and headlines. But we were attacked instead. Why shouldn't the Muslims be subsidized to save millions of dollars a year for the government and the cities? I don't know what addicts' crimes cost nationally, but it is said to be *billions* a year in New York City. An estimated $12 million a year is lost to thieves in Harlem alone.

An addict doesn't work to supply his habit, which may cost anywhere from ten to fifty dollars a day. How could he earn that much? No! The addict steals, he hustles in other ways; he preys upon other human beings like a hawk or a vulture— as I did. Very likely, he is a school drop-out, the same as I was, an Army reject, psychologically unsuited to a job even if he was offered one, the same as I was.

Women addicts "boost" (shoplift), or they prostitute themselves. Muslim sisters talk hard to black prostitutes who are struggling to quit using dope in order to qualify morally to become registered Muslims. "You are helping the white man to regard your body as a garbage can—"

Numerous "exposés" of the Nation of Islam have implied that Mr. Muhammad's followers were chiefly ex-cons and junkies. In the early years, yes, the converts from society's lowest levels were a sizable part of the Nation's broad base of membership. Always Mr. Muhammad instructed us, "Go after the black man in the mud." Often, he said, those converted made the best Muslims.

But gradually we recruited other black people—the "good Christians" whom we "fished" from their churches. Then, an increase began in the membership percentage of educated and trained Negroes. For each rally attracted to the local temple a few more of that particular city's so-called "middle-class" Negroes, the type who previously had scoffed at us "Black Muslims" as "demagogues," and "hate-teachers," "black racists" and all the rest of the names. The Muslim truths— listened to, thought about—reaped for us a growing quota of young black men and women. For those with training and talents, the Nation of Islam had plenty of positions where those abilities were needed.

There were some registered Muslims who would never reveal their membership, except to other Muslims, because of their positions in the white man's world. There were, I know, a few, who because of their positions were known only to their ministers and to Mr. Elijah Muhammad.

In 1961, our Nation flourished. Our newspaper *Muhammad Speaks*' full back page carried an architect's drawing of a $20 million Islamic Center proposed to be built in Chicago. Every Muslim was making personal financial contribution toward the Center. It would include a beautiful mosque, school, library, and hospital, and a museum documenting the black man's glorious history.

Mr. Muhammad visited the Muslim countries, and upon his return he directed that we would begin calling our temples "mosques."

There was a sharp climb now, too, in the number of Muslim-owned small businesses. Our businesses sought to demonstrate to the black people what black people could do for themselves —if they would only unify, trade with each other—exclusively where possible—and hire each other, and in so doing, keep black money within the black communities, just as other minorities did.

Recordings of Mr. Muhammad's speeches were now regularly being broadcast across America over small radio stations. In Detroit and Chicago, school-age Muslim children attended our two Universities of Islam—through high school in Chicago, and through junior high in Detroit. Starting from kindergarten, they learned of the black man's glorious history and from the third grade they studied the black man's original language, Arabic.

Mr. Muhammad's eight children now were all deeply involved in key capacities in the Nation of Islam. I took a deep personal pride in having had something to do with that—at least in some cases, years before. When Mr. Muhammad had sent me out in his service as a minister, I began to feel it was a shame that his children worked as some of them then did for the white man, in factories, construction work, driving taxis, things like that. I felt that I should work for Mr. Muhammad's family as sincerely as I worked for him. I urged Mr. Muhammad to let me put on a special drive within our few small mosques, to raise funds which would enable those of his children working for the white man to be instead employed within our Nation. Mr. Muhammad agreed, the special fund drive did prove successful, and his children gradually did begin working for the Nation. Emanuel, the oldest, today runs the dry-cleaning plant. Sister Ethel (Muhammad) Sharrieff is the Muslim Sisters' Supreme Instructor. (Her husband, Raymond Sharrieff, is Supreme Captain of the Fruit of Islam.) Sister Lottie Muhammad supervises the two Universities of Islam. Nathaniel Muhammad assists Emanuel in the dry-cleaning plant. Herbert Muhammad now publishes *Muhammad Speaks*, the Nation's newspaper that I began. Elijah Muhammad, Jr., is the Fruit of Islam Assistant Supreme Captain. Wallace Muhammad was the Philadelphia Mosque Minister, until finally he was suspended from the Nation along with me—for reasons I will go into. The youngest child, Akbar Muhammad, the family student, attends the University of Cairo at El-Azhar. Akbar also has broken with his father.

I believe that it was too strenuous a marathon of long speeches that Mr. Muhammad made at our big rallies which, abruptly, badly aggravated his long-bothersome bronchial asthmatic condition.

Just in conversation, Mr. Muhammad would suddenly begin coughing, and the coughing tempo would increase until it racked his slight body.

Mr. Muhammad almost doubled up sometimes. Soon, he had to take to his bed. As hard as he tried not to, as deeply as it grieved him, he had to cancel several long-scheduled appearances at big-city rallies. Thousands were disappointed to have to hear me instead, or other poor substitutes for Mr. Muhammad in person.

Members of the Nation were deeply concerned. Doctors recommended a dry climate. The Nation bought Mr. Muhammad a home in Phoenix, Arizona. One of the first times I visited Mr. Muhammad there, I stepped off a plane into flashing and whirring cameras until I wondered who was behind me. Then I saw the cameramen's guns; they were from the Arizona Intelligence Division.

The wire of our Nation of Islam brought all Muslims the joyful news that the Arizona climate did vastly relieve the Messenger's suffering. Since then he has spent most of each year in Phoenix.

Despite the fact that Mr. Muhammad, convalescing, could no longer work the daily long hours he had previously worked in Chicago, he was now more than ever burdened with heavy decision-making and administrative duties. In every respect, the Nation was expanded both internally and externally. Mr. Muhammad simply could no longer allot as much time as previously to considering and deciding which public-speaking, radio, and television requests he felt I should accept—as well as to some organizational matters which I had always brought to him for advice or decision.

Mr. Muhammad evidenced the depth of his trust in me. In those areas I've described, he told me to make the decisions myself. He said that my guideline should be whatever I felt was wise—whatever was in the general good interests of our Nation of Islam.

"Brother Malcolm, I want you to become well known," Mr. Muhammad told me one day. "Because if you are well known, it will make *me* better known," he went on.

"But, Brother Malcolm, there is something you need to know. You will grow to be hated when you become well known. Because usually people get jealous of public figures."

Nothing that Mr. Muhammad ever said to me was more prophetic.

CHAPTER FIFTEEN

ICARUS

The more places I represented Mr. Muhammad on television and radio, and at colleges and elsewhere, the more letters came from people who had heard me. I'd say that ninety-five per cent of the letters were from white people.

Only a few of the letters fell into the "Dear Nigger X" category, or the death-threats. Most of my mail exposed to me the white man's two major dreads. The first one was his own private belief that God wrathfully is going to destroy this civilization. And the white man's second most pervading dread was his image of the black man entering the body of the white woman.

An amazing percentage of the white letter-writers agreed entirely with Mr. Muhammad's analysis of the problem—but not with his solution. One odd ambivalence was how some letters, otherwise all but championing Mr. Muhammad, would recoil at the expression "white devils." I tried to explain this in subsequent speeches:

"Unless we call one white man, by name, a 'devil,' we are not speaking of any *individual* white man. We are speaking of the *collective* white man's *historical* record. We are speaking of the collective white man's cruelties, and evils, and greeds, that have seen him *act* like a devil toward the non-white man. Any intelligent, honest, objective person cannot fail to realize that this white man's slave trade, and his subsequent devilish actions are directly *responsible* for not only the *presence* of this black man in America, but also for the *condition* in which we find this black man here. You cannot find *one* black man, I do not care who he is, who has not been personally damaged in some way by the devilish acts of the collective white man!"

Nearly every day, some attack on the "Black Muslims" would appear in some newspapers. Increasingly, a focal target was something that I had said, "Malcolm X" as a "demagogue." I would grow furious reading any harsh attack upon Mr. Muhammad. I didn't care what they said about me.

Those social workers and sociologists—they tried to take me apart. Especially the black ones, for some reason. Of course, I knew the reason: the white man signed their paychecks. If I wasn't "polarizing the community," according to this bunch, I had "erroneously appraised the racial picture." Or in some statement, I had "over-generalized." Or when I had made some absolutely true point, "Malcolm X conveniently manipulated. . . ."

Once, one of my Mosque Seven Muslim brothers who worked with teenagers in a well-known Harlem community center showed me a confidential report. Some black senior social worker had been given a month off to investigate the "Black Muslims" in the Harlem area. Every paragraph sent me back to the dictionary—I guess that's why I've never forgotten one line about me. Listen to this: "The dynamic interstices of the Harlem sub-culture have been oversimplified and distorted by Malcolm X to meet his own needs."

Which of us, I wonder, knew more about that Harlem ghetto "sub-culture"? I, who had hustled for years in those streets, or that black snob status-symbol-educated social worker?

But that's not important. What's important, to my way of thinking about it, is that among America's 22 million black people so relatively few have been lucky enough to attend a college—and here was one of those who had been lucky. Here was, to my way of thinking, one of those "educated" Negroes who never had understood the true intent, or purpose, or application of education. Here was one of those stagnant educations, never used except for parading a lot of big words.

Do you realize this is one of the major reasons why America's white man has so easily contained and oppressed America's black man? Because until just lately, among the few educated Negroes scarcely any applied their education, as I am forced to say the white man does—in searching and creative thinking, to further themselves and their own kind in this competitive, materialistic, dog-eat-dog white man's world. For generations, the so-called "educated" Negroes have "led" their black brothers by echoing the white man's thinking—which naturally has been to the exploitive white man's advantage.

The white man—give him his due—has an extraordinary intelligence, an extraordinary cleverness. His world is full of proof of it. You can't name a thing the white man can't make. You can hardly name a scientific problem he can't solve. Here he is now solving the problems of sending men exploring into outer space—and returning them safely to earth.

But in the arena of dealing with human beings, the white man's working intelligence is hobbled. His intelligence will fail him altogether if the humans happen to be non-white. The white man's emotions superseded his intelligence. He will commit against non-whites the most incredible spontaneous emotional acts, so psyche-deep is his "white superiority" complex.

Where was the A-bomb dropped . . . "to save American lives"? Can the white man be so naive as to think the clear import of this *ever* will be lost upon the non-white two-thirds of the earth's population?

Before that bomb was dropped—right over here in the United States, what about the one hundred thousand loyal naturalized and native-born Japanese American citizens who were herded into camps, behind barbed wire? But how many German-born naturalized Americans were herded behind barbed wire? They were *white!*

Historically, the non-white complexion has evoked and exposed the "devil" in the very nature of the white man.

What else but a controlling emotional "devil" so blinded American white intelligence that it couldn't foresee that millions of black slaves, "freed," then permitted even limited education, would one day rise up as a terrifying monster within white America's midst?

The white man's brains that today explore space should have told the slavemaster that any slave, if he is educated, will no longer fear his master. History shows that an educated slave always begins to ask, and next demand, equality with his master.

Today, in many ways the black man sees the collective white man in America better than that white man can see himself. And the 22 million blacks realize increasingly that physically, politically, economically, and even to some degree socially, the aroused black man can create a turmoil in white America's vitals—not to mention America's international image.

I had not intended to stray off. I had been telling how in 1963, I was trying to cope with the white newspaper, radio, and television reporters who were determined to defeat Mr. Muhammad's teachings.

I developed a mental image of reporters as human ferrets— steadily sniffing, darting, probing for some way to trick me, somehow to corner me in our interview exchanges.

Let some civil rights "leader" make some statement, displeasing to the white public power structure, and the reporters, in an effort to whip him back into line, would try to use me. I'll give an example. I'd get a question like this: "Mr. Malcolm X, you've often gone on record as disapproving of the sit-ins and similar Negro protest actions—what is your opinion of the Montgomery boycott that Dr. King is leading?"

Now my feeling was that although the civil rights "leaders" kept attacking us Muslims, still they were black people, still they were our own kind, and I would be most foolish to let the white man maneuver me against the civil rights movement.

When I was asked about the Montgomery boycott, I'd carefully review what led up to it. Mrs. Rosa Parks was riding home on a bus and at some bus stop the white cracker bus driver ordered Mrs. Parks to get up and give her seat to some white passenger who had just got on the bus. I'd say, "Now, just *imagine* that! This good, hard-working, Christian-believing black woman, she's paid her money, she's in her seat. Just because she's *black*, she's asked to get up! I mean, sometimes even for *me* it's hard to believe the white man's arrogance!"

Or I might say, "No one will ever know exactly what emotional ingredient made this relatively trivial incident a fuse for those Montgomery Negroes. There had been *centuries* of the worst kind of outrages against Southern black people— lynchings, rapings, shootings, beatings! But you know history has been triggered by trivial-seeming incidents. Once a little nobody Indian lawyer was put off a train, and fed up with injustice, he twisted a knot in the British Lion's tail. *His* name was Mahatma Gandhi!"

Or I might copy a trick I had seen lawyers use, both in life and on television. It was a way that lawyers would slip in before a jury something otherwise inadmissible. (Sometimes I think I really might have made it as a lawyer, as I once told that eighth-grade teacher in Mason, Michigan, I wanted to be, when he advised me to become a carpenter.) I would slide right over the reporter's question to drop into his lap a logical-extension hot potato for him.

"Well, sir, I see the same boycott reasoning for Negroes asked to join the Army, Navy, and Air Force. Why should we go off to die somewhere to preserve a so-called 'democracy' that gives a white immigrant of one day more than it gives the black man with four hundred years of slaving and serving in this country?"

Whites would prefer fifty local boycotts to having 22 million Negroes start thinking about what I had just said. I don't have to tell you that it never got printed the way I said it. It would be turned inside out if it got printed at all. And I could detect when the white reporters had gotten their heads together; they quit asking me certain questions.

If I had developed a good point, though, I'd bait a hook to get it said when I went on radio or television. I'd seem to slip and mention some recent so-called civil rights "advance." You know, where some giant industry had hired ten show-piece Negroes; some restaurant chain had begun making more money by serving Negroes; some Southern university had enrolled a black freshman without bayonets—like that. When I "slipped," the program host would leap on that bait: "Ahhh! Indeed, Mr. Malcolm X—you can't deny *that's* an advance for your race!"

I'd jerk the pole then. "I can't turn around without hearing about some 'civil rights advance'! White people seem to think the black man ought to be shouting 'hallelujah'! Four hundred years the white man has had his foot-long knife in the black man's back—and now the white man starts to *wiggle* the knife out, maybe six inches! The black man's supposed to be *grateful?* Why, if the white man jerked the knife *out,* it's still going to leave a *scar!*"

Similarly, just let some mayor or some city council somewhere boast of having "no Negro problem." That would get off the newsroom teletypes and it would soon be jammed right in my face. I'd say they didn't need to tell me where this was, because I knew that all it meant was that relatively very few Negroes were living there. That's true the world over, you know. Take "democratic" England—when 100,000 black West

Indians got there, England stopped the black migration. Finland welcomed a Negro U. S. Ambassador. Well, let enough Negroes follow him to Finland! Or in Russia, when Khrushchev was in power, he threatened to cancel the visas of black African students whose anti-discrimination demonstration said to the world, "Russia, too. . . ."

The Deep South white press generally blacked me out. But they front-paged what I felt about Northern white and black Freedom Riders going *South* to "demonstrate." I called it "ridiculous"; their own Northern ghettoes, right at home, had enough rats and roaches to kill to keep all of the Freedom Riders busy. I said that ultra-liberal New York had more integration problems that Mississippi. If the Northern Freedom Riders wanted more to do, they could work on the roots of such ghetto evils as the little children out in the streets at midnight, with apartment keys on strings around their necks to let themselves in, and their mothers and fathers drunk, drug addicts, thieves, prostitutes. Or the Northern Freedom Riders could light some fires under Northern city halls, unions, and major industries to give more jobs to Negroes to remove so many of them from the relief and welfare rolls, which created laziness, and which deteriorated the ghettoes into steadily worse places for humans to live. It was all—it *is* all —the absolute truth; but what did I want to *say* it for? Snakes couldn't have turned on me faster than the liberal.

Yes, I will pull off that liberal's halo that he spends such efforts cultivating! The North's liberals have been for so long pointing accusing fingers at the South and getting away with it that they have fits when they are exposed as the world's worst hypocrites.

I believe my own life *mirrors* this hypocrisy. I know nothing about the South. I am a creation of the Northern white man and of his hypocritical attitude toward the Negro.

The white Southerner was always given his due by Mr. Muhammad. The white Southerner, you can say one thing— he is honest. He bares his teeth to the black man; he tells the black man, to his face, that Southern whites never will accept phony "integration." The Southern white goes further, to tell the black man that he means to fight him every inch of the way—against even the so-called "tokenism." The advantage of this is the Southern black man never has been under any illusions about the opposition he is dealing with.

You can say for many Southern white people that, individually, they have been paternalistically helpful to many individual Negroes. But the Northern white man, he grins with his teeth, and his mouth has always been full of tricks and lies of "equality" and "integration." When one day all over America, a black hand touched the white man's shoulder, and the white man turned, and there stood the Negro saying "Me, too . . ." why, that Northern liberal shrank from that black man with as much guilt and dread as any Southern white man.

Actually, America's most dangerous and threatening black man is the one who has been kept sealed up by the Northerner in the black ghettoes—the Northern white power structure's system to keep talking democracy while keeping the black man out of sight somewhere, around the corner.

The word "integration" was invented by a Northern liberal. The word has no real meaning. I ask you: in the racial sense in which it's used so much today, whatever "integration" is supposed to mean, can it precisely be defined? The truth is that "integration" is an *image,* it's a foxy Northern liberal's smoke-screen that confuses the true wants of the American black man. Here in these fifty racist and neo-racist states of North America, this word "integration" has millions of white people confused, and angry, believing wrongly that the black masses want to live mixed up with the white man. That is the case only with the relative handful of these "integration"-mad Negroes.

I'm talking about these "token-integrated" Negroes who flee from their poor, downtrodden black brothers—from their own self-hate, which is what they're really trying to escape. I'm talking about these Negroes you will see who can't get enough of nuzzling up to the white man. These "chosen few" Negroes are more white-minded, more anti-black, than even the white man is.

Human rights! Respect as *human beings!* That's what America's black masses want. That's the true problem. The black masses want not to be shrunk from as though they are plague-ridden. They want not to be walled up in slums, in the ghettoes, like animals. They want to live in an open, free society where they can walk with their heads up, like men, and women!

Few white people realize that many black people today dislike and avoid spending any more time than they must around white people. This "integration" image, as it is popularly interpreted, has millions of vain, self-exalted white people convinced that black people want to sleep in bed with them—and that's a lie! Or you can't *tell* the average white man that the Negro man's prime desire isn't to have a white woman—another lie! Like a black brother recently observed to me, "Look, you ever smell one of them *wet?*"

The black masses prefer the company of their own kind. Why, even these fancy, bourgeois Negroes—when they get back home from the fancy "integrated" cocktail parties, what do they do but kick off their shoes and talk about those white liberals they just left as if the liberals were dogs. And the white liberals probably do the very same thing. I can't be sure about the whites, I am never around them in private—but the bourgeois Negroes know I'm not lying.

I'm telling it like it *is!* You *never* have to worry about me biting my tongue if something I know as truth is on my mind. Raw, naked truth exchanged between the black man and the white man is what a whole lot more of is needed in this country—to clear the air of the racial mirages, clichés, and lies that this country's very atmosphere has been filled with for four hundred years.

In many communities, especially small communities, white people have created a benevolent image of themselves as having had so much "good-will toward our Negroes," every time any "local Negro" begins suddenly letting the local whites know the truth—that the black people are sick of being hind-tit, second-class, disfranchised, that's when you hear, uttered so sadly, "Unfortunately now because of this, our whites of good-will are starting to turn against the Negroes. . . . It's so regrettable . . . progress *was* being made . . . but now our communications between the races have broken down!"

What are they talking about? There never was any *communication.* Until after World War II, there wasn't a single community in the entire United States where the white man heard from any local Negro "leaders" the truth of what Negroes felt about the conditions that the white community imposed upon Negroes.

You need some proof? Well, then, why was it that when Negroes did start revolting across America, virtually all of white America was caught up in surprise and even shock? I would hate to be general of an army as badly informed as the

American white man has been about the Negro in this country.

This is the situation which permitted Negro combustion to slowly build up to the revolution-point, without the white man realizing it. All over America, the local Negro "leader," in order to survive as a "leader," kept reassuring the local white man, in effect, "Everything's all right, everything's right in hand, boss!" When the "leader" wanted a little something for his people: "Er, boss, some of the people talking about we sure need a better school, boss." And if the local Negroes hadn't been causing any "trouble," the "benevolent" white man might nod and give them a school, or some jobs.

The white men belonging to the power structures in thousands of communities across America know that I'm right! They know that I am describing what has been the true pattern of "communications" between the "local whites of good-will" and the local Negroes. It has been a pattern created by domineering, ego-ridden whites. Its characteristic design permitted the white man to feel "noble" about throwing crumbs to the black man, instead of feeling guilty about the local community's system of cruelly exploiting Negroes.

But I want to tell you something. This pattern, this "system" that the white man created, of teaching Negroes to hide the truth from him behind a façade of grinning, "yessir-bossing," foot-shuffling and head-scratching—that system has done the American white man more harm than an invading army would do to him.

Why do I say this? Because all this has steadily helped this American white man to build up, deep in his psyche, absolute conviction that he *is* "superior." In how many, many communities have, thus, white men who didn't finish high school regarded condescendingly university-educated local Negro "leaders," principals of schools, teachers, doctors, other professionals?

The white man's system has been imposed upon non-white peoples all over the world. This is exactly the reason why wherever people who are anything but white live in this world today, the white man's governments are finding themselves in deeper and deeper trouble and peril.

Let's just face truth. Facts! Whether or not the white man of the world is able to face truth, and facts, about the true reasons for his troubles—that's what essentially will determine whether or not *he* will now survive.

Today we are seeing this revolution of the non-white peoples, who just a few years ago would have frozen in horror if the mighty white nations so much as lifted an eyebrow. What it is, simply, is that black and brown and red and yellow peoples have, after hundreds of years of exploitation and imposed "inferiority" and general misuse, become, finally, do-or-die sick and tired of the white man's heel on their necks.

How can the white American government figure on selling "democracy" and "brotherhood" to non-white peoples—if they read and hear every day what's going on right here in America, and see the better-than-a-thousand-words photographs of the American white man denying "democracy" and "brotherhood" even to America's native-born non-whites? The world's non-whites know how this Negro here has loved the American white man, and slaved for him, tended to him, nursed him. This Negro has jumped into uniform and gone off and died when this America was attacked by enemies both white and non-white. Such a faithful, loyal non-white as *this*—and *still* America bombs him, and sets dogs on him, and turns fire hoses on him, and jails him by the thousands, and beats him bloody, and inflicts upon him all manner of other crimes.

Of course these things, known and refreshed every day for the rest of the world's non-whites, are a vital factor in these burnings of ambassadors' limousines, these stonings, defilings, and wreckings of embassies and legations, these shouts of "White man, go home!" these attacks on white Christian missionaries, and these bombings and tearing down of flags.

Is it clear why I have said that the American white man's malignant superiority complex has done him more harm than an invading army?

The American black man should be focusing his every effort toward building his *own* businesses, and decent homes for himself. As other ethnic groups have done, let the black people, wherever possible, however possible, patronize their own kind, hire their own kind, and start in those ways to build up the black race's ability to do for itself. That's the only way the American black man is ever going to get respect. One thing the white man never can give the black man is self-respect! The black man never can become independent and recognized as a human being who is truly equal with other human beings until he has what they have, and until he is doing for himself what others are doing for themselves.

The black man in the ghettoes, for instance, has to start self-correcting his own material, moral, and spiritual defects and evils. The black man needs to start his own program to get rid of drunkenness, drug addiction, prostitution. The black man in America has to lift up his own sense of values.

Only a few thousands of Negroes, relatively a very tiny number, are taking any part in "integration." Here, again, it is those few bourgeois Negroes, rushing to throw away their little money in the white man's luxury hotels, his swanky nightclubs, and big, fine, exclusive restaurants. The white people patronizing those places can afford it. But these Negroes you see in those places can't afford it, certainly most of them can't. Why, what does some Negro one installment payment away from disaster look like somewhere downtown out to dine, grinning at some headwaiter who has more money than the Negro? Those bourgeois Negroes out draping big tablecloth-sized napkins over their knees and ordering quail under glass and stewed snails—why, Negroes don't even *like* snails! What they're doing is proving they're integrated.

If you want to get right down to the real outcome of this so-called "integration," what you've got to arrive at is intermarriage.

I'm right *with* the Southern white man who believes that you can't have so-called "integration," at least not for long, without intermarriage increasing. And what good is this for anyone? Let's again face reality. In a world as color-hostile as this, man or woman, black or white, what do they want with a mate of the other race?

Certainly white people have served enough notice of their hostility to any blacks in their families and neighborhoods. And the way most Negroes feel today, a mixed couple probably finds that black families, black communities, are even more hostile than the white ones. So what's bound to face "integrated" marriages, except being unwelcomed, unwanted, "misfits" in whichever world they try to live in? What we arrive at is that "integration," socially, is no good for either side. "Integration," ultimately, would destroy the white race . . . and destroy the black race.

The white man's "integrating" with black women has already changed the complexion and characteristics of the black race in America. What's been proved by the "blacks" whose complexions are "whiter" than many "white" people? I'm told that there are in America today between two and five million "white Negroes," who are "passing" in white society. Imagine their torture! Living in constant fear that some black person they've known might meet and expose them. Imagine every day living a lie. *Imagine* hearing their own white husbands, their own white wives, even their own white children, talking about "those Negroes."

I would doubt if anyone in America has heard Negroes more bitter against the white man than some of those I have heard. But I will tell you that, without any question, the *most* bitter anti-white diatribes that I have ever heard have come from "passing" Negroes, living as whites, among whites, exposed every day to what white people say among themselves regarding Negroes—things that a recognized Negro never would hear. Why, if there was a racial showdown, these Negroes "passing" within white circles would become the black side's most valuable "spy" and ally.

Europe's "brown babies," now young men and women who are starting to marry, and produce families of their own . . . have their experiences throughout their lives, scarred as racial freaks, proved anything positive for "integration"?

"Integration" is called "assimilation" if white ethnic groups alone are involved: it's fought against tooth and nail by those who want their heritage preserved. Look at how the Irish threw the English out of Ireland. The Irish knew the English would engulf them. Look at the French-Canadians, fanatically fighting to keep their identity.

In fact, history's most tragic result of a mixed, therefore diluted and weakened, ethnic identity has been experienced by a white ethnic group—the Jew in Germany.

He had made greater contributions to Germany than Germans themselves had. Jews had won over half of Germany's Nobel Prizes. Every culture in Germany was led by the Jew; he published the greatest newspaper. Jews were the greatest artists, the greatest poets, composers, stage directors. But those Jews made a fatal mistake—assimilating.

From World War I to Hitler's rise, the Jews in Germany had been increasingly intermarrying. Many changed their names and many took other religions. Their own Jewish religion, their own rich Jewish ethnic and cultural roots, they anesthetized, and cut off . . . until they began thinking of themselves as "Germans."

And the next thing they knew, there was Hitler, rising to power from the beer halls—with his emotional "Aryan master race" theory. And right at hand for a scapegoat was the self-weakened, self-deluded "German" Jew.

Most mysterious is how did those Jews—with all of their brilliant minds, with all of their power in every aspect of Germany's affairs—how did those Jews stand almost as if mesmerized, watching something which did not spring upon them overnight, but which was gradually developed—a monstrous plan for their own *murder*.

Their self-brainwashing had been so complete that not long after, in the gas chambers, a lot of them were still gasping, "It *can't* be true!"

If Hitler *had* conquered the world, as he meant to—that is a shuddery thought for every Jew alive today.

The Jew never will forget that lesson. Jewish intelligence eyes watch every neo-Nazi organization. Right after the war, the Jews' Haganah mediating body stepped up the longtime negotiations with the British. But this time, the Stern gang was shooting the British. And this time the British acquiesced and helped them to wrest Palestine away from the Arabs, the rightful owners, and then the Jews set up Israel, their own country—the one thing that every race of man in the world respects, and understands.

Not long ago, the black man in America was fed a dose of another form of the weakening, lulling and deluding effects of so-called "integration." It was that "Farce on Washington," I call it.

The idea of a mass of blacks marching on Washington was originally the brainchild of the Brotherhood of Sleeping Car Porters' A. Philip Randolph. For twenty or more years the March on Washington idea had floated around among Negroes. And, spontaneously, suddenly now, that idea caught on.

Overalled rural Southern Negroes, small town Negroes, Northern ghetto Negroes, even thousands of previously Uncle Tom Negroes began talking "March!"

Nothing since Joe Louis had so coalesced the masses of Negroes. Groups of Negroes were talking of getting to Washington any way they could—in rickety old cars, on buses, hitch-hiking—walking, even, if they had to. They envisioned thousands of black brothers converging together upon Washington—to lie down in the streets, on airport runways, on government lawns—demanding of the Congress and the White House some concrete civil rights action.

This was a national bitterness; militant, unorganized, and leaderless. Predominantly, it was young Negroes, defiant of whatever might be the consequences, sick and tired of the black man's neck under the white man's heel.

The white man had plenty of good reasons for nervous worry. The right spark—some unpredictable emotional chemistry—could set off a black uprising. The government knew that thousands of milling, angry blacks not only could completely disrupt Washington—but they could erupt in Washington.

The White House speedily invited in the major civil rights Negro "leaders." They were asked to stop the planned March. They truthfully said they hadn't begun it, they had no control over it—the idea was national, spontaneous, unorganized, and leaderless. In other words, it was a black powder keg.

Any student of how "integration" can weaken the black man's movement was about to observe a master lesson.

The White House, with a fanfare of international publicity, "approved," "endorsed," and "welcomed" a March on Washington. The big civil rights organizations right at this time had been publicly squabbling about donations. The *New York Times* had broken the story. The N.A.A.C.P. had charged that other agencies' demonstrations, highly publicized, had attracted a major part of the civil rights donations— while the N.A.A.C.P. got left holding the bag, supplying costly bail and legal talent for the other organizations' jailed demonstrators.

It was like a movie. The next scene was the "big six" civil rights Negro "leaders" meeting in New York City with the white head of a big philanthropic agency. They were told that their money-wrangling in public was damaging their image. And a reported $800,000 was donated to a United Civil Rights Leadership council that was quickly organized by the "big six."

Now, what had instantly achieved black unity? The white man's money. What string was attached to the money? Advice. Not only was there this donation, but another comparable sum was promised, for sometime later on, after the March . . . obviously if all went well.

The original "angry" March on Washington was now about to be entirely changed.

Massive international publicity projected the "big six" as March on Washington leaders. It was news to those angry grass-roots Negroes steadily adding steam to their March plans. They probably assumed that now those famous "leaders" were endorsing and joining them.

Invited next to join the March were four famous white public figures: one Catholic, one Jew, one Protestant, and one labor boss.

The massive publicity now gently hinted that the "big ten" would "supervise" the March on Washington's "mood," and its "direction."

The four white figures began nodding. The word spread fast among so-called "liberal" Catholics, Jews, Protestants, and laborites: it was "democratic" to join this black March. And suddenly, the previously March-nervous whites began announcing *they* were going.

It was as if electrical current shot through the ranks of bourgeois Negroes—the very so-called "middle-class" and "upper-class" who had earlier been deploring the March on Washington talk by grass-roots Negroes.

But white people, now, were going to march.

Why, some downtrodden, jobless, hungry Negro might have gotten trampled. Those "integration"-mad Negroes practically ran over each other trying to find out where to sign up. The "angry blacks" March suddenly had been made chic. Suddenly it had a Kentucky Derby image. For the status-seeker, it was a status symbol. "Were you *there*?" You can hear that right today.

It had become an outing, a picnic.

The morning of the March, any rickety carloads of angry, dusty, sweating small-town Negroes would have gotten lost among the chartered jet planes, railroad cars, and air-conditioned buses. What originally was planned to be an angry riptide, one English newspaper aptly described now as "the gentle flood."

Talk about "integrated"! It was like salt and pepper. And, by now, there wasn't a single logistics aspect uncontrolled.

The marchers had been instructed to bring no signs—signs were provided. They had been told to sing one song: "We Shall Overcome." They had been told *how* to arrive, *when*, *where* to arrive, *where* to assemble, when to *start* marching, the *route* to march. First-aid stations were strategically located—even where to *faint!*

Yes, I was there. I observed that circus. Who ever heard of angry revolutionists all harmonizing "We Shall Overcome

. . . Suum Day . . ." while tripping and swaying along arm-in-arm with the very people they were supposed to be angrily revolting against? Who ever heard of angry revolutionists swinging their bare feet together with their oppressor in lily-pad park pools, with gospels and guitars and "I Have A Dream" speeches?

And the black masses in America were—and still are—having a nightmare.

These "angry revolutionists" even followed their final instructions: to leave early. With all of those thousands upon thousands of "angry revolutionists," so few stayed over that the next morning the Washington hotel association reported a costly loss in empty rooms.

Hollywood couldn't have topped it.

In a subsequent press poll, not one Congressman or Senator with a previous record of opposition to civil rights said he had changed his views. What did anyone expect? How was a one-day "integrated" picnic going to counter-influence these representatives of prejudice rooted deep in the psyche of the American white man for four hundred years?

The very fact that millions, black and white, believed in this monumental farce is another example of how much this country goes in for the surface glossing over, the escape ruse, surfaces, instead of truly dealing with its deep-rooted problems.

What that March on Washington did do was lull Negroes for a while. But inevitably, the black masses started realizing they had been smoothly hoaxed again by the white man. And, inevitably, the black man's anger rekindled, deeper than ever, and there began bursting out in different cities, in the "long, hot summer" of 1964, unprecedented racial crises.

About a month before the "Farce on Washington," the *New York Times* reported me, according to its poll conducted on college and university campuses, as "the second most sought after" speaker at colleges and universities. The only speaker ahead of me was Senator Barry Goldwater.

I believe that what had generated such college popularity for me was Dr. Lincoln's book, *The Black Muslims in America*. It had been made required reading in numerous college courses. Then a long, candid interview with me was carried by *Playboy* magazine, whose circulation on college campuses is the biggest of any magazine's. And many students, having studied first the book and then the *Playboy* interview, wanted to hear in person this so-called "fiery Black Muslim."

When the *New York Times* poll was published, I had spoken at well over fifty colleges and universities, like Brown, Harvard, Yale, Columbia and Rutgers, in the Ivy League, and others throughout the country. Right now, I have invitations from Cornell, Princeton and probably a dozen others, as soon as my time and their available dates can be scheduled together. Among Negro institutions, I had then been to Atlanta University and Clark College down in Atlanta, to Howard University in Washington, D.C., and to a number of others with small student bodies.

Except for all-black audiences, I liked the college audiences best. The college sessions sometimes ran two to four hours— they often ran overtime. Challenges, queries, and criticisms were fired at me by the usually objective and always alive and searching minds of undergraduate and graduate students, and their faculties. The college sessions never failed to be exhilarating. They never failed in helping me to further my own education. I never experienced one college session that didn't show me ways to improve upon my presentation and defense of Mr. Muhammad's teachings. Sometimes in a panel or debate appearance, I'd find a jam-packed audience to hear me, alone, facing six or eight student and faculty scholars—heads of departments such as sociology, psychology, philosophy, history, and religion, and each of them coming at me in his specialty.

At the outset, always I'd confront such panels with something such as: "Gentlemen, I finished the eighth grade in Mason, Michigan. My high school was the black ghetto of Roxbury, Massachusetts. My college was in the streets of Harlem, and my master's was taken in prison. Mr. Muhammad has taught me that I never need fear any man's intellect who tries to defend or to justify the white man's criminal record against the non-white man—especially the white man and the black man here in North America."

It was like being on a battlefield—with intellectual and philosophical bullets. It was an exciting battling with ideas. I got so I could feel my audiences' temperaments. I've talked with other public speakers; they agree that this ability is native to any person who has the "mass appeal" gift, who can get through to and move people. It's a psychic radar. As a doctor, with his finger against a pulse, is able to feel the heart rate, when I am up there speaking, I can *feel* the reaction to what I am saying.

I think I could be speaking blindfolded and after five minutes, I could tell you if sitting out there before me was an all-black or an all-white audience. Black audiences and white audiences feel distinguishably different. Black audiences feel warmer, there is almost a musical rhythm, for me, even in their silent response.

Question-and-answer periods are another area where, by now, again blindfolded, I can often tell you the ethnic source of a question. The most easily recognizable of these to me are a Jew in any audience situation, and a bourgeois Negro in "integrated" audiences.

My clue to the Jew's question and challenges is that among all other ethnic groups, his expressed thinking, his expressed concerns, are the most subjective. And the Jew is usually hypersensitive. I mean, you can't even say "Jew" without him accusing you of anti-Semitism. I don't care what a Jew is professionally, doctor, merchant, housewife, student, or whatever—first he, or she, thinks Jew.

Now, of course I can understand the Jew's hypersensitivity. For two thousand years, religious and personal prejudices against Jews have been vented and exercised, as strong as white prejudices against the non-white. But I know that America's five and a half million Jews (two million of them are concentrated in New York) look at it very practically, whether they know it or not: that all of the bigotry and hatred focused upon the black man keeps off the Jew a lot of heat that would be on him otherwise.

For an example of what I am talking about—in every black ghetto, Jews own the major businesses. Every night the owners of those businesses go home with that black community's money, which helps the ghetto to stay poor. But I doubt that I have ever uttered this absolute truth before an audience without being hotly challenged, and accused by a Jew of anti-Semitism. Why? I will bet that I have told five hundred such challengers that Jews as a group would never watch some other minority systematically siphoning out their community's resources without doing something about it. I have told them that if I tell the simple truth, it doesn't mean that I am anti-Semitic; it means merely that I am anti-exploitation.

The white liberal may be a little taken aback to know that

from all-Negro audiences I never have had one challenge, never one question that defended the white man. That has been true even when a lot of those "black bourgeoisie" and "integration"-mad Negroes were among the blacks. All Negroes, among themselves, admit the white man's criminal record. They may not know as many details as I do, but they know the general picture.

But, let me tell you something significant: This very same bourgeois Negro who, among Negroes, would never make a fool of himself in trying to defend the white man—watch that same Negro in a mixed black and white audience, knowing he's overheard by his beloved "Mr. Charlie." Why, you should hear those Negroes attack me, trying to justify, or forgive the white man's crimes! These Negroes are people who bring me nearest to breaking one of my principal rules, which is never to let myself become over-emotional and angry. Why, sometimes I've felt I ought to jump down off that stand and get *physical* with some of those brainwashed white man's tools, parrots, puppets. At the colleges, I've developed some stock put-downs for them: "You must be a law student, aren't you?" They have to say either yes, or no. And I say, "I thought you were. You defend this criminal white man harder than he defends his guilty self!"

One particular university's "token-integrated" black Ph.D. associate professor I never will forget; he got me so mad I couldn't see straight. As badly as our 22 millions of educationally deprived black people need the help of any brains he has, there he was looking like some fly in the buttermilk among white "colleagues"—and he was trying to *eat me up!* He was ranting about what a "divisive demagogue" and what a "reverse racist" I was. I was racking my head, to spear that fool; finally I held up my hand, and he stopped. "Do you know what white racists call black Ph.D's?" He said something like, "I believe that I happen not to be aware of that" —you know, one of these ultra-proper-talking Negroes. And I laid the word down on him, loud: *"Nigger!"*

Speaking in these colleges and universities was good for the Nation of Islam, I would report to Mr. Muhammad, because the devilish white man's best minds were developed and influenced in the colleges and universities. But for some reason that I could never understand until much later, Mr. Muhammad never really wanted me to speak at these colleges and universities.

I was to learn later, from Mr. Muhammad's own sons, that he was envious because he felt unequipped to speak at colleges himself. But nevertheless, in Mr. Muhammad's behalf at this time, I was finding these highly intelligent audiences amazingly open-minded and objective in their receptions of the raw, naked truths that I would tell them:

"Time and time again, the black, the brown, the red, and the yellow races have witnessed and suffered the white man's small ability to understand the simple notes of the spirit. The white man seems tone deaf to the total orchestration of humanity. Every day, his newspapers' front pages show us the world that he has created.

"God's wrathful judgment is close upon this white man stumbling and groping blindly in wickedness and evil and spiritual darkness.

"Look—remaining today are only two giant white nations, America and Russia, each of them with mistrustful, nervous satellites. America is propping up most of the remaining white world. The French, the Belgians, the Dutch, the Portuguese, the Spanish and other white nations have weakened steadily as non-white Asians and Africans have recovered their lands.

"America is subsidizing what is left of the prestige and strength of the once mighty Britain. The sun has set forever on that monocled, pith-helmeted resident colonialist, sipping tea with his delicate lady in the non-white colonies being systematically robbed of every valuable resource. Britain's superfluous royalty and nobility now exist by charging tourists to inspect the once baronial castles, and by selling memoirs, perfumes, autographs, titles, and even themselves.

"The whole world knows that the white man cannot survive another war. If either of the two giant white nations pushes the button, white civilization will die!

"And we see again that not ideologies, but race, and color, is what binds human beings. Is it accidental that as Red Chinese visit African and Asian countries, Russia and America draw steadily closer to each other?

"The collective white man's history has left the non-white peoples no alternative, either, but to draw closer to each other. Characteristically, as always, the devilish white man lacks the moral strength and courage to cast off his arrogance. He wants, today, to 'buy' friends among the non-whites. He tries, characteristically, to cover up his past record. He does not possess the humility to admit his guilt, to try and atone for his crimes. The white man has perverted the simple message of love that the Prophet Jesus lived and taught when He walked upon this earth."

Audiences seemed surprised when I spoke about Jesus. I would explain that we Muslims believe in the Prophet Jesus. He was one of the three most important Prophets of the religion of Islam, the others being Mohammad and Moses. In Jerusalem there are Muslim shrines built to the Prophet Jesus. I would explain that it was our belief that Christianity did not perform what Christ taught. I never failed to cite that even Billy Graham, challenged in Africa, had himself made the distinction, "I believe in Christ, not Christianity."

I never will forget one little blonde co-ed after I had spoken at her New England college. She must have caught the next plane behind that one I took to New York. She found the Muslim restaurant in Harlem. I just happened to be there when she came in. Her clothes, her carriage, her accent, all showed Deep South white breeding and money. At that college, I had told how the ante-bellum white slavemaster even devilishly manipulated his own woman. He convinced her that she was "too pure" for his base "animal instincts." With this "noble" ruse, he conned his own wife to look away from his obvious preference for the "animal" black woman. So the "delicate mistress" sat and watched the plantation's little mongrel-complexioned children, sired obviously by her father, her husband, her brothers, her sons. I said at that college that the guilt of American whites included their knowledge that in hating Negroes, they were hating, they were rejecting, they were denying, their own blood.

Anyway, I'd never seen anyone I ever spoke before more affected than this little white college girl. She demanded, right up in my face, "Don't you believe there are any *good* white people?" I didn't want to hurt her feelings. I told her, "People's *deeds* I believe in, Miss—not their words."

"What can I *do?*" she exclaimed. I told her, "Nothing." She burst out crying, and ran out and up Lenox Avenue and caught a taxi.

Mr. Muhammad—each time I'd go to see him in Chicago, or in Phoenix—would warm me with his expressions of his approval and confidence in me.

He left me in charge of the Nation of Islam's affairs when he made an Omra pilgrimage to the Holy City Mecca.

I believed so strongly in Mr. Muhammad that I would have hurled myself between him and an assassin.

A chance event brought crashing home to me that there was something—one thing—greater than my reverence for Mr. Muhammad.

It was the awesomeness of my reason to revere him.

I was the invited speaker at the Harvard Law School Forum. I happened to glance through a window. Abruptly, I realized that I was looking in the direction of the apartment house that was my old burglary gang's hideout.

It rocked me like a tidal wave. Scenes from my once depraved life lashed through my mind. *Living* like an animal; *thinking* like an animal!

Awareness came surging up in me—how deeply the religion of Islam had reached down into the mud to lift me up, to save me from being what I inevitably would have been: a dead criminal in a grave, or, if still alive, a flint-hard, bitter, thirty-seven-year-old convict in some penitentiary, or insane asylum. Or, at best, I would have been an old, fading Detroit Red, hustling, stealing enough for food and narcotics, and myself being stalked as prey by cruelly ambitious younger hustlers such as Detroit Red had been.

But Allah had blessed me to learn about the religion of Islam, which had enabled me to lift myself up from the muck and the mire of this rotting world.

And there I stood, the invited speaker, at Harvard.

A story that I had read in prison when I was reading a lot of Greek mythology flicked into my head.

The boy Icarus. Do you remember the story?

Icarus' father made some wings that he fastened with wax. "Never fly but so high with these wings," the father said. But soaring around, this way, that way, Icarus' flying pleased him so that he began thinking he was flying on his own merit. Higher, he flew—higher—until the heat of the sun melted the wax holding those wings. And down came Icarus —tumbling.

Standing there by that Harvard window, I silently vowed to Allah that I never would forget that any wings I wore had been put on by the religion of Islam. That fact I never have forgotten . . . not for one second.

CHAPTER SIXTEEN

OUT

In nineteen sixty-one, Mr. Muhammad's condition grew suddenly worse.

As he talked with me when I visited him, when he talked with anyone, he would unpredictably begin coughing harder, and harder, until his body was wracked and jerking in agonies that were painful to watch, and Mr. Muhammad would have to take to his bed.

We among Mr. Muhammad's officials, and his family, kept the situation to ourselves, while we could. Few other Muslims became aware of Mr. Muhammad's condition until there were last-minute cancellations of long-advertised personal appearances at some big Muslim rallies. Muslims knew that only something really serious would ever have stopped the Messenger from keeping his promise to be with them at their rallies. Their questions had to be answered, and the news of our leader's illness swiftly spread through the Nation of Islam.

Anyone not a Muslim could not conceive what the possible loss of Mr. Muhammad would have meant among his followers. To us, the Nation of Islam was Mr. Muhammad. What bonded us into the best organization black Americans ever had was every Muslim's devout regard for Mr. Muhammad as black America's moral, mental, and spiritual reformer.

Stated another way, we Muslims regarded ourselves as moral and mental and spiritual examples for other black Americans, because we followed the personal example of Mr. Muhammad. Black communities discussed with respect how Muslims were suspended if they lied, gambled, cheated, or smoked. For moral crimes, such as fornication or adultery, Mr. Muhammad personally would mete out sentences of from one to five years of "isolation," if not complete expulsion from the Nation. And Mr. Muhammad would punish his officials more readily than the newest convert in a mosque. He said that any defecting official betrayed both himself and his position as a leader and example for other Muslims. For every Muslim, in his rejection of immoral temptation, the beacon was Mr. Muhammad. All Muslims felt as one that without his light, we would all be in darkness.

As I have related, doctors recommended a dry climate to ease Mr. Muhammad's condition. Quickly we found up for sale in Phoenix the home of the saxophone player, Louis Jordan. The Nation's treasury purchased the home, and Mr. Muhammad soon moved there.

Only by being two people could I have worked harder in the service of the Nation of Islam. I had every gratification that I wanted. I had helped bring about the progress and national impact such that none could call us liars when we called Mr. Muhammad the most powerful black man in America. I had helped Mr. Muhammad and his other ministers to revolutionize the American black man's thinking, opening his eyes until he would never again look in the same fearful, worshipful way at the white man. I had participated in spreading the truths that had done so much to help the American black man rid himself of the mirage that the white race was made up of "superior" beings. I had been a part of the tapping of something in the black secret soul.

If I harbored any personal disappointment whatsoever, it was that privately I was convinced that our Nation of Islam could be an even greater force in the American black man's overall struggle—if we engaged in more *action*. By that, I mean I thought privately that we should have amended, or relaxed, our general non-engagement policy. I felt that, wherever black people committed themselves, in the Little Rocks and the Birminghams and other places, militantly disciplined Muslims should also be there—for all the world to see, and respect, and discuss.

It could be heard increasingly in the Negro communities: "Those Muslims *talk* tough, but they never *do* anything, unless somebody bothers Muslims." I moved around among outsiders more than most other Muslim officials. I felt the very real potentiality that, considering the mercurial moods of the black masses, this labeling of Muslims as "talk only" could see us, powerful as we were, one day suddenly separated from the Negroes' front-line struggle.

But beyond that single personal concern, I couldn't have asked Allah to bless my efforts any more than he had. Islam in New York City was growing faster than anywhere in America. From the one tiny mosque to which Mr. Muhammad had originally sent me, I had now built three of the Nation's most powerful and aggressive mosques—Harlem's Seven-A in Manhattan, Corona's Seven-B in Queens, and Mosque Seven-C in Brooklyn. And on a national basis, I had either directly established, or I had helped to establish, most of the one hundred or more mosques in the fifty states. I was crisscrossing North America sometimes as often as four times a week. Often, what sleep I got was caught in the jet planes. I was maintaining a marathon schedule of press, radio, television, and public-speaking commitments. The only way that I could keep up with my job for Mr. Muhammad was by flying with the wings that he had given me.

As far back as 1961, when Mr. Muhammad's illness took that turn for the worse, I had heard chance negative remarks concerning me. I had heard veiled implications. I had noticed other little evidences of the envy and of the jealousy which Mr. Muhammad had prophesied. For example, it was being said that "Minister Malcolm is trying to take over the Nation," it was being said that I was "taking credit" for Mr. Muhammad's teaching, it was being said that I was trying to "build an empire" for myself. It was being said that I loved playing "coast-to-coast Mr. Big Shot."

When I heard these things, actually, they didn't anger me. They helped me to re-steel my inner resolve that such lies would never become true of me. I would always remember that Mr. Muhammad had prophesied this envy and jealousy. This would help me to ignore it, because I knew that *he* would understand if *he* ever should hear such talk.

A frequent rumor among non-Muslims was "Malcolm X is making a pile of money." All Muslims at least knew better than that. *Me* making money? The F.B.I. and the C.I.A. and the I.R.S. all combined can't turn up a thing I got, beyond a car to drive and a seven-room house to live in. (And by now the Nation of Islam is jealously and greedily trying to take away even that house.) I had *access* to money. Yes! Elijah Muhammad would authorize for me any amount that I asked for. But he knew, as every Muslim official knew, that every nickel and dime I ever got was used to promote the Nation of Islam.

My attitude toward money generated the only domestic quarrel that I have ever had with my beloved wife Betty. As our children increased in number, so did Betty's hints to me that I should put away *something* for our family. But I refused, and finally we had this argument. I put my foot down. I knew I had in Betty a wife who would sacrifice her life for me if such an occasion ever presented itself to her, but still I told her that too many organizations had been destroyed by leaders who tried to benefit personally, often goaded into it by their wives. We nearly broke up over this argument. I finally convinced Betty that if anything ever happened to me, the Nation of Islam would take care of her for the rest of her life, and of our children until they were grown. I could never have been a bigger fool!

In every radio or television appearance, in every newspaper interview, I always made it crystal clear that I was Mr. Muhammad's *representative*. Anyone who ever heard me make a public speech during this time knows that at least once a minute I said, "The Honorable Elijah Muhammad teaches—" I would refuse to talk with any person who ever tried any so-called "joke" about my constant reference to Mr. Muhammad. Whenever anyone said, or wrote, "Malcolm X, the number two Black Muslim—" I would recoil. I have called up reporters and radio and television newscasters long-distance and asked them never to use that phrasing again, explaining to them: "*All* Muslims are number two—after Mr. Muhammad."

My briefcase was stocked with Mr. Muhammad's photographs. I gave them to photographers who snapped my picture. I would telephone editors asking them, "Please use Mr. Muhammad's picture instead of mine." When, to my joy, Mr. Muhammad agreed to grant interviews to white writers, I rarely spoke to a white writer, or a black one either, whom I didn't urge to visit Mr. Muhammad in person in Chicago— "Get the truth from the Messenger in person"—and a number of them did go there and meet and interview him.

Both white people and Negroes—even including Muslims— would make me uncomfortable, always giving me so much credit for the steady progress that the Nation of Islam was making. "All praise is due to Allah," I told everybody. "Anything creditable that I do is due to Mr. Elijah Muhammad."

I believe that no man in the Nation of Islam could have gained the international prominence I gained with the wings Mr. Muhammad had put on me—plus having the freedom

that he granted me to take liberties and do things on my own
—and still have remained as faithful and as selfless a servant
to him as I was.

I would say that it was in 1962 when I began to notice
that less and less about me appeared in our Nation's
Muhammad Speaks. I learned that Mr. Muhammad's son,
Herbert, now the paper's publisher, had instructed that as
little as possible be printed about me. In fact, there was more
in the Muslim paper about integrationist Negro "leaders"
than there was about me. I could read more about myself in
the European, Asian, and African press.

I am not griping about publicity for myself. I already had
received more publicity than many world personages. But
I resented the fact that the Muslims' own newspaper denied
them news of important things being done in their behalf,
simply because it happened that I had done the things. I was
conducting rallies, trying to propagate Mr. Muhammad's
teachings, and because of jealousy and narrow-mindedness
finally I got no coverage at all—for by now an order had
been given to completely black me out of the newspaper.
For instance, I spoke to eight thousand students at the University of California, and the press there gave big coverage
to what I said of the power and program of Mr. Muhammad.
But when I got to Chicago, expecting at least a favorable
response and some coverage, I met only a chilly reaction.
The same thing happened when, in Harlem, I staged a rally
that drew seven thousand people. At that time, Chicago headquarters was even discouraging me from staging large rallies.
But the next week, I held another Harlem rally that was even
bigger and more successful than the first one—and obviously
this only increased the envy of the Chicago headquarters.

But I would put these things out of my mind, as they
occurred. At least, as much as I humanly could, I put them
out of my mind. I am not trying to make myself seem right
and noble. I am telling the truth. I *loved* the Nation, and
Mr. Muhammad. I *lived for* the Nation, and for Mr. Muhammad.

It made other Muslim officials jealous because my picture
was often in the daily press. They wouldn't remember that
my picture was there because of my fervor in championing
Mr. Muhammad. They wouldn't simply reason that as vulnerable as the Nation of Islam was to distorted rumors and
outright lies, we needed nothing so little as to have our public

spokesman constantly denying the rumors. Common sense would have told any official that certainly Mr. Muhammad couldn't be running all over the country as his own spokesman. And whoever he appointed as his spokesman couldn't avoid a lot of press focus.

Whenever I caught any resentful feelings hanging on in my mind, I would be ashamed of myself, considering it a sign of weakness in myself. I knew that at least Mr. Muhammad knew that my life was totally dedicated to representing him.

But during 1963, I couldn't help being very hypersensitive to my critics in high posts within our Nation. I quit selecting certain of my New York brothers and giving them money to go and lay groundwork for new mosques in other cities—because slighting remarks were being made about "Malcolm's ministers." In a time in America when it was of arch importance for a militant black voice to reach mass audiences, *Life* magazine wanted to do a personal story of me, and I refused. I refused again when a cover story was offered by *Newsweek*. I refused again when I could have been a guest on the top-rated "Meet the Press" television program. Each refusal was a general loss for the black man, and, for the Nation of Islam, each refusal was a specific loss—and each refusal was made because of Chicago's attitude. There was jealousy because I had been requested to make these featured appearances.

When a high-powered-rifle slug tore through the back of the N.A.A.C.P. Field Secretary Medgar Evers in Mississippi, I wanted to say the blunt truths that needed to be said. When a bomb was exploded in a Negro Christian church in Birmingham, Alabama, snuffing out the lives of those four beautiful little black girls, I made comments—but not what should have been said about the climate of hate that the American white man was generating and nourishing. The more hate was permitted to lash out when there were ways it could have been checked, the more bold the hate became—until at last it was flaring out at even the white man's own kind, including his own leaders. In Dallas, Texas, for instance, the then Vice President and Mrs. Johnson were vulgarly insulted. And the U. S. Ambassador to the United Nations, Adlai Stevenson, was spat upon and hit on the head by a white woman picket.

Mr. Muhammad made me the Nation's first National Minister. At a late 1963 rally in Philadelphia, Mr. Muhammad, embracing me, said to that audience before us, "This is my most faithful, hardworking minister. He will follow me until he dies."

He had never paid such a compliment to any Muslim. No praise from any other earthly person could have meant more to me.

But this would be Mr. Muhammad's and my last public appearance together.

Not long before, I had been on the Jerry Williams radio program in Boston, when someone handed me an item hot off the Associated Press machine. I read that a chapter of the Louisiana Citizens Council had just offered a $10,000 reward for my death.

But the threat of death was much closer to me than somewhere in Louisiana.

What I am telling you is the truth. When I discovered who else wanted me dead, I am telling you—it nearly sent me to Bellevue.

In my twelve years as a Muslim minister, I had always taught so strongly on the moral issues that many Muslims accused me of being "anti-woman." The very keel of my teaching, and my most bone-deep personal belief, was that Elijah Muhammad in every aspect of his existence was a symbol of moral, mental, and spiritual reform among the American black people. For twelve years, I had taught that within the entire Nation of Islam; my own transformation was the best example I knew of Mr. Muhammad's power to reform black men's lives. From the time I entered prison until I married, about twelve years later, because of Mr. Muhammad's influence upon me, I had never touched a woman.

But around 1963, if anyone had noticed, I spoke less and less of religion. I taught social doctrine to Muslims, and current events, and politics. I stayed wholly off the subject of morality.

And the reason for this was that my faith had been shaken in a way that I can never fully describe. For I had discovered Muslims had been betrayed by Elijah Muhammad himself.

I want to make this as brief as I can, only enough so that my position and my reactions will be understood. As to whether or not I should reveal this, there's no longer any need for any question in my mind—for now the public knows. To make it concise, I will quote from one wire service story as it appeared in newspapers, and was reported over radio and television, across the United States:

"Los Angeles, July 3 (UPI)—Elijah Muhammad, 67-year-old leader of the Black Muslim movement, today faced paternity suits from two former secretaries who charged he fathered their four children. . . . Both women are in their twenties. . . . Miss Rosary and Miss Williams charged they had intimacies with Elijah Muhammad from 1957 until this year. Miss Rosary alleged he fathered her two children and said she was expecting a third child by him . . . the other plaintiff said he was the father of her daughter. . . ."

As far back as 1955, I had heard hints. But believe me when I tell you this: for me even to consider believing anything as insane-sounding as any slightest implication of any immoral behavior of Mr. Muhammad—why, the very idea made me shake with fear.

And so my mind simply refused to accept anything so grotesque as adultery mentioned in the same breath with Mr. Muhammad's name.

Adultery! Why, any Muslim guilty of adultery was summarily ousted in disgrace. One of the Nation's most closely kept scandals was that a succession of the personal secretaries of Mr. Muhammad had become pregnant. They were brought before Muslim courts and charged with adultery and they confessed. Humiliated before the general body, they received sentences of from one to five years of "isolation." That meant they were to have no contact whatsoever with any other Muslims.

I don't think I could say anything which better testifies to my depth of faith in Mr. Muhammad than that I totally and absolutely rejected my own intelligence. I simply refused to believe. I didn't want Allah to "burn my brain" as I felt the brain of my brother Reginald had been burned for harboring evil thoughts about Mr. Elijah Muhammad. The last time I had seen Reginald, one day he walked into the Mosque Seven restaurant. I saw him coming in the door. I went and met him. I looked into my own brother's eyes; I told him he wasn't welcome among Muslims, and he turned around and left, and I haven't seen him since. I did that to my own blood brother because, years before, Mr. Muhammad had sentenced Reginald to "isolation" from all other Muslims—and I considered that I was a Muslim before I was Reginald's brother.

No one in the world could have convinced me that Mr. Muhammad would betray the reverence bestowed upon him by all of the mosques full of poor, trusting Muslims nickeling and diming up to faithfully support the Nation of Islam—

when many of these faithful were scarcely able to pay their own rents.

But by late 1962, I learned reliably that numerous Muslims were leaving Mosque Two in Chicago. The ugly rumor was spreading swiftly—even among non-Muslim Negroes. When I thought how the press constantly sought ways to discredit the Nation of Islam, I trembled to think of such a thing reaching the ears of some newspaper reporter, either black or white.

I actually began to have nightmares . . . I saw *headlines*.

I was burdened with a leaden fear as I kept speaking engagements all over America. Any time a reporter came anywhere near me, I could *hear* him ask, "Is it true, Mr. Malcolm X, this report we hear, that . . ." And what was I going to say?

There was never any specific moment when I admitted the situation to myself. In the way that the human mind can do, somehow I slid over admitting to myself the ugly fact, even as I began dealing with it.

Both in New York and Chicago, non-Muslims whom I knew began to tell me indirectly they had heard—or they would ask me if I had heard. I would act as if I had no idea whatever of what they were talking about—and I was grateful when they chose not to spell out what they knew. I went around knowing that I looked to them like a total fool. I felt like a total fool, out there every day preaching, and apparently not knowing what was going on right under my nose, in my own organization, involving the very man I was praising so. To look like a fool unearthed emotions I hadn't felt since my Harlem hustler days. The worst thing in the hustler's world was to be a dupe.

I will give you an example. Backstage at the Apollo Theater in Harlem one day, the comedian Dick Gregory looked at me. "Man," he said, "Muhammad's nothing but a . . ."—I can't say the word he used. *Bam!* Just like that. My Muslim instincts said to attack Dick—but, instead, I felt weak and hollow. I think Dick sensed how upset I was and he let me get him off the subject. I knew Dick, a Chicagoan, was wise in the ways of the streets, and blunt-spoken. I wanted to plead with him not to say to anyone else what he had said to me—but I couldn't; it would have been my own admission.

I can't describe the torments I went through.

Always before, in any extremity, I had caught the first plane to Mr. Elijah Muhammad. He had virtually raised me from the dead. Everything I was that was creditable, he had made me. I felt that no matter what, I could not let him down.

There was no one I could turn to with this problem, except Mr. Muhammad himself. Ultimately that had to be the case. But first I went to Chicago to see Mr. Muhammad's second youngest son, Wallace Muhammad. I felt that Wallace was Mr. Muhammad's most strongly spiritual son, the son with the most objective outlook. Always, Wallace and I had shared an exceptional closeness and trust.

And Wallace knew, when he saw me, why I had come to see him. "I know," he said. I said I thought we should rally to help his father. Wallace said he didn't feel that his father would welcome any efforts to help him. I told myself that Wallace must be crazy.

Next, I broke the rule that no Muslim is supposed to have any contact with another Muslim in the "isolated" state. I looked up, and I talked with three of the former secretaries to Mr. Muhammad. From their own mouths, I heard their stories of who had fathered their children. And from their own mouths I heard that Elijah Muhammad had told them I was the best, the greatest minister he ever had, but that someday I would leave him, turn against him—so I was "dangerous." I learned from these former secretaries of Mr. Muhammad that while he was praising me to my face, he was tearing me apart behind my back.

That deeply hurt me.

Every day, I was meeting the microphones, cameras, press reporters, and other commitments, including the Muslims of my own Mosque Seven. I felt almost out of my mind.

Finally, the thing crystallized for me. As long as I did nothing, I felt it was the same as being disloyal. I felt that as long as I sat down, I was not helping Mr. Muhammad—when somebody needed to be standing up.

So one night I wrote to Mr. Muhammad about the poison being spread about him. He telephoned me in New York. He said that when he saw me he would discuss it.

I desperately wanted to find some way—some kind of a bridge—over which I was certain the Nation of Islam could be saved from self-destruction. I had faith in the Nation: we weren't some group of Christian Negroes, jumping and shouting and full of sins.

I thought of one bridge that could be used if and when the shattering disclosure should become public. Loyal Muslims could be taught that a man's accomplishments in his life outweigh his personal, human weaknesses. Wallace Muhammad helped me to review the Quran and the Bible for documentation. David's adultery with Bathsheba weighed less on history's scales, for instance, than the positive fact of David's killing Goliath. Thinking of Lot, we think not of incest, but of his saving the people from the destruction of Sodom and Gomorrah. Or, our image of Noah isn't of his getting drunk—but of his building the ark and teaching people to save themselves from the flood. We think of Moses leading the Hebrews from bondage, not of Moses' adultery with the Ethiopian women. In all of the cases I reviewed, the positive outweighed the negative.

I began teaching in New York Mosque Seven that a man's accomplishments in his life outweighed his personal, human weaknesses. I taught that a person's good deeds outweigh his bad deeds. I never mentioned the previously familiar subjects of adultery and fornication, and I never mentioned immoral evils.

By some miracle, the adultery talk which was so widespread in Chicago seemed to only leak a little in Boston, Detroit, and New York. Apparently, it hadn't reached other mosques around the country at all. In Chicago, increasing numbers of Muslims were leaving Mosque Two, I heard, and many non-Muslims who had been sympathetic to the Nation were now outspokenly anti-Muslim. In February, 1963, I officiated at the University of Islam graduation exercises; when I introduced various members of the Muhammad family, I could feel the cold chill toward them from the Muslims in the audience.

Elijah Muhammad had me fly to Phoenix to see him in April, 1963.

We embraced, as always—and amost immediately he took me outside, where we began to walk by his swimming pool.

He was The Messenger of Allah. When I was a foul, vicious convict, so evil that other convicts had called me Satan, this man had rescued me. He was the man who had trained me, who had treated me as if I were his own flesh and blood. He was the man who had given me wings—to go places, to do things I otherwise never would have dreamed of. We walked, with me caught up in a whirlwind of emotions.

"Well, son," Mr. Muhammad said, "what is on your mind?"

Plainly, frankly, pulling no punches, I told Mr. Muhammad what was being said. And without waiting for any response from him, I said that with his son Wallace's help I had found in the Quran and the Bible that which might be taught to

Muslims—if it became necessary—as the fulfillment of prophecy.

"Son, I'm not surprised," Elijah Muhammad said. "You always have had such a good understanding of prophecy, and of spiritual things. You recognize that's what all of this is— prophecy. You have the kind of understanding that only an old man has.

"I'm David," he said. "When you read about how David took another man's wife, I'm that David. You read about Noah, who got drunk—that's me. You read about Lot, who went and laid up with his own daughters. I have to fulfill all of those things."

I remembered that when an epidemic is about to hit some- where, that community's people are inoculated against expos- ure with some of the same germs that are anticipated—and this prepares them to resist the oncoming virus.

I decided I had better prepare six other East Coast Muslim officials whom I selected.

I told them. And then I told them why I had told them— that I felt they should not be caught by surprise and shock if it became their job to teach the Muslims in their mosques the "fulfillment of prophecy." I found then that some had already heard it; one of them, Minister Louis X of Boston, as much as seven months before. They had been living with the dilemma themselves.

I never dreamed that the Chicago Muslim officials were going to make it appear that I was throwing gasoline on the fire instead of water. I never dreamed that they were going to try to make it appear that instead of inoculating against an epidemic, I had started it.

The stage in Chicago even then was being set for Muslims to shift their focus off the epidemic—and onto me.

Hating me was going to become the cause for people of shattered faith to rally around.

Non-Muslim Negroes who knew me well, and even some of the white reporters with whom I had some regular con- tact, were telling me, almost wherever I went, "Malcolm X, you're looking tired. You need a rest."

They didn't know a fraction of it. Since I had been a Muslim, this was the first time any white people really got to me in a personal way. I could tell that some of them were really honest and sincere. One of these, whose name I won't call—he might lose his job—said, "Malcolm X, the whites need your voice worse than the Negroes." I remember so well his saying this because it prefaced the first time since I became a Muslim that I had ever talked with any white man at any length about anything except the Nation of Islam and the American black man's struggle today.

I can't remember how, or why, he somehow happened to mention the Dead Sea Scrolls. I came back with something like, "Yes, those scrolls are going to take Jesus off the stained-glass windows and the frescoes where he has been lily-white, and put Him back into the true mainstream of history where Jesus actually was non-white." The reporter was surprised, and I went on that the Dead Sea Scrolls were going to reaffirm that Jesus was a member of that brotherhood of Egyptian seers called the Essene—a fact already known from Philo, the famous Egyptian historian of Jesus' time. And the reporter and I got off on about two good hours of talking in the areas of archaeology, history, and religion. It was *so* pleasant. I almost forgot the heavy worries on my mind—for that brief respite. I remember we wound up agreeing that by the year 2000, every schoolchild will be taught the true color of great men of antiquity.

I've said that I expected headlines momentarily. I hadn't expected the kind which came.

No one needs to be reminded of who got assassinated in Dallas, Texas, on November 22, 1963.

Within hours after the assassination—I am telling nothing but the truth—every Muslim minister received from Mr. Elijah Muhammad a directive—in fact, *two* directives. Every minister was ordered to make no remarks at all concerning the assassination. Mr. Muhammad instructed that if pressed for comment, we should say: "No comment."

During that three-day period where there was no other news to be heard except relating to the murdered President, Mr. Muhammad had a previously scheduled speaking engagement in New York at the Manhattan Center. He cancelled his coming to speak, and as we were unable to get back the money already paid for the rental of the center, Mr. Muhammad told me to speak in his stead. And so I spoke.

Many times since then, I've looked at the speech notes I used that day, which had been prepared at least a week before the assassination. The title of my speech was "God's Judgment of White America." It was on the theme, familiar to me, of "as you sow, so shall you reap," or how the hypocritical American white man was reaping what he had sowed.

The question-and-answer period opened, I suppose inevitably, with someone asking me, "What do you think about President Kennedy's assassination? What is your opinion?"

Without a second thought, I said what I honestly felt—that it was, as I saw it, a case of "the chickens coming home to roost." I said that the hate in white men had not stopped with the killing of defenseless black people, but that hate, allowed to spread unchecked, finally had struck down this country's Chief of State. I said it was the same thing as had happened with Medgar Evers, with Patrice Lumumba, with Madame Nhu's husband.

The headlines and the news broadcasts promptly had it: *"Black Muslims' Malcolm X: 'Chickens Come Home To Roost.'"*

It makes me feel weary to think of it all now. All over America, all over the world, some of the world's most important personages were saying in various ways, and in far stronger ways than I did, that America's climate of hate had been responsible for the President's death. But when Malcolm X said the same thing, it was ominous.

My regular monthly visit to Mr. Muhammad was due the next day. Somehow, on the plane, I expected something. I've always had this strong intuition.

Mr. Muhammad and I embraced each other in greeting. I sensed some ingredient missing from his usual amiability. And I was suddenly tense—to me also very significant. For years, I had prided myself that Mr. Muhammad and I were so close that I knew how he felt by how I felt. If he was nervous, I was nervous. If I was relaxed, then I knew he was relaxed. Now, I felt the *tension. . . .*

First we talked of other things, sitting in his living room. Then he asked me, "Did you see the papers this morning?"

I said, "Yes, sir, I did."

"That was a very bad statement," he said. "The country loved this man. The whole country is in mourning. That was very ill-timed. A statement like that can make it hard on Muslims in general."

And then, as if Mr. Muhammad's voice came from afar, I

heard his words: "I'll have to silence you for the next ninety days—so that the Muslims everywhere can be disassociated from the blunder."

I was numb.

But I was a follower of Mr. Muhammad. Many times I had said to my own assistants that anyone in a position to discipline others must be able to take disciplining himself.

I told Mr. Muhammad, "Sir, I agree with you, and I submit, one hundred per cent."

I flew back to New York psychologically preparing myself to tell my Mosque Seven assistants that I had been suspended —or "silenced."

But to my astonishment, upon arrival I learned that my assistants already had been informed.

What astonished me even more—a telegram had been sent to every New York City newspaper and radio and television station. It was the most quick and thorough publicity job that I had ever seen the Chicago officials initiate.

Every telephone where I could possibly be reached was ringing. London. Paris. A.P., U.P.I. Every television and radio network, and all of the newspapers were calling. I told them all, "I disobeyed Mr. Muhammad. I submit completely to his wisdom. Yes, I expect to be speaking again after ninety days."

"Malcolm X Silenced!" It was headlines.

My first worry was that if a scandal broke for the Nation of Islam within the next ninety days, I would be gagged when I could be the most experienced Muslim in dealing with the news media that would make the most of any scandal within the Nation.

I learned next that my "silencing" was even more thorough than I had thought. I was not only forbidden to talk with the press, I was not even to teach in my own Mosque Seven.

Next, an announcement was made throughout the Nation of Islam that I would be reinstated within ninety days, *"if he submits."*

This made me suspicious—for the first time. I had completely submitted. But, deliberately, Muslims were being given the impression that I had rebelled.

I hadn't hustled in the streets for years for nothing. I knew when I was being set up.

Three days later, the first word came to me that a Mosque Seven official who had been one of my most immediate assistants was telling certain Mosque Seven brothers: "If you knew what the Minister did, you'd go out and kill him yourself."

And then I knew. As any official in the Nation of Islam would instantly have known, any death-talk for me could have been approved of—if not actually initiated—by only one man.

My head felt like it was bleeding inside. I felt like my brain was damaged. I went to see Dr. Leona A. Turner, who has been my family doctor for years, who practices in East Elmhurst, Long Island. I asked her to give me a brain examination.

She did examine me. She said I was under great strain—and I needed rest.

Cassius Clay and I are not together today. But always I must be grateful to him that at just this time, when he was in Miami training to fight Sonny Liston, Cassius invited me, Betty, and the children to come there as his guests—as a sixth wedding anniversary present to Betty and me.

I had met Cassius Clay in Detroit in 1962. He and his brother Rudolph came into the Student's Luncheonette next door to the Detroit Mosque where Elijah Muhammad was about to speak at a big rally. Every Muslim present was impressed by the bearing and the obvious genuineness of the striking, handsome pair of prizefighter brothers. Cassius came up and pumped my hand, introducing himself as he later presented himself to the world, "I'm Cassius Clay." He acted as if I was supposed to know who he was. So I acted as though I did. Up to that moment, though, I had never even heard of him. Ours were two entirely different worlds. In fact, Elijah Muhammad instructed us Muslims against all forms of sports.

As Elijah Muhammad spoke, the two Clay brothers practically led the applause, further impressing everyone with their sincerity—since a Muslim rally was about the world's last place to seek fight fans.

Thereafter, now and then I heard how Cassius showed up in Muslim mosques and restaurants in various cities. And if I happened to be speaking anywhere within reasonable distance of wherever Cassius was, he would be present. I liked him. Some contagious quality about him made him one of the very few people I ever invited to my home. Betty liked him. Our children were crazy about him. Cassius was simply a likeable, friendly, clean-cut, down-to-earth youngster. I noticed

how alert he was even in little details. I suspected that there
was a plan in his public clowning. I suspected, and he confirmed to me, that he was doing everything possible to con and
to "psyche" Sonny Liston into coming into the ring angry,
poorly trained, and overconfident, expecting another of his
vaunted one-round knockouts. Not only was Cassius receptive
to advice, he solicited it. Primarily, I impressed upon him to
what a great extent a public figure's success depends upon
how alert and knowledgeable he is to the true natures and
to the true motives of all of the people who flock around him.
I warned him about the "foxes," his expression for the aggressive, cute young females who flocked after him; I told Cassius
that instead of "foxes," they really were wolves.

This was Betty's first vacation since we had married. And
our three girls romped and played with the heavyweight con-
tender.

I don't know what I might have done if I had stayed in
New York during that crucial time—besieged by insistently
ringing telephones, and by the press, and by all of the other
people so anxious to gloat, to speculate and to "commiserate."

I was in a state of emotional shock. I was like someone who
for twelve years had had an inseparable, beautiful marriage
—and then suddenly one morning at breakfast the marriage
partner had thrust across the table some divorce papers.

I felt as though something in *nature* had failed, like the sun,
or the stars. It was that incredible a phenomenon to me—
something too stupendous to conceive. I am not sparing myself. Around Cassius Clay's fight camp, around the Hampton
House Motel where my family was staying, I talked with my
own wife, and with other people, and actually I was only
mouthing words that really meant nothing to me. Whatever I
was saying at any time was being handled by a small corner
of my mind. The rest of my mind was filled with a parade of
a thousand and one different scenes from the past twelve
years . . . scenes in the Muslim mosques . . . scenes with Mr.
Muhammad . . . scenes with Mr. Muhammad's family . . .
scenes with Muslims, individually, as my audiences, and at
our social gatherings . . . and scenes with the white man in
audiences, and the press.

I walked, I talked, I functioned. At the Cassius Clay fight
camp, I told the various sportswriters repeatedly what I gradually had come to know within myself was a lie—that I would
be reinstated within ninety days. But I could not yet let

myself psychologically face what I knew: that already the Nation of Islam and I were physically divorced. Do you understand what I mean? A judge's signature on a piece of paper can grant to a couple a physical divorce—but for either of them, or maybe for both of them, if they have been a very close marriage team, to actually become *psychologically* divorced from each other might take years.

But in the physical divorce, I could not evade the obvious strategy and plotting coming out of Chicago to eliminate me from the Nation of Islam . . . if not from this world. And I felt that I perceived the anatomy of the plotting.

Any Muslim would have known that my "chickens coming home to roost" statement had been only an excuse to put into action the plan for getting me out. And step one had been already taken: the Muslims were given the impression that I had rebelled against Mr. Muhammad. I could now anticipate step two: I would remain "suspended" (and later I would be "isolated") indefinitely. Step three would be either to provoke some Muslim ignorant of the truth to take it upon himself to kill me as a "religious duty"—or to "isolate" me so that I would gradually disappear from the public scene.

The only person who knew was my wife. I never would have dreamed that I would ever depend so much upon any woman for strength as I now leaned upon Betty. There was no exchange between us; Betty said nothing, being the caliber of wife that she is, with the depth of understanding that she has—but I could feel the envelopment of her comfort. I knew that she was as faithful a servant of Allah as I was, and I knew that whatever happened, she was with me.

The death talk was not my fear. Every second of my twelve years with Mr. Muhammad, I had been ready to lay down my life for him. The thing to me worse than death was the betrayal. I could conceive death. I couldn't conceive betrayal—not of the loyalty which I had given to the Nation of Islam, and to Mr. Muhammad. During the previous twelve years, if Mr. Muhammad had committed any civil crime punishable by death, I would have said and tried to prove that I did it—to save him—and I would have gone to the electric chair, as Mr. Muhammad's servant.

There as Cassius Clay's guest in Miami, I tried desperately to push my mind off my troubles and onto the Nation's troubles. I still struggled to persuade myself that Mr. Muhammad had been fulfilling prophecy. Because I actually had believed that if Mr. Muhammad was not God, then he surely stood next to God.

What began to break my faith was that, try as I might, I couldn't hide, I couldn't evade, that Mr. Muhammad, instead of facing what he had done before his followers, as a human weakness or as fulfillment of prophecy—which I sincerely believe that Muslims would have understood, or at least they would have accepted—Mr. Muhammad had, instead, been willing to hide, to cover up what he had done.

That was my major blow.

That was how I first began to realize that I had believed in Mr. Muhammad more than he believed in himself.

And that was how, after twelve years of never thinking for as much as five minutes about myself, I became able finally to muster the nerve, and the strength, to start facing the facts, to think for myself.

Briefly I left Florida to return Betty and the children to our Long Island home. I learned that the Chicago Muslim officials were further displeased with me because of the newspaper reports of me in the Cassius Clay camp. They felt that Cassius hadn't a prayer of a chance to win. They felt the Nation would be embarrassed through my linking the Muslim image with him. (I don't know if the champion today cares to remember that most newspapers in America were represented at the pre-fight camp—except *Muhammad Speaks*. Even though Cassius was a Muslim brother, the Muslim newspaper didn't consider his fight worth covering.)

I flew back to Miami feeling that it was Allah's intent for me to help Cassius prove Islam's superiority before the world —through proving that mind can win over brawn. I don't have to remind you how people everywhere scoffed at Cassius Clay's chances of beating Liston.

This time, I brought from New York with me some photographs of Floyd Patterson and Sonny Liston in their fight camps, with white priests as their "spiritual advisors." Cassius Clay, being a Muslim, didn't need to be told how white Christianity had dealt with the American black man. "This fight is the *truth*," I told Cassius. "It's the Cross and the Crescent fighting in a prize ring—for the first time. It's a modern Crusades—a Christian and a Muslim facing each other with television to beam it off Telstar for the whole world to see what happens!" I told Cassius, "Do you think Allah has brought about all this intending for you to leave the ring as anything but the champion?" (You may remember that at the weighing-in, Cassius was yelling such things as "It is prophesied for me to be successful! I cannot be beaten!")

Sonny Liston's handlers and advisors had him fighting harder to "integrate" than he was training to meet Cassius. Liston finally had managed to rent a big, fine house over in a rich, wall-to-wall white section. To give you an idea, the owner of the neighboring house was the New York Yankees baseball club owner, Dan Topping. In the early evenings, when Cassius and I would sometimes walk where the black people lived, those Negroes' mouths would hang open in surprise that he was among them instead of whites as most black champions preferred. Again and again, Cassius startled those Negroes, telling them, "You're my own kind. I get my strength from being around my own black people."

What Sonny Liston was about to meet, in fact, was one of the most awesome frights that ever can confront any person —one who worships Allah, and who is completely without fear.

Among over eight thousand other seat holders in Miami's big Convention Hall, I received Seat Number Seven. Seven has always been my favorite number. It has followed me throughout my life. I took this to be Allah's message confirming to me that Cassius Clay was going to win. Along with Cassius, I really was more worried about how his brother Rudolph was going to do, fighting his first pro fight in the preliminaries.

While Rudolph was winning a four-round decision over a Florida Negro named "Chip" Johnson, Cassius stood at the rear of the auditorium watching calmly, dressed in a black tuxedo. After all of his months of antics, after the weighing-in act that Cassius had put on, this calmness should have tipped off some of the sportswriters who were predicting Clay's slaughter.

Then Cassius disappeared, dressing to meet Liston. As we had agreed, I joined him in a silent prayer for Allah's blessings. Finally, he and Liston were in their corners in the ring. I folded my arms and tried to appear the coolest man in the place, because a television camera can show you looking like a fool yelling at a prizefight.

Except for whatever chemical it was that got into Cassius' eyes and blinded him temporarily in the fourth and fifth rounds, the fight went according to his plan. He evaded Liston's

powerful punches. The third round automatically began the
tiring of the aging Liston, who was overconfidently trained
to go only two rounds. Then, desperate, Liston lost. The secret
of one of fight history's greatest upsets was that months before
that night, Clay had out-thought Liston.

There probably never has been as quiet a new-champion
party. The boyish king of the ring came over to my motel.
He ate ice cream, drank milk, talked with football star
Jimmy Brown and other friends, and some reporters. Sleepy,
Cassius took a quick nap on my bed, then he went back home.

We had breakfast together the next morning, just before
the press conference when Cassius calmly made the announcement which burst into international headlines that he was a
"Black Muslim."

But let me tell you something about that. Cassius never
announced himself a member of any "Black Muslims." The
press reporters made that out of what he told them, which
was this: "I believe in the religion of Islam, which means I
believe there is no God but Allah, and Muhammad is His
Apostle. This is the same religion that is believed in by over
seven hundred million dark-skinned peoples throughout Africa
and Asia."

Nothing in all of the furor which followed was more
ridiculous than Floyd Patterson announcing that as a Catholic,
he wanted to fight Cassius Clay—to save the heavyweight
crown from being held by a Muslim. It was such a sad case
of a brainwashed black Christian ready to do battle for the
white man—who wants no part of him. Not three weeks later,
the newspapers reported that in Yonkers, New York, Patterson was offering to sell his $140,000 house for a $20,000 loss.
He had "integrated" into a neighborhood of whites who had
made his life miserable. None were friendly. Their children
called his children "niggers." One neighbor trained his dog
to deface Patterson's property. Another erected a fence to
hide the Negroes from sight. "I tried, it just didn't work,"
Patterson told the press.

The first direct order for my death was issued through a
Mosque Seven official who previously had been a close assistant. Another previously close assistant of mine was assigned
to do the job. He was a brother with a knowledge of demoli-
tion; he was asked to wire my car to explode when I turned
the ignition key. But this brother, it happened, had seen too

much of my total loyalty to the Nation to carry out his order. Instead, he came to me. I thanked him for my life. I told him what was really going on in Chicago. He was stunned almost beyond belief.

This brother was close to others in the Mosque Seven circle who might subsequently be called upon to eliminate me. He said he would take it upon himself to enlighten each of them enough so that they wouldn't allow themselves to be used.

This first direct death-order was how, finally, I began to arrive at my psychological divorce from the Nation of Islam.

I began to see, wherever I went—on the streets, in business places, on elevators, sidewalks, in passing cars—the faces of Muslims whom I knew, and I knew that any of them might be waiting the opportunity to try and put a bullet into me.

I was racking my brain. What was I going to do? My life was inseparably committed to the American black man's struggle. I was generally regarded as a "leader." For years, I had attacked so many so-called "black leaders" for their shortcomings. Now, I had to honestly ask myself what I could offer, how I was genuinely qualified to help the black people win their struggle for human rights. I had enough experience to know that in order to be a good organizer of anything which you expect to succeed—including yourself—you must almost mathematically analyze cold facts.

I had, as one asset, I knew, an international image. No amount of money could have bought that. I knew that if I said something newsworthy, people would read or hear of it, maybe even around the world, depending upon what it was. More immediately, in New York City, where I would naturally base any operation, I had a large, direct personal following of non-Muslims. This had been building up steadily ever since I had led Muslims in the dramatic protest to the police when our brother Hinton was beaten up. Hundreds of Harlem Negroes had seen, and hundreds of thousands of them had later heard how we had shown that almost anything could be accomplished by black men who would face the white man without fear. All of Harlem had seen how from then on, the police gave Muslims respect. (This was during the time that the Deputy Chief Inspector at the 28th Precinct had said of me, "No one man should have that much power.")

Over the ensuing years, I'd had various kinds of evidence that a high percentage of New York City's black people responded to what I said, including a great many who would not publicly say so. For instance, time and again when I spoke at street rallies, I would draw ten and twelve times as many people as most other so-called "Negro leaders." I knew that in any society, a true leader is one who earns and deserves the following he enjoys. True followers are bestowed by themselves, out of their own volition and emotions. I knew that the great lack of most of the big-named "Negro leaders" was their lack of any true rapport with the ghetto Negroes. How could they have rapport when they spent most of their time "integrating" with white people? I knew that the ghetto people knew that I never left the ghetto in spirit, and I never left it physically any more than I had to. I had a ghetto instinct; for instance, I could feel if tension was beyond normal in a ghetto audience. And I could speak and understand the ghetto's language. There was an example of this that always flew to my mind every time I heard some of the "big name" Negro "leaders" declaring they "spoke for" the ghetto black people.

After a Harlem street rally, one of these downtown "leaders" and I were talking when we were approached by a Harlem hustler. To my knowledge I'd never seen this hustler before; he said to me, approximately: "Hey, baby! I dig you holding this all-originals scene at the track . . . I'm going to lay a vine under the Jew's balls for a dime—got to give you a play . . . Got the shorts out here trying to scuffle up on some bread . . . Well, my man, I'll get on, got to go peck a little, and cop me some z's—" And the hustler went on up Seventh Avenue.

I would never have given it another thought, except that this downtown "leader" was standing, staring after that hustler, looking as if he'd just heard Sanskrit. He asked me what had been said, and I told him. The hustler had said he was aware that the Muslims were holding an all-black bazaar at Rockland Palace, which is primarily a dancehall. The hustler intended to pawn a suit for ten dollars to attend and patronize the bazaar. He had very little money but he was trying hard to make some. He was going to eat, then he would get some sleep.

The point I am making is that, as a "leader," I could talk over the ABC, CBS, or NBC microphones, at Harvard or at Tuskegee; I could talk with the so-called "middle class" Negro and with the ghetto blacks (whom all the other leaders just talked *about*). And because I had been a hustler, I knew better than all whites knew, and better than nearly all of the black "leaders" knew, that actually the most dangerous black man in America was the ghetto hustler.

Why do I say this? The hustler, out there in the ghetto jungles, has less respect for the white power structure than any other Negro in North America. The ghetto hustler is internally restrained by nothing. He has no religion, no concept of morality, no civic responsibility, no fear—nothing. To survive, he is out there constantly preying upon others, probing for any human weakness like a ferret. The ghetto hustler is forever frustrated, restless, and anxious for some "action." Whatever he undertakes, he commits himself to it fully, absolutely.

What makes the ghetto hustler yet more dangerous is his "glamor" image to the school-dropout youth in the ghetto. These ghetto teen-agers see the hell caught by their parents struggling to get somewhere, or see that they have given up struggling in the prejudiced, intolerant white man's world. The ghetto teen-agers make up their own minds they would rather be like the hustlers whom they see dressed "sharp" and flashing money and displaying no respect for anybody or anything. So the ghetto youth become attracted to the hustler worlds of dope, thievery, prostitution, and general crime and immorality.

It scared me the first time I really saw the danger of these ghetto teen-agers if they are ever sparked to violence. One sweltering summer afternoon, I attended a Harlem street rally which contained a lot of these teen-agers in the crowd. I had been invited by some "responsible" Negro leaders who normally never spoke to me; I knew they had just used my name to help them draw a crowd. The more I thought about it on the way there, the hotter I got. And when I got on the stand, I just told that crowd in the street that I wasn't really wanted up there, that my name had been used—and I walked off the speaker's stand.

Well, what did I want to do that for? Why, those young, teen-age Negroes got upset, and started milling around and yelling, upsetting the older Negroes in the crowd. The first thing you know traffic was blocked in four directions by a crowd whose mood quickly grew so ugly that I really got apprehensive. I got up on top of a car and began waving my arms and yelling at them to quiet down. They did quiet, and then I asked them to disperse—and they did.

This was when it began being said that I was America's only Negro who "could stop a race riot—or start one." I don't know if I could do either one. But I know one thing: it had taught me in a very few minutes to have a whole lot of respect for the human combustion that is packed among the hustlers and their young admirers who live in the ghettoes where the Northern white man has sealed-off the Negro— away from whites—for a hundred years.

The "long hot summer" of 1964 in Harlem, in Rochester, and in other cities, has given an idea of what could happen— and that's all, only an idea. For all of those riots were kept contained within where the Negroes lived. You let any of these bitter, seething ghettoes all over America receive the right igniting incident, and become really inflamed, and explode, and burst out of their boundaries into where whites live! In New York City, you let enraged blacks pour out of Harlem across Central Park and fan down the tunnels of Madison and Fifth and Lexington and Park Avenues. Or, take Chicago's South Side, an older, even worse slum—you let those Negroes swarm downtown. You let Washington, D.C.'s festering blacks head down Pennsylvania Avenue. Detroit has already seen a peaceful massing of more than a *hundred thousand* blacks—think about that. You name the city. Black social dynamite is in Cleveland, Philadelphia, San Francisco, Los Angeles . . . the black man's anger is there, fermenting.

I've strayed off onto some of the incidents and situations which have taught me to respect the danger in the ghettoes. I had been trying to explain how I honestly evaluated my own qualifications to be worthy of presenting myself as an independent "leader" among black men.

In the end, I reasoned that the decision already had been made for me. The ghetto masses already had entrusted me with an image of leadership among them. I knew the ghetto instinctively extends that trust only to one who had demonstrated that he would never sell them out to the white man. I not only had no such intention—to sell out was not even in my nature.

I felt a challenge to plan, and build, an organization that could help to cure the black man in North America of the sickness which has kept him under the white man's heel.

The black man in North America was mentally sick in his cooperative, sheeplike acceptance of the white man's culture.

The black man in North America was spiritually sick because for centuries he had accepted the white man's Christianity—which asked the black so-called Christian to expect no true Brotherhood of Man, but to endure the cruelties of the white so-called Christians. Christianity had made black men fuzzy, nebulous, confused in their thinking. It had taught the black man to think if he had no shoes, and was hungry, "we gonna get shoes and milk and honey and fish fries in Heaven."

The black man in North America was economically sick and that was evident in one simple fact: as a consumer, he got less than his share, and as a producer gave *least*. The black American today shows us the perfect parasite image—the black tick under the delusion that he is progressing because he rides on the udder of the fat, three-stomached cow that is white America. For instance, annually, the black man spends over $3 billion for automobiles, but America contains hardly any franchised black automobile dealers. For instance, forty per cent of the expensive imported Scotch whisky consumed in America goes down the throats of the status-sick black man; but the only black-owned distilleries are in bathtubs, or in the woods somewhere. Or for instance—a scandalous shame—in New York City, with over a million Negroes, there aren't twenty black-owned businesses employing over ten people. It's because black men don't own and control their own community's retail establishments that they can't stabilize their own community.

The black man in North America was sickest of all politically. He let the white man divide him into such foolishness as considering himself a black "Democrat," a black "Republican," a black "Conservative," or a black "Liberal" . . . when a ten-million black vote bloc could be the deciding balance of power in American politics, because the white man's vote is almost always evenly divided. The polls are one place where every black man could fight the black man's cause with dignity, and with the power and the tools that the white man understands, and respects, and fears, and cooperates with. Listen, let me tell you something! If a black bloc committee told Washington's worst "nigger-hater," "We represent ten million votes," why, that "nigger-hater" would leap up: 'Well, how *are* you? Come on *in* here!" Why, if the Mississippi black man voted in a bloc, Eastland would pretend to be more liberal than Jacob Javits—or Eastland would not survive in his office. Why else is it that racist politicians fight to keep black men from the polls?

Whenever any group can vote in a bloc, and decide the outcome of elections, and it *fails* to do this, then that group is politically sick. Immigrants once made Tammany Hall the most powerful single force in American politics. In 1880, New York City's first Irish Catholic Mayor was elected and by 1960 America had its first Irish Catholic President. America's black man, voting as a bloc, could wield an even more powerful force.

U.S. politics is ruled by special-interest blocs and lobbies. What group has a more urgent special interest, what group needs a bloc, a lobby, more than the black man? Labor owns one of Washington's largest non-government buildings—situated where they can literally watch the White House—and no political move is made that doesn't involve how Labor feels about it. A lobby got Big Oil its depletion allowance. The farmer, through his lobby, is the most government-subsidized special-interest group in America today, because a million farmers vote, not as Democrats, or Republicans, liberals, conservatives, but as farmers.

Doctors have the best lobby in Washington. Their special-interest influence successfully fights the Medicare program that's wanted, and needed, by millions of other people. Why, there's a Beet Growers' Lobby! A Wheat Lobby! A Cattle Lobby! A China Lobby! Little countries no one ever heard of have their Washington lobbies, representing their special interests.

The government has departments to deal with the special-interest groups that make themselves heard and felt. A Department of Agriculture cares for the farmers' needs. There is a Department of Health, Education and Welfare. There is a Department of the Interior—in which the Indians are included. Is the farmer, the doctor, the Indian, the greatest problem in America today? No—it is the black man! There ought to be a Pentagon-sized Washington department dealing with every segment of the black man's problems.

Twenty-two million black men! They have given America four hundred years of toil; they have bled and died in every battle since the Revolution; they were in America before the Pilgrims, and long before the mass immigrations—and they are still today at the bottom of everything!

Why, twenty-two million black people should tomorrow give

a dollar apiece to build a skyscraper lobby building in Washington, D.C. Every morning, every legislator should receive a communication about what the black man in America expects and wants and needs. The demanding voice of the black lobby should be in the ears of every legislator who votes on any issue.

The cornerstones of this country's operation are economic and political strength and power. The black man doesn't have the economic strength—and it will take time for him to build it. But right now the American black man has the political strength and power to change his destiny overnight.

It was a big order—the organization I was creating in my mind, one which would help to challenge the American black man to gain his human rights, and to cure his mental, spiritual, economic, and political sicknesses. But if you ever intend to do anything worthwhile, you have to start with a worthwhile plan.

Substantially, as I saw it, the organization I hoped to build would differ from the Nation of Islam in that it would embrace all faiths of black men, and it would carry into practice what the Nation of Islam had only preached.

Rumors were swirling, particularly in East Coast cities—what was I going to do? Well, the first thing I was going to have to do was to attract far more willing heads and hands than my own. Each day, more militant, action brothers who had been with me in Mosque Seven announced their break from the Nation of Islam to come with me. And each day, I learned, in one or another way, of more support from non-Muslim Negroes, including a surprising lot of the "middle" and "upper class" black bourgeoisie, who were sick of the status-symbol charade. There was a growing clamor: "When are you going to call a meeting, to get organized?"

To hold a first meeting, I arranged to rent the Carver Ballroom of the Hotel Theresa, which is at the corner of 125th Street and Seventh Avenue, which might be called one of Harlem's fusebox locations.

The *Amsterdam News* reported the planned meeting and many readers inferred that we were establishing our beginning mosque in the Theresa. Telegrams and letters and telephone calls came to the hotel for me, from across the country. Their general tone was that this was a move that people had waited for. People I'd never heard of expressed confidence in me in moving ways. Numerous people said that the Nation of Islam's stringent moral restrictions had repelled them—and they wanted to join me.

A doctor who owned a small hospital telephoned long-distance to join. Many others sent contributions—even before our policies had been publicly stated. Muslims wrote from other cities that they would join me, their remarks being generally along the lines that "Islam is too inactive" . . . "The Nation is moving too slow."

Astonishing numbers of white people called, and wrote, offering contributions, or asking could *they* join? The answer was, no, they couldn't join; our membership was all black— but if their consciences dictated, they could financially help our constructive approach to America's race problems.

Speaking-engagement requests came in—twenty-two of them in one particular Monday morning's mail. It was startling to me that an unusual number of the requests came from groups of white Christian ministers.

I called a press conference. The microphones stuck up before me. The flashbulbs popped. The reporters, men and women, white and black, representing media that reached around the world, sat looking at me with their pencils and open notebooks.

I made the announcement: "I am going to organize and head a new mosque in New York City known as the Muslim Mosque, Inc. This will give us a religious base, and the spiritual force necessary to rid our people of the vices that destroy the moral fiber of our community.

"Muslim Mosque, Inc. will have its temporary headquarters in the Hotel Theresa in Harlem. It will be the working base for an action program designed to eliminate the political oppression, the economic exploitation, and the social degradation suffered daily by twenty-two million Afro-Americans."

Then the reporters began firing questions at me.

It was not all as simple as it may sound. I went few places without constant awareness that any number of my former brothers felt they would make heroes of themselves in the Nation of Islam if they killed me. I knew how Elijah Muhammad's followers thought; I had taught so many of them to think. I knew that no one would kill you quicker than a Muslim if he felt that's what Allah wanted him to do.

There was one further major preparation that I knew I needed. I'd had it in my mind for a long time—as a servant of Allah. But it would require money that I didn't have.

I took a plane to Boston. I was turning again to my sister Ella. Though at times I'd made Ella angry at me, beneath it all, since I had first come to her as a teen-aged hick from Michigan, Ella had never once really wavered from my corner.

"Ella," I said, "I want to make the pilgrimage to Mecca."

Ella said, "How much do you need?"

CHAPTER SEVENTEEN

MECCA

The pilgrimage to Mecca, known as Hajj, is a religious obligation that every orthodox Muslim fulfills, if humanly able, at least once in his or her lifetime.

The Holy Quran says it, "Pilgrimage to the Ka'ba is a duty men owe to God; those who are able, make the journey."

Allah said: "And proclaim the pilgrimage among men; they will come to you on foot and upon each lean camel, they will come from every deep ravine."

At one or another college or university, usually in the informal gatherings after I had spoken, perhaps a dozen generally white-complexioned people would come up to me, identifying themselves as Arabian, Middle Eastern or North African Muslims who happened to be visiting, studying, or living in the United States. They had said to me that, my white-indicting statements notwithstanding, they felt that I was sincere in considering myself a Muslim—and they felt if I was exposed to what they always called "true Islam," I would "understand it, and embrace it." Automatically, as a follower of Elijah Muhammad, I had bridled whenever this was said.

But in the privacy of my own thoughts after several of these experiences, I did question myself: if one was sincere in professing a religion, why should he balk at broadening his knowledge of that religion?

Once in a conversation I broached this with Wallace Muhammad, Elijah Muhammad's son. He said that yes, certainly, a Muslim should seek to learn all that he could about Islam. I had always had a high opinion of Wallace Muhammad's opinion.

Those orthodox Muslims whom I had met, one after another, had urged me to meet and talk with a Dr. Mahmoud

Youssef Shawarbi. He was described to me as an eminent, learned Muslim, a University of Cairo graduate, a University of London Ph.D., a lecturer on Islam, a United Nations advisor and the author of many books. He was a full professor of the University of Cairo, on leave from there to be in New York as the Director of the Federation of Islamic Associations in the United States and Canada. Several times, driving in that part of town, I had resisted the impulse to drop in at the F.I.A. building, a brownstone at 1 Riverside Drive. Then one day Dr. Shawarbi and I were introduced by a newspaperman.

He was cordial. He said he had followed me in the press; I said I had been told of him, and we talked for fifteen or twenty minutes. We both had to leave to make appointments we had, when he dropped on me something whose logic never would get out of my head. He said, "No man has believed perfectly until he wishes for his brother what he wishes for himself."

Then, there was my sister Ella herself. I couldn't get over what she had done. I've said before, this is a *strong* big, black, Georgia-born woman. Her domineering ways had gotten her put out of the Nation of Islam's Boston Mosque Eleven; they took her back, then she left on her own. Ella had started studying under Boston orthodox Muslims, then she founded a school where Arabic was taught! *She* couldn't speak it, she hired teachers who did. That's Ella! She deals in real estate, and *she* was saving up to make the pilgrimage. Nearly all night, we talked in her living room. She told me there was no question about it; it was more important that I go. I thought about Ella the whole flight back to New York. A *strong* woman. She had broken the spirits of three husbands, more driving and dynamic than all of them combined. She had played a very significant role in my life. No other woman ever was strong enough to point me in directions; I pointed women in directions. I had brought Ella into Islam, and now she was financing me to Mecca.

Allah always gives you signs, when you are with Him, that He is with you.

When I applied for a visa to Mecca at the Saudi Arabian Consulate, the Saudi Ambassador told me that no Muslim converted in America could have a visa for the Hajj pilgrimage without the signed approval of Dr. Mahmoud Shawarbi. But that was only the beginning of the sign from Allah.

When I telephoned Dr. Shawarbi, he registered astonishment. "I was just going to get in touch with you," he said, "by all means come right over."

When I got to his office, Dr. Shawarbi handed me the signed letter approving me to make the Hajj in Mecca, and then a book. It was *The Eternal Message of Muhammad* by Abd ar-Rahman Azzam.

The author had just sent the copy of the book to be given to me, Dr. Shawarbi said, and he explained that this author was an Egyptian-born Saudi citizen, an international statesman, and one of the closest advisors of Prince Faisal, the ruler of Arabia. "He has followed you in the press very closely." It was hard for me to believe.

Dr. Shawarbi gave me the telephone number of his son, Muhammad Shawarbi, a student in Cairo, and also the number of the author's son, Omar Azzam, who lived in Jedda, "your last stop before Mecca. Call them both, by all means."

I left New York quietly (little realizing that I was going to return noisily). Few people were told I was leaving at all. I didn't want some State Department or other roadblocks put in my path at the last minute. Only my wife, Betty, and my three girls and a few close associates came with me to Kennedy International Airport. When the Lufthansa Airlines jet had taken off, my two seatrow mates and I introduced ourselves. Another sign! Both were Muslims, one was bound for Cairo, as I was, and the other was bound for Jedda, where I would be in a few days.

All the way to Frankfurt, Germany, my seatmates and I talked, or I read the book I had been given. When we landed in Frankfurt, the brother bound for Jedda said his warm good-bye to me and the Cairo-bound brother. We had a few hours layover before we would take another plane to Cairo. We decided to go sightseeing in Frankfurt.

In the men's room there at the airport, I met the first American abroad who recognized me, a white student from Rhode Island. He kept eyeing me, then he came over. "Are you X?" I laughed and said I was, I hadn't ever heard it that way. He exclaimed, "You can't be! Boy, I know no one will believe me when I tell them this!" He was attending school, he said, in France.

The brother Muslim and I both were struck by the cordial hospitality of the people in Frankfurt. We went into a lot of shops and stores, looking more than intending to buy anything. We'd walk in, any store, every store, and it would be Hello! People who never saw you before, and knew you were strangers. And the same cordiality when we left, without buying anything. In America, you walk in a store and spend a hundred dollars, and leave, and you're still a stranger. Both you and the clerks act as though you're doing each other a favor. Europeans act more human, or humane, whichever the right word is. My brother Muslim, who could speak enough German to get by, would explain that we were Muslims, and I saw something I had already experienced when I was looked upon as a Muslim and not as a Negro, right in America. People seeing you as a Muslim saw you as a human being and they had a different look, different talk, everything. In one Frankfurt store—a little shop, actually—the storekeeper leaned over his counter to us and waved his hand, indicating the German people passing by: "This way one day, that way another day—" My Muslim brother explained to me that what he meant was that the Germans would rise again.

Back at the Frankfurt airport, we took a United Arab Airlines plane on to Cairo. Throngs of people, obviously Muslims from everywhere, bound on the pilgrimage, were hugging and embracing. They were of all complexions, the whole atmosphere was of warmth and friendliness. The feeling hit me that there really wasn't any color problem here. The effect was as though I had just stepped out of a prison.

I had told my brother Muslim friend that I wanted to be a tourist in Cairo for a couple of days before continuing to Jedda. He gave me his number and asked me to call him, as he wanted to put me with a party of his friends, who could speak English, and would be going on the pilgrimage, and would be happy to look out for me.

So I spent two happy days sightseeing in Cairo. I was impressed by the modern schools, housing developments for the masses, and the highways and the industrialization that I saw. I had read and heard that President Nasser's administration had built up one of the most highly industrialized countries on the African continent. I believe what most surprised me was that in Cairo, automobiles were being manufactured, and also buses.

I had a good visit with Dr. Shawarbi's son, Muhammad Shawarbi, a nineteen-year-old, who was studying economics and political science at Cairo University. He told me that his father's dream was to build a University of Islam in the United States.

The friendly people I met were astounded when they learned I was a Muslim—from America! They included an Egyptian scientist and his wife, also on their way to Mecca for the Hajj, who insisted I go with them to dinner in a restaurant in Heliopolis, a suburb of Cairo. They were an extremely well-informed and intelligent couple. Egypt's rising industrialization was one of the reasons why the Western powers were so anti-Egypt, it was showing other African countries what they should do, the scientist said. His wife asked me, "Why are people in the world starving when America has so much surplus food? What do they do, dump it in the ocean?" I told her, "Yes, but they put some of it in the holds of surplus ships, and in subsidized granaries and refrigerated space and let it stay there, with a small army of caretakers, until it's unfit to eat. Then another army of disposal people get rid of it to make space for the next surplus batch." She looked at me in something like disbelief. Probably she thought I was kidding. But the American taxpayer knows it's the truth. I didn't go on to tell her that right in the United States, there are hungry people.

I telephoned my Muslim friend, as he had asked, and the Hajj party of his friends was waiting for me. I made it eight of us, and they included a judge and an official of the Ministry of Education. They spoke English beautifully, and accepted me like a brother. I considered it another of Allah's signs, that wherever I turned, someone was there to help me, to guide me.

The literal meaning of Hajj in Arabic is to set out toward a definite objective. In Islamic law, it means to set out for Ka'ba, the Sacred House, and to fulfill the pilgrimage rites. The Cairo airport was where scores of Hajj groups were becoming *Muhrim*, pilgrims, upon entering the state of Ihram, the assumption of a spiritual and physical state of consecration. Upon advice, I arranged to leave in Cairo all of my luggage and four cameras, one a movie camera. I had bought in Cairo a small valise, just big enough to carry one suit, shirt, a pair of underwear sets and a pair of shoes into Arabia. Driving to the airport with our Hajj group, I began to get nervous, knowing that from there in, it was going to be watching others who knew what they were doing, and trying to do what they did.

Entering the state of Ihram, we took off our clothes and put on two white towels. One, the *Izar*, was folded around the loins. The other, the *Rida*, was thrown over the neck and shoulders, leaving the right shouder and arm bare. A pair of simple sandals, the *na'l*, left the ankle-bones bare. Over the *Izar* waist-wrapper, a money belt was worn, and a bag, something like a woman's big handbag, with a long strap, was for carrying the passport and other valuable papers, such as the letter I had from Dr. Shawarbi.

Every one of the thousands at the airport, about to leave for Jedda, was dressed this way. You could be a king or a peasant and no one would know. Some powerful personages, who were discreetly pointed out to me, had on the same thing I had on. Once thus dressed, we all had begun intermittently calling out *"Labbayka! Labbayka!"* (Here I come, O Lord!) The airport sounded with the din of *Muhrim* expressing their intention to perform the journey of the Hajj.

Planeloads of pilgrims were taking off every few minutes, but the airport was jammed with more, and their friends and relatives waiting to see them off. Those not going were asking others to pray for them at Mecca. We were on our plane, in the air, when I learned for the first time that with the crush, there was not supposed to have been space for me, but strings had been pulled, and someone had been put off because they didn't want to disappoint an American Muslim. I felt mingled emotions of regret that I had inconvenienced and discomfited whoever was bumped off the plane for me, and, with that, an utter humility and gratefulness that I had been paid such an honor and respect.

Packed in the plane were white, black, brown, red, and yellow people, blue eyes and blond hair, and my kinky red hair—all together, brothers! All honoring the same God Allah, all in turn giving equal honor to each other.

From some in our group, the word was spreading from seat to seat that I was a Muslim from America. Faces turned, smiling toward me in greeting. A box lunch was passed out and as we ate that, the word that a Muslim from America was aboard got up into the cockpit.

The captain of the plane came back to meet me. He was an Egyptian, his complexion was darker than mine; he could have walked in Harlem and no one would have given him a second glance. He was delighted to meet an American Muslim. When he invited me to visit the cockpit, I jumped at the chance.

The co-pilot was darker than he was. I can't tell you the feeling it gave me. I had never seen a black man flying a jet. That instrument panel: no one ever could know what all of those dials meant! Both of the pilots were smiling at me, treating me with the same honor and respect I had received ever since I left America. I stood there looking through the glass at the sky ahead of us. In America, I had ridden in more planes than probably any other Negro, and I never had been invited up into the cockpit. And there I was, with two Muslim seatmates, one from Egypt, the other from Arabia, all of us bound for Mecca, with me up in the pilots' cabin. Brother, I *knew* Allah was with me.

I got back to my seat. All of the way, about an hour's flight, we pilgrims were loudly crying out, *"Labbayka! Labbayka!"* The plane landed at Jedda. It's a seaport town on the Red Sea, the arrival or disembarkation point for all pilgrims who come to Arabia to go to Mecca. Mecca is about forty miles to the east, inland.

The Jedda airport seemed even more crowded than Cairo's had been. Our party became another shuffling unit in the shifting mass with every race on earth represented. Each party was making its way toward the long line waiting to go through Customs. Before reaching Customs, each Hajj party was assigned a *Mutawaf,* who would be responsible for transferring that party from Jedda to Mecca. Some pilgrims cried *"Labbayka!"* Others, sometimes large groups, were chanting in unison a prayer that I will translate, "I submit to no one but Thee, O Allah, I submit to no one but Thee. I submit to Thee because Thou hast no partner. All praise and blessings come from Thee, and Thou art alone in Thy kingdom." The essence of the prayer is the Oneness of God.

Only officials were not wearing the *Ihram* garb, or the white skull caps, long, white, nightshirt-looking gown and the little slippers of the *Mutawaf,* those who guided each pilgrim party, and their helpers. In Arabic, an *mmmm* sound before a verb makes a verbal noun, so *"Mutawaf"* meant "the one who guides" the pilgrims on the *"Tawaf,"* which is the circumambulation of the Ka'ba in Mecca.

I was nervous, shuffling in the center of our group in the

line waiting to have our passports inspected. I had an appre-
hensive feeling. Look what I'm handing them. I'm in the
Muslim world, right at The Fountain. I'm handing them the
American passport which signifies the exact opposite of what
Islam stands for.

The judge in our group sensed my strain. He patted my
shoulder. Love, humility, and true brotherhood was almost
a physical feeling wherever I turned. Then our group reached
the clerks who examined each passport and suitcase carefully and nodded to the pilgrim to move on.

I was so nervous that when I turned the key in my bag,
and it didn't work, I broke open the bag, fearing that they
might think I had something in the bag that I shouldn't have.
Then the clerk saw that I was handing him an American
passport. He held it, he looked at me and said something
in Arabic. My friends around me began speaking rapid
Arabic, gesturing and pointing, trying to intercede for me.
The judge asked me in English for my letter from Dr.
Shawarbi, and he thrust it at the clerk, who read it. He gave
the letter back, protesting—I could tell that. An argument
was going on, *about* me. I felt like a stupid fool, unable to
say a word, I couldn't even understand what was being
said. But, finally, sadly, the judge turned to me.

I had to go before the *Mahgama Sharia*, he explained. It
was the Muslim high court which examined all possibly non-
authentic converts to the Islamic religion seeking to enter
Mecca. It was absolute that no non-Muslim could enter
Mecca.

My friends were going to have to go on to Mecca without
me. They seemed stricken with concern for me. And *I* was
stricken. I found the words to tell them, "Don't worry, I'll
be fine. Allah guides me." They said they would pray hourly
in my behalf. The white-garbed *Mutawaf* was urging them
on, to keep schedule in the airport's human crush. With all
of us waving, I watched them go.

It was then about three in the morning, a Friday morning.
I never had been in such a jammed mass of people, but I
never had felt more alone, and helpless, since I was a baby.
Worse, Friday in the Muslim world is a rough counterpart
of Sunday in the Christian world. On Friday, all the members of a Muslim community gather, to pray together. The
event is called *yaum al-jumu'a*—"the day of gathering." It

meant that no courts were held on Friday. I would have to wait until Saturday, at least.

An official beckoned a young Arab *Mutawaf's* aide. In broken English, the official explained that I would be taken to a place right at the airport. My passport was kept at Customs. I wanted to object, because it is a traveler's first law never to get separated from his passport, but I didn't. In my wrapped towels and sandals, I followed the aide in his skull cap, long white gown, and slippers. I guess we were quite a sight. People passing us were speaking all kinds of languages. I couldn't speak anybody's language. I was in bad shape.

Right outside the airport was a mosque, and above the airport was a huge, dormitory-like building, four tiers high. It was semi-dark, not long before dawn, and planes were regularly taking off and landing, their landing lights sweeping the runways, or their wing and tail lights blinking in the sky. Pilgrims from Ghana, Indonesia, Japan, and Russia, to mention some, were moving to and from the dormitory where I was being taken. I don't believe that motion picture cameras ever have filmed a human spectacle more colorful than my eyes took in. We reached the dormitory and began climbing, up to the fourth, top, tier, passing members of every race on earth. Chinese, Indonesians, Afghanistanians. Many, not yet changed into the *Ihram* garb, still wore their national dress. It was like pages out of the *National Geographic* magazine.

My guide, on the fourth tier, gestured me into a compartment that contained about fifteen people. Most lay curled up on their rugs asleep. I could tell that some were women, covered head and foot. An old Russian Muslim and his wife were not asleep. They stared frankly at me. Two Egyptian Muslims and a Persian roused and also stared as my guide moved us over into a corner. With gestures, he indicated that he would demonstrate to me the proper prayer ritual postures. Imagine, being a Muslim minister, a leader in Elijah Muhammad's Nation of Islam, and not knowing the prayer ritual.

I tried to do what he did. I knew I wasn't doing it right. I could feel the other Muslims' eyes on me. Western ankles won't do what Muslim ankles have done for a lifetime. Asians squat when they sit, Westerners sit upright in chairs. When my guide was down in a posture, I tried everything I could to get down as he was, but there I was, sticking up. After about an hour, my guide left, indicating that he would return later.

I never even thought about sleeping. Watched by the Muslims, I kept practicing prayer posture. I refused to let myself think how ridiculous I must have looked to them. After a while, though, I learned a little trick that would let me get down closer to the floor. But after two or three days, my ankle was going to swell.

As the sleeping Muslims woke up, when dawn had broken, they almost instantly became aware of me, and we watched each other while they went about their business. I began to see what an important role the rug played in the overall cultural life of the Muslims. Each individual had a small prayer rug, and each man and wife, or large group, had a larger communal rug. These Muslims prayed on their rugs there in the compartment. Then they spread a tablecloth over the rug and ate, so the rug became the dining room. Removing the dishes and cloth, they sat on the rug—a living room. Then they curl up and sleep on the rug—a bedroom. In that compartment, before I was to leave it, it dawned on me for the first time why the fence had paid such a high price for Oriental rugs when I had been a burglar in Boston. It was because so much intricate care was taken to weave fine rugs in countries where rugs were so culturally versatile. Later, in Mecca, I would see yet another use of the rug. When any kind of a dispute arose, someone who was respected highly and who was not involved would sit on a rug with the disputers around him, which made the rug a courtroom. In other instances it was a classroom.

One of the Egyptian Muslims, particularly, kept watching me out of the corner of his eye. I smiled at him. He got up and came over to me. "Hel-lo—" he said. It sounded like the Gettysburg Address. I beamed at him, "Hello!" I asked his name. "Name? Name?" He was trying hard, but he didn't get it. We tried some words on each other. I'd guess his English vocabulary spanned maybe twenty words. Just enough to frustrate me. I was trying to get him to comprehend anything. "Sky." I'd point. He'd smile. "Sky," I'd say again, gesturing for him to repeat it after me. He would. "Airplane . . . rug . . . foot . . . sandal . . . eyes. . . ." Like that. Then an amazing thing happened. I was so glad I had some communication with a human being, I was just saying whatever came to mind. I said "Muhammad Ali Clay—" All of the Muslims listening lighted up like a Christmas tree. "You? You?" My friend was pointing at me. I shook my head, "No, no. Muhammad Ali Clay my friend—*friend!*" They half understood me. Some of them didn't understand, and that's how it began to get around that I was Cassius Clay, world heavyweight champion. I was later to learn that apparently every man, woman and child in the Muslim world had heard how Sonny Liston (who in the Muslim world had the image of a man-eating ogre) had been beaten in Goliath-David fashion by Cassius Clay, who then had told the world that his name was Muhammad Ali and his religion was Islam and Allah had given him his victory.

Establishing the rapport was the best thing that could have happened in the compartment. My being an American Muslim changed the attitudes from merely watching me to wanting to look out for me. Now, the others began smiling steadily. They came closer, they were frankly looking me up and down. Inspecting me. Very friendly. I was like a man from Mars.

The *Mutawaf's* aide returned, indicating that I should go with him. He pointed from our tier down at the mosque and I knew that he had come to take me to make the morning prayer, *El Sobh,* always before sunrise. I followed him down, and we passed pilgrims by the thousands, babbling languages, everything but English. I was angry with myself for not having taken the time to learn more of the orthodox prayer rituals before leaving America. In Elijah Muhammad's Nation of Islam, we hadn't prayed in Arabic. About a dozen or more years before, when I was in prison, a member of the orthodox Muslim movement in Boston, named Abdul Hameed, had visited me and had later sent me prayers in Arabic. At that time, I had learned those prayers phonetically. But I hadn't used them since.

I made up my mind to let the guide do everything first and I would watch him. It wasn't hard to get him to do things first. He wanted to anyway. Just outside the mosque there was a long trough with rows of faucets. Ablutions had to precede praying. I knew that. Even watching the *Mutawaf's* helper, I didn't get it right. There's an exact way that an orthodox Muslim washes, and the exact way is very important.

I followed him into the mosque, just a step behind, watching. He did his prostration, his head to the ground. I did mine. *"Bi-smi-llahi-r-Rahmain-r-Rahim—"* ("In the name of Allah, the Beneficent, the Merciful—") All Muslim prayers began that way. After that, I may not have been mumbling the right thing, but I was mumbling.

I don't mean to have any of this sound joking. It was far from a joke with me. No one who happened to be watching could tell that I wasn't saying what the others said.

After that Sunrise Prayer, my guide accompanied me back up to the fourth tier. By sign language, he said he would return within three hours, then he left.

Our tier gave an excellent daylight view of the whole airport area. I stood at the railing, watching. Planes were landing and taking off like clockwork. Thousands upon thousands of people from all over the world made colorful patterns of movement. I saw groups leaving for Mecca, in buses, trucks, cars. I saw some setting out to walk the forty miles. I wished that I could start walking. At least, I knew how to do that.

I was afraid to think what might lie ahead. Would I be rejected as a Mecca pilgrim? I wondered what the test would consist of, and when I would face the Muslim high court.

The Persian Muslim in our compartment came up to me at the rail. He greeted me, hesitantly, "Amer . . . American?" He indicated that he wanted me to come and have breakfast with him and his wife, on their rug. I knew that it was an immense offer he was making. You don't have tea with a Muslim's wife. I didn't want to impose, I don't know if the Persian understood or not when I shook my head and smiled, meaning "No, thanks." He brought me some tea and cookies, anyway. Until then, I hadn't even thought about eating.

Others made gestures. They would just come up and smile and nod at me. My first friend, the one who had spoken a little English, was gone. I didn't know it, but he was spreading the word of an American Muslim on the fourth tier. Traffic had begun to pick up, going past our compartment. Muslims in the *Ihram* garb, or still in their national dress, walked slowly past, smiling. It would go on for as long as I was there to be seen. But I hadn't yet learned that I was the attraction.

I have always been restless, and curious. The *Mutawaf's*

aide didn't return in the three hours he had said, and that made me nervous. I feared that he had given up on me as beyond help. By then, too, I was really getting hungry. All of the Muslims in the compartment had offered me food, and I had refused. The trouble was, I have to admit it, at that point I didn't know if I could go for their manner of eating. Everything was in one pot on the dining-room rug, and I saw them just fall right in, using their hands.

I kept standing at the tier railing observing the courtyard below, and I decided to explore a bit on my own. I went down to the first tier. I thought, then, that maybe I shouldn't get too far, someone might come for me. So I went back up to our compartment. In about forty-five minutes, I went back down. I went further this time, feeling my way. I saw a little restaurant in the courtyard. I went straight in there. It was jammed, and babbling with languages. Using gestures, I bought a whole roasted chicken and something like thick potato chips. I got back out in the courtyard and I tore up that chicken, using my hands. Muslims were doing the same thing all around me. I saw men at least seventy years old bringing both legs up under them, until they made a human knot of themselves, eating with as much aplomb and satisfaction as though they had been in a fine restaurant with waiters all over the place. All ate as One, and slept as One. Everything about the pilgrimage atmosphere accented the Oneness of Man under One God.

I made, during the day, several trips up to the compartment and back out in the courtyard, each time exploring a little further than before. Once, I nodded at two black men standing together. I nearly shouted when one spoke to me in British-accented English. Before their party approached, ready to leave for Mecca, we were able to talk enough to exchange that I was American and they were Ethiopians. I was heartsick. I had found two English-speaking Muslims at last—and they were leaving. The Ethiopians had both been schooled in Cairo, and they were living in Ryadh, the political capital of Arabia. I was later going to learn to my surprise that in Ethiopia, with eighteen million people, ten million are Muslims. Most people think Ethiopia is Christian. But only its government is Christian. The West has always helped to keep the Christian government in power.

I had just said my Sunset Prayer, *El Maghrib;* I was lying

on my cot in the fourth-tier compartment, feeling blue and alone, when out of the darkness came a sudden light!

It was actually a sudden thought. On one of my venturings in the yard full of activity below, I had noticed four men, officials, seated at a table with a telephone. Now, I thought about seeing them there, and with *telephone*, my mind flashed to the connection that Dr. Shawarbi in New York had given me, the telephone number of the son of the author of the book which had been given to me. Omar Azzam lived right there in Jedda!

In a matter of a few minutes, I was downstairs and rushing to where I had seen the four officials. One of them spoke functional English. I excitedly showed him the letter from Dr. Shawarbi. He read it. Then he read it aloud to the other three officials. "A Muslim from America!" I could almost see it capture their imaginations and curiosity. They were very impressed. I asked the English-speaking one if he would please do me the favor of telephoning Dr. Omar Azzam at the number I had. He was glad to do it. He got someone on the phone and conversed in Arabic.

Dr. Omar Azzam came straight to the airport. With the four officials beaming, he wrung my hand in welcome, a young, tall, powerfully built man. I'd say he was six foot three. He had an extremely polished manner. In America, he would have been called a white man, but—it struck me, hard and instantly—from the way he acted, I had no *feeling* of him being a white man. "Why didn't you call before?" he demanded of me. He showed some identification to the four officials, and he used their phone. Speaking in Arabic, he was talking with some airport officials. "Come!" he said.

In something less than half an hour, he had gotten me released, my suitcase and passport had been retrieved from Customs, and we were in Dr. Azzam's car, driving through the city of Jedda, with me dressed in the *Ihram* two towels and sandals. I was speechless at the man's attitude, and at my own physical feeling of no difference between us as human beings. I had heard for years of Muslim hospitality, but one couldn't quite imagine such warmth. I asked questions. Dr. Azzam was a Swiss-trained engineer. His field was city planning. The Saudi Arabian government had borrowed him from the United Nations to direct all of the reconstruction work being done on Arabian holy places. And Dr. Azzam's sister

332 THE AUTOBIOGRAPHY OF MALCOLM X

was the wife of Prince Faisal's son. I was in a car with the
brother-in-law of the son of the ruler of Arabia. Nor was
that all that Allah had done. "My father will be so happy
to meet you," said Dr. Azzam. The author who had sent me
the book!

I asked questions about his father. Abd ir-Rahman Azzam
was known as Azzam Pasha, or Lord Azzam, until the Egyptian revolution, when President Nasser eliminated all "Lord"
and "Noble" titles. "He should be at my home when we get
there," Dr. Azzam said. "He spends much time in New York
with his United Nations work, and he has followed you with
great interest."

I was speechless.

It was early in the morning when we reached Dr. Azzam's
home. His father was there, his father's brother, a chemist,
and another friend—all up that early, waiting. Each of
them embraced me as though I were a long-lost child. I had
never seen these men before in my life, and they treated
me so good! I am going to tell you that I had never been
so honored in my life, nor had I ever received such true
hospitality.

A servant brought tea and coffee, and disappeared. I was
urged to make myself comfortable. No women were anywhere in view. In Arabia, you could easily think there were
no females.

Dr. Abd ir-Rahman Azzam dominated the conversation.
Why hadn't I called before? They couldn't understand why
I hadn't. Was I comfortable? They seemed embarrassed that
I had spent the time at the airport; that I had been delayed
in getting to Mecca. No matter how I protested that I felt no
inconvenience, that I was fine, they would not hear it. "You
must rest," Dr. Azzam said. He went to use the telephone.

I didn't know what this distinguished man was doing. I
had no dream. When I was told that I would be brought
back for dinner that evening, and that, meanwhile, I should
get back in the car, how could I have realized that I was
about to see the epitome of Muslim hospitality?

Abd ir-Rahman Azzam, when at home, lived in a suite
at the Jedda Palace Hotel. Because I had come to them with
a letter from a friend, he was going to stay at his son's home,
and let me use his suite, until I could get on to Mecca.

When I found out, there was no use protesting: I was in

the suite; young Dr. Azzam was gone; there was no one to protest to. The three-room suite had a bathroom that was as big as a double at the New York Hilton. It was suite number 214. There was even a porch outside, affording a beautiful view of the ancient Red Sea city.

There had never before been in my emotions such an impulse to pray—and I did, prostrating myself on the living-room rug.

Nothing in either of my two careers as a black man in America had served to give me any idealistic tendencies. My instincts automatically examined the reasons, the motives, of anyone who did anything they didn't have to do for me. Always in my life, if it was any white person, I could see a selfish motive.

But there in that hotel that morning, a telephone call and a few hours away from the cot on the fourth-floor tier of the dormitory, was one of the few times I had been so awed that I was totally without resistance. That white man—at least he would have been considered "white" in America—related to Arabia's ruler, to whom he was a close advisor, truly an international man, with nothing in the world to gain, had given up his suite to me, for my transient comfort. He had *nothing* to gain. He didn't need me. He had everything. In fact, he had more to lose than gain. He had followed the American press about me. If he did that, he knew there was only stigma attached to me. I was supposed to have horns. I was a "racist." I was "anti-white"—and he from all appearances was white. I was supposed to be a criminal; not only that, but everyone was even accusing me of using his religion of Islam as a cloak for my criminal practices and philosophies. Even if he had had some motive to use me, he knew that I was separated from Elijah Muhammad and the Nation of Islam, my "power base," according to the press in America. The only organization that I had was just a few weeks old. I had no job. I had no money. Just to get over there, I had had to borrow money from my sister.

That morning was when I first began to reappraise the "white man." It was when I first began to perceive that "white man," as commonly used, means complexion only secondarily; primarily it described attitudes and actions. In America, "white man" meant specific attitudes and actions toward the black man, and toward all other non-white men.

But in the Muslim world, I had seen that men with white complexions were more genuinely brotherly than anyone else had ever been.

That morning was the start of a radical alteration in my whole outlook about "white" men.

I should quote from my notebook here. I wrote this about noon, in the hotel: "My excitement, sitting here, waiting to go before the Hajj Committee, is indescribable. My window faces to the sea westward. The streets are filled with the incoming pilgrims from all over the world. The prayers are to Allah and verses from the Quran are on the lips of everyone. Never have I seen such a beautiful sight, nor witnessed such a scene, nor felt such an atmosphere. Although I am excited, I feel safe and secure, thousands of miles from the totally different life that I have known. Imagine that twenty-four hours ago, I was in the fourth-floor room over the airport, surrounded by people with whom I could not communicate, feeling uncertain about the future, and very lonely, and then *one* phone call, following Dr. Shawarbi's instructions. I have met one of the most powerful men in the Muslim world. I will soon sleep in his bed at the Jedda Palace. I know that I am surrounded by friends whose sincerity and religious zeal I can feel. I must pray again to thank Allah for this blessing, and I must pray again that my wife and children back in America will always be blessed for their sacrifices, too."

I did pray, two more prayers, as I had told my notebook. Then I slept for about four hours, until the telephone rang. It was young Dr. Azzam. In another hour, he would pick me up to return me there for dinner. I tumbled words over one another, trying to express some of the thanks I felt for all of their actions. He cut me off. "Ma sha'a-llah"—which means, "It is as Allah has pleased."

I seized the opportunity to run down into the lobby, to see it again before Dr. Azzam arrived. When I opened my door, just across the hall from me a man in some ceremonial dress, who obviously lived there, was also headed downstairs, surrounded by attendants. I followed them down, then through the lobby. Outside, a small caravan of automobiles was waiting. My neighbor appeared through the Jedda Palace Hotel's front entrance and people rushed and crowded him, kissing his hand. I found out who he was: the Grand Mufti of Jerusalem. Later, in the hotel, I would have the opportunity to talk with him for about a half-hour. He was a cordial man of great dignity. He was well up on world affairs, and even the latest events in America.

I will never forget the dinner at the Azzam home. I quote my notebook again: "I couldn't say in my mind that these were 'white' men. Why, the men acted as if they were brothers of mine, the elder Dr. Azzam as if he were my father. His fatherly, scholarly speech. I *felt* like he was my father. He was, you could tell, a highly skilled diplomat, with a broad range of mind. His knowledge was so worldly. He was as current on world affairs as some people are to what's going on in their living room.

"The more we talked, the more his vast reservoir of knowledge and its variety seemed unlimited. He spoke of the racial lineage of the descendants of Muhammad the Prophet, and he showed how they were both black and white. He also pointed out how color, the complexities of color, and the problems of color which exist in the Muslim world, exist only where, and to the extent that, that area of the Muslim world has been influenced by the West. He said that if one encountered any differences based on attitude toward color, this directly reflected the degree of Western influence."

I learned during dinner that while I was at the hotel, the Hajj Committee Court had been notified about my case, and that in the morning I should be there. And I was.

The Judge was Sheikh Muhammad Harkon. The Court was empty except for me and a sister from India, formerly a Protestant, who had converted to Islam, and was, like me, trying to make the Hajj. She was brown-skinned, with a small face that was mostly covered. Judge Harkon was a kind, impressive man. We talked. He asked me some questions, having to do with my sincerity. I answered him as truly as I could. He not only recognized me as a true Muslim, but he gave me two books, one in English, the other in Arabic. He recorded my name in the Holy Register of true Muslims, and we were ready to part. He told me, "I hope you will become a great preacher of Islam in America." I said that I shared that hope, and I would try to fulfill it.

The Azzam family were very elated that I was qualified and accepted to go to Mecca. I had lunch at the Jedda Palace. Then I slept again for several hours, until the telephone awakened me.

It was Muhammad Abdul Azziz Maged, the Deputy Chief

of Protocol for Prince Faisal. "A special car will be waiting to take you to Mecca, right after your dinner," he told me. He advised me to eat heartily, as the Hajj rituals require plenty of strength.

I was beyond astonishment by then.

Two young Arabs accompanied me to Mecca. A well-lighted, modern turnpike highway made the trip easy. Guards at intervals along the way took one look at the car, and the driver made a sign, and we were passed through, never even having to slow down. I was, all at once, thrilled, important, humble, and thankful.

Mecca, when we entered, seemed as ancient as time itself. Our car slowed through the winding streets, lined by shops on both sides and with buses, cars, and trucks, and tens of thousands of pilgrims from all over the earth were everywhere.

The car halted briefly at a place where a *Mutawaf* was waiting for me. He wore the white skullcap and long night-shirt garb that I had seen at the airport. He was a short, dark-skinned Arab, named Muhammad. He spoke no English whatever.

We parked near the Great Mosque. We performed our ablution and entered. Pilgrims seemed to be on top of each other, there were so many, lying, sitting, sleeping, praying, walking.

My vocabulary cannot describe the new mosque that was being built around the Ka'ba. I was thrilled to realize that it was only one of the tremendous rebuilding tasks under the direction of young Dr. Azzam, who had just been my host. The Great Mosque of Mecca, when it is finished, will surpass the architectural beauty of India's Taj Mahal.

Carrying my sandals, I followed the *Mutawaf*. Then I saw the Ka'ba, a huge black stone house in the middle of the Great Mosque. It was being circumambulated by thousands upon thousands of praying pilgrims, both sexes, and every size, shape, color, and race in the world. I knew the prayer to be uttered when the pilgrim's eyes first perceive the Ka'ba. Translated, it is "O God, You are peace, and peace derives from You. So greet us, O Lord, with peace." Upon entering the Mosque, the pilgrim should try to kiss the Ka'ba if possible, but if the crowds prevent him getting that close, he touches it, and if the crowds prevent that, he raises his hand and cries out "Takbir!" ("God is great!") I could not get within yards. "Takbir!"

My feeling there in the House of God was a numbness. My *Mutawaf* led me in the crowd of praying, chanting pilgrims, moving seven times around the Ka'ba. Some were bent and wizened with age; it was a sight that stamped itself on the brain. I saw incapacitated pilgrims being carried by others. Faces were enraptured in their faith. The seventh time around, I prayed two *Rak'a*, prostrating myself, my head on the floor. The first prostration, I prayed the Quran verse "Say He is God, the one and only"; the second prostration: "Say O you who are unbelievers, I worship not that which you worship. . . ."

As I prostrated, the *Mutawaf* fended pilgrims off to keep me from being trampled.

The *Mutawaf* and I next drank water from the well of Zem Zem. Then we ran between the two hills, Safa and Marwa, where Hajar wandered over the same earth searching for water for her child Ishmael.

Three separate times, after that, I visited the Great Mosque and circumambulated the Ka'ba. The next day we set out after sunrise toward Mount Arafat, thousands of us, crying in unison: "Labbayka! Labbayka!" and "Allah Akbar!" Mecca is surrounded by the crudest-looking mountains I have ever seen; they seem to be made of the slag from a blast furnace. No vegetation is on them at all. Arriving about noon, we prayed and chanted from noon until sunset, and the *asr* (afternoon) and *Maghrib* (sunset) special prayers were performed.

Finally, we lifted our hands in prayer and thanksgiving, repeating Allah's words: "There is no God but Allah. He has no partner. His are authority and praise. Good emanates from Him, and He has power over all things."

Standing on Mount Arafat had concluded the essential rites of being a pilgrim to Mecca. No one who missed it could consider himself a pilgrim.

The *Ihram* had ended. We cast the traditional seven stones at the devil. Some had their hair and beards cut. I decided that I was going to let my beard remain. I wondered what my wife Betty, and our little daughters, were going to say when they saw me with a beard, when I got back to New York. New York seemed a million miles away. I hadn't seen a newspaper that I could read since I left New York. I had no idea what was happening there. A Negro rifle club that had been in existence for over twelve years in Harlem had been "discovered" by the police; it was being trumpeted that I was "behind it." Elijah Muhammad's Nation of Islam had a lawsuit going against me, to force me and my family to vacate the house in which we lived on Long Island.

The major press, radio, and television media in America had representatives in Cairo hunting all over, trying to locate me, to interview me about the furor in New York that I had allegedly caused—when I knew nothing about any of it.

I only knew what I had left in America, and how it contrasted with what I had found in the Muslim world. About twenty of us Muslims who had finished the Hajj were sitting in a huge tent on Mount Arafat. As a Muslim from America, I was the center of attention. They asked me what about the Hajj had impressed me the most. One of the several who spoke English asked; they translated my answers for the others. My answer to that question was not the one they expected, but it drove home my point.

I said, "The *brotherhood!* The people of all races, colors, from all over the world coming together as *one!* It has proved to me the power of the One God."

It may have been out of taste, but that gave me an opportunity, and I used it, to preach them a quick little sermon on America's racism, and its evils.

I could tell the impact of this upon them. They had been aware that the plight of the black man in America was "bad," but they had not been aware that it was inhuman, that it was a psychological castration. These people from elsewhere around the world were shocked. As Muslims, they had a very tender heart for all unfortunates, and very sensitive feelings for truth and justice. And in everything I said to them, as long as we talked, they were aware of the yardstick that I was using to measure everything—that to me the earth's most explosive and pernicious evil is racism, the inability of God's creatures to live as One, especially in the Western world.

I have reflected since that the letter I finally sat down to compose had been subconsciously shaping itself in my mind.

The *color-blindness* of the Muslim world's religious society and the *color-blindness* of the Muslim world's human society: these two influences had each day been making a greater impact, and an increasing persuasion against my previous way of thinking.

The first letter was, of course, to my wife, Betty. I never had a moment's question that Betty, after initial amazement, would change her thinking to join mine. I had known a thousand reassurances that Betty's faith in me was total. I knew that she would see what I had seen—that in the land of Muhammad and the land of Abraham, I had been blessed by Allah with a new insight into the true religion of Islam, and a better understanding of America's entire racial dilemma.

After the letter to my wife, I wrote next essentially the same letter to my sister Ella. And I knew where Ella would stand. She had been saving to make the pilgrimage to Mecca herself.

I wrote to Dr. Shawarbi, whose belief in my sincerity had enabled me to get a passport to Mecca.

All through the night, I copied similar long letters for others who were very close to me. Among them was Elijah Muhammad's son Wallace Muhammad, who had expressed to me his conviction that the only possible salvation for the Nation of Islam would be its accepting and projecting a better understanding of Orthodox Islam.

And I wrote to my loyal assistants at my newly formed Muslim Mosque, Inc. in Harlem, with a note appended, asking that my letter be duplicated and distributed to the press.

I knew that when my letter became public knowledge back in America, many would be astounded—loved ones, friends, and enemies alike. And no less astounded would be millions whom I did not know—who had gained during my twelve years with Elijah Muhammad a "hate" image of Malcolm X.

Even I was myself astounded. But there was precedent in my life for this letter. My whole life had been a chronology of—*changes*.

Here is what I wrote . . . from my heart:

"Never have I witnessed such sincere hospitality and the overwhelming spirit of true brotherhood as is practiced by people of all colors and races here in this Ancient Holy Land, the home of Abraham, Muhammad, and all the other prophets of the Holy Scriptures. For the past week, I have been utterly speechless and spellbound by the graciousness I see displayed all around me by people *of all colors*.

"I have been blessed to visit the Holy City of Mecca. I have made my seven circuits around the Ka'ba, led by a young *Mutawaf* named Muhammad. I drank water from the well of Zem Zem. I ran seven times back and forth between the hills of Mt. Al-Safa and Al-Marwah. I have prayed in the ancient city of Mina, and I have prayed on Mt. Arafat.

"There were tens of thousands of pilgrims, from all over the world. They were of all colors, from blue-eyed blonds to black-skinned Africans. But we were all participating in the same ritual, displaying a spirit of unity and brotherhood that my experiences in America had led me to believe never could exist between the white and the non-white.

"America needs to understand Islam, because this is the one religion that erases from its society the race problem. Throughout my travels in the Muslim world, I have met, talked to, and even eaten with people who in America would have been considered 'white'—but the 'white' attitude was removed from their minds by the religion of Islam. I have never before seen *sincere* and *true* brotherhood practiced by all colors together, irrespective of their color.

"You may be shocked by these words coming from me. But on this pilgrimage, what I have seen, and experienced, has forced me to *re-arrange* much of my thought-patterns previously held, and to *toss aside* some of my previous conclusions. This was not too difficult for me. Despite my firm convictions, I have been always a man who tries to face facts, and to accept the reality of life as new experience and new knowledge unfolds it. I have always kept an open mind, which is necessary to the flexibility that must go hand in hand with every form of intelligent search for truth.

"During the past eleven days here in the Muslim world, I have eaten from the same plate, drunk from the same glass, and slept in the same bed (or on the same rug)—while praying to the *same God*—with fellow Muslims, whose eyes were the bluest of blue, whose hair was the blondest of blond, and whose skin was the whitest of white. And in the *words* and in the *actions* and in the *deeds* of the 'white' Muslims, I felt the same sincerity that I felt among the black African Muslims of Nigeria, Sudan, and Ghana.

"We were *truly* all the same (brothers)—because their belief in one God had removed the 'white' from their *minds*, the 'white' from their *behavior*, and the 'white' from their *attitude*.

"I could see from this, that perhaps if white Americans could accept the Oneness of God, then perhaps, too, they could accept *in reality* the Oneness of Man—and cease to measure, and hinder, and harm others in terms of their 'differences' in color.

"With racism plaguing America like an incurable cancer, the so-called 'Christian' white American heart should be more receptive to a proven solution to such a destructive problem. Perhaps it could be in time to save America from imminent disaster—the same destruction brought upon Germany by racism that eventually destroyed the Germans themselves.

"Each hour here in the Holy Land enables me to have greater spiritual insights into what is happening in America between black and white. The American Negro never can be blamed for his racial animosities—he is only reacting to four hundred years of the conscious racism of the American whites. But as racism leads America up the suicide path, I do believe, from the experiences that I have had with them, that the whites of the younger generation, in the colleges and universities, will see the handwriting on the wall and many of them will turn to the *spiritual* path of *truth*—the *only* way left to America to ward off the disaster that racism inevitably must lead to.

"Never have I been so highly honored. Never have I been made to feel more humble and unworthy. Who would believe the blessings that have been heaped upon an *American Negro?* A few nights ago, a man who would be called in America a 'white' man, a United Nations diplomat, an ambassador, a companion of kings, gave me *his* hotel suite, *his* bed. By this man, His Excellency Prince Faisal, who rules this Holy Land, was made aware of my presence here in Jedda. The very next morning, Prince Faisal's son, in person, informed me that by the will and decree of his esteemed father, I was to be a State Guest.

"The Deputy Chief of Protocol himself took me before the Hajj Court. His Holiness Sheikh Muhammad Harkon himself okayed my visit to Mecca. His Holiness gave me two books on Islam, with his personal seal and autograph, and he told me that he prayed that I would be a successful preacher of Islam in America. A car, a driver, and a guide, have been placed at my disposal, making it possible for me to travel about this Holy Land almost at will. The government provides air-conditioned quarters and servants in each city that I visit. Never would I have even thought of dreaming that I would ever be a recipient of such honors—honors that in America would be bestowed upon a King—not a Negro.

"All praise is due to Allah, the Lord of all the Worlds.
                                        "Sincerely,

                                        "El-Hajj Malik El-Shabazz
                                        "(Malcolm X)"

CHAPTER EIGHTEEN

EL-HAJJ MALIK EL-SHABAZZ

Prince Faisal, the absolute ruler of Arabia, had made me a guest of the state. Among the courtesies and privileges which this brought to me, especially—shamelessly—I relished the chauffeured car which toured me around in Mecca with the chauffeur-guide pointing out sights of particular significance. Some of the Holy City looked as ancient as time itself. Other parts of it resembled a modern Miami suburb. I cannot describe with what feelings I actually pressed my hands against the earth where the great Prophets had trod four thousand years before.

"The Muslim from America" excited everywhere the most intense curiosity and interest. I was mistaken time and again for Cassius Clay. A local newspaper had printed a photograph of Cassius and me together at the United Nations. Through my chauffeur-guide-interpreter I was asked scores of questions about Cassius. Even children knew of him, and loved him there in the Muslim world. By popular demand, the cinemas throughout Africa and Asia had shown his fight. At that moment in young Cassius' career, he had captured the imagination and the support of the entire dark world.

My car took me to participate in special prayers at Mt. Arafat, and at Mina. The roads offered the wildest drives that I had ever known: nightmare traffic, brakes squealing, skidding cars, and horns blowing. (I believe that all of the driving in the Holy Land is done in the name of Allah.) I had begun to learn the prayers in Arabic; now, my biggest prayer difficulty was physical. The unaccustomed prayer posture had caused my big toe to swell, and it pained me.

But the Muslim world's customs no longer seemed strange to me. My hands now readily plucked up food from a common

343

dish shared with brother Muslims; I was drinking without hesitation from the same glass as others; I was washing from the same little pitcher of water; and sleeping with eight or ten others on a mat in the open. I remember one night at Muzdalifa with nothing but the sky overhead I lay awake amid sleeping Muslim brothers and I learned that pilgrims from every land—every color, and class, and rank; high officials and the beggar alike—all snored in the same language.

I'll bet that in the parts of the Holy Land that I visited a million bottles of soft drinks were consumed—and ten million cigarettes must have been smoked. Particularly the Arab Muslims smoked constantly, even on the Hajj pilgrimage itself. The smoking evil wasn't invented in Prophet Muhammad's days—if it had been, I believe he would have banned it.

It was the largest Hajj in history, I was later told. Kasem Gulek, of the Turkish Parliament, beaming with pride, informed me that from Turkey alone over six hundred buses—over fifty thousand Muslims—had made the pilgrimage. I told him that I dreamed to see the day when shiploads and planeloads of American Muslims would come to Mecca for the Hajj.

There was a color pattern in the huge crowds. Once I happened to notice this, I closely observed it thereafter. Being from America made me intensely sensitive to matters of color. I saw that people who looked alike drew together and most of the time stayed together. This was entirely voluntary; there being no other reason for it. But Africans were with Africans. Pakistanis were with Pakistanis. And so on. I tucked it into my mind that when I returned home I would tell Americans this observation; that where true brotherhood existed among all colors, where no one felt segregated, where there was no "superiority" complex, no "inferiority" complex—then voluntarily, naturally, people of the same kind felt drawn together by that which they had in common.

It is my intention that by the time of my next Hajj pilgrimage, I will have at least a working vocabulary of Arabic. In my ignorant, crippled condition in the Holy Land, I had been lucky to have met patient friends who enabled me to talk by interpreting for me. Never before in my life had I felt so deaf and dumb as during the times when no interpreter was with me to tell me what was being said around me, or about me, or even to me, by other Muslims—before they learned that "the Muslim from America" knew only a few prayers in Arabic and, beyond that, he could only nod and smile.

Behind my nods and smiles, though, I was doing some American-type thinking and reflection. I saw that Islam's conversions around the world could double and triple if the colorfulness and the true spiritualness of the Hajj pilgrimage were properly advertised and communicated to the outside world. I saw that the Arabs are poor at understanding the psychology of non-Arabs and the importance of public relations. The Arabs said *"insha Allah"* ("God willing")—then they waited for converts. Even by this means, Islam was on the march, but I knew that with improved public relations methods the number of new converts turning to Allah could be turned into millions.

Constantly, wherever I went, I was asked questions about America's racial discrimination. Even with my background, I was astonished at the degree to which the major single image of America seemed to be discrimination.

In a hundred different conversations in the Holy Land with Muslims high and low, and from around the world—and, later, when I got to Black Africa—I don't have to tell you never once did I bite my tongue or miss a single opportunity to tell the truth about the crimes, the evils and the indignities that are suffered by the black man in America. Through my interpreter, I lost no opportunity to advertise the American black man's real plight. I preached it on the mountain at Arafat, I preached it in the busy lobby of the Jedda Palace Hotel. I would point at one after another—to bring it closer to home; "You . . . you . . . you—because of your dark skin, in America you, too, would be called 'Negro.' You could be bombed and shot and cattle-prodded and fire-hosed and beaten because of your complexions."

As some of the poorest pilgrims heard me preach, so did some of the Holy World's most important personages. I talked at length with the blue-eyed, blond-haired Hussein Amini, Grand Mufti of Jerusalem. We were introduced on Mt. Arafat by Kasem Gulick of the Turkish Parliament. Both were learned men; both were especially well-read on America. Kasem Gulick asked me why I had broken with Elijah Muhammad. I said that I preferred not to elaborate upon our differences, in the interests of preserving the American black man's unity. They both understood and accepted that.

I talked with the Mayor of Mecca, Sheikh Abdullah Eraif, who when he was a journalist had criticized the methods of the Mecca municipality—and Prince Faisal made him the Mayor, to see if he could do any better. Everyone generally acknowledged that Sheikh Eraif was doing fine. A filmed feature "The Muslim From America" was made by Ahmed Horyallah and his partner Essid Muhammad of Tunis' television station. In America once, in Chicago, Ahmed Horyallah had interviewed Elijah Muhammad.

The lobby of the Jedda Palace Hotel offered me frequent sizable informal audiences of important men from many different countries who were curious to hear the "American Muslim." I met many Africans who had either spent some time in America, or who had heard other Africans' testimony about America's treatment of the black man. I remember how before one large audience, one cabinet minister from Black Africa (he knew more about world-wide current events than anyone else I've ever met) told of his occasionally traveling in the United States, North and South, deliberately not wearing his national dress. Just recalling the indignities he had met as a black man seemed to expose some raw nerve in this highly educated, dignified official. His eyes blazed in his passionate anger, his hands hacked the air: "Why is the American black man so complacent about being trampled upon? Why doesn't the American black man *fight* to be a human being?"

A Sudanese high official hugged me, "You champion the American black people!" An Indian official wept in his compassion "for my brothers in your land." I reflected many, many times to myself upon how the American Negro has been entirely brainwashed from ever seeing or thinking of himself, as he should, as a part of the non-white peoples of the world. The American Negro has no conception of the hundreds of millions of other non-whites' concern for him: he has no conception of their feeling of brotherhood for and with him.
. It was there in the Holy Land, and later in Africa, that I formed a conviction which I have had ever since—that a topmost requisite for any Negro leader in America ought to be extensive traveling in the non-white lands on this earth, and the travel should include many conferences with the ranking men of those lands. I guarantee that any honest, open-minded Negro leader would return home with more effective thinking about alternative avenues to solutions of the American black man's problem. Above all, the Negro leaders would find that many non-white officials of the highest standing, especially Africans, would tell them—privately—that they would be glad to throw their weight behind the Negro cause, in the United

Nations, and in other ways. But these officials understandably feel that the Negro in America is so confused and divided that he doesn't himself know what his cause is. Again, it was mainly Africans who variously expressed to me that no one would wish to be embarrassed trying to help a brother who shows no evidence that he wants that help—and who seems to refuse to cooperate in his own interests.

The American black "leader's" most critical problem is lack of imagination! His thinking, his strategies, if any, are always limited, at least basically, to only that which is either advised, or approved by the white man. And the first thing the American power structure doesn't want any Negroes to start is thinking *internationally*.

I think the single worst mistake of the American black organizations, and their leaders, is that they have failed to establish direct brotherhood lines of communication between the independent nations of Africa and the American black people. Why, every day, the black African heads of state should be receiving direct accounts of the latest developments in the American black man's struggles—instead of the U.S. State Department's releases to Africans which always imply that the American black man's struggle is being "solved."

Two American authors, best-sellers in the Holy Land, had helped to spread and intensify the concern for the American black man. James Baldwin's books, translated, had made a tremendous impact, as had the book *Black Like Me*, by John Griffin. If you're unfamiliar with that book, it tells how the white man Griffin blackened his skin and spent two months traveling as a Negro about America; then Griffin wrote of the experiences that he met. "A frightening experience!" I heard exclaimed many times by people in the Holy World who had read the popular book. But I never heard it without opening their thinking further: "Well, if it was a frightening experience for him as nothing but a make-believe Negro for sixty days—then you think about what *real* Negroes in America have gone through for four hundred years."

One honor that came to me, I had prayed for: His Eminence, Prince Faisal, invited me to a personal audience with him.

As I entered the room, tall, handsome Prince Faisal came from behind his desk. I never will forget the reflection I had at that instant, that here was one of the world's most important men, and yet with his dignity one saw clearly his sincere humility. He indicated for me a chair opposite from his. Our interpreter was the Deputy Chief of Protocol, Muhammad Abdul Azziz Maged, an Egyptian-born Arab, who looked like a Harlem Negro.

Prince Faisal impatiently gestured when I began stumbling for words trying to express my gratitude for the great honor he had paid me in making me a guest of the State. It was only Muslim hospitality to another Muslim, he explained, and I was an unusual Muslim from America. He asked me to understand above all that whatever he had done had been his pleasure, with no other motives whatever.

A gliding servant served a choice of two kinds of tea as Prince Faisal talked. His son, Muhammad Faisal, had "met" me on American television while attending a Northern California university. Prince Faisal had read Egyptian writers' articles about the American "Black Muslims." "If what these writers say is true, the Black Muslims have the wrong Islam," he said. I explained my role of the previous twelve years, of helping to organize and to build the Nation of Islam. I said that my purpose for making the Hajj was to get an understanding of true Islam. "That is good," Prince Faisal said, pointing out that there was an abundance of English-translation literature about Islam—so that there was no excuse for ignorance, and no reason for sincere people to allow themselves to be misled.

The last of April, 1964, I flew to Beirut, the seaport capital of Lebanon. A part of me, I left behind in the Holy City of Mecca. And, in turn, I took away with me—forever—a part of Mecca.

I was on my way, now, to Nigeria, then Ghana. But some friends I had made in the Holy Land had urged and insisted that I make some stops en route and I had agreed. For example, it had been arranged that I would first stop and address the faculty and the students at the American University of Beirut.

In Beirut's Palm Beach Hotel, I luxuriated in my first long sleep since I had left America. Then, I went walking—fresh from weeks in the Holy Land: immediately my attention was struck by the mannerisms and attire of the Lebanese women. In the Holy Land, there had been the very modest, very feminine Arabian women—and there was this sudden contrast of the half-French, half-Arab Lebanese women who projected in their dress and street manners more liberty, more boldness. I saw clearly the obvious European influence upon the Lebanese culture. It showed me how any country's moral strength, or its moral weakness, is quickly measurable by the street attire and attitude of its women—especially its young women. Wherever the spiritual values have been submerged, if not destroyed, by an emphasis upon the material things, invariably, the women reflect it. Witness the women, both young and old, in America—where scarcely any moral values are left. There seems in most countries to be either one extreme or the other. Truly a paradise could exist wherever material progress and spiritual values could be properly balanced.

I spoke at the University of Beirut the truth of the American black man's condition. I've previously made the comment that any experienced public speaker can feel his audience's reactions. As I spoke, I felt the subjective and defensive reactions of the American white students present—but gradually their hostilities lessened as I continued to present the unassailable facts. But the students of African heritage—well, I'll *never* get over how the African displays his emotions.

Later, with astonishment, I heard that the American press carried stories that my Beirut speech caused a "riot." What kind of a riot? I don't know how any reporter, in good conscience, could have cabled that across the ocean. The Beirut *Daily Star* front-page report of my speech mentioned no "riot" —because there was none. When I was done, the African students all but besieged me for autographs; some of them even hugged me. Never have even American Negro audiences accepted me as I have been accepted time and again by the less inhibited, more down-to-earth Africans.

From Beirut, I flew back to Cairo, and there I took a train to Alexandria, Egypt. I kept my camera busy during each brief stopover. Finally I was on a plane to Nigeria.

During the six-hour flight, when I was not talking with the pilot (who had been a 1960 Olympics swimmer), I sat with a passionately political African. He almost shouted in his fervor. "When people are in a stagnant state, and are being brought out of it, there is no *time* for voting!" His central theme was that no new African nation, trying to decolonize itself, needed any political system that would permit division and bickering. "The people don't know what the vote means! It is the job of the enlightened leaders to raise the people's intellect."

In Lagos, I was greeted by Professor Essien-Udom of the

Ibadan University. We were both happy to see each other. We had met in the United States as he had researched the Nation of Islam for his book, *Black Nationalism*. At his home, that evening, a dinner was held in my honor, attended by other professors and professional people. As we ate, a young doctor asked me if I knew that New York City's press was highly upset about a recent killing in Harlem of a white woman—for which, according to the press, many were blaming me at least indirectly. An elderly white couple who owned a Harlem clothing store had been attacked by several young Negroes, and the wife was stabbed to death. Some of these young Negroes, apprehended by the police, had described themselves as belonging to an organization they called "Blood Brothers." These youths, allegedly, had said or implied that they were affiliated with "Black Muslims" who had split away from the Nation of Islam to join up with me.

I told the dinner guests that it was my first word of any of it, but that I was not surprised when violence happened in any of America's ghettoes where black men had been living packed like animals and treated like lepers. I said that the charge against me was typical white man scapegoat-seeking—that whenever something white men disliked happened in the black community, typically white public attention was directed not at the cause, but at a selected scapegoat.

As for the "Blood Brothers," I said I considered all Negroes to be my blood brothers. I said that the white man's efforts to make my name poison actually succeeded only in making millions of black people regard me like Joe Louis.

Speaking in the Ibadan University's Trenchard Hall, I urged that Africa's independent nations needed to see the necessity of helping to bring the Afro-American's case before the United Nations. I said that just as the American Jew is in political, economic, and cultural harmony with world Jewry, I was convinced that it was time for all Afro-Americans to join the world's Pan-Africanists. I said that physically we Afro-Americans might remain in America, fighting for our Constitutional rights, but that philosophically and culturally we Afro-Americans badly needed to "return" to Africa—and to develop a working unity in the framework of Pan-Africanism.

Young Africans asked me politically sharper questions than one hears from most American adults. Then an astonishing thing happened when one old West Indian stood and began attacking me—for attacking America. "Shut up! Shut up!" students yelled, booing, and hissing. The old West Indian tried to express defiance of them, and in a sudden rush a group of students sprang up and were after him. He barely escaped ahead of them. I never saw anything like it. Screaming at him, they ran him off the campus. (Later, I found out that the old West Indian was married to a white woman, and he was trying to get a job in some white-influenced agency which had put him up to challenge me. Then, I understood his problem.)

This wasn't the last time I'd see the Africans' almost fanatic expression of their political emotions.

Afterward, in the Students' Union, I was plied with questions, and I was made an honorary member of the Nigerian Muslim Students' Society. Right here in my wallet is my card: "Alhadji Malcolm X. Registration No. M-138." With the membership, I was given a new name: "Omowale." It means, in the Yoruba language, "the son who has come home." I meant it when I told them I had never received a more treasured honor.

Six hundred members of the Peace Corps were in Nigeria, I learned. Some white Peace Corps members who talked with me were openly embarrassed at the guilt of their race in America. Among the twenty Negro Peace Corpsmen I talked with, a very impressive fellow to me was Larry Jackson, a Morgan State College graduate from Fort Lauderdale, Florida, who had joined the Peace Corps in 1962.

I made Nigerian radio and television program appearances. When I remember seeing black men operating their *own* communications agencies, a thrill still runs up my spine. The reporters who interviewed me included an American Negro from *Newsweek* magazine—his name was Williams. Traveling through Africa, he had recently interviewed Prime Minister Nkrumah.

Talking with me privately, one group of Nigerian officials told me how skillfully the U.S. Information Agency sought to spread among Africans the impression that American Negroes were steadily advancing, and that the race problem soon would be solved. One high official told me, "Our informed leaders and many, many others know otherwise." He said that behind the "diplomatic front" of every African U.N. official was recognition of the white man's gigantic duplicity and conspiracy to keep the world's peoples of African heritage separated—both physically and ideologically—from each other.

"In your land, how many black people think about it that South and Central and North America contain over *eighty million* people of African descent?" he asked me.

"The world's course will change the day the African-heritage peoples come together as brothers!"

I never had heard that kind of global black thinking from any black man in America.

From Lagos, Nigeria, I flew on to Accra, Ghana.

I think that nowhere is the black continent's wealth and the natural beauty of its people richer than in Ghana, which is so proudly the very fountainhead of Pan-Africanism.

I stepped off the plane into a jarring note. A red-faced American white man recognized me; he had the nerve to come up grabbing my hand and telling me in a molasses drawl that he was from Alabama, and then he invited me to his home for dinner!

My hotel's dining room, when I went to breakfast, was full of more of those whites—discussing Africa's untapped wealth as though the African waiters had no ears. It nearly ruined my meal, thinking how in America they sicked police dogs on black people, and threw bombs in black churches, while blocking the doors of their white churches—and now, once again in the land where their forefathers had stolen blacks and thrown them into slavery, was that white man.

Right there at my Ghanaian breakfast table was where I made up my mind that as long as I was in Africa, every time I opened my mouth, I was going to make things hot for that white man, grinning through his teeth wanting to exploit Africa again—it had been her human wealth the last time, now he wanted Africa's mineral wealth.

And I knew that my reacting as I did presented no conflict with the convictions of brotherhood which I had gained in the Holy Land. The Muslims of "white" complexions who had changed my opinions were men who had showed me that they practiced genuine brotherhood. And I knew that any American white man with a genuine brotherhood for a black man was hard to find, no matter how much he grinned.

The author Julian Mayfield seemed to be the leader of Ghana's little colony of Afro-American expatriates. When I telephoned Mayfield, in what seemed no time at all I was sitting in his home surrounded by about forty black American expatriates; they had been waiting for my arrival. There were business and professional people, such as the militant former

Brooklynites Dr. and Mrs. Robert E. Lee, both of them dentists, who had given up their United States' citizenship. Such others as Alice Windom, Maya Angelou Make, Victoria Garvin, and Leslie Lacy had even formed a "Malcolm X Committee" to guide me through a whirlwind calendar of appearances and social events.

In my briefcase here are some of the African press stories which had appeared when it was learned that I was en route:

"Malcolm X's name is almost as familiar to Ghanaians as the Southern dogs, fire hoses, cattle prods, people sticks, and the ugly, hate-contorted white faces. . . ."

"Malcolm X's decision to enter the mainstream of the struggle heralds a hopeful sign on the sickeningly dismal scene of brutalized, non-violent, passive resistance. . . ."

"An extremely important fact is that Malcolm X is the first Afro-American leader of national standing to make an independent trip to Africa since Dr. Du Bois came to Ghana. This may be the beginning of a new phase in our struggle. Let's make sure we don't give it less thought than the State Department is doubtless giving it right now."

And another: "Malcolm X is one of our most significant and miltant leaders. We are in a battle. Efforts will be made to malign and discredit him. . . ."

I simply couldn't believe this kind of reception five thousand miles from America! The officials of the press had even arranged to pay my hotel expenses, and they would hear no objection that I made. They included T. D. Baffoe, the Editor-in-Chief of the *Ghanaian Times;* G. T. Anim, the Managing Director of the Ghana News Agency; Kofi Batsa, the Editor of *Spark* and the Secretary-General of the Pan-African Union of Journalists; and Mr. Cameron Duodu; and others. I could only thank them all. Then, during the beautiful dinner which had been prepared by Julian Mayfield's pretty Puerto Rican wife, Ana Livia (she was in charge of Accra's district health program), I was plied with questions by the eagerly interested black expatriates from America who had returned to Mother Africa.

I can only wish that every American black man could have shared my ears, my eyes, and my emotions throughout the round of engagements which had been made for me in Ghana. And my point in saying this is not the reception that I personally received as an individual of whom they had heard, but it was the reception tendered to me as the symbol of the militant American black man, as I had the honor to be regarded.

At a jam-packed press club conference, I believe the very first question was why had I split with Elijah Muhammad and the Nation of Islam. The Africans had heard such rumors as that Elijah Muhammad had built a palace in Arizona. I straightened out that falsehood, and I avoided any criticism. I said that our disagreement had been in terms of political direction and involvement in the extra-religious struggle for human rights. I said I respected the Nation of Islam for its having been a psychologically revitalizing movement and a source of moral and social reform, and that Elijah Muhammad's influence upon the American black man had been basic.

I stressed to the assembled press the need for mutual communication and support between the Africans and Afro-Americans whose struggles were interlocked. I remember that in the press conference, I used the word "Negro," and I was firmly corrected. "The word is not favored here, Mr. Malcolm X. The term Afro-American has greater meaning, and dignity." I sincerely apologized. I don't think that I said "Negro" again as long as I was in Africa. I said that the 22 million Afro-Americans in the United States could become for Africa a great positive force—while, in turn, the African nations could and should exert positive force at diplomatic levels against America's racial discrimination. I said, "All of Africa unites in opposition to South Africa's apartheid, and to the oppression in the Portuguese territories. But you waste your time if you don't realize that Verwoerd and Salazar, and Britain and France, never could last a day if it were not for United States support. So until you expose the man in Washington, D.C., you haven't accomplished anything."

I knew that the State Department's G. Mennen Williams was officially visiting in Africa. I said, "Take my word for it —you be suspicious of all these American officials who come to Africa grinning in your faces when they don't grin in ours back home." I told them that my own father was murdered by whites in the state of Michigan where G. Mennen Williams once was the Governor.

I was honored at the Ghana Club, by more press representatives and dignitaries. I was the guest at the home of the late black American author Richard Wright's daughter, beautiful, slender, soft-voiced Julia, whose young French husband publishes a Ghanaian paper. Later, in Paris, I was to meet Richard Wright's widow, Ellen, and a younger daughter, Rachel.

I talked with Ambassadors, at their embassies. The Algerian Ambassador impressed me as a man who was dedicated totally to militancy, and to world revolution, as the way to solve the problems of the world's oppressed masses. His perspective was attuned not just to Algerians, but to include the Afro-Americans and all others anywhere who were oppressed. The Chinese Ambassador, Mr. Huang Ha, a most perceptive, and also most militant man, focused upon the efforts of the West to divide Africans from the peoples of African heritage elsewhere. The Nigerian Ambassador was deeply concerned about the Afro-Americans' plight in America. He had personal knowledge of their suffering, having lived and studied in Washington, D.C. Similarly, the most sympathetic Mali Ambassador had been in New York at the United Nations. I breakfasted with Dr. Makonnen of British Guiana. We discussed the need for the type of Pan-African unity that would also include the Afro-Americans. And I had a talk in depth about Afro-American problems with Nana Nketsia, the Ghanaian Minister of Culture.

Once when I returned to my hotel, a New York City call was waiting for me from Mal Goode of the American Broadcasting Company. Over the telephone Mal Goode asked me questions that I answered for his beeping tape recorder, about the "Blood Brothers" in Harlem, the rifle clubs for Negroes, and other subjects with which I was being kept identified in the American press.

In the University of Ghana's Great Hall, I addressed the largest audience that I would in Africa—mostly Africans, but also numerous whites. Before this audience, I tried my best to demolish the false image of American race relations that I knew was spread by the U.S. Information Agency. I tried to impress upon them all the true picture of the Afro-American's plight at the hands of the white man. I worked on those whites there in the audience:

"I've never *seen* so many whites so nice to so many blacks as you white people here in Africa. In America, Afro-Americans are struggling for integration. They should come here— to Africa—and see how you grin at Africans. You've really got integration here. But can you tell the Africans that in America you grin at the black people? No, you can't! And you don't honestly like these Africans any better, either—but what you *do* like is the *minerals* Africa has under her soil. . . ."

Those whites out in the audience turned pink and red. They knew I was telling the truth. "I'm not anti-American, and I didn't come here to *condemn* America—I want to make that very clear!" I told them. "I came here to tell the truth—and if the *truth* condemns America, then she stands condemned!"

One evening I met most of the officials in Ghana—all of those with whom I had previously talked, and more—at a party that was given for me by the Honorable Kofi Baako, the Ghanaian Minister of Defense, and the Leader of the National Assembly. I was told that this was the first time such an honor was accorded to a foreigner since Dr. W. E. B. Du Bois had come to Ghana. There was music, dancing, and fine Ghanaian food. Several persons at the party were laughing among themselves, saying that at an earlier party that day, U.S. Ambassador Mahomey was knocking himself out being exceptionally friendly and jovial. Some thought that he was making a strong effort to counteract the truth about America that I was telling every chance I got.

Then an invitation came to me which exceeded my wildest dream. I would never have imagined that I would actually have an opportunity to address the members of the Ghanaian Parliament!

I made my remarks brief—but I made them strong: "How can you condemn Portugal and South Africa while our black people in America are being bitten by dogs and beaten with clubs?" I said I felt certain that the only reason black Africans —our black brothers—could be so silent about what happened in America was that they had been misinformed by the American government's propaganda agencies.

At the end of my talk, I heard "Yes! We support the Afro-American . . . morally, physically, materially if necessary!"

In Ghana—or in all of black Africa—my highest single honor was an audience at the Castle with Osagyefo Dr. Kwame Nkrumah.

Before seeing him, I was searched most thoroughly. I respected the type of security the Ghanaians erect around their leader. It gave me that much more respect for independent black men. Then, as I entered Dr. Nkrumah's long office, he came out from behind his desk at the far end. Dr. Nkrumah wore ordinary dress, his hand was extended and a smile was on his sensitive face. I pumped his hand. We sat on a couch and talked. I knew that he was particularly well-informed on the Afro-American's plight, as for years he had lived and studied in America. We discussed the unity of Africans and peoples of African descent. We agreed that Pan-Africanism was the key also to the problems of those of African heritage. I could feel the warm, likeable and very down-to-earth qualities of Dr. Nkrumah. My time with him was up all too soon. I promised faithfully that when I returned to the United States, I would relay to Afro-Americans his personal warm regards.

That afternoon, thirty-nine miles away in Winneba, I spoke at the Kwame Nkrumah Ideological Institute—where two hundred students were being trained to carry forward Ghana's intellectual revolution, and here again occurred one of those astounding demonstrations of the young African's political fervor. After I had spoken, during the question-and-answer period, some young Afro-American stood up, whom none there seemed to know. "I am an American Negro," he announced himself. Vaguely, he defended the American white man. The African students booed and harassed him. Then instantly when the meeting was over, they cornered this fellow with verbal abuse, "Are you an agent of Rockefeller?" . . . "Stop corrupting our children!" (The fellow had turned out to be a local secondary school teacher, placed in the job by an American agency.) . . . "Come to this Institute for some orientation!" Temporarily, a teacher rescued the fellow —but then the students rushed him and drove him away, shouting, "Stooge!" . . . "C.I.A." . . . "American agent!"

Chinese Ambassador and Mrs. Huang Hua gave a state dinner in my honor. The guests included the Cuban and the Algerian ambassadors, and also it was here that I met Mrs. W. E. B. Du Bois. After the excellent dinner, three films were shown. One, a color film, depicted the People's Republic of China in celebration of its Fourteenth Anniversary. Prominently shown in this film was the militant former North Carolina Afro-American Robert Williams, who has since taken refuge in Cuba after his advocacy that the American black people should take up arms to defend and protect themselves. The second film focused upon the Chinese people's support for the Afro-American struggle. Chairman Mao Tsetung was shown delivering his statement of that support, and the film offered sickening moments of graphic white brutality —police and civilian—to Afro-Americans who were demonstrating in various U.S. cities, seeking civil rights. And the final film was a dramatic presentation of the Algerian Revolution.

The "Malcolm X Committee" rushed me from the Chinese Embassy dinner to where a soiree in my honor had already begun at the Press Club. It was my first sight of Ghanaians dancing the high-life. A high and merry time was being had by everyone, and I was pressed to make a short speech. I stressed again the need for unity between Africans and Afro-Americans. I cried out of my heart, "Now, dance! Sing! But as you do—remember Mandela, remember Sobokwe! Remember Lumumba in his grave! Remember South Africans now in jail!"

I said, "You wonder why *I* don't dance? Because I want you to remember twenty-two million Afro-Americans in the U.S.!"

But I sure felt like dancing! The Ghanaians performed the high-life as if possessed. One pretty African girl sang "Blue Moon" like Sarah Vaughan. Sometimes the band sounded like Milt Jackson, sometimes like Charlie Parker.

The next morning, a Saturday, I heard that Cassius Clay and his entourage had arrived. There was a huge reception for him at the airport. I thought that if Cassius and I happened to meet, it would likely prove embarrassing for Cassius, since he had elected to remain with Elijah Muhammad's version of Islam. I would not have been embarrassed, but I knew that Cassius would have been forbidden to associate with me. I knew that Cassius knew I had been with him, and for him, and believed in him, when those who later embraced him felt that he had no chance. I decided to avoid Cassius so as not to put him on the spot.

A luncheon was given for me that afternoon by the Nigerian High Commissioner, His Excellency Alhadji Isa Wali, a short, bespectacled, extremely warm and friendly man who had lived in Washington, D.C. for two years. After lunch, His Excellency spoke to the guests of his American encounters with discrimination, and of friendships he had made with Afro-Americans, and he reaffirmed the bonds between Africans and Afro-Americans.

His Excellency held up before the luncheon guests a large and handsome issue of an American magazine, *Horizon;* it was opened to an article about the Nation of Islam, written by Dr. Morroe Berger of Princeton University. One full page was a photograph of me; the opposite full page was a beautiful color illustration of a black royal Nigerian Muslim, stalwart and handsome, of hundreds of years ago.

"When I look at these photographs, I know these two people are one," said His Excellency. "The only difference is in their attire—and one was born in America and the other in Africa.

"So to let everyone know that I believe we are brothers, I am going to give to Alhadji Malcolm X a robe like that worn by the Nigerian in this photo."

I was overwhelmed by the splendor of the beautiful blue robe and the orange turban which His Excellency then presented to me. I bent over so that he, a short man, could properly arrange the turban on my head. His Excellency Alhadji Isa Wali also presented me with a two-volume translation of the Holy Quran.

After this unforgettable luncheon, Mrs. Shirley Graham Du Bois drove me to her home, so that I could see and photograph the home where her famed late husband, Dr. W. E. B. Du Bois, had spent his last days. Mrs. Du Bois, a writer, was the Director of Ghanaian television, which was planned for educational purposes. When Dr. Du Bois had come to Ghana, she told me, Dr. Nkrumah had set up the aging great militant Afro-American scholar like a king, giving to Dr. Du Bois everything he could wish for. Mrs. Du Bois told me that when Dr. Du Bois was failing fast, Dr. Nkrumah had visited, and the two men had said good-bye, both knowing that one's death was near—and Dr. Nkrumah had gone away in tears.

My final Ghanaian social event was a beautiful party in my honor given by His Excellency Mr. Armando Entralgo Gonzalez, the Cuban Ambassador to Ghana. The next morning—it was Sunday—the "Malcolm X Committee" was waiting at my hotel, to accompany me to the airport. As we left the hotel, we met Cassius Clay with some of his entourage, returning from his morning walk. Cassius momentarily seemed uncertain—then he spoke, something almost monosyllabic, like "How are you?" It flashed through my mind how close we had been before the fight that had changed the course of his life. I replied that I was fine—something like that—and that I hoped he was, which I sincerely meant. Later on, I sent Cassius a message by wire, saying that I hoped that he would realize how much he was loved by Muslims wherever they were; and that he would not let anyone use him and maneuver him into saying and doing things to tarnish his image.

The "Malcolm X Committee" and I were exchanging good-byes at the Accra airport when a small motorcade of *five Ambassadors* arrived—to see me off!

I no longer had any words.

In the plane, bound for Monrovia, Liberia, to spend a day, I knew that after what I had experienced in the Holy Land, the second most indelible memory I would carry back to America would be the Africa seething with serious awareness of itself, and of Africa's wealth, and of her power, and of her destined role in the world.

From Monrovia, I flew to Dakar, Senegal. The Senegalese in the airport, hearing about the Muslim from America, stood in line to shake my hand, and I signed many autographs. "Our people can't speak Arabic, but we have Islam in our hearts," said one Senegalese. I told them that exactly described their fellow Afro-American Muslims.

From Dakar, I flew to Morocco, where I spent a day sightseeing. I visited the famous Casbah, the ghetto which had resulted when the ruling white French wouldn't let the dark-skinned natives into certain areas of Casablanca. Thousands upon thousands of the subjugated natives were crowded into the ghetto, in the same way that Harlem, in New York City, became America's Casbah.

It was Tuesday, May 19, 1964—my thirty-ninth birthday —when I arrived in Algiers. A lot of water had gone under the bridge in those years. In some ways, I had had more experiences than a dozen men. The taxi driver, while taking me to the Hotel Aletti, described the atrocities the French had committed, and personal measures that he had taken to get even. I walked around Algiers, hearing rank-and-file expressions of hatred for America for supporting the oppressors of the Algerians. They were true revolutionists, not afraid of death. They had, for so long, faced death.

The Pan American jet which took me home—it was Flight 115—landed at New York's Kennedy Air Terminal on May 21, at 4:25 in the afternoon. We passengers filed off the plane and toward Customs. When I saw the crowd of fifty or sixty reporters and photographers, I honestly wondered what celebrity I had been on the plane with.

But I was the "villain" they had come to meet.

In Harlem especially, and also in some other U.S. cities, the 1964 long, hot summer's predicted explosions had begun.

Article after article in the white man's press had cast me as a symbol—if not a causative agent—of the "revolt" and of the "violence" of the American black man, wherever it had sprung up.

In the biggest press conference that I had ever experienced anywhere, the camera bulbs flashed, and the reporters fired questions.

"Mr. Malcolm X, what about those "Blood Brothers," reportedly affiliated with your organization, reportedly trained for violence, who have killed innocent white people?" . . . "Mr. Malcolm X, what about your comment that Negroes should form rifle clubs? . . ."

I answered the questions. I knew I was back in America again, hearing the subjective, scapegoat-seeking questions of the white man. New York white youth were killing victims; that was a "sociological" problem. But when black youth killed somebody, the power structure was looking to hang somebody. When black men had been lynched or otherwise murdered in cold blood, it was always said, "Things will get better." When whites had rifles in their homes, the Constitution gave them the right to protect their home and themselves. But when black people even spoke of having rifles in their homes, that was "ominous."

I slipped in on the reporters something they hadn't been expecting. I said that the American black man needed to quit thinking what the white man had taught him—which was that the black man had no alternative except to beg for his so-called "civil rights." I said that the American black man needed to recognize that he had a strong, airtight case to take the United States before the United Nations on a formal accusation of "denial of human rights"—and that if Angola and South Africa were precedent cases, then there would be no easy way that the U.S. could escape being censured, right on its own home ground.

Just as I had known, the press wanted to get me off that subject. I was asked about my "Letter From Mecca"—I was all set with a speech regarding that:

"I hope that once and for all my Hajj to the Holy City of Mecca has established our Muslim Mosque's authentic religious affiliation with the 750 million Muslims of the orthodox Islamic World. And I *know* once and for all that the Black Africans look upon America's 22 million blacks as long-lost *brothers!* They *love* us! They *study* our struggle for freedom!

They were so *happy* to hear how we are awakening from our long sleep—after so-called 'Christian' white America had taught us to be *ashamed* of our African brothers and homeland!

"Yes—I wrote a letter from Mecca. You're asking me 'Didn't you say that now you accept white men as brothers?' Well, my answer is that in the Muslim World, I saw, I felt, and I wrote home how my thinking was broadened! Just as I wrote, I shared true, brotherly love with many white-complexioned Muslims who never gave a single thought to the race, or to the complexion, of another Muslim.

"My pilgrimage broadened my scope. It blessed me with a new insight. In two weeks in the Holy Land, I saw what I never had seen in thirty-nine years here in America. I saw all *races,* all *colors,*—blue-eyed blonds to black-skinned Africans —in *true* brotherhood! In unity! Living as one! Worshiping as one! No segregationists—no liberals; they would not have known how to interpret the meaning of those words.

"In the past, yes, I have made sweeping indictments of *all* white people. I never will be guilty of that again—as I know now that some white people *are* truly sincere, that some truly are capable of being brotherly toward a black man. The true Islam has shown me that a blanket indictment of all white people is as wrong as when whites make blanket indictments against blacks.

"Yes, I have been convinced that *some* American whites do want to help cure the rampant racism which is on the path to *destroying* this country!

"It was in the Holy World that my attitude was changed, by what I experienced there, and by what I witnessed there, in terms of brotherhood—not just brotherhood toward me, but brotherhood between all men, of all nationalities and complexions, who were there. And now that I am back in America, my attitude here concerning white people has to be governed by what my black brothers and I experience here, and what we witness here—in terms of brotherhood. The *problem* here in America is that we meet such a small minority of individual so-called 'good,' or 'brotherly' white people. Here in the United States, notwithstanding those few 'good' white people, it is the *collective* 150 million white people whom the *collective* 22 million black people have to deal with!

"Why, here in America, the seeds of racism are so deeply

rooted in the white people collectively, their belief that they are 'superior' in some way is so deeply rooted, that these things are in the national white subconsciousness. Many whites are even actually unaware of their own racism, until they face some test, and then their racism emerges in one form or another.

"Listen! The white man's racism toward the black man here in America is what has got him in such trouble all over this world, with other non-white peoples. The white man can't separate himself from the stigma that he automatically feels about anyone, no matter who, who is not his color. And the non-white peoples of the world are sick of the condescending white man! That's why you've got all of this trouble in places like Viet Nam. Or right here in the Western Hemisphere— probably 100 million people of African descent are divided against each other, taught by the white man to hate and to mistrust each other. In the West Indies, Cuba, Brazil, Venezuela, all of South America, Central America! All of those lands are full of people with African blood! On the African continent, even, the white man has maneuvered to divide the black African from the brown Arab, to divide the so-called 'Christian African' from the Muslim African. Can you imagine what can happen, what would certainly happen, if all of these African-heritage peoples ever *realize* their blood bonds, if they ever realize they all have a common goal—if they ever *unite?*"

The press was glad to get rid of me that day. I believe that the black brothers whom I had just recently left in Africa would have felt that I did the subject justice. Nearly through the night, my telephone at home kept ringing. My black brothers and sisters around New York and in some other cities were calling to congratulate me on what they had heard on the radio and television news broadcasts, and people, mostly white, were wanting to know if I would speak here or there.

The next day I was in my car driving along the freeway when at-a red light another car pulled alongside. A white woman was driving and on the passenger's side, next to me, was a white man. *"Malcolm X!"* he called out—and when I looked, he stuck his hand out of his car, across at me, grinning. "Do you mind shaking hands with a white man?" Imagine that! Just as the traffic light turned green, I told him, "I don't mind shaking hands with human beings. Are you one?"

CHAPTER NINETEEN

1965

I must be honest. Negroes—Afro-Americans—showed no inclination to rush to the United Nations and demand justice for themselves here in America. I really had known in advance that they wouldn't. The American white man has so thoroughly brainwashed the black man to see himself as only a domestic "civil rights" problem that it will probably take longer than I live before the Negro sees that the struggle of the American black man is international.

And I had known, too, that Negroes would not rush to follow me into the orthodox Islam which had given me the insight and perspective to see that the black men and white men truly could be brothers. America's Negroes—especially older Negroes—are too indelibly soaked in Christianity's double standard of oppression.

So, in the "public invited" meetings which I began holding each Sunday afternoon or evening in Harlem's well-known Audubon Ballroom, as I addressed predominantly non-Muslim Negro audiences, I did not immediately attempt to press the Islamic religion, but instead to embrace all who sat before me:

"—not Muslim, nor Christian, Catholic, nor Protestant . . . Baptist nor Methodist, Democrat nor Republican, Mason nor Elk! I mean the black people of America—and the black people all over this earth! Because it is as this collective mass of black people that we have been deprived not only of our civil rights, but even of our human rights, the right to human dignity. . . ."

On the streets, after my speeches, in the faces and the voices of the people I met—even those who would pump my hands and want my autograph—I would feel the wait-and-see attitude. I would feel—and I understood—their uncertainty about where I stood. Since the Civil War's "freedom," the black man has gone down so many fruitless paths. His leaders, very largely, had failed him. The religion of Christianity had failed him. The black man was scarred, he was cautious, he was apprehensive.

I understood it better now than I had before. In the Holy World, away from America's race problem, was the first time I ever had been able to think clearly about the basic divisions of white people in America, and how their attitudes and their motives related to, and affected Negroes. In my thirty-nine years on this earth, the Holy City of Mecca had been the first time I had ever stood before the Creator of All and felt like a complete human being.

In that peace of the Holy World—in fact, the very night I have mentioned when I lay awake surrounded by snoring brother pilgrims—my mind took me back to personal memories I would have thought were gone forever . . . as far back, even, as when I was just a little boy, eight or nine years old. Out behind our house, out in the country from Lansing, Michigan, there was an old, grassy "Hector's Hill," we called it—which may still be there. I remembered there in the Holy World how I used to lie on the top of Hector's Hill, and look up at the sky, at the clouds moving over me, and daydream, all kinds of things. And then, in a funny contrast of recollections, I remembered how years later, when I was in prison, I used to lie on my cell bunk—this would be especially when I was in solitary: what we convicts called "The Hole"—and I would picture myself talking to large crowds. I don't have any idea why such previsions came to me. But they did. To tell that to anyone then would have sounded crazy. Even I didn't have, myself, the slightest inkling. . . .

In Mecca, too, I had played back for myself the twelve years I had spent with Elijah Muhammad as if it were a motion picture. I guess it would be impossible for anyone ever to realize fully how complete was my belief in Elijah Muhammad. I believed in him not only as a leader in the ordinary *human* sense, but also I believed in him as a *divine* leader. I believed he had no human weaknesses or faults, and that, therefore, he could make no mistakes and that he could do no wrong. There on a Holy World hilltop, I realized how very dangerous it is for people to hold any human being in such esteem, especially to consider anyone some sort of "divinely guided" and "protected" person.

My thinking had been opened up wide in Mecca. In the long letters I wrote to friends, I tried to convey to them my new insights into the American black man's struggle and his problems, as well as the depths of my search for truth and justice.

"I've had enough of someone else's propaganda," I had written to these friends. "I'm for truth, no matter who tells it. I'm for justice, no matter who it is for or against. I'm a human being first and foremost, and as such I'm for whoever and whatever benefits humanity *as a whole*."

Largely, the American white man's press refused to convey that I was now attempting to teach Negroes a new direction. With the 1964 "long, hot summer" steadily producing new incidents, I was constantly accused of "stirring up Negroes." Every time I had another radio or television microphone at my mouth, when I was asked about "stirring up Negroes" or "inciting violence," I'd get hot.

"It takes no one to stir up the sociological dynamite that stems from the unemployment, bad housing, and inferior education already in the ghettoes. This explosively criminal condition has existed for so long, it needs no fuse; it fuses itself; it spontaneously combusts from within itself. . . ."

They called me "the angriest Negro in America." I wouldn't deny that charge. I spoke exactly as I felt. "I *believe* in anger. The Bible says there is a *time* for anger." They called me "a teacher, a fomentor of violence." I would say point blank, "That is a lie. I'm not for wanton violence, I'm for justice. I feel that if white people were attacked by Negroes—if the forces of law prove unable, or inadequate, or reluctant to protect those whites from those Negroes—then those white people should protect and defend themselves from those Negroes, using arms if necessary. And I feel that when the law fails to protect Negroes from whites' attack, then those Negroes should use arms, if necessary, to defend themselves."

"Malcolm X Advocates Armed Negroes!"

What was wrong with that? I'll tell you what was wrong. I was a black man talking about physical defense against the white man. The white man can lynch and burn and bomb and beat Negroes—that's all right: "Have patience" . . . "The customs are entrenched" . . . "Things are getting better."

Well, I believe it's a crime for anyone who is being brutalized to continue to accept that brutality without doing something to defend himself. If that's how "Christian" philosophy is interpreted, if that's what Gandhian philosophy teaches, well, then, I will call them criminal philosophies.

I tried in every speech I made to clarify my new position regarding white people—"I don't speak against the sincere, well-meaning, good white people. I have learned that there *are* some. I have learned that not all white people are racists. I am speaking against and my fight is against the white *racists*. I firmly believe that Negroes have the right to fight against these racists, by any means that are necessary."

But the white reporters kept wanting me linked with that word "violence." I doubt if I had one interview without having to deal with that accusation.

"I *am* for violence if non-violence means we continue postponing a solution to the American black man's problem—just to *avoid* violence. I don't go for non-violence if it also means a delayed solution. To me a delayed solution is a non-solution. Or I'll say it another way. If it must take violence to get the black man his human rights in this country, I'm *for* violence exactly as you know the Irish, the Poles, or Jews would be if they were flagrantly discriminated against. I am just as they would be in that case, and they would be for violence—no matter what the consequences, no matter who was hurt by the violence."

White society *hates* to hear anybody, especially a black man, talk about the crime the white man has perpetrated on the black man. I have always understood that's why I have been so frequently called "a revolutionist." It sounds as if *I* have done some crime! Well, it may be the American black man does need to become involved in a *real* revolution. The word for "revolution" in German is *Umwälzung*. What it means is a complete overturn—a complete change. The overthrow of King Farouk in Egypt and the succession of President Nasser is an example of a true revolution. It means the destroying of an old system, and its replacement with a new system. Another example is the Algerian revolution, led by Ben Bella; they threw out the French who had been there over 100 years. So how does anybody sound talking about the Negro in America waging some "revolution"? Yes, he is condemning a system—but he's not trying to overturn the system, or to destroy it. The Negro's so-called "revolt" is merely an asking to be *accepted* into the existing system! A *true* Negro revolt might entail, for instance, fighting for separate black states within this country—which several groups and individuals have advocated, long before Elijah Muhammad came along.

When the white man came into this country, he certainly wasn't demonstrating any "non-violence." In fact, the very man whose name symbolizes non-violence here today has stated:

"Our nation was born in genocide when it embraced the doctrine that the original American, the Indian, was an inferior race. Even before there were large numbers of Negroes on our shores, the scar of racial hatred had already disfigured colonial society. From the sixteenth century forward, blood flowed in battles over racial supremacy. We are perhaps the only nation which tried as a matter of national policy to wipe out its indigenous population. Moreover, we elevated that tragic experience into a noble crusade. Indeed, even today we have not permitted ourselves to reject or to feel remorse for this shameful episode. Our literature, our films, our drama, our folklore all exalt it. Our children are still taught to respect the violence which reduced a red-skinned people of an earlier culture into a few fragmented groups herded into impoverished reservations."

"Peaceful coexistence!" That's another one the white man has always been quick to cry. Fine! But what have been the deeds of the white man? During his entire advance through history, he has been waving the banner of Christianity . . . and carrying in his other hand the sword and the flintlock.

You can go right back to the very beginning of Christianity. Catholicism, the genesis of Christianity as we know it to be presently constituted, with its hierarchy, was conceived in Africa—by those whom the Christian church calls "The Desert Fathers." The Christian church became infected with racism when it entered white Europe. The Christian church returned to Africa under the banner of the Cross—conquering, killing, exploiting, pillaging, raping, bullying, beating—and teaching white supremacy. This is how the white man thrust himself into the position of leadership of the world —through the use of naked physical power. And he was totally inadequate spiritually. Mankind's history has proved from one era to another that the true criterion of leadership is spiritual. Men are attracted by spirit. By power, men are *forced*. Love is engendered by spirit. By power, anxieties are created.

I am in agreement one hundred per cent with those racists who say that no government laws ever can *force* brotherhood.

The only true world solution today is governments guided by true religion—of the spirit. Here in race-torn America, I am convinced that the Islam religion is desperately needed, particularly by the American black man. The black man needs to reflect that he has been America's most fervent Christian—and where has it gotten him? In fact, in the white man's hands, in the white man's interpretation . . . where has Christianity brought this *world?*

It has brought the non-white two-thirds of the human population to rebellion. Two-thirds of the human population today is telling the one-third minority white man, "Get out!" And the white man is leaving. And as he leaves, we see the non-white peoples returning in a rush to their original religions, which had been labeled "pagan" by the conquering white man. Only one religion—Islam—had the power to stand and fight the white man's Christianity for a *thousand years!* Only Islam could keep white Christianity at bay.

The Africans are returning to Islam and other indigenous religions. The Asians are returning to being Hindus, Buddhists and Muslims.

As the Christian Crusade once went East, now the Islamic Crusade is going West. With the East—Asia—closed to Christianity, with Africa rapidly being converted to Islam, with Europe rapidly becoming un-Christian, generally today it is accepted that the "Christian" civilization of America—which is propping up the white race around the world—is Christianity's remaining strongest bastion.

Well, if *this* is so—if the so-called "Christianity" now being practiced in America displays the best that world Christianity has left to offer—no one in his right mind should need any much greater proof that very close at hand is the *end* of Christianity.

Are you aware that some Protestant theologians, in their writings, are using the phrase "post-Christian era"—and they mean *now?*

And what is the greatest single reason for this Christian church's failure? It is its failure to combat racism. It is the old "You sow, you reap" story. The Christian church sowed racism —blasphemously; now it reaps racism.

Sunday mornings in this year of grace 1965, imagine the "Christian conscience" of congregations guarded by deacons barring the door to black would-be worshipers, telling them "You can't enter *this* House of God!"

Tell me, if you can, a sadder irony than that St. Augustine,

Florida—a city named for the black African saint who saved Catholicism from heresy—was recently the scene of bloody race riots.

I believe that God now is giving the world's so-called "Christian" white society its last opportunity to repent and atone for the crimes of exploiting and enslaving the world's non-white peoples. It is exactly as when God gave Pharaoh a chance to repent. But Pharaoh persisted in his refusal to give justice to those whom he oppressed. And, we know, God finally destroyed Pharaoh.

Is white America really sorry for her crimes against the black people? Does white America have the capacity to repent—and to atone? Does the capacity to repent, to atone, exist in a majority, in one-half, in even one-third of American white society?

Many black men, the victims—in fact most black men—would like to be able to forgive, to forget, the crimes.

But most American white people seem not to have it in them to make any serious atonement—to do justice to the black man.

Indeed, how *can* white society atone for enslaving, for raping, for unmanning, for otherwise brutalizing *millions* of human beings, for centuries? What atonement would the God of Justice demand for the robbery of the black people's labor, their lives, their true identities, their culture, their history— and even their human dignity?

A desegregated cup of coffee, a theater, public toilets— the whole range of hypocritcal "integration"—these are not atonement.

After a while in America, I returned abroad—and this time, I spent eighteen weeks in the Middle East and Africa.

The world leaders with whom I had private audiences this time included President Gamal Abdel Nasser, of Egypt; President Julius K. Nyerere, of Tanzania; President Nnamoi Azikiwe, of Nigeria; Osagyefo Dr. Kwame Nkrumah, of Ghana; President Sekou Touré, of Guinea; President Jomo Kenyatta, of Kenya; and Prime Minister Dr. Milton Obote, of Uganda.

I also met with religious leaders—African, Arab, Asian, Muslim, and non-Muslim. And in all of these countries, I talked with Afro-Americans and whites of many professions and backgrounds.

An American white ambassador in one African country was Africa's most respected American ambassador: I'm glad to say that this was told to me by one ranking African leader. We talked for an entire afternoon. Based on what I had heard of him, I had to believe him when he told me that as long as he was on the African continent, he never thought in terms of race, that he dealt with human beings, never noticing their color. He said he was more aware of language differences than of color differences. He said that only when he returned to America would he become aware of color differences.

I told him, "What you are telling me is that it isn't the American white *man* who is a racist, but it's the American political, economic, and social *atmosphere* that automatically nourishes a racist psychology in the white man." He agreed.

We both agreed that American society makes it next to impossible for humans to meet in America and not be conscious of their color differences. And we both agreed that if racism could be removed, America could offer a society where rich and poor could truly live like human beings.

That discussion with the ambassador gave me a new insight —one which I like: that the white man is *not* inherently evil, but America's racist society influences him to act evilly. The society has produced and nourishes a psychology which brings out the lowest, most base part of human beings.

I had a totally different kind of talk with another white man I met in Africa—who, to me, personified exactly what the ambassador and I had discussed. Throughout my trip, I was of course aware that I was under constant surveillance. The agent was a particularly obvious and obnoxious one; I am not sure for what agency, as he never identified it, or I would say it. Anyway, this one finally got under my skin when I found I couldn't seem to eat a meal in the hotel without seeing him somewhere around watching me. You would have thought I was John Dillinger or somebody.

I just got up from my breakfast one morning and walked over to where he was and I told him I knew he was following me, and if he wanted to know anything, why didn't he ask me. He started to give me one of those too-lofty-to-descend-to-you attitudes. I told him then right to his face he was a fool, that he didn't know me, or what I stood for, so that made him one of those people who let somebody else do their thinking; and that no matter what job a man had, at least he ought to be able to think for himself. That stung him; he let me have it.

I was, to hear him tell it, anti-American, un-American, seditious, subversive, and probably Communist. I told him that what he said only proved how little he understood about me. I told him that the only thing the F.B.I., the C.I.A., or anybody else could ever find me guilty of, was being open-minded. I said I was seeking for the truth, and I was trying to weigh —objectively—everything on its own merit. I said what I was against was strait-jacketed thinking, and strait-jacketed societies. I said I respected every man's right to believe whatever his intelligence tells him is intellectually sound, and I expect everyone else to respect my right to believe likewise.

This super-sleuth then got off on my "Black Muslim" religious beliefs. I asked him hadn't his headquarters bothered to brief him—that my attitudes and beliefs were changed? I told him that the Islam I believed in now was the Islam which was taught in Mecca—that there was no God but Allah, and that Muhammad ibn Abdullah who lived in the Holy City of Mecca fourteen hundred years ago was the Last Messenger of Allah.

Almost from the first I had been guessing about something; and I took a chance—and I really shook up that "super-sleuth." From the consistent subjectivity in just about every thing he asked and said, I had deduced something, and I told him, "You know, I think you're a Jew with an Anglicized name." His involuntary expression told me I'd hit the button. He asked me how I knew. I told him I'd had so much experience with how Jews would attack me that I usually could identify them. I told him all I held against the Jew was that so many Jews actually were hypocrites in their claim to be friends of the American black man, and it burned me up to be so often called "anti-Semitic" when I spoke things I knew to be the absolute truth about Jews. I told him that, yes, I gave the Jew credit for being among all other whites the most active, and the most vocal, financier, "leader" and "liberal" in the Negro civil rights movement. But I said at the same time I knew that the Jew played these roles for a very careful strategic reason: the more prejudice in America could be focused upon the Negro, then the more the white Gentiles' prejudice would keep diverted off the Jew. I said that to me, one proof that all the civil rights posturing of so many Jews wasn't sincere was that so often in the North the quickest segregationists were Jews themselves. Look at practically everything the black man is trying to "integrate" into for instance;

if Jews are not the actual owners, or are not in controlling positions, then they have major stockholdings or they are otherwise in powerful leverage positions—and do they really sincerely exert these influences? No!

And an even clearer proof for me of how Jews truly regard Negroes, I said, was what invariably happened wherever a Negro moved into any white residential neighborhood that was thickly Jewish. Who would always lead the whites' exodus? The Jews! Generally in these situations, some whites stay put —you just notice who they are: they're Irish Catholics, they're Italians; they're rarely ever any Jews. And, ironically, the Jews themselves often still have trouble being "accepted."

Saying this, I know I'll hear "anti-Semitic" from every direction again. Oh, yes! But truth is truth.

Politics dominated the American scene while I was traveling abroad this time. In Cairo and again in Accra, the American press wire services reached me with trans-Atlantic calls, asking whom did I favor, Johnson—or Goldwater?

I said I felt that as far as the American black man was concerned they were both just about the same. I felt that it was for the black man only a question of Johnson, the fox, or Goldwater, the wolf.

"Conservatism" in America's politics means "Let's keep the niggers in their place." And "liberalism" means "Let's keep the knee-grows in their place—but tell them we'll treat them a little better; let's fool them more, with more promises." With these choices, I felt that the American black man only needed to choose which one to be eaten by, the "liberal" fox or the "conservative" wolf—because both of them would eat him.

I didn't go for Goldwater any more than for Johnson— except that in a wolf's den, I'd always know exactly where I stood; I'd watch the dangerous wolf closer than I would the smooth, sly fox. The wolf's very growling would keep me alert and fighting him to survive, whereas I might be lulled and fooled by the tricky fox. I'll give you an illustration of the fox. When the assassination in Dallas made Johnson President, who was the first person he called for? It was for his best friend, "Dicky"—Richard Russell of Georgia. Civil rights was "a moral issue," Johnson was declaring to everybody—while his best friend was the Southern racist who led the civil rights opposition. How would some sheriff sound, declaring himself so against bank robbery—and Jesse James his best friend?

Goldwater as a man, I respected for speaking out his true convictions—something rarely done in politics today. He wasn't whispering to racists and smiling at integrationists. I felt Goldwater wouldn't have risked his unpopular stand without conviction. He flatly told black men he wasn't for them—and there is this to consider: always, the black people have advanced further when they have seen they had to rise up against a system that they clearly saw was outright against them. Under the steady lullabys sung by foxy liberals, the Northern Negro became a beggar. But the Southern Negro, facing the honestly snarling white man, rose up to battle that white man for his freedom—long before it happened in the North.

Anyway, I didn't feel that Goldwater was any better for black men than Johnson, or vice-versa. I wasn't in the United States at election time, but if I had been, I wouldn't have put myself in the position of voting for either candidate for the Presidency, or of recommending to any black man to do so. It has turned out that it's Johnson in the White House—and black votes were a major factor in his winning as decisively as he wanted to. If it had been Goldwater, all I am saying is that the black people would at least have known they were dealing with an honestly growling wolf, rather than a fox who could have them half-digested before they even knew what was happening.

I kept having all kinds of troubles trying to develop the kind of Black Nationalist organization I wanted to build for the American Negro. Why Black Nationalism? Well, in the competitive American society, how can there ever be any white-black solidarity before there is first some black solidarity? If you will remember, in my childhood I had been exposed to the Black Nationalist teachings of Marcus Garvey —which, in fact, I had been told had led to my father's murder. Even when I was a follower of Elijah Muhammad, I had been strongly aware of how the Black Nationalist political, economic and social philosophies had the ability to instill within black men the racial dignity, the incentive, and the confidence that the black race needs today to get up off its knees, and to get on its feet, and get rid of its scars, and to take a stand for itself.

One of the major troubles that I was having in building

the organization that I wanted—an all-black organization
whose ultimate objective was to help create a society in which
there could exist honest white-black brotherhood—was that
my earlier public image, my old so-called "Black Muslim"
image, kept blocking me. I was trying to gradually reshape
that image. I was trying to turn a corner, into a new regard
by the public, especially Negroes; I was no less angry than
I had been, but at the same time the true brotherhood I had
seen in the Holy World had influenced me to recognize that
anger can blind human vision.

Every free moment I could find, I did a lot of talking to
key people whom I knew around Harlem, and I made a lot
of speeches, saying: "True Islam taught me that it takes *all*
of the religious, political, economic, psychological, and racial
ingredients, or characteristics, to make the Human Family
and the Human Society complete.

"Since I learned the *truth* in Mecca, my dearest friends
have come to include *all* kinds—some Christians, Jews,
Buddhists, Hindus, agnostics, and even atheists! I have friends
who are called capitalists, Socialists, and Communists! Some
of my friends are moderates, conservatives, extremists—
some are even Uncle Toms! My friends today are black,
brown, red, yellow, and *white!*"

I said to Harlem street audiences that ony when mankind
would submit to the One God who created all—only then
would mankind even approach the "peace" of which so much
talk could be heard . . . but toward which so little *action*
was seen.

I said that on the American racial level, we had to approach
the black man's struggle against the white man's racism as a
human problem, that we had to forget hypocritical politics
and propaganda. I said that both races, as human beings, had
the obligation, the responsibility, of helping to correct America's human problem. The well-meaning white people, I said,
had to combat, actively and directly, the racism in other white
people. And the black people had to build within themselves
much greater awareness that along with equal rights there
had to be the bearing of equal responsibilities.

I knew, better than most Negroes, how many white people
truly wanted to see American racial problems solved. I knew
that many whites were as frustrated as Negroes. I'll bet I got
fifty letters some days from white people. The white people
in meeting audiences would throng around me, asking me,

after I had addressed them somewhere, "What *can* a sincere white person do?"

When I say that here now, it makes me think about that little co-ed I told you about, the one who flew from her New England college down to New York and came up to me in the Nation of Islam's restaurant in Harlem, and I told her that there was "nothing" she could do. I regret that I told her that. I wish that now I knew her name, or where I could telephone her, or write to her, and tell her what I tell white people now when they present themselves as being sincere, and ask me, one way or another, the same thing that she asked.

The first thing I tell them is that at least where my own particular Black Nationalist organization, the Organization of Afro-American Unity, is concerned, they can't *join* us. I have these very deep feelings that white people who want to join black organizations are really just taking the escapist way to salve their consciences. By visibly hovering near us, they are "proving" that they are "with us." But the hard truth is this *isn't* helping to solve America's racist problem. The Negroes aren't the racists. Where the really sincere white people have got to do their "proving" of themselves is not among the black *victims*, but out on the battle lines of where America's racism really *is*—and that's in their own home communities; America's racism is among their own fellow whites. That's where the sincere whites who really mean to accomplish something have got to work.

Aside from that, I mean nothing against any sincere whites when I say that as members of black organizations, generally whites' very presence subtly renders the black organization automatically less effective. Even the best white members will slow down the Negroes' discovery of what they need to do, and particularly of what they can do—for themselves, working by themselves, among their own kind, in their own communities.

I sure don't want to hurt anybody's feelings, but in fact I'll even go so far as to say that I never really trust the kind of white people who are always so anxious to hang around Negroes, or to hang around in Negro communities. I don't trust the kind of whites who love having Negroes always hanging around them. I don't know—this feeling may be a throwback to the years when I was hustling in Harlem and all of those red-faced, drunk whites in the afterhours clubs were always grabbing hold of some Negroes and talking about

"I just want you to know you're just as good as I am—"
And then they got back in their taxicabs and black limousines
and went back downtown to the places where they lived and
worked, where no blacks except servants had better get
caught. But, anyway, I know that every time that whites
join a black organization, you watch, pretty soon the blacks
will be leaning on the whites to support it, and before you
know it a black may be up front with a title, but the whites,
because of their money, are the real controllers.

I tell sincere white people, "Work in conjunction with us—
each of us working among our own kind." Let sincere white
individuals find all other white people they can who feel as
they do—and let them form their own all-white groups, to
work trying to convert other white people who are thinking
and acting so racist. Let sincere whites go and teach non-
violence to white people!

We will completely respect our white co-workers. They will
deserve every credit. We will give them every credit. We will
meanwhile be working among our own kind, in our own
black communities—showing and teaching black men in ways
that only other black men can—that the black man has got
to help himself. Working separately, the sincere white people
and sincere black people actually will be working together.

In our mutual sincerity we might be able to show a road
to the salvation of America's very soul. It can only be salvaged
if human rights and dignity, in full, are extended to black men.
Only such real, meaningful actions as those which are sincerely
motivated from a deep sense of humanism and moral responsibility can get at the basic causes that produce the racial
explosions in America today. Otherwise, the racial explosions
are only going to grow worse. Certainly nothing is ever going
to be solved by throwing upon me and other so-called black
"extremists" and "demagogues" the blame for the racism that
is in America.

Sometimes, I have dared to dream to myself that one day,
history may even say that my voice—which disturbed the
white man's smugness, and his arrogance, and his complacency
—that my voice helped to save America from a grave, possibly
even a fatal catastrophe.

The goal has always been the same, with the approaches
to it as different as mine and Dr. Martin Luther King's non-
violent marching, that dramatizes the brutality and the evil
of the white man against defenseless blacks. And in the racial

climate of this country today, it is anybody's guess which of the "extremes" in approach to the black man's problems might *personally* meet a fatal catastrophe first—"non-violent" Dr. King, or so-called "violent" me.

Anything I do today, I regard as urgent. No man is given but so much time to accomplish whatever is his life's work. My life in particular never has stayed fixed in one position for very long. You have seen how throughout my life, I have often known unexpected drastic changes.

I am only facing the facts when I know that any moment of any day, or any night, could bring me death. This is particularly true since the last trip that I made abroad. I have seen the nature of things that are happening, and I have heard things from sources which are reliable.

To speculate about dying doesn't disturb me as it might some people. I never have felt that I would live to become an old man. Even before I was a Muslim—when I was a hustler in the ghetto jungle, and then a criminal in prison, it always stayed on my mind that I would die a violent death. In fact, it runs in my family. My father and most of his brothers died by violence—my father because of what he believed in. To come right down to it, if I take the kind of things in which I believe, then add to that the kind of temperament that I have, plus the one hundred per cent dedication I have to whatever I believe in—these are ingredients which make it just about impossible for me to die of old age.

I have given to this book so much of whatever time I have because I feel, and I hope, that if I honestly and fully tell my life's account, read objectively it might prove to be a testimony of some social value.

I think that an objective reader may see how in the society to which I was exposed as a black youth here in America, for me to wind up in a prison was really just about inevitable. It happens to so many thousands of black youth.

I think that an objective reader may see how when I heard "The white man is the devil," when I played back what had been my own experiences, it was inevitable that I would respond positively; then the next twelve years of my life were devoted and dedicated to propagating that phrase among the black people.

I think, I hope, that the objective reader, in following my

life—the life of only one ghetto-created Negro—may gain a better picture and understanding than he has previously had of the black ghettoes which are shaping the lives and the thinking of almost all of the 22 million Negroes who live in America.

Thicker each year in these ghettoes is the kind of teen-ager that I was—with the wrong kinds of heroes, and the wrong kinds of influences. I am not saying that all of them become the kind of parasite that I was. Fortunately, by far most do not. But still, the small fraction who do add up to an annual total of more and more costly, dangerous youthful criminals. The F.B.I. not long ago released a report of a shocking rise in crime each successive year since the end of World War II —ten to twelve per cent each year. The report did not say so in so many words, but I am saying that the majority of that crime increase is annually spawned in the black ghettoes which the American racist society permits to exist. In the 1964 "long, hot summer" riots in major cities across the United States, the socially disinherited black ghetto youth were always at the forefront.

In this year, 1965, I am certain that more—and worse— riots are going to erupt, in yet more cities, in spite of the conscience-salving Civil Rights Bill. The reason is that the *cause* of these riots, the racist malignancy in America, has been too long unattended.

I believe that it would be almost impossible to find any-where in America a black man who has lived further down in the mud of human society than I have; or a black man who has been any more ignorant than I have been; or a black man who has suffered more anguish during his life than I have. But it is only after the deepest darkness that the greatest joy can come; it is only after slavery and prison that the sweetest appreciation of freedom can come.

For the freedom of my 22 million black brothers and sisters here in America, I do believe that I have fought the best that I knew how, and the best that I could, with the short-comings that I have had. I know that my shortcomings are many.

My greatest lack has been, I believe, that I don't have the kind of academic education I wish I had been able to get— to have been a lawyer, perhaps. I do believe that I might have made a good lawyer. I have always loved verbal battle, and challenge. You can believe me that if I had the time right now, I would not be one bit ashamed to go back into any New York City public school and start where I left off at the ninth grade, and go on through a degree. Because I don't begin to be academically equipped for so many of the interests that I have. For instance, I love languages. I wish I were an accomplished linguist. I don't know anything more frustrating than to be around people talking something you can't understand. Especially when they are people who look just like you. In Africa, I heard original mother tongues, such as Hausa, and Swahili, being spoken, and there I was standing like some little boy, waiting for someone to tell me what had been said; I never will forget how ignorant I felt.

Aside from the basic African dialects, I would try to learn Chinese, because it looks as if Chinese will be the most powerful political language of the future. And already I have begun studying Arabic, which I think is going to be the most powerful spiritual language of the future.

I would just like to *study*. I mean ranging study, because I have a wide-open mind. I'm interested in almost any subject you can mention. I know this is the reason I have come to really like, as individuals, some of the hosts of radio or television panel programs I have been on, and to respect their minds—because even if they have been almost steadily in disagreement with me on the race issue, they still have kept their minds open and objective about the truths of things happening in this world. Irv Kupcinet in Chicago, and Barry Farber, Barry Gray and Mike Wallace in New York—people like them. They also let me see that they respected my mind—in a way I know they never realized. The way I knew was that often they would invite my opinion on subjects off the race issue. Sometimes, after the programs, we would sit around and talk about all kinds of things, current events and other things, for an hour or more. You see, most whites, even when they credit a Negro with some intelligence, will still feel that all he can talk about is the race issue; most whites never feel that Negroes can contribute anything to other areas of thought, and ideas. You just notice how rarely you will ever hear whites asking any Negroes what they think about the problem of world health, or the space race to land men on the moon.

Every morning when I wake up, now, I regard it as having another borrowed day. In any city, wherever I go, making speeches, holding meetings of my organization, or attending to other business, black men are watching every move I make, awaiting their chance to kill me. I have said publicly many times that I know that they have their orders. Anyone who chooses not to believe what I am saying doesn't know the Muslims in the Nation of Islam.

But I am also blessed with faithful followers who are, I believe, as dedicated to me as I once was to Mr. Elijah Muhammad. Those who would hunt a man need to remember that a jungle also contains those who hunt the hunters.

I know, too, that I could suddenly die at the hands of some white racists. Or I could die at the hands of some Negro hired by the white man. Or it could be some brainwashed Negro acting on his own idea that by eliminating me he would be helping out the white man, because I talk about the white man the way I do.

Anyway, now, each day I live as if I am already dead, and I tell you what I would like for you to do. When I *am* dead —I say it that way because from the things I *know*, I do not expect to live long enough to read this book in its finished form—I want you to just watch and see if I'm not right in what I say: that the white man, in his press, is going to identify me with "hate."

He will make use of me dead, as he has made use of me alive, as a convenient symbol of "hatred"—and that will help him to escape facing the truth that all I have been doing is holding up a mirror to reflect, to show, the history of un-speakable crimes that his race has committed against my race.

You watch. I will be labeled as, at best, an "irresponsible" black man. I have always felt about this accusation that the black "leader" whom white men consider to be "responsible" is invariably the black "leader" who never gets any results. You only get action as a black man if you are regarded by the white man as "irresponsible." In fact, this much I had learned when I was just a little boy. And since I have been some kind of a "leader" of black people here in the racist society of America, I have been more reassured each time the white man resisted me, or attacked me harder—because each time made me more certain that I was on the right track in the American black man's best interests. The racist white man's opposition automatically made me know that I did offer the black man something worthwhile.

Yes, I have cherished my "demagogue" role. I know that societies often have killed the people who have helped to

change those societies. And if I can die having brought any
light, having exposed any meaningful truth that will help to
destroy the racist cancer that is malignant in the body of
America—then, all of the credit is due to Allah. Only the
mistakes have been mine.

EPILOGUE

During nineteen fifty-nine, when the public was becoming aware of the Muslims after the New York telecast "The Hate That Hate Produced," I was in San Francisco, about to retire after twenty years in the U.S. Coast Guard. A friend returned from a visit to her Detroit home and told me of a startling "black man's" religion, "The Nation of Islam," to which, to her surprise, her entire family was converted. I listened with incredulity to how a "mad scientist Mr. Yacub" had genetically "grafted" the white race from an original black people. The organization's leader was described as "The Honorable Elijah Muhammad" and a "Minister Malcolm X" was apparently chief of staff.

When I entered a civilian writing career in New York City, I collected, around Harlem, a good deal of provocative material and then proposed an article about the cult to the *Reader's Digest*. Visiting the Muslim restaurant in Harlem, I asked how I could meet Minister Malcolm X, who was pointed out talking in a telephone booth right behind me. Soon he came out, a gangling, tall, reddish-brownskinned fellow, at that time thirty-five years old; when my purpose was made known, he bristled, his eyes skewering me from behind the horn-rimmed glasses. "You're another one of the white man's tools sent to spy!" he accused me sharply. I said I had a legitimate writing assignment and showed him my letter from the magazine stating that an objective article was wanted, one that would balance what the Muslims said of themselves and what their attackers said about them. Malcolm X snorted that no white man's promise was worth the paper it was on;

he would need time to decide if he would cooperate or not. Meanwhile, he suggested that I could attend some of the Harlem Temple Number 7 meetings ("temples" have since been renamed "mosques") which were open to non-Muslim Negroes.

Around the Muslim's restaurant, I met some of the converts, all of them neatly dressed and almost embarrassingly polite. Their manners and miens reflected the Spartan personal discipline the organization demanded, and none of them would utter anything but Nation of Islam clichés. Even excellent weather was viewed as a blessing from Allah, with corollary credit due to "The Honorable Elijah Muhammad."

Finally, Minister Malcolm X told me that he would not take personal responsibility. He said that I should talk about an article with Mr. Muhammad personally. I expressed willingness, an appointment was made, and I flew to Chicago. The slightly built, shy-acting, soft-voiced Mr. Muhammad invited me to dinner with his immediate family in his mansion. I was aware that I was being carefully sized up while he talked primarily of F.B.I. and Internal Revenue Service close surveillance of his organization, and of a rumored forthcoming Congressional probe. "But I have no fear of any of them; I have all that I need—the truth," Mr. Muhammad said. The subject of my writing an article somehow never got raised, but Malcolm X proved far more cooperative when I returned.

He would sit with me at a white-topped table in the Muslim restaurant and answer guardedly any questions I asked between constant interruptions by calls from the New York press in the telephone booth. When I asked if I could see Muslim activities in some other cities, he arranged with other ministers for me to attend meetings at temples in Detroit, Washington, and Philadelphia.

My article entitled "Mr. Muhammad Speaks" appeared in early 1960, and it was the first featured magazine notice of the phenomenon. A letter quickly came from Mr. Muhammad appreciating that the article kept my promise to be objective, and Malcolm X telephoned similar compliments. About this time, Dr. C. Eric Lincoln's book *The Black Muslims in America* was published and the Black Muslims became a subject of growing interest. During 1961 and 1962, the *Saturday Evening Post* teamed me with a white writer, Al Balk, to do an article; next I did a personal interview of Malcolm X for *Playboy* magazine, which had promised to print verbatim whatever response he made to my questions. During that interview of several days' duration, Malcolm X repeatedly exclaimed, after particularly blistering anti-Christian or anti-white statements: "You know that devil's not going to print that!" He was very much taken aback when *Playboy* kept its word.

Malcolm X began to warm up to me somewhat. He was most aware of the national periodicals' power, and he had come to regard me, if still suspiciously, as one avenue of access. Occasionally now he began to telephone me advising me of some radio, television, or personal speaking appearance he was about to make, or he would invite me to attend some Black Muslim bazaar or other public affair.

I was in this stage of relationship with the Malcolm X who often described himself on the air as "the angriest black man in America" when in early 1963 my agent brought me together with a publisher whom the *Playboy* interview had given the idea of the autobiography of Malcolm X. I was asked if I felt I could get the now nationally known firebrand to consent to telling the intimate details of his entire life. I said I didn't know, but I would ask him. The editor asked me if I could sketch the likely highlights of such a book, and as I commenced talking, I realized how little I knew about the man personally, despite all my interviews. I said that the question had made me aware of how careful Malcolm X had always been to play himself down and to play up his leader Elijah Muhammad.

All that I knew, really, I said, was that I had heard Malcolm X refer in passing to his life of crime and prison before he became a Black Muslim; that several times he had told me: "You wouldn't believe my past," and that I had heard others say that at one time he had peddled dope and women and committed armed robberies.

I knew that Malcolm X had an almost fanatical obsession about time. "I have less patience with someone who doesn't wear a watch than with anyone else, for this type is not time-conscious," he had once told me. "In all our deeds, the proper value and respect for time determines success or failure." I knew how the Black Muslim membership was said to increase wherever Malcolm X lectured, and I knew his pride that

Negro prisoners in most prisons were discovering the Muslim religion as he had when he was a convict. I knew he professed to eat only what a Black Muslim (preferably his wife Betty) had cooked and he drank innumerable cups of coffee which he lightened with cream, commenting wryly, "Coffee is the only thing I like integrated." Over our luncheon table, I told the editor and my agent how Malcolm X could unsettle non-Muslims—as, for instance, once when he offered to drive me to a subway, I began to light a cigarette and he drily observed, "That woud make you the first person ever to smoke in this automobile."

Malcolm X gave me a startled look when I asked him if he would tell his life story for publication. It was one of the few times I have ever seen him uncertain. "I will have to give a book a lot of thought," he finally said. Two days later, he telephoned me to meet him again at the Black Muslim restaurant. He said, "I'll agree. I think my life story may help people to appreciate better how Mr. Muhammad salvages black people. But I don't want my motives for this misinterpreted by anybody—the Nation of Islam must get every penny that might come to me." Of course, Mr. Muhammad's agreement would be necessary, and I would have to ask Mr. Muhammad myself.

So I flew again to see Mr. Muhammad, but this time to Phoenix, Arizona, where the Nation of Islam had bought him the house in the hot, dry climate that relieved his severe bronchial condition. He and I talked alone this time. He told me how his organization had come far with largely uneducated Muslims and that truly giant strides for the black man could be made if his organization were aided by some of the talents which were available in the black race. He said, "And one of our worst needs is writers"—but he did not press me to answer. He suddenly began coughing, and rapidly grew worse and worse until I rose from my seat and went to him, alarmed, but he waved me away, gasping that he would be all right. Between gasps, he told me he felt that "Allah approves" the book. He said, "Malcolm is one of my most outstanding ministers." After arranging for his chauffeur to return me to the Phoenix airport, Mr. Muhammad quickly bade me good-bye and rushed from the room coughing.

Back East, Malcolm X carefully read and then signed the

publication contract, and he withdrew from his wallet a piece of paper filled with his sprawling longhand. "This is this book's dedication," he said. I read: "This book I dedicate to The Honorable Elijah Muhammad, who found me here in America in the muck and mire of the filthiest civilization and society on this earth, and pulled me out, cleaned me up, and stood me on my feet, and made me the man that I am today."

The contract provided that all monies accruing to Malcolm X "shall be made payable by the agent to 'Muhammad's Mosque No. 2,'" but Malcolm X felt this was insufficient. He dictated to me a letter to type for his signature, which I did: "Any and all monies representing my contracted share of the financial returns should be made payable by the literary agent to Muhammad's Mosque No. 2. These payments should be mailed to the following address: Mr. Raymond Sharrieff, 4847 Woodlawn Avenue, Chicago 15, Illinois."

Another letter was dictated, this one an agreement between him and me: "Nothing can be in this book's manuscript that I didn't say, and nothing can be left out that I want in it."

In turn, I asked Malcolm X to sign for me a personal pledge that however busy he was, he would give me a priority quota of his time for the planned 100,000-word "as told to" book which would detail his entire life. And months later, in a time of strain between us, I asked for—and he gave—his permission that at the end of the book I could write comments of my own about him which would not be subject to his review.

Malcolm X promptly did begin to pay me two- and three-hour visits, parking his blue Oldsmobile outside the working studio I then had in Greenwich Village. He always arrived around nine or ten at night carrying his flat tan leather briefcase which along with his scholarly look gave him a resemblance to a hardworking lawyer. Inevitably, he was tired after his long busy day, and sometimes he was clearly exhausted.

We got off to a very poor start. To use a word he liked, I think both of us were a bit "spooky." Sitting right there and staring at me was the fiery Malcolm X who could be as acid toward Negroes who angered him as he was against whites in general. On television, in press conferences, and at Muslim rallies, I had heard him bitterly attack other Negro writers as "Uncle Toms," "yard Negroes," "black men in white clothes." And there I sat staring at him, proposing to spend a year plumbing his innermost secrets when he had developed a near phobia for secrecy during his years of crime and his years in the Muslim hierarchy. My twenty years in military service and my Christian religious persuasion didn't help, either; he often jeered publicly at these affiliations for Negroes. And although he now would indirectly urge me to write for national magazines about the Muslims, he had told me several times, in various ways, that "you blacks with professional abilities of any kind will one of these days wake up and find out that you must unite under the leadership of The Honorable Elijah Muhammad for your own salvation." Malcolm X was also convinced that the F.B.I. had "bugged" my studio; he probably suspected that it may even have been done with my cooperation. For the first several weeks, he never entered the room where we worked without exclaiming, "Testing, testing—one, two, three. . . ."

Tense incidents occurred. One night a white friend was in the studio when Malcolm X arrived a little earlier than anticipated, and they passed each other in the corridor. Malcolm X's manner during all of that session suggested that his worst doubts had been confirmed. Another time when Malcolm X sat haranguing me about the glories of the Muslim organization, he was gesturing with his passport in his hand; he saw that I was trying to read its perforated number and suddenly he thrust the passport toward me, his neck flushed reddish: "Get the number straight, but it won't be anything the white devil doesn't already know. He issued me the passport."

For perhaps a month I was afraid we weren't going to get any book. Malcolm X was still stiffly addressing me as "Sir!" and my notebook contained almost nothing but Black Muslim philosophy, praise of Mr. Muhammad, and the "evils" of "the white devil." He would bristle when I tried to urge him that the proposed book was *his* life. I was thinking that I might have to advise the publisher that I simply couldn't seem to get through to my subject when the first note of hope occurred. I had noticed that while Malcolm X was talking, he often simultaneously scribbled with his red-ink ball-point pen on any handy paper. Sometimes it was the margin of a newspaper he brought in, sometimes it was on index cards that he carried in the back of a small, red-backed appointment book. I began leaving two white paper napkins by him every time I served him more coffee, and the ruse worked when he sometimes scribbled on the napkins, which I retrieved when he left. Some examples are these:

"Here lies a YM, killed by a BM, fighting for the WM, who killed all the RM." (Decoding that wasn't difficult, knowing Malcolm X. "YM" was for yellow man, "BM" for black man, "WM" for white man, and "RM" was for red man.)

"Nothing ever happened without cause. Cause BM condition WM won't face. WM obsessed with hiding his guilt."

"If Christianity had asserted itself in Germany, six million Jews would have lived."

"WM so quick to tell BM 'Look what I have done for you!' No! Look what you have done *to* us!"

"BM dealing with WM who put our eyes out, now he condemns us because we cannot see."

"Only persons really changed history those who changed men's thinking about themselves. Hitler as well as Jesus, Stalin as well as Buddha . . . Hon. Elijah Muhammad. . . ."

It was through a clue from one of the scribblings that finally I cast a bait that Malcolm X took. "Woman who cries all the time is only because she knows she can get away with it," he had scribbled. I somehow raised the subject of women. Suddenly, between sips of coffee and further scribbling and doodling, he vented his criticisms and skepticisms of women. "You never can fully trust any woman," he said. "I've got the only one I ever met whom I would trust seventy-five per cent. I've told her that," he said. "I've told her like I tell you I've seen too many men destroyed by their wives, or their women.

"I don't *completely* trust anyone," he went on, "not even myself. I have seen too many men destroy themselves. Other people I trust from not at all to highly, like The Honorable Elijah Muhammad." Malcolm X looked squarely at me. "You I trust about twenty-five percent."

Trying to keep Malcolm X talking, I mined the woman theme for all it was worth. Triumphantly, he exclaimed, "Do you know why Benedict Arnold turned traitor—a woman!" He said, "Whatever else a woman is, I don't care who the woman is, it starts with her being vain. I'll prove it, something you can do anytime you want, and I know what I'm talking about, I've done it. You think of the hardest-looking, meanest-acting woman you know, one of those women who never smiles. Well, every day you see that woman you look her right in the eyes and tell her 'I think you're beautiful,' and you watch what happens. The first day she may curse you out, the second day, too—but you watch, you keep on, after a while one day she's going to start smiling just as soon as you come in sight."

When Malcolm X left that night, I retrieved napkin scribblings that further documented how he could be talking about one thing and thinking of something else:

"Negroes have too much righteousness. WM says, 'I want this piece of land, how do I get those couple of thousand BM on it off?'"

"I have wife who understands, or even if she doesn't she at least pretends."

"BM struggle never gets open support from abroad it needs unless BM first forms own united front."

"Sit down, talk with people with brains I respect, all of us want same thing, do some brainstorming."

"Would be shocking to reveal names of the BM leaders who have secretly met with THEM." (The capitalized letters stood for The Honorable Elijah Muhammad.)

Then one night, Malcolm X arrived nearly out on his feet from fatigue. For two hours, he paced the floor delivering a tirade against Negro leaders who were attacking Elijah Muhammad and himself. I don't know what gave me the inspiration to say once when he paused for breath, "I wonder if you'd tell me something about your mother?"

Abruptly he quit pacing, and the look he shot at me made me sense that somehow the chance question had hit him. When I look back at it now, I believe I must have caught him so physically weak that his defenses were vulnerable.

Slowly, Malcolm X began to talk, now walking in a tight circle. "She was always standing over the stove, trying to stretch whatever we had to eat. We stayed so hungry that we were dizzy. I remember the color of dresses she used to wear—they were a kind of faded-out gray. . . ." And he kept on talking until dawn, so tired that the big feet would often almost stumble in their pacing. From this stream-of-consciousness reminiscing I finally got out of him the foundation for this book's beginning chapters, "Nightmare" and "Mascot." After that night, he never again hesitated to tell me even the most intimate details of his personal life, over the next two years. His talking about his mother triggered something.

Malcolm X's mood ranged from somber to grim as he recalled his childhood. I remember his making a great point of how he learned what had been a cardinal awareness of his ever since: "It's the hinge that squeaks that gets the grease." When his narration reached his moving to Boston to live with his half-sister Ella, Malcolm X began to laugh about how "square" he had been in the ghetto streets. "Why, I'm telling you things I haven't thought about since then!" he would exclaim. Then it was during recalling the early Harlem days that Malcolm X really got carried away. One night, suddenly, wildly, he jumped up from his chair and, incredibly, the fearsome black demagogue was scat-singing and popping his fingers, "re-bop-de-bop-blap-blam—" and then grabbing a vertical pipe with one hand (as the girl partner) he went jubilantly lindy-hopping around, his coattail and the long legs and the big feet flying as they had in those Harlem days. And then almost as suddenly, Malcolm X caught himself and sat back down, and for the rest of that session he was decidedly grumpy. Later on in the Harlem narrative, he grew somber again. "The only thing I considered wrong was what I got caught doing wrong. I had a jungle mind, I was living in a jungle, and everything I did was done by instinct to survive." But he stressed that he had no regrets about his crimes, "because it was all a result of what happens to thousands upon thousands of black men in the white man's Christian world."

His enjoyment resumed when the narrative entered his prison days. "Let me tell you how I'd get those white devil convicts and the guards, too, to do anything I wanted. I'd whisper to them, 'If you don't, I'll start a rumor that you're really a light Negro just passing as white.' That shows you what the white devil thinks about the black man. He'd rather die than be thought a Negro!" He told me about the reading he had been able to do in prison: "I didn't know what I was doing, but just by instinct I liked the books with intellectual vitamins." And another time: "In the hectic pace of the world today, there is no time for meditation, or for deep thought. A prisoner has time that he can put to good use. I'd put prison second to college as the best place for a man to go if he needs to do some thinking. If he's *motivated*, in prison he can change his life."

Yet another time, Malcolm X reflected, "Once a man has been to prison, he never looks at himself or at other people the same again. The 'squares' out here whose boat has been in smooth waters all the time turn up their noses at an ex-con. But an ex-con can keep his head up when the 'squares' sink."

He scribbled that night (I kept both my notebooks and the paper napkins dated): "This WM created and dropped A-bomb on non-whites; WM now calls 'Red' and lives in fear of other WM he knows may bomb us."

Also: "Learn wisdom from the pupil of the eye that looks upon all things and yet to self is blind. Persian poet."

At intervals, Malcolm X would make a great point of stressing to me, "Now, I don't want anything in this book to make it sound that I think I'm somebody important." I would assure him that I would try not to, and that in any event he would be checking the manuscript page by page, and ultimately the galley proofs. At other times, he would end an attack upon the white man and, watching me take the notes, exclaim, "That devil's not going to print that, I don't care what he says!" I would point out that the publishers had made a binding contract and had paid a sizable sum in advance. Malcolm X would say, "You trust them, and I don't. You studied what he wanted you to learn about him in schools, I studied him in the streets and in prison, where you see the truth."

Experiences which Malcolm X had had during a day could flavor his interview mood. The most wistful, tender anecdotes generally were told on days when some incident had touched him. Once, for instance, he told me that he had learned that a Harlem couple, not Black Muslims, had named their newborn son "Malcolm" after him. "What do you know about *that?*" he kept exclaiming. And that was the night he went back to his own boyhood again and this time recalled how he used to lie on his back on Hector's Hill and think. That night, too: "I'll never forget the day they elected me the class president. A girl named Audrey Slaugh, whose father owned a car repair shop, nominated me. And a boy named James Cotton seconded the nomination. The teacher asked me to leave the room while the class voted. When I returned I was the class president. I couldn't believe it."

Any interesting book which Malcolm X had read could get him going about his love of books. "People don't realize how a man's whole life can be changed by *one* book." He came back again and again to the books that he had studied when in prison. "Did you ever read *The Loom of Language?*" he asked me and I said I hadn't. "You should. Philology, it's a tough science—all about how words can be recognized, no matter where you find them. Now, you take 'Caesar,' it's Latin, in Latin it's pronounced like 'Kaiser,' with a hard C. But we anglicize it by pronouncing a soft C. The Russians say 'Czar' and mean the same thing. Another Russian dialect says 'Tsar.' Jakob Grimm was one of the foremost philologists, I studied his 'Grimm's Law' in prison—all about consonants. Philology is related to the science of etymology, dealing in root words. I dabbled in both of them."

When I turn that page in my notebook, the next bears a note that Malcolm X had telephoned me saying "I'm going to be out of town for a few days." I assumed that as had frequently been the case before, he had speaking engagements or other Muslim business to attend somewhere and I was glad for the respite in which to get my notes separated under the chapter headings they would fit. But when Malcolm X returned this time, he reported triumphantly, "I have something to tell you that will surprise you. Ever since we discussed my mother, I've been thinking about her. I realized that I had blocked her out of my mind—it was just unpleasant to think about her having been twenty-some years in that mental hospital." He said, "I don't want to take the credit. It was really my sister Yvonne who thought it might be possible to get her out. Yvonne got my brothers Wilfred, Wesley and Philbert together, and I went out there, too. It was Philbert who really handled it.

"It made me face something about myself," Malcolm X said. "My mind had closed about our mother. I simply didn't feel the problem could be solved, so I had shut it out. I had built up subconscious defenses. The white man does this. He shuts out of his mind, and he builds up subconscious defenses against anything he doesn't want to face up to. I've just become aware how closed my mind was now that I've opened it up again. That's one of the characteristics I don't like about myself. If I meet a problem I feel I can't solve, I shut it out. I make believe that it doesn't exist. But it exists."

It was my turn to be deeply touched. Not long afterward, he was again away for a few days. When he returned this time, he said that at his brother Philbert's home, "we had dinner with our mother for the first time in all those years!" He said, "She's sixty-six, and her memory is better than mine and she looks young and healthy. She has more of her teeth than those who were instrumental in sending her to the institution."

When something had angered Malcolm X during the day, his face would be flushed redder when he visited me, and he generally would spend much of the session lashing out bitterly. When some Muslims were shot by Los Angeles policemen, one of them being killed, Malcolm X, upon his return from a trip he made there, was fairly apoplectic for a week. It had been in this mood that he had made, in Los Angeles, the statement which caused him to be heavily censured by members of both races. "I've just heard some good news!"— referring to a plane crash at Orly Field in Paris in which thirty-odd white Americans, mostly from Atlanta, Georgia, had been killed instantly. (Malcolm X never publicly recanted this statement, to my knowledge, but much later he said to me simply, "That's one of the things I wish I had never said.")

Anytime the name of the present Federal Judge Thurgood Marshall was raised, Malcolm X still practically spat fire in memory of what the judge had said years before when he was the N.A.A.C.P. chief attorney: "The Muslims are run by a bunch of thugs organized from prisons and jails and financed, I am sure, by some Arab group." The only time that I have ever heard Malcolm X use what might be construed as a curse word, it was a "hell" used in response to a statement that Dr. Martin Luther King made that Malcolm X's talk brought "misery upon Negroes." Malcolm X exploded to me, "How in the hell can my talk do this? It's always a Negro responsible, not what the white man does!" The "extremist" or "demagogue" accusation invariably would burn Malcolm X. "Yes, I'm an extremist. The black race here in North America is in extremely bad condition. You show me a black man who isn't an extremist and I'll show you one who needs psychiatric attention!"

Once when he said, "Aristotle shocked people. Charles

Darwin outraged people. Aldous Huxley scandalized millions!" Malcolm X immediately followed the statement with "Don't print that, people would think I'm trying to link myself with them." Another time, when something provoked him to exclaim, "These Uncle Toms make me think about how the Prophet Jesus was criticized in his own country!" Malcolm X promptly got up and silently took my notebook, tore out that page and crumpled it and put it into his pocket, and he was considerably subdued during the remainder of that session.

I remember one time we talked and he showed me a newspaper clipping reporting where a Negro baby had been bitten by a rat. Malcolm X said, "Now, just read that, just think of that a minute! Suppose it was *your* child! Where's that slumlord—on some beach in Miami!" He continued fuming throughout our interview. I did not go with him when later that day he addressed a Negro audience in Harlem and an incident occurred which Helen Dudar reported in the *New York Post*.

"Malcolm speaking in Harlem stared down at one of the white reporters present, the only whites admitted to the meeting, and went on, 'Now, there's a reporter who hasn't taken a note in half an hour, but as soon as I start talking about the Jews, he's busy taking notes to prove that I'm anti-Semitic.'

"Behind the reporter, a male voice spoke up, 'Kill the bastard, kill them all.' The young man, in his unease, smiled nervously and Malcolm jeered, 'Look at him laugh. He's really not laughing, he's just laughing with his teeth.' An ugly tension curled the edges of the atmosphere. Then Malcolm went on: 'The white man doesn't know how to laugh. He just shows his teeth. But *we* know how to laugh. We laugh deep down, from the bottom up.' The audience laughed, deep down, from the bottom up and, as suddenly as Malcolm had stirred it, so, skillfully and swiftly, he deflected it. It had been at once a masterful and shabby performance."

I later heard somewhere, or read, that Malcolm X telephoned an apology to the reporter. But this was the kind of evidence which caused many close observers of the Malcolm X phenomenon to declare in absolute seriousness that he was the only Negro in America who could either start a race riot—or stop one. When I once quoted this to him, tacitly inviting his comment, he told me tartly, "I don't know if I could start one. I don't know if I'd want to stop one." It was the kind of statement he relished making.

Over the months, I had gradually come to establish something of a telephone acquaintance with Malcolm X's wife, whom I addressed as "Sister Betty," as I had heard the Muslims do. I admired how she ran a home, with, then, three small daughters, and still managed to take all of the calls which came for Malcolm X, surely as many calls as would provide a job for an average switchboard operator. Sometimes when he was with me, he would telephone home and spend as much as five minutes rapidly jotting on a pad the various messages which had been left for him.

Sister Betty, generally friendly enough on the phone with me, sometimes would exclaim in spontaneous indignation, "The man never gets any *sleep!*" Malcolm X rarely put in less than an 18-hour workday. Often when he had left my studio at four A.M. and a 40-minute drive lay between him and home in East Elmhurst, Long Island, he had asked me to telephone him there at nine A.M. Usually this would be when he wanted me to accompany him somewhere, and he was going to tell me, after reviewing his commitments, when and where he wanted me to meet him. (There were times when I didn't get an awful lot of sleep myself.) He was always accompanied, either by some of his Muslim colleagues like James 67X (the 67th man named "James" who had joined Harlem's Mosque Number 7), or Charles 37X, or by me, but he never asked me to be with him when they were. I went with him to college and university lectures, to radio and television stations for his broadcasts, and to public appearances in a variety of situations and locations.

If we were driving somewhere, motorists along the highway would wave to Malcolm X, the faces of both whites and Negroes spontaneously aglow with the wonderment that I had seen evoked by other "celebrities." No few airline hostesses had come to know him, because he flew so much; they smiled prettily at him, he was in turn the essence of courtly gentlemanliness, and inevitably the word spread and soon an unusual flow of bathroom traffic would develop, passing where he sat. Whenever we arrived at our destination, it became familiar to hear "There's Malcolm X!" *"Where?"* "The tall one." Passers-by of both races stared at him. A few of both races, more Negroes than whites, would speak or nod to him in greeting. A high percentage of white people were visibly uncomfortable in his presence, especially within the confines of small areas, such as in elevators. "I'm the only black man they've ever been close to who they know speaks the *truth* to them," Malcolm X once explained to me. "It's their guilt that upsets them, not me." He said another time, "The white man is afraid of truth. The truth takes the white man's breath and drains his strength—you just watch his face get red anytime you tell him a little truth."

There was something about this man when he was in a room with people. He commanded the room, whoever else was present. Even out of doors; once I remember in Harlem he sat on a speaker's stand between Congressman Adam Clayton Powell and the former Manhattan Borough President Hulan Jack, and when the street rally was over the crowd focus was chiefly on Malcolm X. I remember another time that we had gone by railway from New York City to Philadelphia where he appeared in the Philadelphia Convention Hall on the radio station WCAU program of Ed Harvey. "You are the man who has said 'All Negroes are angry and I am the angriest of all'; is that correct?" asked Harvey, on the air, introducing Malcolm X, and as Malcolm X said crisply, "That quote is correct!" the gathering crowd of bystanders stared at him, riveted.

We had ridden to Philadelphia in reserved parlor car seats. "I can't get caught on a coach, I could get into trouble on a coach," Malcolm X had said. Walking to board the parlor car, we had passed a dining car toward which he jerked his head, "I used to work on that thing." Riding to our destination, he conversationally told me that the F.B.I. had tried to bribe him for information about Elijah Muhammad; that he wanted me to be sure and read a new book, *Crisis in Black and White* by Charles Silberman—"one of the very few white writers I know with the courage to tell his kind the truth"; and he asked me to make a note to please telephone the *New York Post's* feature writer Helen Dudar and tell her he thought very highly of her recent series—he did not want to commend her directly.

After the Ed Harvey Show was concluded, we took the train to return to New York City. The parlor car, packed with businessmen behind their newspapers, commuting homeward after their workdays, was electric with Malcolm X's presence. After the white-jacketed Negro porter had made several trips up and down the aisle, he was in the middle of another trip when Malcolm X *sotto-voced* in my ear, "He used to work with me, I forget his name, we worked right on this very train together. He knows it's me. He's trying to make up his mind what to do." The porter went on past us, poker-faced. But when he came through again, Malcolm X suddenly leaned forward from his seat, smiling at the porter. "Why, sure, I know who you are!" the porter suddenly said, loudly. "You washed dishes right on this train! I was just telling some of the fellows you were in my car here. We all follow you!"

The tension in the car could have been cut with a knife. Then, soon, the porter returned to Malcolm X, his voice expansive. "One of our guests would like to meet you." Now a young, clean-cut white man rose and came up, his hand extended, and Malcolm X rose and shook the proffered hand firmly. Newspapers dropped just below eye-level the length of the car. The young white man explained distinctly, loudly, that he had been in the Orient for awhile, and now was studying at Columbia. "I don't agree with everything you say," he told Malcolm X, "but I have to admire your presentation."

Malcolm's voice in reply was cordiality itself. "I don't think you could search America, sir, and find two men who agree on everything." Subsequently, to another white man, an older businessman, who came up and shook hands, he said evenly, "Sir, I know how you feel. It's a hard thing to speak out against me when you are agreeing with so much that I say." And we rode on into New York under, now, a general open gazing.

In Washington, D.C., Malcolm X slashed at the government's reluctance to take positive steps in the Negro's behalf. I gather that even the White House took notice, for not long afterward I left off interviewing Malcolm X for a few days and went to the White House to do a *Playboy* interview of the then White House Press Secretary Pierre Salinger, who grimaced spontaneously when I said I was writing the life story of Malcolm X. Another time I left Malcolm X to interview the U.S. Nazi Party Commander George Lincoln Rockwell, who frankly stated that he admired the courage of Malcolm X, and he felt that the two of them should speak together across the United States, and they could thus begin a real solution to the race problem—one of voluntary separation of the white and black races, with Negroes returning to Africa. I reported this to Malcolm X, who snorted, "He must think I'm nuts! What am *I* going to look like going speaking with a *devil!*" Yet another time, I went off to Atlanta and interviewed for *Playboy* Dr. Martin Luther King. He was privately intrigued to hear little-known things about Malcolm X that I told him; for publication, he discussed him with reserve, and he did say that he would sometime like to have an opportunity to talk with him. Hearing this, Malcolm X said drily, "You think I ought to send him a telegram with my telephone number?" (But from other things that Malcolm X said to me at various times, I deduced that he actually had a reluctant admiration for Dr. King.)

Malcolm X and I reached the point, ultimately, where we shared a mutual camaraderie that, although it was never verbally expressed, was a warm one. He was for me unquestionably one of the most engaging personalities I had ever met, and for his part, I gathered, I was someone he had learned he could express himself to, with candor, without the likelihood of hearing it repeated, and like any person who lived amid tension, he enjoyed being around someone, another man, with whom he could psychically relax. When I made trips now, he always asked me to telephone him when I would be returning to New York, and generally, if he could squeeze it into his schedule, he met me at the airport. I would see him coming along with his long, gangling strides, and wearing the wide, toothy, good-natured grin, and as he drove me into New York City he would bring me up to date on things of interest that had happened since I left. I remember one incident within the airport that showed me how Malcolm X never lost his racial perspective. Waiting for my baggage, we witnessed a touching family reunion scene as part of which several cherubic little children romped and played, exclaiming in another language. "By tomorrow night, they'll know how to say their first English word—*nigger*," observed Malcolm X.

When Malcolm X made long trips, such as to San Francisco or Los Angeles, I did not go along, but frequently, usually very late at night, he would telephone me, and ask how the book was coming along, and he might set up the time for our next interview upon his return. One call that I never will forget came at close to four A.M., waking me; he must have just gotten up in Los Angeles. His voice said, "Alex Haley?" I said, sleepily, "Yes? Oh, *hey,* Malcolm!" His voice said, "I trust you seventy per cent"—and then he hung up. I lay a short time thinking about him and I went back to sleep feeling warmed by that call, as I still am warmed to remember it. Neither of us ever mentioned it.

Malcolm X's growing respect for individual whites seemed to be reserved for those who ignored on a personal basis the things he said about whites and who jousted with him as a *man.* He, moreover, was convinced that he could tell a lot about any person by listening. "There's an art to listening well," he told me. "I listen closely to the sound of a man's voice when he's speaking. I can hear sincerity." The newspaper person whom he ultimately came to admire probably more than any other was the *New York Times'* M. S. Handler. (I was very happy when I learned that Handler had agreed to write this book's Introduction; I know that Malcolm X would have liked that.) The first time I ever heard Malcolm X speak of Handler, whom he had recently met, he began, "I was talking with this devil—" and abruptly he cut himself off in obvious embarrassment. "It's a reporter named Handler, from the *Times*—" he resumed. Malcolm X's respect for the man steadily increased, and Handler, for his part, was an influence upon the inner Malcolm X. "He's the most genuinely unprejudiced white man I ever met," Malcolm X said to me, speaking of Handler months later. "I have asked him things and tested him. I have listened to him talk, closely."

I saw Malcolm X too many times exhilarated in after-lecture give-and-take with predominantly white student bodies at colleges and universities to ever believe that he nurtured at his core any blanket white-hatred. "The young whites, and blacks, too, are the only hope that America has," he said to me once. "The rest of us have always been living in a lie."

Several Negroes come to mind now who I know, in one way or another, had vastly impressed Malcolm X. (Some others come to mind whom I know he has vastly abhorred, but these I will not mention.) Particularly high in his esteem, I know, was the great photographer, usually associated with *Life* magazine, Gordon Parks. It was Malcolm X's direct influence with Elijah Muhammad which got Parks permitted to enter and photograph for publication in *Life* the highly secret self-defense training program of the Black Muslim Fruit of Islam, making Parks, as far as I know, the only non-Muslim who ever has witnessed this, except for policemen and other agency representatives who had feigned "joining" the Black Muslims to infiltrate them. "His success among the white man never has made him lose touch with black reality," Malcolm X said of Parks once.

Another person toward whom Malcolm X felt similarly was the actor Ossie Davis. Once in the middle of one of our interviews, when we had been talking about something else, Malcolm X suddenly asked me, "Do you know Ossie Davis?" I said I didn't. He said, "I ought to introduce you sometime, that's one of the finest black men." In Malcolm X's long dealings with the staff of the Harlem weekly newspaper *Amsterdam News,* he had come to admire Executive Editor James Hicks and the star feature writer James Booker. He said that Hicks had "an open mind, and he never panics for the white man." He thought that Booker was an outstanding reporter; he also was highly impressed with Mrs. Booker when he met her.

It was he who introduced me to two of my friends today, Dr. C. Eric Lincoln who was at the time writing the book *The Black Muslims in America,* and Louis Lomax who was then writing various articles about the Muslims. Malcolm X deeply respected the care and depth which Dr. Lincoln was putting into his research. Lomax, he admired for his ferreting ear and eye for hot news. "If I see that rascal Lomax running somewhere, I'll grab my hat and get behind him," Malcolm X said once, "because I know he's onto something." Author James Baldwin Malcolm X also admired. "He's so brilliant he confuses the white man with words on paper." And another time, "He's upset the white man more than anybody except The Honorable Elijah Muhammad."

Malcolm X had very little good to say of Negro ministers, very possibly because most of them had attacked the Black Muslims. Excepting reluctant admiration of Dr. Martin Luther King, I heard him speak well of only one other, The Reverend Eugene L. Callender of Harlem's large Presbyterian Church of the Master. "He's a preacher, but he's a fighter for the black man," said Malcolm X. I later learned that somewhere the direct, forthright Reverend Callender had privately cornered Malcolm X and had read him the riot act about his general attacks upon the Negro clergy. Malcolm X also admired The Reverend Adam Clayton Powell, in his Congressman political role: "I'd think about retiring if the black man had ten like him in Washington." He had similar feelings about the N.A.A.C.P. lawyer, now a New York State Assemblyman, Percy Sutton, and later Sutton was retained as his personal attorney. Among Negro educators, of whom Malcolm X met many in his college and university lecturing, I never heard him speak well of any but one, Dr. Kenneth B. Clark. "There's a black man with brains gone to bed," Malcolm X told me once, briefly lapsing into his old vernacular. He had very distinct reservations about Negro professional intelligentsia as a category. They were the source from which most of the Black Muslims' attackers came. It was for this reason that some of his most bristling counter-attacks against "these so-called educated Uncle Thomases, Ph.D." were flung out at his audiences at Negro institutions of higher learning.

Where I witnessed the Malcolm X who was happiest and most at ease among members of our own race was when sometimes I chanced to accompany him on what he liked to call "my little daily rounds" around the streets of Harlem, among the Negroes that he said the "so-called black leaders" spoke of "as black masses statistics." On these tours, Malcolm X generally avoided the arterial 125th Street in Harlem; he plied the side streets, especially in those areas which were thickest with what he described as "the black man down in the gutter where I came from," the poverty-ridden with a high incidence of dope addicts and winos.

Malcolm X here indeed was a hero. Striding along the sidewalks, he bathed all whom he met in the boyish grin, and his conversation with any who came up was quiet and pleasant. "It's just what the white devil wants you to do, brother," he might tell a wino, "he wants you to get drunk so he will have an excuse to put a club up beside your head." Or I remember once he halted at a stoop to greet several older women: "Sisters, let me ask you something," he said conversationally, "have you ever known *one* white man who either didn't do something to you, or take something from you?" One among that audience exclaimed after a moment, "I sure *ain't!*" whereupon all of them joined in laughter and we walked on with

Malcolm X waving back to cries of "He's *right!*"

I remember that once in the early evening we rounded a corner to hear a man, shabbily dressed, haranguing a small crowd around his speaking platform of an upturned oblong wooden box with an American flag alongside. "I don't respect or believe in this damn flag, it's there because I can't hold a public meeting without it unless I want the white man to put me in jail. And that's what I'm up here to talk about— these crackers getting rich off the blood and bones of your and my people!" Said Malcolm X, grinning, "He's *working!*"

Malcolm X rarely exchanged any words with those Negro men with shiny, "processed" hair without giving them a nudge. Very genially: "Ahhhh, brother, the white devil has taught you to hate yourself so much that you put hot lye in your hair to make it look more like his hair."

I remember another stoopful of women alongside the door of a small grocery store where I had gone for something, leaving Malcolm X talking across the street. As I came out of the store, one woman was excitedly describing for the rest a Malcolm X lecture she had heard in Mosque Number 7 one Sunday. "Oooooh, he *burnt* that white man, burnt him *up,* chile . . . chile, he told us we descendin' from black kings an' queens—Lawd, I didn't know it!" Another woman asked, "You believe that?" and the first vehemently responded, "Yes, I *do!*"

And I remember a lone, almost ragged guitarist huddled on a side street playing and singing just for himself when he glanced up and instantly recognized the oncoming, striding figure. "Huh-*ho!*" the guitarist exclaimed, and jumping up, he snapped into a mock salute. "My *man!*"

Malcolm X loved it. And they loved him. There was no question about it: whether he was standing tall beside a street lamp chatting with winos, or whether he was firing his radio and television broadsides to unseen millions of people, or whether he was titillating small audiences of sophisticated whites with his small-talk such as, "My hobby is stirring up Negroes, that's spelled *knee*-grows the way you liberals pronounce it"—the man had charisma, and he had *power.* And I was not the only one who at various times marveled at how he could continue to receive such an awesome amount of international personal publicity and still season liberally practically everything he said, both in public and privately, with credit and hosannas to "The Honorable Elijah Muhammad." Often I made side notes to myself about this. I kept, in effect, a double-entry set of notebooks. Once, noting me switching from one to the other, Malcolm X curiously asked me what for? I told him some reason, but not that one notebook was things he said for his book and the other was for my various personal observations about him; very likely he would have become self-conscious. "You must have written a million words by now," said Malcolm X. "Probably," I said. "This white man's crazy," he mused. "I'll prove it to you. Do you think I'd publicize somebody knocking me like I do him?"

"Look, tell me the truth," Malcolm X said to me one evening, "you travel around. Have you heard anything?"

Truthfully, I told him I didn't know what he had reference to. He dropped it and talked of something else.

From Malcolm X himself, I had seen, or heard, a few unusual things which had caused me some little private wonder and speculation, and then, with nothing to hang them onto, I had dismissed them. One day in his car, we had stopped for the red light at an intersection; another car with a white man driving had stopped alongside, and when this white man saw Malcolm X, he instantly called across to him, "I don't blame your people for turning to you. If I were a Negro I'd follow you, too. Keep up the fight!" Malcolm X said to the man very sincerely, "I wish I could have a white chapter of the people I meet like you." The light changed, and as both cars drove on, Malcolm X quickly said to me, firmly, "Not only don't write that, never repeat it. Mr. Muhammad would have a fit." The significant thing about the incident, I later reflected, was that it was the first time I had ever heard him speak of Elijah Muhammad with anything less than reverence.

About the same time, one of the scribblings of Malcolm X's that I had retrieved had read, enigmatically, "My life has always been one of changes." Another time, this was in September, 1963, Malcolm X had been highly upset about something during an entire session, and when I read the *Amsterdam News* for that week, I guessed that he had been upset about an item in Jimmy Booker's column that Booker had heard that Elijah Muhammad and Malcolm X were feuding. (Booker was later to reveal that after his column was written, he had gone on vacation, and on his return he learned that Malcolm X "stormed into the *Amsterdam News* with three followers . . . 'I want to see Jimmy Booker. I don't like what he wrote. There is no fight between me and Elijah Muhammad. I believe in Mr. Muhammad and will lay down my life for him.'")

Also, now and then, when I chanced to meet a few other key Muslims, mainly when I was with Malcolm X, but when he was not immediately present, I thought I detected either in subtle phrasing, or in manner, something less than total admiration of their famous colleague—and then I would tell myself I had misinterpreted. And during these days, Dr. C. Eric Lincoln and I would talk on the phone fairly often. We rarely would fail to mention how it seemed almost certain that seeds of trouble lay in the fact that however much Malcolm X praised Elijah Muhammad, it was upon dramatic, articulate Malcolm X that the communications media and hence the general public focused the great bulk of their attention. I never dreamed, though, what Malcolm X was actually going through. He never breathed a word, at least not to me, until the actual rift became public.

When Malcolm X left me at around two A.M. on that occasion, he asked me to call him at nine A.M. The telephone in the home in East Elmhurst rang considerably longer than usual, and Sister Betty, when she answered, sounded strained, choked up. When Malcolm X came on, he, too, sounded different. He asked me, "Have you heard the radio or seen the newspapers?" I said I hadn't. He said, "Well, do!" and that he would call me later.

I went and got the papers. I read with astonishment that Malcolm X had been suspended by Elijah Muhammad—the stated reason being the "chickens coming home to roost" remark that Malcolm X recently had made as a comment upon the assassination of President Kennedy.

Malcolm X did telephone, after about an hour, and I met him at the Black Muslims' newspaper office in Harlem, a couple of blocks further up Lenox Avenue from their mosque and restaurant. He was seated behind his light-brown metal desk and his brown hat lay before him on the green blotter. He wore a dark suit with a vest, a white shirt, the inevitable leaping-sailfish clip held his narrow tie, and the big feet in the shined black shoes pushed the swivel chair pendulously back and forth as he talked into the telephone.

"I'm always hurt over any act of disobedience on my part concerning Mr. Muhammad. . . . Yes, sir—anything The Honorable Elijah Muhammad does is all right with me. I believe absolutely in his wisdom and authority." The telephone would ring again instantly every time he put it down. "Mr. Peter Goldman! I haven't heard your voice in a good while! Well, sir, I just should have kept my big mouth shut." To the *New York Times*: "Sir? Yes—he suspended me from making public appearances for the time being, which I fully understand. I say the same thing to you that I have told others, I'm in complete submission to Mr. Muhammad's judgment, because I have always found his judgment to be based on sound thinking." To C.B.S.: "I think that anybody who is in a position to discipline others should first learn to accept discipline himself."

He brought it off, the image of contriteness, the best he could—throughout the harshly trying next several weeks. But the back of his neck was reddish every time I saw him. He did not yet put into words his obvious fury at the public humiliation. We did very little interviewing now; he was so busy on telephones elsewhere, but it did not matter too much because by now I had the bulk of the needed life story material in hand. When he did find some time to visit me, he was very preoccupied, and I could *feel* him rankling with anger and with inactivity, but he tried hard to hide it.

He scribbled one night, "You have not converted a man because you have silenced him. John Viscount Morley." And the same night, almost illegibly, "I was going downhill until he picked me up, but the more I think of it, we picked each other up."

When I did not see him for several days, a letter came. "I have cancelled all public appearances and speaking engagements for a number of weeks. So within that period it should be possible to finish this book. With the fast pace of newly developing incidents today, it is easy for something that is done or said tomorrow to be outdated even by sunset on the same day. Malcolm X."

I pressed to get the first chapter, "Nightmare," into a shape that he could review. When it was ready in a readable rough draft, I telephoned him. He came as quickly as he could drive from his home—which made me see how grinding an ordeal it was to him to just be sitting at home, inactive, and knowing his temperament, my sympathies went out to Sister Betty.

He pored over the manuscript pages, raptly the first time, then drawing out his red-ink ball-point pen he read through the chapter again, with the pen occasionally stabbing at something. "You can't bless Allah!" he exclaimed, changing "bless" to "praise." In a place that referred to himself and his brothers and sisters, he scratched red through "we kids." "Kids are *goats!*" he exclaimed sharply.

Soon, Malcolm X and his family flew to Miami. Cassius Clay had extended the invitation as a sixth wedding anniversary present to Malcolm X and Sister Betty, and they had accepted most gratefully. It was Sister Betty's first vacation in the six years of the taut regimen as a Black Muslim wife, and it was for Malcolm X both a saving of face and something to *do*.

Very soon after his arrival, he telegraphed me his phone number at a motel. I called him and he told me, "I just want to tell you something. I'm not a betting man anymore, but if you are, you bet on Cassius to beat Liston, and you will win." I laughed and said he was prejudiced. He said, "Remember what I told you when the fight's over." I received later a picture postcard, the picture in vivid colors being of a chimpanzee at the Monkey Jungle in Miami. Malcolm X had written on the reverse side, "One hundred years after the Civil War, and these *chimpanzees* get more recognition, respect and freedom in America than our people do. Bro. Malcolm X." Another time, an envelope came, and inside it was a clipping of an Irv Kupcinet column in the Chicago *Sun-Times*. Malcolm X's red pen had encircled an item which read, "Insiders are predicting a split in the Black Muslims. Malcolm X, ousted as No. 2 man in the organization, may form a splinter group to oppose Elijah Muhammad." Alongside the item, Malcolm X had scribbled "Imagine this!!!"

The night of the phenomenal upset, when Clay *did* beat Liston, Malcolm X telephoned me, and sounds of excitement were in the background. The victory party was in his motel suite, Malcolm X told me. He described what was happening, mentioned some of those who were present, and that the new heavyweight king was "in the next room, my bedroom here" taking a nap. After reminding me of the fight prediction he had made, Malcolm X said that I should look forward now to Clay's "quick development into a major world figure. I don't know if you really realize the world significance that this is the first *Muslim* champion."

It was the following morning when Cassius Clay gave the press interview which resulted in national headlines that he was actually a "Black Muslim," and soon after, the newspapers were carrying pictures of Malcolm X introducing the heavyweight champion to various African diplomats in the lobbies of the United Nations headquarters in New York City. Malcolm X toured Clay about in Harlem, and in other places, functioning, he said, as Clay's "friend and religious advisor."

I had now moved upstate to finish my work on the book, and we talked on the telephone every three or four days. He said things suggesting that he might never be returned to his former Black Muslim post, and he now began to say things quietly critical of Elijah Muhammad. *Playboy* magazine asked me to do an interview with the new champion Cassius Clay, and when I confidently asked Malcolm X to arrange for me the needed introduction to Clay, Malcolm X hesitantly said, "I think you had better ask somebody else to do that." I was highly surprised at the reply, but I had learned never to press him for information. And then, very soon after, I received a letter. "Dear Alex Haley: A quick note. Would you prepare a properly worded letter that would enable me to change the reading of the contract so that all remaining proceeds now would go to the Muslim Mosque, Inc., or in the case of my death then to go directly to my wife, Mrs. Betty X Little? The sooner this letter or contract is changed, the more easily I will rest." Under the signature of Malcolm X, there was a P.S.: "How is it possible to write one's autobiography in a world so fast-changing as this?"

Soon, I read in the various newspapers that rumors were being heard of threats on Malcolm X's life. Then there was an article in the *Amsterdam News*: The caption was "Malcolm X Tells Of Death Threat," and the story reported that he had said that former close associates of his in the New York mosque had sent out "a special squad" to "try to kill me in cold blood. Thanks to Allah, I learned of the plot from the very same brothers who had been sent out to murder me. These brothers had heard me represent and defend Mr. Muhammad for too long for them to swallow the lies about me without first asking me some questions for their own clarification."

I telephoned Malcolm X, and expressed my personal concern for him. His voice sounded weary. He said that his "uppermost interest" was that any money which might come due him in the future would go directly to his new organization, or to his wife, as the letter he had signed and mailed had specified. He told me, "I know I've got to get a will made for myself, I never did because I never have had anything to will to anybody, but if I don't have one and something happened to me, there could be a mess." I expressed concern for him, and he told me that he had a loaded rifle in his home, and "I can take care of myself."

The "Muslim Mosque, Inc." to which Malcolm X had referred was a new organization which he had formed, which at that time consisted of perhaps forty or fifty Muslims who had left the leadership of Elijah Muhammad.

Through a close associate of Cassius Clay, whom Malcolm X had finally suggested to me, my interview appointment was arranged with the heavyweight champion, and I flew down to New York City to do the interview for *Playboy*. Malcolm X was "away briefly," Sister Betty said on the phone—and she spoke brusquely. I talked with one Black Muslim lady whom I had known before she had joined, and who had been an admirer of Malcolm X. She had elected to remain in the original fold, "but I'll tell you, brother, what a lot in the mosque are saying, you know, it's like if you divorced your husband, you'd still like to see him once in a while." During my interviews with Cassius Clay in his three-room suite at Harlem's Theresa Hotel, inevitably the questions got around to Clay's Muslim membership, then to a query about what had happened to his formerly very close relationship with Malcolm X. Evenly, Clay said, "You just don't buck Mr. Muhammad and get away with it. I don't want to talk about him no more."

Elijah Muhammad at his headquarters in Chicago grew "emotionally affected" whenever the name of Malcolm X had to be raised in his presence, one of the Muslims in Clay's entourage told me. Mr. Muhammad reportedly had said,

"Brother Malcolm got to be a *big* man. I made him big. I was about to make him a *great* man." The faithful Black Muslims predicted that soon Malcolm X would be turned upon by the defectors from Mosque Number 7 who had joined him: "They will feel betrayed." Said others, "A great chastisement of Allah will fall upon a hypocrite." Mr. Muhammad reportedly had said at another time, "Malcolm is destroying himself," and that he had no wish whatever to see Malcolm X die, that he "would rather see him live and suffer his treachery."

The general feeling among Harlemites, non-Muslims, with whom I talked was that Malcolm X had been powerful and influential enough a minister that eventually he would split the mosque membership into two hostile camps, and that in New York City at least, Elijah Muhammad's unquestioned rule would be ended.

Malcolm X returned. He said that he had been in Boston and Philadelphia. He spent ample time with me, now during the day, in Room 1936 in the Hotel Americana. His old total ease was no longer with him. As if it was the most natural thing in the world to do, at sudden intervals he would stride to the door; pulling it open, he would look up and down the corridor, then shut the door again. "If I'm alive when this book comes out, it will be a miracle," he said by way of explanation. "I'm not saying it distressingly—" He leaned forward and touched the buff gold bedspread. "I'm saying it like I say that's a bedspread."

For the first time he talked with me in some detail about what had happened. He said that his statement about President Kennedy's assassination was not why he had been ousted from the Muslims. "It wasn't the reason at all. Nobody said anything when I made stronger statements before." The real reason, he said, was "jealousy in Chicago, and I had objected to the immorality of the man who professed to be more moral than anybody."

Malcolm X said that he had increased the Nation of Islam membership from about 400 when he had joined to around 40,000. "I don't think there were more than 400 in the country when I joined, I really don't. They were mostly older people, and many of them couldn't even pronounce Mr. Muhammad's name, and he stayed mostly in the background."

Malcolm X worked hard not to show it, but he was upset.

"There is nothing more frightful than ignorance in action. Goethe," he scribbled one day. He hinted about Cassius Clay a couple of times, and when I responded only with anecdotes about my interview with Clay, he finally asked what Clay had said of him. I dug out the index card on which the question was typed in advance and Clay's response was beneath in longhand. Malcolm X stared at the card, then out of the window, and he got up and walked around; one of the few times I ever heard his voice betray his hurt was when he said, "I felt like a blood big-brother to him." He paused. "I'm not against him now. He's a fine young man. Smart. He's just let himself be used, led astray."

And at another time there in the hotel room he came the nearest to tears that I ever saw him, and also the only time I ever heard him use, for his race, one word. He had been talking about how hard he had worked building up the Muslim organization in the early days when he was first moved to New York City, when abruptly he exclaimed hoarsely, "We had the *best* organization the black man's ever had—*niggers* ruined it!"

A few days later, however, he wrote in one of his memo books this, which he let me read, "Children have a lesson adults should learn, to not be ashamed of failing, but to get up and try again. Most of us adults are so afraid, so cautious, so 'safe,' and therefore so shrinking and rigid and afraid that it is why so many humans fail. Most middle-aged adults have resigned themselves to failure."

Telephone calls came frequently for Malcolm X when he was in the room with me, or he would make calls; he would talk in a covert, guarded manner, clearly not wishing me to be able to follow the discussion. I took to going into the bathroom at these times, and closing the door, emerging when the murmuring of his voice had stopped—hoping that made him more comfortable. Later, he would tell me that he was hearing from some Muslims who were still ostensibly Elijah Muhammad's followers. "I'm a marked man," he said one day, after such a call. "I've had highly placed people tell me to be very careful every move I make." He thought about it. "Just as long as my family doesn't get hurt, I'm not frightened for myself." I have the impression that Malcolm X heard in advance that the Muslim organization was going to sue to make him vacate the home he and his family lived in.

I had become worried that Malcolm X, bitter, would want to go back through the chapters in which he had told of his Black Muslim days and re-edit them in some way. The day before I left New York City to return upstate, I raised my concern to Malcolm X. "I have thought about that," he said. "There are a lot of things I could say that passed through my mind at times even then, things I saw and heard, but I threw them out of my mind. I'm going to let it stand the way I've told it. I want the book to be the way it was."

Then—March 26, 1964—a note came from Malcolm X: "There is a chance that I may make a quick trip to several very important countries in Africa, including a pilgrimage to the Muslim Holy Cities of Mecca and Medina, beginning about April 13th. Keep this to yourself."

While abroad, Malcolm X wrote letters and postcards to almost everyone he knew well. His letters now were signed "El-Hajj Malik El-Shabazz."

Then, in mid-May, Sister Betty telephoned me, her voice jubilant: Malcolm X was returning. I flew to New York City. On May 21, the phone rang in my hotel room and Sister Betty said, "Just a minute, please—," then the deep voice said, "How are you?"

"Well! El-Hajj Malik El-Shabazz! How are *you?*"

He said, "Just a little bit tired." He had arrived on a Pan-American Airlines flight at 4:30. He was going to have a press conference at seven P.M. at the Hotel Theresa. "I'll pick you up at 6:30 at 135th and Lenox, on the uptown side—all right?"

When the blue Oldsmobile stopped, and I got in, El Hajj Malcolm, broadly beaming, wore a seersucker suit, the red hair needed a barber's attention, and he had grown a beard. Also in the car was Sister Betty. It was the first time we had ever seen each other after more than a year of talking several times a week on the telephone. We smiled at each other. She wore dark glasses, a blue maternity suit, and she was pregnant with what would be her fourth child.

There must have been fifty still and television photographers and reporters jockeying for position, up front, and the rest of the Skyline Ballroom was filling with Negro followers of Malcolm X, or his well-wishers, and the curious. The room lit up with flickering and flooding lights as he came in the door squiring Sister Betty, holding her arm tenderly, and she was smiling broadly in her pride that this man was her man. I recognized the *Times'* M. S. Handler and introduced myself; we warmly shook hands and commandeered a little two-chair table. The reporters in a thick semicircle before Malcolm X seated on the podium fired questions at him, and he gave the impression that all of his twelve years' oratorical practice had prepared him for this new image.

"Do we correctly understand that you now do not think that all whites are evil?"

"*True*, sir! My trip to Mecca has opened my eyes. I no longer subscribe to racism. I have adjusted my thinking to the point where I believe that whites are human beings"—a significant pause—"as long as this is borne out by their humane attitude toward Negroes."

They picked at his "racist" image. "I'm *not* a racist. I'm not condemning whites for being whites, but for their deeds. I condemn what whites collectively have done to our people collectively."

He almost continually flashed about the room the ingratiating boyish smile. He would pick at the new reddish beard. They asked him about that, did he plan to keep it? He said he hadn't decided yet, he would have to see if he could get used to it or not. Was he maneuvering to now join the major civil-rights leaders whom he had previously bitterly attacked? He answered that one sideways: "I'll explain it this way, sir. If some men are in a car, driving with a destination in mind, and you know they are going the wrong way, but they are convinced they are going the right way, then you get into the car with them, and ride with them, talking—and finally when they see they are on the wrong road, not getting where they were intending, then you tell them, and they will listen to you *then*, what road to take." He had never been in better form, weighing, parrying, answering the questions.

The *Times'* Handler, beside me, was taking notes and muttering under his breath, "Incredible! Incredible!" I was thinking the same thing. I was thinking, some of the time, that if a pebble were dropped from the window behind Malcolm X, it would have struck on a sidewalk eight floors below where years before he had skulked, selling dope.

As I resumed writing upstate, periodic notes came from Malcolm X. "I hope the book is proceeding rapidly, for events concerning my life happen so swiftly, much of what has already been written can easily be outdated from month to month. In life, nothing is permanent; not even life itself (smile). So I would advise you to rush it on out as fast as possible." Another note, special delivery, had a tone of irritation with me: he had received from the publisher a letter which indicated that he had received a $2500 check when the book contract was signed, "and therefore I will be expected to pay *personal* income tax on this. As you know, it was my repeated specification that this entire transaction was to be made at that time directly with and to the Mosque. In fact, I have never seen that check to this very day."

The matter was straightened out, and I sent Malcolm X some rough chapters to read. I was appalled when they were soon returned, red-inked in many places where he had told of his almost father-and-son relationship with Elijah Muhammad. Telephoning Malcolm X, I reminded him of his previous decision, and I stressed that if those chapters contained such telegraphing to readers of what would lie ahead, then the book would automatically be robbed of some of its building suspense and drama. Malcolm X said, gruffly, "Whose book is this?" I told him "yours, of course," and that I only made the objection in my position as a writer. He said that he would have to think about it. I was heart-sick at the prospect that he might want to re-edit the entire book into a polemic against Elijah Muhammad. But late that night, Malcolm X telephoned. "I'm sorry. You're right. I was upset about something. Forget what I wanted changed, let what you already had stand." I never again gave him chapters to review unless I was with him. Several times I would covertly watch him frown and wince as he read, but he never again asked for any change in what he had originally said. And the only thing that he ever indicated that he wished had been different in his life came when he was reading the chapter "Laura." He said, "That was a smart girl, a *good* girl. She tried her best to make something out of me, and look what I started her into—dope and prostitution. I wrecked that girl."

Malcolm X was busy, busy, busy; he could not visit my hotel room often, and when he did, it shortly would get the feeling of Grand Central Station. It seemed that when the telephone was not ringing for him, he was calling someone else, consulting the jotted numbers in his ever-ready memorandum book. Now he had begun to talk a great deal with various people from the Middle East or Africa who were in New York. Some of these came to see him at the hotel room. At first, I would sit by the window engrossed in reading while they talked by the room's door in low tones. He was very apologetic when this occurred, and I told him I felt no sensitivity about it; then, afterwards, I would generally step out into the hallway, or perhaps take the elevator down to the lobby, then watch the elevators until I saw the visitor leave. One day, I remember, the phone had rung steadily with such callers as C.B.S., A.B.C., N.B.C., every New York City paper, the London *Daily Express,* and numerous individuals—he and I had gotten no work at all accomplished; then a television camera crew arrived and filled the room to tape an interview with Malcolm X by A.B.C.'s commentator Bill Beutel. As the crew was setting up its floodlights on tripods, a Dayton, Ohio, radio station called, wishing to interview Malcolm X by telephone. He asked me to ask them to call him the following day at his sister Ella's home in Boston. Then the Ghana Ministry of Information called. I turned with a note to Malcolm X to whom the commentator Beutel had just said, "I won't take much of your time, I just have a few probably stupid questions." Glancing at my note, Malcolm X said to Beutel, "Only the unasked question is stupid," and then to me, "Tell them I'll call them back, please." Then just as the television cameras began rolling, with Beutel and Malcolm X talking, the telephone rang again and it was *Life* magazine reporter Marc Crawford to whom I whispered what was happening. Crawford, undaunted, asked if the open receiver could be placed where he could hear the interview, and I complied, relieved that it was one way to let the interview proceed without interruption.

The manuscript copy which Malcolm X was given to review was in better shape now, and he pored through page by page, intently, and now and then his head would raise with some comment. "You know," he said once, "why I have been able to have some effect is because I make a study of the weaknesses of this country and because the more the white man yelps, the more I know I have struck a nerve." Another time, he put down upon the bed the manuscript he was reading, and he got up from his chair and walked back and forth, stroking his chin, then he looked at me. "You know this place here in this chapter where I told you how I put the pistol up to my head and kept pulling the trigger and scared them so when I was starting the burglary ring—well," he paused, "I don't know if I ought to tell you this or not, but I want to tell the truth." He eyed me, speculatively. "I palmed the bullet." We laughed together. I said, "Okay, give that page here, I'll fix it." Then he considered, "No, leave it that way. Too many people would be so quick to say that's what I'm doing today, bluffing."

Again when reading about the period when he had discovered the prison library, Malcolm X's head jerked up. "Boy! I never will forget that old aardvark!" The next evening, he came into the room and told me that he had been to the Museum of Natural History and learned something about the aardvark. "Now, aardvark actually means 'earth hog.' That's a good example of root words, as I was telling you. When you study the science of philology, you learn the laws governing how a consonant can lose its shape, but it keeps its identity from language to language." What astonished me here was that I knew that on that day, Malcolm X's schedule had been crushing, involving both a television and radio appearance and a live speech, yet he had gone to find out something about the aardvark.

Before long, Malcolm X called a press conference, and announced, "My new Organization of Afro-American Unity is a non-religious and non-sectarian group organized to unite Afro-Americans for a constructive program toward attainment of human rights." The new OAAU's tone appeared to be one of militant black nationalism. He said to the questions of various reporters in subsequent interviews that the OAAU would seek to convert the Negro population from non-violence to active self-defense against white supremacists across America. On the subject of politics he offered an enigma, "Whether you use bullets or ballots, you've got to aim well; don't strike at the puppet, strike at the puppeteer." Did he envision any special area of activity? "I'm going to join in the fight wherever Negroes ask for my help." What about alliance with other Negro organizations? He said that he would consider forming some united front with certain selected Negro leaders. He conceded under questioning that the N.A.A.C.P. was "doing some good." Could any whites join his OAAU? "If John Brown were alive, maybe him." And he answered his critics with such statements as that he would send "armed guerrillas" into Mississippi. "I am dead serious. We will send them not only to Mississippi, but to any place where black people's lives are threatened by white bigots. As far as I am concerned, Mississippi is anywhere south of the Canadian border." At another time, when Evelyn Cunningham of the *Pittsburgh Courier* asked Malcolm X in a kidding way, "Say something startling for my column," he told her, "Anyone who wants to follow me and my movement has got to be ready to go to jail, to the hospital, and to the cemetery before he can be truly free." Evelyn Cunningham, printing the item, commented, "He smiled and chuckled, but he was in dead earnest."

His fourth child, yet another daughter, was born and he and Sister Betty named the baby Gamilah Lumumbah. A young waitress named Helen Lanier, at Harlem's Twenty Two Club where Malcolm X now often asked people to meet him, gave him a layette for the new baby. He was very deeply touched by the gesture. "Why, I hardly know that girl!"

He was clearly irked when a *New York Times* poll among New York City Negroes reflected that three-fourths had named Dr. Martin Luther King as "doing the best work for Negroes," and another one-fifth had voted for the N.A.A.C.P.'s Roy Wilkins, while only six percent had voted for Malcolm X. "Brother," he said to me, "do you realize that some of history's greatest leaders never were recognized until they were safely in the ground!"

One morning in mid-summer 1964, Malcolm X telephoned me and said that he would be leaving "within the next two or three days" for a planned six weeks abroad. I heard from him first in Cairo, about as the predicted "long, hot summer" began in earnest, with riots and other uprisings of Negroes occurring in surburban Philadelphia, in Rochester, in Brooklyn, in Harlem, and other cities. The *New York Times* reported that a meeting of Negro intellectuals had agreed that Dr. Martin Luther King could secure the allegiance of the middle and upper classes of Negroes, but Malcolm X alone could secure the allegiance of Negroes at the bottom. "The Negroes respect Dr. King and Malcolm X because they sense in these men absolute integrity and know they will never sell them out. Malcolm X cannot be corrupted and the Negroes know this and therefore respect him. They also know that he comes from the lower depths, as they do, and regard him as one of their own. Malcolm X is going to play a formidable role, because the racial struggle has now shifted to the urban North . . . if Dr. King is convinced that he has sacrificed ten years of brilliant leadership, he will be forced to revise his concepts. There is only one direction in which he can move, and that is in the direction of Malcolm X." I sent a clipping of that story to Malcolm X in Cairo.

In Washington, D.C. and New York City, at least, powerful civic, private, and governmental agencies and individuals were keenly interested in what Malcolm X was saying abroad, and were speculating upon what would he say, and possibly do, when he returned to America. In upstate New York, I received a telephone call from a close friend who said he had been asked to ask me if I would come to New York City on an appointed day to meet with "a very high government official" who was interested in Malcolm X. I did fly down to the city. My friend accompanied me to the offices of a large private foundation well known for its activities and donations in the civil-rights area. I met the foundation's president and he introduced me to the Justice Department Civil Rights Section head, Burke Marshall. Marshall was chiefly interested in Malcolm X's finances, particularly how his extensive traveling since his Black Muslim ouster had been paid for. I told him that to the best of my knowledge the several payments from the publisher had financed Malcolm X, along with fees he received for some speeches, and possible donations that his organization received, and that Malcolm X had told me of borrowing money from his Sister Ella for the current trip, and that recently the *Saturday Evening Post* had bought the condensation rights of the book for a substantial sum that was soon to be received. Marshall listened quietly, intently, and asked a few questions concerning other aspects of Malcolm X's life, then thanked me. I wrote to Malcolm X in Cairo that night about the interview. He never mentioned it.

The *Saturday Evening Post* flew photographer John Launois to Cairo to locate Malcolm X and photograph him in color. The magazine's September 12 issue appeared, and I sent a copy by airmail to Malcolm X. Within a few days, I received a stinging note, expressing his anger at the magazine's editorial regarding his life story. (The editorial's opening sentence read, "If Malcolm X were not a Negro, his autobiography would be little more than a journal of abnormal psychology, the story of a burglar, dope pusher, addict and jailbird—with a family history of insanity—who acquires messianic delusions and sets forth to preach an upside-down religion of 'brotherly' hatred.") I wrote to Malcolm X that he could not fairly hold me responsible for what the magazine had written in a separate editorial opinion. He wrote an apology, "but the greatest care must be exercised in the future."

His return from Africa was even more auspicious than when he had returned from the Hajj pilgrimage to Mecca. A large group of Negroes, his followers and well-wishers, kept gathering in the Overseas Arrival Building at Kennedy Airport. When I entered, white men with cameras were positioned on the second level, taking pictures of all the Negroes who entered, and almost as obvious were Negro plain-clothesmen moving about. Malcolm's greeters had draped across the glass overlooking the U.S. Customs Inspection line some large cloth banners on which were painted in bold letters, "Welcome Home, Malcolm."

He came in sight, stepping into one of the Customs Inspection lines; he heard the cheering and he looked up, smiling his pleasure.

Malcolm X wanted to "huddle" with me to fill me in on details from his trip that he wanted in the book. He said that he was giving me only the highlights, because he felt that his carefully kept diary might be turned into another book. We had intensive sessions in my hotel room, where he read what he selected from the diary, and I took notes. "What I want to stress is that I was trying to internationalize our problem," he said to me, "to make the Africans feel their *kinship* with us Afro-Americans. I made them *think* about it, that they are our blood brothers, and we all came from the same foreparents. That's why the Africans loved me, the same way the Asians loved me because I was religious."

Within a few days, he had no more time to see me. He would call and apologize; he was beset by a host of problems, some of which he mentioned, and some of which I heard from other people. Most immediately, there was discontent within his organization, the OAAU. His having stayed away almost three times as long as he had said he would be gone had sorely tested the morale of even his key members, and there was a general feeling that his interest was insufficient to expect his followers' interest to stay high. I heard from one member that "a growing disillusion" could be sensed throughout the organization.

In Harlem at large, in the bars and restaurants, on the street corners and stoops, there could be heard more blunt criticism of Malcolm X than ever before in his career. There were, variously expressed, two primary complaints. One was that actually Malcolm X only talked, but other civil-rights organizations were *doing*. "All he's *ever* done was talk, CORE and SNCC and some of them people of Dr. King's are out getting beat over the head." The second major complaint was that Malcolm X was himself too confused to be seriously followed any longer. "He doesn't know *what* he believes in. No sooner do you hear one thing than he's switched to something else." The two complaints were not helping the old firebrand Malcolm X image any, nor were they generating the local public interest that was badly needed by his small, young OAAU.

A court had made it clear that Malcolm X and his family would have to vacate the Elmhurst house for its return to the adjudged legal owners, Elijah Muhammad's Nation of Islam. And other immediate problems which Malcolm X faced included finances. Among his other expenses, a wife and four daughters had to be supported, along with at least one full-time OAAU official. Upon his return from Africa, our agent for the book had delivered to me for Malcolm X a check for a sizable sum; soon afterward Malcolm X told me, laughing wryly, "It's *evaporated*. I don't know where!"

Malcolm X plunged into a welter of activities. He wrote and telephoned dozens of acceptances to invitations to speak, predominantly at colleges and universities—both to expound his philosophies and to earn the $150-$300 honorariums above traveling expenses. When he was in New York City, he spent all the time he could in his OAAU's sparsely furnished office on the mezzanine floor of the Hotel Theresa, trying to do something about the OAAU's knotty problems. "I'm not exposing our size in numbers," he evaded the query of one reporter. "You know, the strongest part of a tree is the root, and if you expose the root, the tree dies. Why, we have many 'invisible' members, of all types. Unlike other leaders, I've practiced the flexibility to put myself into contact with every kind of Negro in the country."

Even at mealtimes, at his favorite Twenty Two Club, or elsewhere in Harlem, he could scarcely eat for the people who came up asking for appointments to discuss with him topics ranging from personal problems to his opinions on international issues. It seemed not in him to say "No" to such requests. And aides of his, volunteering their time, as often as not had to wait lengthy periods to get his ear for matters important to the OAAU, or to himself; often, even then, he most uncharacteristically showed an impatience with their questions or their suggestions, and they chafed visibly. And at least once weekly, generally on Sunday evenings, he would address as many Negroes as word of mouth and mimeographed advertising could draw to hear him in Harlem's Audubon Ballroom on West 166th Street between Broadway and St. Nicholas Avenue, near New York City's famous Columbia-Presbyterian Medical Center.

Malcolm X for some reason suddenly began to deliver a spate of attacks against Elijah Muhammad, making more bitter accusations of "religious fakery" and "immorality" than he ever had. Very possibly, Malcolm X had grown increasingly incensed by the imminence of the court's deadline for him to have to move his wife and four little daughters from the comfortable home in which they had lived for years in Elmhurst. And Sister Betty was again pregnant. "A home is really the only thing I've ever provided Betty since we've been married," he had told me, discussing the court's order, "and they want to take that away. Man, I can't keep on putting her through changes, all she's put up with—man, I've *got* to love this woman!"

A rash of death threats were anonymously telephoned to the police, to various newspapers, to the OAAU office, and to the family's home in Elmhurst. When he went to court again, fighting to keep the house, he was guarded by a phalanx of eight OAAU men, twenty uniformed policemen, and twelve plain-clothes detectives. The court's decision was that the order to vacate would not be altered. When Malcolm X reached home in Long Island, one of his followers, telephoning him there, got, instead, a telephone company operator who said that the OL 1-6320 number was "disconnected." A carload of his OAAU followers, racing to Long Island, found Malcolm X and his family perfectly safe. Inquiry of the telephone company revealed that a "Mrs. Small" had called and requested that the service for that number be disconnected, "for vacation." The OAAU followers drove back to Harlem. There was an ensuing confrontation between them and followers of Elijah Muhammad in front of the Black Muslim restaurant at 116th Street and Lenox Avenue. The incident wound up with policemen who rushed to the scene finding two guns in the OAAU car, and the six OAAU men were arrested.

Malcolm X had a date to speak in Boston, but he was too busy to go, and he sent an OAAU assistant who spoke instead. The car returning him to the Boston Airport was blocked at the East Boston Tunnel by another car. Reportedly, men with knives rushed out of the blockade car, but the Malcolm X forces showed a shotgun, and the attackers dispersed.

Malcolm X steadily accused the Black Muslims as the source of the various attacks and threats. "There is no group in the United States more able to carry out this threat than the Black Muslims," he said. "I know, because I taught them myself." Asked why he had attacked the Black Muslims and Elijah Muhammad when things had seemed to be cooled down, he said, "I would not have revealed any of this if they had left me alone." He let himself be photographed in his home holding an automatic carbine rifle with a full double clip of ammunition that he said he kept ready for action against any possible assassination efforts. "I have taught my wife to use it, and instructed her to fire on anyone, white, black, or yellow, who tries to force his way inside."

I went to New York City in December for Malcolm X's reading of final additions to the manuscript, to include the latest developments. He was further than I had ever seen him from his old assured self, it seemed to me. He kept saying that the press was making light of his statements about the threats on his life. "They act like I'm jiving!" He brought up again the *Saturday Evening Post* editorial. "You can't trust the publishing people, I don't care what they tell you." The agent for the book sent to my hotel a contract dealing with foreign publication rights which needed Malcolm X's and my signature. I signed it as he observed and handed the pen to him. He looked suspiciously at the contract, and said, "I had better show this thing to my lawyer," and put the contract in his inside coat pocket. Driving in Harlem about an hour later, he suddenly stopped the car across the street from the 135th Street Y.M.C.A. Building. Withdrawing the contract, he signed it, and thrust it to me. "I'll trust you," he said, and drove on.

With Christmas approaching, upon an impulse I bought for Malcolm X's two oldest daughters two large dolls, with painted brown complexions, the kind of dolls that would "walk" when held by the left hand. When Malcolm X next came to my room in the Hotel Wellington, I said, "I've gotten something for you to take to Attilah and Qubilah for Christmas gifts," and I "walked" out the dolls. Amazement, then a wide grin spread over his face. "Well, what do you know about that? Well, how about that!" He bent to examine the dolls. His expression showed how touched he was. "You know," he said after a while, "this isn't something I'm proud to say, but I don't think I've ever bought one gift for my children. Everything they play with, either Betty got it for them, or somebody gave it to them, never me. That's not good, I know it. I've always been too *busy*."

In early January, I flew from upstate New York to Kennedy Airport where I telephoned Malcolm X at home and told him that I was waiting for another plane to Kansas City to witness the swearing-in of my younger brother George who had recently been elected a Kansas State Senator. "Tell your brother for me to remember us in the alley," Malcolm X said. "Tell him that he and all of the other moderate Negroes who are getting somewhere need to always remember that it was us extremists who made it possible." He said that when I was ready to leave Kansas, to telephone him saying when I would arrive back in New York, and if he could we could get together. I did this, and he met me at Kennedy Airport. He had only a little while, he was so pressed, he said; he had to leave that afternoon himself for a speaking engagement which had come up. So I made reservations for the next flight back upstate, then we went outside and sat and talked in his car in a parking lot. He talked about the pressures on him everywhere he turned, and about the frustrations, among them that no one wanted to accept anything relating to him except "my old 'hate' and 'violence' image." He said "the so-called moderate" civil-rights organizations avoided him as "too militant" and the "so-called militants" avoided him as "too moderate." "They won't let me turn the corner!" he once exclaimed, "I'm caught in a trap!"

In a happier area, we talked about the coming baby. We laughed about the four girls in a row already. "This one will be the boy," he said. He beamed, "If not, the *next* one!" When I said it was close to time for my plane to leave, he said he had to be getting on, too. I said, "Give my best to Sister Betty," he said that he would, we shook hands and I got outside and stood as he backed the blue Oldsmobile from its parking space. I called out "See you!" and we waved as he started driving away. There was no way to know that it was the last time I would see him alive.

On January 19, Malcolm X appeared on the Pierre Berton television show in Canada and said, in response to a question about integration and intermarriage:

"I believe in recognizing every human being as a human being—neither white, black, brown, or red; and when you are dealing with humanity as a family there's no question of integration or intermarriage. It's just one human being marrying another human being or one human being living around and with another human being. I may say, though, that I don't think it should ever be put upon a black man, I don't think the burden to defend any position should ever be put upon the black man, because it is the white man collectively who has shown that he is hostile toward integration and toward intermarriage and toward these other strides toward oneness. So as a black man and especially as a black American, any stand that I formerly took, I don't think that I would have to defend it because it's still a reaction to the society, and it's a reaction that was produced by the society; and I think that it is the society that produced this that should be attacked, not the reaction that develops among the people who are the victims of that negative society."

From this, it would be fair to say that one month before his death, Malcolm had revised his views on intermarriage to the point where he regarded it as simply a personal matter.

On the 28th of January, Malcolm X was on TWA's Flight No. 9 from New York that landed at about three P.M. in Los Angeles. A special police intelligence squad saw Malcolm

X greeted by two close friends, Edward Bradley and Allen Jamal, who drove him to the Statler-Hilton Hotel where Malcolm X checked into Room 1129. Said Bradley, "As we entered the lobby, six men came in right after us. I recognized them as Black Muslims." When Malcolm X returned downstairs to the lobby, he "practically bumped into the Muslim entourage. The Muslims were stunned. Malcolm's face froze, but he never broke his gait. Then, we knew we were facing trouble." Malcolm X's friends drove him to pick up "two former secretaries of Elijah Muhammad, who (had) filed paternity suits against him," and they went to the office of the colorful Los Angeles attorney Gladys Root. Mrs. Root said that Malcolm X made accusations about Elijah Muhammad's conduct with various former secretaries.

After dinner, Malcolm X's two friends drove him back to the hotel. "Black Muslims were all over the place," Bradley related. "Some were in cars and others stood around near the hotel. They had the hotel completely surrounded. Malcolm sized up the situation and jumped out of the car. He warned me to watch out and ran into the lobby. He went to his room and remained there for the rest of his stay in Los Angeles."

The car in which Malcolm X left the hotel, bound for the airport, was followed, said Bradley. "Hardly had we got on the Freeway when we saw two carloads of Black Muslims following us. The cars started to pull alongside. Malcolm picked up my walking cane and stuck it out of a back window as if it were a rifle. The two cars fell behind. We picked up speed, pulled off the airport ramp, and roared up to the front of the terminal. The police were waiting and Malcolm was escorted to the plane through an underground passageway. Then I saw Malcolm to the plane."

Chicago police were waiting when the plane landed at O'Hare Airport that night at eight o'clock. Driven to the Bristol Hotel, Malcolm X checked in, and the adjoining suite was taken by members of the police force who would keep him under steady guard for the next three days in Chicago. Malcolm X testified at the office of the Attorney General of the State of Illinois which had been investigating the Nation of Islam. Another day he appeared on the television program of Irv Kupcinet; he described attempts that had been made to kill him. He said he had on his desk a letter naming the persons assigned to kill him. When police returned Malcolm X to his hotel "at least 15 grim-faced Negroes (were) loitering nearby." Whispered Malcolm X to Detective Sergeant Edward McClellan, "Those are all Black Muslims. At least two of them I recognize as being from New York. Elijah seems to know every move I make." Later, in his room, he told the detective, "It's only going to be a matter of time before they catch up with me. I know too much about the Muslims. But their threats are not going to stop me from what I am determined to do." After that night spent in the hotel, Malcolm X was police-escorted back to O'Hare where he caught a plane to New York City's Kennedy Airport.

Right away, he was served with a court order of eviction from the Elmhurst home. He telephoned me upstate. His voice was strained. He told me that he had filed an appeal to the court order, that on the next day he was going to Alabama, and thence to England and France for scheduled speeches, and soon after returning he would go to Jackson, Mississippi, to address the Mississippi Freedom Democratic Party, on February 19. Then he said—the first time he had ever voiced to me such an admission—"Haley, my nerves are shot, my brain's tired." He said that upon his return from Mississippi, he would like to come and spend two or three days in the town where I was, and read the book's manuscript again. "You say it's a quiet town. Just a couple of days of peace and quiet, that's what I need." I said that he knew he was welcome, but there was no need for him to tax himself reading through the long book again, as it had only a few very minor editing changes since he had only recently read it. "I just want to read it one more time," he said, "because I don't expect to read it in finished form." So we made a tentative agreement that the day after his projected return from Mississippi, he would fly upstate to visit for a weekend with me. The projected date was the Saturday and Sunday of February 20-21.

Jet magazine reported Malcolm X's trip to Selma, Alabama, on the invitation of two members of the Student Nonviolent Coordinating Committee. Dr. Martin Luther King was in a Selma jail when Malcolm X's arrival sent officials of Dr. King's Southern Christian Leadership Conference "into a tailspin." Quickly, the SCLC's Executive Director Reverend Andrew Young and Reverend James Bevel met with Malcolm X, urging him not to incite any incidents and cautioning him that his presence could cause violence. "He listened with a smile," said Miss Faye Bellamy, secretary of the SNCC, who accompanied Malcolm X to a Negro church where he would address a mass meeting. "Remember this: nobody puts words in my mouth," he told Miss Bellamy. He told her that "in about two weeks" he planned to start Southern recruiting for his Harlem-based OAAU. At the church where he would speak, Malcolm X was seated on the platform next to Mrs. Martin Luther King, to whom he leaned and whispered that he was "trying to help," she told *Jet*. "He said he wanted to present an alternative; that it might be easier for whites to accept Martin's proposals after hearing him (Malcolm X). I didn't understand him at first," said Mrs. King. "He seemed rather anxious to let Martin know he was not causing trouble or making it difficult, but that he was trying to make it easier. . . . Later, in the hallway, he reiterated this. He seemed sincere. . . ."

Addressing the mass meeting Malcolm X reportedly shouted: "I don't advocate violence, but if a man steps on my toes, I'll step on his." . . . "Whites better be glad Martin Luther King is rallying the people because other forces are waiting to take over if he fails."

Returned to New York City, Malcolm X soon flew to France. He was scheduled to speak before a Congress of African Students. But he was formally advised that he would not be permitted to speak and, moreover, that he could consider himself officially barred forever from France as "an undesirable person." He was asked to leave—and he did, fuming with indignation. He flew on to London, and reporters of the British Broadcasting Corporation took him on an interviewing tour in Smethwick, a town near Birmingham with a large colored population. Numerous residents raised a storm of criticism that the B.B.C. was a party to a "fanning of racism" in the already tension-filled community. On this visit, he spoke also at the London School of Economics.

Malcolm X returned to New York City on Saturday, February 13th. He was asleep with his family when at about a quarter of three the following Sunday morning, a terrifying blast awakened them. Sister Betty would tell me later that Malcolm X, barking commands and snatching up screaming, frightened children, got the family safely out of the back door into the yard. Someone had thrown flaming Molotov cocktail gasoline bombs through the front picture window. It took the fire department an hour to extinguish the flames.

Half the house was destroyed. Malcolm X had no fire insurance.

Pregnant, distraught Sister Betty and the four little daughters went to the home of close friends. Malcolm X steeled himself to catch a plane as scheduled that morning to speak in Detroit. He wore an open-necked sweater shirt under his suit. Immediately afterward, he flew back to New York. Monday morning, amid a flurry of emergency re-housing plans for his family, Malcolm X was outraged when he learned that Elijah Muhammad's New York Mosque Number 7 Minister James X had told the press that Malcolm X himself had fire-bombed the home "to get publicity."

Monday night, Malcolm X spoke to an audience in the familiar Audubon Ballroom. If he had possessed the steel nerves not to become rattled in public before, now he was: "I've reached the end of my rope!" he shouted to the audience of five hundred. "I wouldn't care for myself if they would not harm my family!" He declared flatly, "My house was bombed by the *Muslims!*" And he hinted at revenge. "There are hunters; there are also those who hunt the hunters!"

Tuesday, February 16th, Malcolm X telephoned me. He spoke very briefly, saying that the complications following the bombing of his home had thrown his plans so awry that he would be unable to visit me upstate on the weekend as he had said he would. He said he had also had to cancel his planned trip to Jackson, Mississippi, which he was going to try and make later. He said he had to hurry to an appointment, and hung up. I would read later where also on that day, he told a close associate, "I have been marked for death in the next five days. I have the names of five Black Muslims who have been chosen to kill me. I will announce them at the meeting." And Malcolm X told a friend that he was going to apply to the Police Department for a permit to carry a pistol. "I don't know whether they will let me have one or not, as I served time in prison."

On Thursday he told a reporter, in an interview which did not appear until after his death: "I'm man enough to tell you that I can't put my finger on exactly what my philosophy is now, but I'm flexible."

The blackboard in the OAAU office counseled members and visitors that "Bro. Malcolm Speaks Thurs. Feb. 18, WINS Station, 10:30 P.M." Earlier Thursday, Malcolm X discussed locating another home with a real estate dealer. On Friday, he had an appointment with Gordon Parks, the *Life* magazine photographer-author whom he had long admired and respected. "He appeared calm and somewhat resplendent with his goatee and astrakhan hat," Parks would report later in *Life*. "Much of the old hostility and bitterness seemed to have left him, but the fire and confidence were still there." Malcolm X, speaking of the old Mosque Number 7 days, said, "That was a bad scene, brother. The sickness and madness of those days —I'm glad to be free of them. It's a time for martyrs now. And if I'm to be one, it will be in the cause of brotherhood. That's the only thing that can save this country. I've learned it the hard way—but I've learned it. . . ."

Parks asked Malcolm X if it was really true that killers were after him. "It's as true as we are standing here," Malcolm X said, "They've tried it twice in the last two weeks." Parks asked him about police protection, and Malcolm X laughed, "Brother, nobody can protect you from a Muslim but a Muslim—or someone trained in Muslim tactics. I know. I invented many of those tactics."

Recalling the incident of the young white college girl who had come to the Black Muslim restaurant and asked "What can I *do?*" and he told her "Nothing," and she left in tears, Malcolm X told Gordon Parks, "Well, I've lived to regret that incident. In many parts of the African continent I saw white students helping black people. Something like this kills a lot of argument. I did many things as a Muslim that I'm sorry for now. I was a zombie then—like all Muslims—I was hypnotized, pointed in a certain direction and told to march. Well, I guess a man's entitled to make a fool of himself if he's ready to pay the cost. It cost me twelve years."

Saturday morning, he drove Sister Betty to see a real estate man. The house that the man then showed them that Malcolm X particularly liked, in a predominantly Jewish neighborhood also on Long Island, required a $3000 down payment. Sister Betty indicated her approval, too, and Malcolm X told the real estate man he thought they would take it. Driving Sister Betty back to the friends' home where she was staying with the children, they estimated that it would cost them about another $1000 to make the move. He stayed until mid-afternoon with Sister Betty at the friends' home, talking. He told her that he realized that she had been under protracted great strain, and that he was sorry about it. When he got his hat to leave, to drive into Manhattan, standing in the hallway, he told Sister Betty, "We'll all be together. I want my family with me. Families shouldn't be separated. I'll never make another long trip without you. We'll get somebody to keep the children. I'll never leave you so long again."

"I couldn't help but just break out grinning," Sister Betty would later tell me.

She figured that he must have stopped at a nearby drugstore to use the telephone booth when I later told her that Malcolm X had telephoned me upstate at about 3:30 that afternoon.

For the first time in nearly two years, I did not recognize immediately that the voice on the other end of the phone belonged to Malcolm X. He sounded as if he had a heavy, deep cold. He told me that in the middle of the night he and some friends had helped a moving company's men take out of the other house all of the family's furniture and other belongings salvagable after the fire-bombing—before a sheriff's eviction party would set the things out on the sidewalk. "Betty and I have been looking at a house we want to buy"— he tried a chuckle—"you know nobody's going to *rent,* not to *me,* these days!" He said, "All I've got is about $150," and that he needed a $3000 down-payment plus $1000 moving costs; he asked if I thought the publisher would advance him $4000 against the projected profits from the book. I said that when our agent's offices opened on Monday morning, I would telephone and I knew that he would query the publisher to see if it couldn't be arranged, then Monday night I would call him back and let him know.

He said that he and Sister Betty had decided that although they were going to pay for the house, to avoid possible trouble they had gotten the agreement of his sister Ella who lived in Boston to let the house be bought in her name. He said that he still owed $1500 to his sister Ella which she had loaned him to make one trip abroad. Eventually they would change the house's title into Sister Betty's name, he said, or maybe into the name of their oldest daughter, Attilah.

He digressed on the dangers he faced. "But, you know, I'm going to tell you something, brother—the more I keep thinking about this thing, the things that have been happening lately, I'm not all that sure it's the Muslims. I know what they can do, and what they can't, and they can't do some of the stuff recently going on. Now, I'm going to tell you, the more I keep thinking about what happened to me in France, I think I'm going to quit saying it's the Muslims."

Then—it seemed to me such an odd, abrupt change of subject: "You know, I'm glad I've been the first to establish official ties between Afro-Americans and our blood brothers in Africa." And saying good-bye, he hung up.

After that telephone call, Malcolm X drove on into Manhattan and to the New York Hilton Hotel between 53rd and 54th Streets at Rockefeller Center. He checked the blue Oldsmobile into the hotel garage and then, in the lobby, he checked himself in and was assigned a twelfth-floor room, to which a bellman accompanied him.

Soon some Negro men entered the giant hotel's busy lobby. They began asking various bellmen what room Malcolm X was in. The bellmen, of course, never would answer that question concerning any guest—and considering that it was Malcolm X whom practically everyone who read New York City newspapers knew was receiving constant death threats, the bellmen quickly notified the hotel's security chief. From then until Malcolm X checked out the next day, extra security vigilance was continuously maintained on the twelfth floor. During that time, Malcolm X left the room only once, to have dinner in the hotel's lobby-level, dimly lit Bourbon Room.

Sunday morning at nine o'clock, Sister Betty in Long Island was surprised when her husband telephoned her and asked if she felt it would be too much trouble for her to get all of the four children dressed and bring them to the two o'clock meeting that afternoon at the Audubon Ballroom in Harlem. She said, "Of course it won't!" On Saturday he had told her that she couldn't come to the meeting. He said to her, "You know what happened an hour ago? Exactly at eight o'clock, the phone woke me up. Some man said 'Wake up, brother' and hung up." Malcolm X said good-bye to Sister Betty.

And four hours later, Malcolm X left his room and took an elevator down to the lobby, where he checked out. He got his car and in the clear, warm midday of Sunday, February 21, he drove uptown to the Audubon Ballroom.

The Audubon Ballroom, between Broadway and St. Nicholas

Avenue, on the south side of West 166th Street, is a two-story building frequently rented for dances, organization functions, and other affairs. A dark, slender, pretty young lady, occupationally a receptionist and avocationally a hardworking OAAU assistant to Malcolm X, has since told me that she arrived early, about 1:30 P.M., having some preliminary work to do. Entering, she saw that the usual 400 wooden chairs had been set up, with aisles on either side, but no center aisle; the young lady (she wishes to be nameless) noticed that several people were already seated in the front rows, but she gave it no thought since some always came early, liking to get seats up close to the stage, to savor to the fullest the dramatic orator Malcolm X. On the stage, behind the speaker's stand were eight straight brown chairs arranged in a row and behind him was the stage's painted backdrop, a mural of a restful country scene. The young lady's responsibilities for this day had included making arrangements and subsequent confirmations with the scheduled co-speaker, the Reverend Milton Galamison, the militant Brooklyn Presbyterian who in 1964 had led the two one-day Negro boycotts in New York City public schools, protesting "racial imbalance." She had similarly made arrangements with some other prominent Negroes who were due to appeal to the audience for their maximum possible contributions to aid the work of Malcolm X and his organization.

The people who entered the ballroom were not searched at the door. In recent weeks, Malcolm X had become irritable about this, saying "It makes people uncomfortable" and that it reminded him of Elijah Muhammad. "If I can't be safe among my own kind, where can I be?" he had once said testily. For this day, also, he had ordered the press—as such—barred, white or black. He was angry at what he interpreted as "slanted" press treatment recently; he felt especially that the newspapers had not taken seriously his statements of the personal danger he was in. United Press International reporter Stanley Scott, a Negro, had been admitted, he later said, when a Malcolm lieutenant decided, "As a Negro, you will be allowed to enter as a citizen if you like, but you must remove your press badge." The same criterion had applied to WMCA newsman Hugh Simpson. Both he and Scott came early enough so that they obtained seats up near the stage.

Malcolm X entered the ballroom at shortly before two o'clock, trudging heavily instead of with his usual lithe strides, his young lady assistant has told me. By this time several other of his assistants were filtering in and out of the small anteroom alongside the stage. He sat down sideways on a chair, his long legs folded around its bottom, and he leaned one elbow on a kind of counter before a rather rickety make-up mirror that entertainers used when dances were held in the ballroom. He wore a dark suit, white shirt and narrow dark tie. He said to a little group of his assistants that he wasn't going to talk about his personal troubles, "I don't want that to be the reason for anyone to come to hear me." He stood up and paced about the little room. He said he was going to state that he had been hasty to accuse the Black Muslims of bombing his home. "Things have happened since that are bigger than what they can do. I know what they can do. Things have gone beyond that."

Those in the anteroom could hear the sounds of the enlarging audience outside taking seats. "The way I feel, I ought not to go out there at all today," Malcolm X said. "In fact, I'm going to ease some of this tension by telling the black man not to fight himself—that's all a part of the white man's big maneuver, to keep us fighting among ourselves, against each other. I'm not fighting anyone, that's not what we're here for." He kept glancing at his wristwatch, anticipating the arrival of Reverend Galamison. "Whenever you make any appointment with a minister," he said to his young lady assistant, "you have to call them two or three hours before time, because they will change their mind. This is typical of ministers."

"I felt bad, I felt that it was my fault," the young lady told me. "It was time for the meeting to start, too." She turned to Malcolm X's stalwart assistant Benjamin X, known as a highly able speaker himself. "Brother, will you speak?" she asked—then, turning to Malcolm X, "Is it all right if he speaks? And maybe he could introduce you." Malcolm X abruptly whirled on her, and barked, "You know you shouldn't ask me right in front of him!" Then, collecting himself quickly, he said "Okay." Brother Benjamin X asked how long he should speak. Malcolm X said, glancing again at his wrist watch, "Make it half an hour." And Brother Benjamin

X went through the door leading onto the stage. They heard him expertly exhorting the audience about what is needed today by "the black man here in these United States."

The Reverend Galamison and other notables due hadn't arrived by three o'clock. "Brother Malcolm looked so disappointed," the young lady says. "He said to me 'I don't think any of them are coming, either.' I felt so terrible for him. It did seem as if no one cared. I told him 'Oh, don't worry, they're just late, they'll be here.'" (It was also reported by another source that Galamison, unable to come to the meeting, did telephone earlier, and that Malcolm X was told of this before he went out to speak.)

Then Brother Benjamin X's half-hour was up, and the young lady and Malcolm X, alone back there in the anteroom could hear him entering the introduction: "And now, without further remarks, I present to you one who is willing to put himself on the line for you, a man who would give his life for you—I want you to hear, listen, to understand—one who is a *trojan* for the black man!"

Applause rose from the audience; at the anteroom door, Malcolm X turned and looked back at his young lady assistant. "You'll have to forgive me for raising my voice to you—I'm just about at my wit's end."

"Oh, don't *mention* it!" she said quickly, "I understand."

His voice sounded far away, "I wonder if anybody *really* understands—" And he walked out onto the stage, into the applause, smiling and nodding at Brother Benjamin X who passed him en route to the anteroom.

The young lady had picked up some paperwork she had to do when Benjamin X came in, perspiring. She patted his hand, saying, "That was good!" Through the anteroom door, just ajar, she and Benjamin X heard the applause diminishing, then the familiar ringing greeting, "*Asalaikum,* brothers and sisters!"

"Asalaikum salaam!" some in the audience responded.

About eight rows of seats from the front, then, a disturbance occurred. In a sudden scuffling, a man's voice was raised angrily, "Take your hand out of my pocket!" The entire audience was swiveling to look. "Hold it! Hold it! Don't get excited," Malcolm X said crisply, "Let's cool it, brothers—"

With his own attention distracted, it is possible that he never saw the gunmen. One woman who was seated near the front says, "The commotion back there diverted me just for an instant, then I turned back to look at Malcolm X just in time to see at least three men in the front row stand and take aim and start firing simultaneously. It looked like a firing squad." Numerous persons later said they saw two men rushing toward the stage, one with a shotgun, the other with two revolvers. Said U.P.I. reporter Stanley Scott: "Shots rang out. Men, women and children ran for cover. They stretched out on the floor and ducked under tables." Radio Station WMCA reporter Hugh Simpson said, "Then I heard this muffled sound, I saw Malcolm hit with his hands still raised, then he fell back over the chiars behind him. Everybody was shouting. I saw one man firing a gun from under his coat behind me as I hit it [the floor], too. He was firing like he was in some Western, running backward toward the door and firing at the same time."

The young lady who was in the backstage anteroom told me, "It sounded like an army had taken over. Somehow, I knew. I wouldn't go and look. I wanted to remember him as he was."

Malcolm X's hand flew to his chest as the first of sixteen shotgun pellets or revolver slugs hit him. Then the other hand flew up. The middle finger of the left hand was bullet-shattered, and blood gushed from his goatee. He clutched his chest. His big body suddenly fell back stiffly, knocking over two chairs; his head struck the stage floor with a thud.

In the bedlam of shouting, screaming, running people, some ran toward the stage. Among them Sister Betty scrambled up from where she had thrown her body over her children, who were shrieking; she ran crying hysterically, "My husband! They're killing my husband!" An unidentified photographer snapped shots of Malcolm X prone on the stage floor with people bent over him snatching apart his bloody shirt, loosening his tie, trying to give him mouth-to-mouth artificial respiration, first a woman, then a man. Said the woman, who identified herself only as a registered nurse, "I don't know how I got up on the stage, but I threw myself down on who I thought was Malcolm—but it wasn't. I was willing to die for the man, I would have taken the bullets myself; then I saw Malcolm, and the firing had stopped, and I tried to give him artificial respiration." Then Sister Betty came through the people, herself a nurse, and people recognizing her moved back; she fell on her knees looking down on his bare, bullet-pocked chest, sobbing, "They killed him!"

Patrolman Thomas Hoy, 22, was stationed outside the Audubon Ballroom entrance. "I heard the shooting and the place exploded." He rushed inside, he saw Malcolm X lying on the stage, and then some people chasing a man. Patrolman Hoy "grabbed the suspect."

Louis Michaux, the owner of the Nationalist Memorial Bookstore at 125th Street and Seventh Avenue in Harlem, said "I was arriving late at the meeting where Malcolm X had invited me, I met a large number of people rushing out."

Sergeant Alvin Aronoff and Patrolman Louis Angelos happened to be cruising by in their radio car when they heard shots. "When we got there," said Aronoff, "the crowds were pushing out and screaming 'Malcolm's been shot!' and 'Get 'im, get 'im, don't let him go!'" The two policemen grabbed by the arms a Negro who was being kicked as he tried to escape. Firing a warning shot into the air, the policemen pushed the man into their police car, not wanting the angry crowd to close in, and drove him quickly to the police station.

Someone had run up to the Columbia-Presbyterian Hospital's Vanderbilt Clinic emergency entrance at 167th Street and grabbed a poles-and-canvas stretcher and brought it back to the Audubon Ballroom stage. Malcolm X was put on the stretcher and an unidentified photographer got a macabre picture of him, with his mouth open and his teeth bared, as men rushed him up to the hospital clinic emergency entrance. A hospital spokesman said later that it was about 3:15 P.M. when Malcolm X reached a third-floor operating room. He was "either dead, or in a death-appearing state," said the spokesman.

A team of surgeons cut through his chest to attempt to massage the heart. The effort was abandoned at 3:30 P.M.

Reporters who had descended upon the hospital office fired questions at the spokesman, who kept saying brusquely, "I don't know." Then he took the elevator upstairs to the emergency operating room. A small crowd of friends and Sister Betty had also pushed into the hospital office when the hospital spokesman returned. Collecting himself, he made an announcement: "The gentleman you know as Malcolm X is dead. He died from gunshot wounds. He was apparently dead before he got here. He was shot in the chest several times, and once in the cheek."

The group filed out of the hospital office. The Negro men were visibly fighting their emotions; one kept smashing his fist into the other cupped palm. Among the women, many were openly crying.

Moments after the news flashed throughout Harlem (and throughout the entire world), a crowd began to gather outside the Hotel Theresa where Malcolm X's OAAU had its headquarters. They learned over transistor radios that the man whom the two policemen had taken from the murder scene initially identified himself as Thomas Hagan, 22 (he was later identified as Talmadge Hayer), in whose right trousers pocket the policemen had found a .45 caliber cartridge clip containing four unused cartridges, and then at Jewish Memorial Hospital doctors had reported that Hayer had been shot in the left thigh, his forehead was bruised and his body was beaten. "If we hadn't gotten him away, they would have kicked him to death," Sergeant Aronoff had said, and Hayer had been taken to the Bellevue Hospital Prison Ward.

By five P.M., the crowd in front of the Theresa Hotel had been quietly, carefully dispersed, and the Black Muslim Mosque Number 7 and its restaurant around the corner, at 116th Street and Lenox Avenue, had been ordered closed as a precautionary measure, on the orders of the local 28th Precinct's Captain Lloyd Sealy, New York City's first Negro to command a precinct. When reporters telephoned the Black Muslim restaurant, a man's voice stated, "No one is available to make any statement." When the OAAU office in the Theresa Hotel was tried, the telephone kept ringing, unanswered. Precinct Captain Sealy soon appeared, walking by himself along 125th Street, swinging his nightstick and conversing with people he met.

At the 28th Precinct station house on West 123rd Street, the forty policemen who were to have gone off duty at four P.M. had been told they must remain on duty, and two full busloads of the highly trained New York City Police Tactical Patrol Force had arrived at the precinct. Various high police officials made press statements. A Tactical Patrol Force Captain, Harry Kaiser, said no unusual occurrences had been noted, and he anticipated no trouble. Deputy Police Com-

missioner Walter Arm said that "hundreds" of extra policemen would be put into the Harlem area, including some members of the Bureau of Special Services. An Assistant Chief
Inspector, Harry Taylor, speculated that the assassins had
not rushed from the ballroom among the crowd, but had
kept running past the stage and escaped on 165th Street. In
the early evening, the police department's Chief of Detectives
Philip J. Walsh quit a vacation he was on to join the hunt
for the killers, and he said he looked forward to "a long-
drawn-out investigation." Police and reporters at the shooting
scene had pictures taken of the stage, with white chalk marks
now circling five bullet holes in the speaker's stand; there
were other holes in the stage's mural backdrop, indicating
slugs or shotgun pellets which had either missed Malcolm X
or passed through him. Police declined to discuss a rumor
sweeping Harlem that they had some motion pictures which
had been taken in the Audubon Ballroom as the murder took
place. Another rumor that gained swift momentum was that
when Sister Betty had leaned over her husband's body, she
had removed from his coat pocket a paper on which he had
written the names of those he had supposedly learned were
assigned to execute him.

Deputy Police Commissioner Walter Arm stressed that the
department had made efforts to protect Malcolm X. Twenty
different times the department had offered protection to Malcolm X or to some of his assistants, and the protection was
refused, said Commissioner Arm, and seventeen times uniformed police guards had been offered for the OAAU meetings at the Audubon Ballroom, the most recent time being
"last Sunday." Asked about the pistol permit that Malcolm X
had said publicly he planned to request, Commissioner Arm
said that as far as he knew, Malcolm X had never actually
filed a request.

A number of questions have been raised. The "suspect"
arrested by Patrolman Hoy as he was being chased from the
meeting has, at present writing, not been identified publicly.
Deputy Police Commissioner Walter Arm's statement that
Malcolm X refused police protection conflicts directly with
the statements of many of his associates that during the week
preceding his assassination Malcolm X complained repeatedly
that the police would not take his requests for protection seriously. Finally, although police sources said that a special detail

of twenty men had been assigned to the meeting and that it had even been attended by agents of the Bureau of Special Services, these men were nowhere in evidence during or after the assassination, and Talmadge Hayer, rescued from the crowd and arrested as a suspect immediately after the assassination, was picked up by two patrolmen in a squad car cruising by.

On long-distance telephones, reporters reached the Chicago mansion headquarters of Elijah Muhammad. He would not come to the telephone, but a spokesman of his said that Muhammad "has no comment today, but he might have something to say tomorrow." No statement could be obtained either from Malcolm X's oldest brother, Wilfred X, the Black Muslim minister of Mosque Number 1 in Detroit. At his home, a woman told reporters that Minister Wilfred X was not there, that he had not gone to New York, and she didn't believe he had any plans to do so. (Minister Wilfred X, reached later, said that he anticipated attending the Black Muslim convention in Chicago on the following Sunday, and regarding his brother, "My brother is dead and there is nothing we can do to bring him back.")

As dark fell, many Negro men and women assembled before Louis Michaux's bookstore, where most of Harlem's Black Nationalist public activity centered. A small group of OAAU members opened their Hotel Theresa headquarters and sat in the room and would not make any statements to reporters.

The New York *Daily News* came onto the newsstands with its cover page devoted to "Malcolm X Murdered" over the photograph of him being borne away on the stretcher, and a sub-caption, "Gunned Down At Rally." In Long Island, where she had been taken just after her father's murder, six-year-old Attilah carefully wrote a letter to him, "Dear Daddy, I love you so. O dear, O dear, I wish you wasn't dead."

The body—still listed as "John Doe" because it had not yet been formally identified—had been moved late Sunday to the New York City Medical Examiner's office at 520 First Avenue. The autopsy confirmed that shotgun pellet wounds in the heart had killed Malcolm X. Chief Medical Examiner Dr. Milton Helpern said that death followed the first sawed-off shotgun blast which caused thirteen wounds in the heart and chest, and he said that .38 and .45 caliber bullet wounds in the thighs and legs evidenced that Malcolm X had been shot at after he had fallen.

Monday morning the official identification was made at the Medical Examiner's office by Sister Betty, who was accompanied by Percy Sutton, Malcolm X's Boston half-sister Mrs. Ella Collins, and Joseph E. Hall, General Manager of the large Unity Funeral Home in Harlem. Leaving the Medical Examiner's office at about noon to go and complete funeral arrangements, Sister Betty told reporters, "No one believed what he said. They never took him seriously, even after the bombing of our home they said he did it himself!"

At the Unity Funeral Home on the east side of Eighth Avenue between 126th and 127th streets, Sister Betty chose a six-foot-nine-inch bronze casket lined with egg-shell velvet. At her request, the funeral would be delayed until the following Saturday, five days away. The funeral home's manager Hall announced to the press that the body would be dressed in a business suit, and it would be put on view under a glass shield from Tuesday through Friday, then the Saturday services would be at a Harlem church.

Soon posted on the funeral home's directory was "El-Hajj Malik El-Shabazz." In Brooklyn, orthodox Moslem Sheik Al-Hajh Daoud Ahmed Faisal of the Islamic Mission of America said that the delayed funeral services violated a Moslem practice that the sun should not set twice on a believer's body, that the Koran prescribed burial inside twenty-four hours if possible, and Moslems believed that when a body grows cold the soul leaves it and when the body is put into the earth it comes alive again.

In Chicago, where policemen were watching all bus depots, railways, terminals, O'Hare Airport and highway entrances, Elijah Muhammad, under heavy guard in his three-story mansion, said, "Malcolm died according to his preaching. He seems to have taken weapons as his god. Therefore, we couldn't tolerate a man like that. He preached war. We preach peace. We are permitted to fight if we are attacked—that's the Scripture, the Koran, and the Bible, too. But we will never be the aggressor. I don't have the right to be frightened, because I was chosen by Allah. If Allah gives me up to the hands of the wicked, I am satisfied. My life is in the hands of Allah." The grounds outside the mansion were patrolled by both Chicago police and Fruit of Islam bodyguards. More of both patrolled before the University of Islam high school, and the offices of the newspaper *Muhammad Speaks*.

Malcolm X's lawyer, Assemblyman Percy Sutton, said that the police now had the names of those whom Malcolm X had said planned to kill him. All over Harlem, reporters were interviewing people, and microphones were being put before the mouths of the man-in-the-street. At police precinct station houses, people being questioned were leaving by side entrances. Said Assistant Chief Inspector Joseph Coyle, in charge of Manhattan North detectives, ". . . . a well-planned conspiracy. We're doing a screening process of the four hundred people who were in the hall at the time." Fifty detectives were on the case, he said, and he had been in touch with police in other cities.

Harlem was mostly asleep when around the Black Muslim Mosque Number 7, on the top floor of a four-story building at 116th Street and Lenox Avenue, an explosive sound at 2:15 P.M. ripped the night. Firemen were instantly summoned by the four policemen who had been guarding the sidewalk entrance to the mosque. Within a few minutes flames burst through the building's roof and leaped thirty feet into the air. For the next seven hours firemen would pour water into the building. On an adjacent roof they found an empty five-gallon gasoline can, a brown, gasoline-stained shopping bag, and oily rags. Southbound IRT subway service was re-routed for a while, also three bus lines. At the spectacular five-alarm fire's height, a wall of the building collapsed; it smashed two fire engines at the curb and injured five firemen, one seriously, and also a pedestrian who had been across the street buying a newspaper. By daybreak, when the fire was declared "under control," the Black Muslim mosque and the Gethsemane Church of God in Christ on the floor beneath it were gutted, and seven street-level stores, including the Black Muslim restaurant, were "total losses." Fire Department sources said that replacing the ruined equipment would cost "around $50,000." Joseph X of the Black Muslims, who once had been the immediate assistant of Malcolm X, said that Elijah Muhammad's followers had two alternative mosques to meet in, one in Brooklyn and the other in Queens, Long Island. Both these mosques were under continuous police guard.

Across the nation in San Francisco on Tuesday afternoon two policemen discovered a fire beginning in the San Francisco Black Muslim Mosque, and quickly extinguished it. Kerosene had been splashed on the sidewalk and door and set afire.

The body of El-Hajj Malik El-Shabazz originally had been scheduled to go on public view at 2:30 P.M. Tuesday. Crowds stood in line behind police barricades waiting to be admitted and the policemen wherever one looked included numerous patrol cars and even sharpshooters on the roofs around the Unity Funeral Home. But the telephoned bomb-threats which had begun shortly after noon made necessary two evacuations of the funeral home for bomb-squad searches, which proved futile. A search was conducted even in the 43rd Street offices of the *New York Times* after a man telephoned complaining of an editorial about Malcolm X and said, "Your plant will be destroyed at four o'clock."

At the funeral home in Harlem, policemen inspected all packages and floral pieces being delivered, as well as the large handbags of women mourners. It was 6:15 P.M. when a cordon of policemen arrived flanking Sister Betty and four close relatives and friends who entered the funeral home in a glare of flashbulbs. "She's a black Jacqueline Kennedy," observed a white reporter. "She has class, she knows what to do and when, she handles herself beautifully."

It was 7:10 P.M. when the family party emerged and left. After ten minutes, the first of the waiting public was admitted. Between then and an hour before midnight, two thousand people, including scores of whites, had filed past the open coffin in which the body lay dressed in a dark business suit, a white shirt and dark tie, with a small, oblong brass plate above it inscribed, *"El-Hajj Malik El-Shabazz— May 19, 1925—Feb. 21, 1965."*

Malcolm X followers had been canvassing with growing anxiety for a Harlem church that would accept the Saturday funeral. Officials of several churches had refused, including a spokesman for the community's largest church, Abyssinian Baptist, of which Congressman-Reverend Adam Clayton Powell is the pastor; others which turned down requests, according to the *Amsterdam News,* included the Williams C.M.E. Church and The Refuge Temple of The Church of Our Lord Jesus Christ. Then the funeral was accepted by Bishop Alvin A. Childs for the Faith Temple, Church of God in Christ located at 147th Street and Amsterdam Avenue. The Faith Temple, a former movie theater which had been converted fifteen years previously, could seat a thousand in its auditorium and another seven hundred in its basement. Bishop Childs, who in 1964 had been elected as Harlem's "locality mayor," told the press that it was "as a humanitarian gesture" that he made his church available, and of Malcolm X, he said, ". . . a militant and vocal person. I did not agree with all of his philosophy, but this did not affect our friendship." Shortly after the news became known, Bishop Childs and his wife began to receive the first of a succession of bomb threats telephoned both to the church and to their home.

Prominent Negro figures were being quoted by the various press media. The famed psychologist Dr. Kenneth B. Clark told *Jet* magazine, "I had a deep respect for this man. I believe that he was sincerely groping to find a place in the fight for Civil Rights, on a level where he would be respected and understood fully. I looked forward to his growth along those lines. It doesn't matter so much about his past. It is tragic that he was cut down at the point when he seemed on the verge of achieving the position of respectability he sought." A *New York Times* correspondent in a London press conference quoted the author and dramatist James Baldwin, who thought the death of Malcolm X was "a major setback for the Negro movement." Pointing at white reporters, Baldwin accused, "You did it . . . whoever did it was formed in the crucible of the Western world, of the American Republic!" European "rape" of Africa began racial problems and was therefore the beginning of the end for Malcolm X, Baldwin said.

The bookstore owner in Harlem, Louis Michaux, a major voice in the community, told the *Amsterdam News,* "It's things like the murder of Malcolm X that drive the masses closer together. He died in the same manner that Patrice Lumumba met his death in the Congo. . . . We must unite, not fight."

"Malcolm X caused many young Negroes to take a new vision of themselves," said Bayard Rustin, a main figure in organizing the March on Washington in 1963. A "third party" was suspected of killing Malcolm X by CORE's National Director James Farmer, who said, "Malcolm's murder was calculated to produce more violence and murder and vengeance killings." A few days later, asked for his opinion of a rumor circulating about that a "Red Chinese" plot brought about the murder, Farmer said, "I would not say it is impossible."

"For the Negroes in America, the death of Malcolm X is the most portentous event since the deportation of Marcus Garvey in the 1920's," said Dr. C. Eric Lincoln, author of *The Black Muslims in America,* who talked to the press at Brown University in Providence, R.I., where he was a visiting professor and research fellow. "I doubt there are 'international implications' in the slaying. The answer is closer to home. The answer is in the local struggle among contending rivals for leadership of the black masses, which are potentially the most volatile sub-group in America." Said Roy Wilkins, Executive Secretary of the National Association for the Advancement of Colored People, "Master spell-binder that he was, Malcolm X in death cast a spell more far-flung and more disturbing than any he cast in life."

The New York City police investigators who were pursuing the case were unhappy that Malcolm's followers had "not come forward" to aid the investigation. At police request, the press printed a telephone number, SW 5-8117, for "strictly confidential" information that anyone might offer concerning the slaying. The police had picked up and were holding Reuben Francis, described as a Malcolm X "bodyguard," who was believed to be the person who had shot the suspected assassin Talmadge Hayer during the melee the previous Sunday at the Audubon Ballroom. Hayer remained in the Bellevue Prison Ward, awaiting surgery.

As thousands continued viewing the body of the slain Malcolm X amid intermittent new bomb threats telephoned to the funeral home, and to the Faith Temple where his funeral was scheduled for Saturday, a new organization, the Federation of Independent Political Action, threatened to picket all Harlem business establishments which would not close from Thursday afternoon until Monday morning "in tribute to Malcolm X." The FIPA's spokesman was Jesse Gray, the well-known rent-strike leader; Harlem pedestrians began to be handed printed sheets reading, in part, "If the stores refuse to close, they identify with our enemy—therefore we must close them—pass them by. Those that shop along 125th Street during the hours that the stores are to be closed identify with the murderous stooge that allowed the power structure to use his hands to kill Brother Malcolm." At a late evening FIPA rally before Louis Michaux's bookstore, Jesse Gray declared that in 1965 a Negro should run for Mayor of New York "in the name of Malcolm," and speculated that such a candidate should receive 100,000 votes. Shortly after the FIPA rally, merchants and other members of the Uptown Chamber of Commerce met and swiftly passed a resolution urging all Harlem stores to remain open and "continue to serve their customers," and recommendation was made that full pay be given to any store employees who might wish to attend Malcolm X's funeral on Saturday morning. Then one after another, Harlem leaders sharply criticized the FIPA proposal as "irresponsible." Finally, nearly all of the Harlem stores kept their doors open for business. The FIPA got together about twenty pickets who patrolled for a while before Harlem's largest store, Blumstein's; leading the pickets were two white men carrying signs reading "All Stores Should Close. Honor Malcolm X."

The weather had turned very cold. Icicles hung from the collapsed roof of the fire-ruined building that had housed Black Muslim Mosque Number 7. The *Amsterdam News*, its offices barely a block down Eighth Avenue from the funeral home where Malcolm X's body lay, editorialized, "Steady, Eddie!" saying that orderly tributes to Malcolm X would "confound his critics, who would like nothing better than to see black people rioting over his remains."

The fear of serious mass rioting set off by some unpredictable spark hung steadily in the air. An increasing number of Harlem leaders declared that the principal reason for this was the downtown white press media, sensationalizing what was going on in a calm, dignified community. Finally the Harlem Ministers' Interfaith Association would issue a formal accusation: "The screaming headlines of many of our newspapers make it seem as if all of Harlem was an armed camp, ready to explode at any moment. The vast majority of the citizens of the Harlem community is not involved in the unfortunate acts of violence that have been grossly overplayed by the press. Many times the slanting of the news is able to bring about an atmosphere through which a few depraved and reckless individuals can take advantage."

"Malcolm X Died Broke"—that headline in Harlem's *Amsterdam News* came as a shock to many in the community.

Few had reflected that Malcolm X, upon becoming a Black Muslim minister, had signed an oath of poverty, so that for twelve years he never acquired anything in his own name. (Somewhere I have read that Malcolm X in his Black Muslim days received about $175 weekly to cover his living and other expenses exclusive of travel.) "He left his four daughters and pregnant wife with no insurance of any kind, no savings, and no income," the *Amsterdam News* story said (and it might have added that he never drew up a will; he had made a February 26th appointment with his lawyer— five days after his death.) Within the week, two groups had organized and were asking Harlemites for contributions to help Sister Betty raise and educate the children (since organized as the Malcolm X Daughters' Fund at Harlem's Freedom National Bank, 275 West 125th Street).

In Boston, Malcolm X's half-sister, Mrs. Ella Mae Collins, told a news conference that she would choose the leaders of the OAAU to succeed Malcolm X. Mrs. Collins operated the Sarah A. Little School of Preparatory Arts where, she said, children were taught Arabic, Swahili, French, and Spanish. In 1959, she, too, had broken away from Elijah Muhammad's Black Muslims, to which she had originally been converted by Malcolm X.

Far from Harlem, in lands where Malcolm X had traveled, the press had given the murder a coverage that had highly irritated the Director of the United States Information Agency, Carl T. Rowan, himself a Negro. In Washington, addressing the American Foreign Service Association, Rowan said that when he first heard of the murder, he knew it would be grossly misconstrued in some countries where people were unaware what Malcolm X represented, and he said the USIA had worked hard to inform the African press of the facts about Malcolm X and his preachments, but still there had been "a host of African reaction based on misinformation and misrepresentation."

Said USIA Director Rowan, "Mind you, here was a Negro who preached segregation and race hatred, killed by another Negro, presumably from another organization that preaches segregation and race hatred, and neither of them representative of more than a tiny minority of the Negro population of America—" Rowan held up some foreign newspapers. "All this about an ex-convict, ex-dope peddler who became a racial fanatic," continued Rowan. "I can only conclude that we Americans know less about what goes on in the minds of other peoples than we thought, or the need to inform is even greater than we in USIA thought it to be."

The *Daily Times* of Lagos, in Nigeria, had said: "Like all mortals, Malcolm X was not without his faults . . . but that he was a dedicated and consistent disciple of the movement for the emancipation of his brethren, no one can doubt . . . Malcolm X has fought and died for what he believed to be right. He will have a place in the palace of martyrs." The *Ghanaian Times,* Accra, called Malcolm X "the militant and most popular of Afro-American anti-segregationist leaders" and it added his name to "a host of Africans and Americans" ranging from John Brown to Patrice Lumumba "who were martyred in freedom's cause." Also in Accra, the *Daily Graphic*: "The assassination of Malcolm X will go down in history as the greatest blow the American integrationist movement has suffered since the shocking assassination of Medgar Evers and John F. Kennedy."

The Pakistan *Hurriyet of Karachi* said: "A great Negro leader"; the *Pakistan Times* said, "His death is a definite setback to the Negro movement for emancipation." The Peking, China *People's Daily* said the killing happened "because Malcolm X . . . fought for the emancipation of the 23,000,000 American Negroes." According to correspondents' reports, the first Algerian headline said "the Ku Klux Klan" assassinated Malcolm X; the pro-Communist *Alger Republican's* editorial on the slaying accused "American Fascism," and the *Times*' Algerian correspondent said Algerians showed "signs" of raising Malcolm X to martyrdom. The U.S. Consulate in Georgetown, British Guiana, was marched on by pickets accusing "American imperialists." Another Peking, China paper, *Jenmin Jihpao,* said that the death showed that "in dealing with imperialist oppressors, violence must be met with violence." *Pravda* in Moscow carried only brief stories and no editorial comment, the *New York Times* Moscow correspondent said, and another in Poland said there was no noticeable reaction of any kind, and that "few Poles had heard of Malcolm or were interested in the racial issue." Reportedly, the murder was only routinely reported with little special interest by the press in Cairo, Beirut, New Delhi, and Saigon. In Paris and Western Europe, the story was "essentially a one-day sensation," with the West German press handling it "as if it were in the Chicago gangster tradition." The *New York Times* said: "The London newspapers have probably played the story harder and longer than most, giving continuing emphasis to the police work on the murder. The *London Times* and the *London Daily Telegraph* both carried editorial comments, but neither treated Malcolm X as a major figure." Also reported by the *New York Times* London correspondent was that "a London group calling itself the Council of African Organizations has violently attacked the United States over the murder. This group is made up of students and other unofficial African representatives here. A press release described Malcolm as a 'leader in the struggle against American imperialism, oppression and racialism.' It said, 'the butchers of Patrice Lumumba are the very same monsters who have murdered Malcolm X in cold blood.'"

Friday morning New York City press headlines concerning Malcolm X's slaying were devoted to the police department's apprehension of a second slaying suspect. He was a stocky, round-faced, twenty-six-year-old karate expert named Norman 3X Butler, allegedly a Black Muslim, and a week later, this was followed by the arrest of Thomas 15X Johnson, also allegedly a Black Muslim. Both men had been earlier indicted in the January, 1965, shooting of Benjamin Brown, a New York City Correction Officer and a Black Muslim defector. Both men were indicted, along with Hayer, for the murder of Malcolm X on March 10.

With the news announcement of Butler's arrest, and his at least tentative identification as a member of Elijah Muhammad's organization, tension reached a new high among all who had any role in the feud. The Black Muslim National Convention was scheduled to begin that Friday in Chicago, to last for three days. Early Friday morning in New York at the Kennedy Airport dozens of policemen spent forty minutes searching a plane belonging to Capital Airlines, which back in December 1964 had accepted a Mosque Number 7 charter flight to Chicago and return, at a fee of $5,175.54 which the mosque had subsequently paid in increments.

Altogether, about three thousand Black Muslims from their mosques in most sizable cities were in Chicago for their annual "Saviour's Day" convention, regarded by them as similar to the holiday of Christmas. In the order of arrival, each group from the different mosques and cities assembled outside the big sports coliseum south of Chicago's business district, the brothers of all ages dressed in neat, dark suits and white shirts and the sisters garbed in flowing silk gowns and headdresses—and every individual was filtered through an intense security check that Chicago police sources said was unprecedented in Chicago except for a visiting President.

Searched even more closely were the relatively few non-Muslim Negroes who came to be spectators, and the press representatives both white and black. "Take off your hat, show some respect!" snapped a Black Muslim guard at a white reporter. As each person was "cleared" a Fruit of Islam man ushered him or her to a specific seat in the drafty interior of the 7500-seat coliseum. (Later, Muslim sources would blame the half-full house upon "the white man's dividing of Negroes," but observers who recalled the packed coliseum in 1964 said that bombing fears kept away many non-Muslim Negroes.) The audience sat lightly murmuring under the two huge hanging banners proclaiming "Welcome Elijah Muhammad—We Are Glad To Have You With Us" and "We Must Have Some Of This Land" (referring to Elijah Muhammad's demand that "one or more states" be turned over to the "23 million so-called Negroes" in America as partial reparation for "over a century of our free blood and sweat as slaves which helped to develop this wealthy nation where still today you show us you do not wish or intend to accept us as equals"). In front of the wide, raised speaker's platform were two nearly life-sized photographic blowups of Elijah Muhammad. Standing between the stage and the audience were Fruit of Islam guards. Others were prowling the aisles, scanning rows of faces, with intermittent peremptory demands for identification, "What mosque, brother?" Still more Fruit of Islam men were inspecting the coliseum's vacant balcony, backstage, downstairs, and rafters and roof.

The ghost of Malcolm X was in the coliseum. First, in a high drama for the Muslims, Elijah Muhammad's son, Wallace Delaney Muhammad, who once had sided with Malcolm X, faced the audience and begged forgiveness for his defection. Next, two brothers of Malcolm X, Wilfred and Philbert, both of them Black Muslim ministers, urged unity with Elijah Muhammad. Said Minister Wilfred X of the Detroit mosque, "We would be ignorant to get confused and go to arguing and fighting among ourselves and forget who the real enemy is." Said Minister Philbert X, of the Lansing mosque, "Malcolm was my own blood brother, next to me. . . . I was shocked. No man wants to see his own brother destroyed. But I knew that he was traveling on a very reckless and dangerous road. I made attempts to change his course. When he was living, I tried to keep him living; now that he is dead, there is nothing I can do." Indicating the seated Elijah Muhammad, Minister Philbert X declared, "Where he leads me, I will follow"— and then he introduced the Black Muslim leader to make his address.

Only the head of Elijah Muhammad was visible above the grim-faced Fruit of Islam men in a living wall, Cassius Clay among them. Crescents, stars, moons and suns were in gold-thread embroidery on the small fez that Elijah Muhammad wore. He said in his speech: "For a long time, Malcolm stood here where I stand. In those days, Malcolm was safe, Malcolm was loved. God, Himself, protected Malcolm. . . . For more than a year, Malcolm was given his freedom. He went every-where—Asia, Europe, Africa, even to Mecca, trying to make enemies for me. He came back preaching that we should not hate the enemy. . . . He came here a few weeks ago to blast away his hate and mud-slinging; everything he could think of to disgrace me. . . . We didn't want to kill Malcolm and didn't try to kill him. They know I didn't harm Malcolm. They know I loved him. His foolish teaching brought him to his own end. . . ."

Both physically and emotionally worked up, often Elijah Muhammad would begin coughing. "Take it easy! Take your time!" his audience pleaded with him. "He had no right to reject me!" Elijah Muhammad declared. "He was a star, who went astray! . . . They knew I didn't harm Malcolm, but he tried to make war against me." He said that Malcolm X would have been given "the most glorious of burials" if he had stayed with the Black Muslims and had died a natural death; "instead, we stand beside the grave of a hypocrite! . . . *Malcolm!* Who was he leading? Who was he teaching? He has no truth! We didn't want to kill Malcolm! His foolish teaching would bring him to his own end! I am not going to let the crackpots destroy the good things Allah sent to you and me!"

Elijah Muhammad drove his frail energy to speak for about

an hour and a half. He challenged any would-be assassins: "If you seek to snuff out the life of Elijah Muhammad, you are inviting your own doom! The Holy Quran tells us not to pick a fight but to defend ourselves. We will fight!" It was mid-afternoon when Elijah Muhammad turned back to his seat with some three thousand Black Muslim men, women, and children shouting "Yes, *sir!* . . . So sweet! . . . All praise to Muhammad!"

In the Unity Funeral Home in the Harlem community of New York City in the mid-afternoon, the public's viewing of the body of Malcolm X was interrupted by the arrival of a party of about a dozen people whose central figure was a white-turbaned, dark-robed elderly man whose white beard fell to his chest and who carried a forked stick. When reporters rushed to attempt interviews, another man in the party waved them away, saying, "A silent tongue does not betray its owner." The man was Sheik Ahmed Hassoun, a Sudanese, a member of the Sunni Moslems, who had taught in Mecca for 35 years when he had met Malcolm X there, and then had soon come to the United States to serve as Malcolm X's spiritual advisor and to teach at the Muslim Mosque, Inc.

Sheik Hassoun prepared the body for burial in accordance with Moslem ritual. Removing the Western clothing in which the body had been on display, Sheik Hassoun washed the body with special holy oil. Then he draped the body in the traditional seven white linen shrouds, called the *kafan*. Only the face with its reddish moustache and goatee was left exposed. The mourners who had come with Sheik Hassoun filed to the bier and he read passages from the Koran. Then he turned to a funeral home representative: "Now the body is ready for burial." Soon, the sheik and his retinue left, and the viewing by the public resumed. When the word spread, numbers of persons who had come before returned for another wait in the long, slowly moving line, wanting to see the Moslem burial dress.

It was late during this Friday afternoon that I got into the quietly moving line, thinking about the Malcolm X with whom I had worked closely for about two years. Blue-uniformed policemen stood at intervals watching us shuffle along within the wooden gray-painted police barricades. Just across the street several men were looking at the line from behind a large side window of the "Lone Star Barber Shop, Eddie

Johns, Prop., William Ashe, Mgr." Among the policemen were a few press representatives talking to each other to pass the time. Then we were inside the softly lit, hushed, cool, large chapel. Standing at either end of the long, handsome bronze coffin were two big, dark policemen, mostly looking straight ahead, but moving their lips when some viewer tarried. Within minutes I had reached the coffin. Under the glass lid, I glimpsed the delicate white shrouding over the chest and up like a hood about the face on which I tried to concentrate for as long as I could. All that I could think was that it was he, all right—Malcolm X. "Move on"—the policeman's voice was soft. Malcolm looked to me—just waxy and *dead*. The policeman's hand was gesturing at his waist level. I thought, *"Well—good-bye."* I moved on.

Twenty-two thousand people had viewed the body when the line was stopped that night for good, at eleven P.M. Quietly, between midnight and dawn, a dozen police cars flanked a hearse that went the twenty-odd blocks farther uptown to the Faith Temple. The bronze coffin was wheeled inside and placed upon a platform draped in thick dark red velvet, in front of the altar, and the coffin's lid was reopened. As the hearse pulled away, policemen stood at posts of vigil both inside and outside Faith Temple. It was crispy cold outside.

About six A.M., people began forming a line on the east side of Amsterdam Avenue. By nine A.M., an estimated six thousand persons thronged the nearby blocks, behind police barriers, and faces were in every window of the apartment buildings across the street; some stood shivering on fire escapes. From 145th Street to 149th Street, policemen had blocked off all automobile traffic except for their own cars, the newspapers' cars, and the equipment trucks for radio and television on-the-spot coverage. There were hundreds of policemen, some on the rooftops in the immediate area. Combing the crowd's edges were reporters with microphones and notebooks. "He was fascinating, a remarkably fascinating man, that's why I'm here," a white girl in her mid-twenties told a *New York Times* man; and a Negro woman, "I'm paying my respects to the greatest black man in this century. He's a black man. Don't say colored." Another woman, noticing steel helmets inside a television network car, laughed to the driver, "You getting ready for next summer?"

When the Faith Temple doors were opened at 9:20, a corps

of OAAU members entered. Within the next quarter-hour, twenty of the men had ushered in six hundred seat-holders. Fifty press reporters, photographers and television cameramen clustered beneath religious murals to the rear of the altar, and some stood on chairs to see better. A Negro engineer monitored recording equipment between the altar and the coffin which was guarded by eight uniformed Negro policemen and two uniformed Negro policewomen. One Negro plain-clothes policeman sat on either side of heavily veiled Sister Betty in the second row. The raised lid of the coffin hid the Faith Temple's brass tithe box and candelabra; the head of the Islamic Mission of America, in Brooklyn, Sheik Al-Haj Daoud Ahmed Faisal, had counseled that any hint of Christianity in the services would make the deceased a *kafir*, an unbeliever. (The sheik had also dissented with the days of public exhibition of the body: "Death is a private matter between Allah and the deceased.")

Before the services began, OAAU ushers brought in one floral wreath—a two-by-five arrangement of the Islamic Star and Crescent in white carnations against a background of red carnations.

First, the actor Ossie Davis and his wife, actress Ruby Dee, read the notes, telegrams and cables of condolence. They came from every major civil-rights organization; from individual figures such as Dr. Martin Luther King; from organizations and governments abroad, such as The Africa-Pakistan-West-Indian Society of the London School of Economics, the Pan-African Congress of Southern Africa, the Nigerian Ambassador from Lagos, the President of the Republic of Ghana, Dr. Kwame Nkrumah: "The death of Malcolm X shall not have been in vain."

Next, Omar Osman stood, a representative of the Islam Center of Switzerland and the United States: "We knew Brother Malcolm as a blood brother, particularly after his pilgrimage to Mecca last year. The highest thing that a Moslem can aspire to is to die on the battlefield and not die at his bedside—" He paused briefly to wait out the applause from among the mourners. "Those who die on the battlefield are not dead, but are alive!" The applause was louder, and cries rose, "Right! Right!" Omar Osman then critically commented upon the remarks which USIA Director Carl Rowan had made in Washington, D.C. about the foreign press reaction to the death of the deceased. From the audience then hisses rose.

Again, the actor Ossie Davis stood. His deep voice delivered the eulogy to Malcolm X which was going to cause Davis subsequently to be hailed more than ever among Negroes in Harlem:

"Here—at this final hour, in this quiet place, Harlem has come to bid farewell to one of its brightest hopes—extinguished now, and gone from us forever. . . .

"Many will ask what Harlem finds to honor in this stormy, controversial and bold young captain—and we will smile. . . . They will say that he is of hate—a fanatic, a racist—who can only bring evil to the cause for which you struggle!

"And we will answer and say unto them: Did you ever talk to Brother Malcolm? Did you ever touch him, or have him smile at you? Did you ever really listen to him? Did he ever do a mean thing? Was he ever himself associated with violence or any public disturbance? For if you did you would know him. And if you knew him you would know why we must honor him: Malcolm was our manhood, our living, black manhood! This was his meaning to his people. And, in honoring him, we honor the best in ourselves. . . . And we will know him then for what he was and is—a Prince—our own black shining Prince!—who didn't hesitate to die, because he loved us so."

Brief speeches were made by others. Then, the family, the OAAU members and other Muslims present stood and filed by the coffin to view the body for the last time. Finally, the two plain-clothes policemen ushered Sister Betty to have her last sight of her husband. She leaned over, kissing the glass over him; she broke into tears. Until then almost no crying had been heard in the services, but now Sister Betty's sobs were taken up by other women.

The services had lasted a little over an hour when the three minutes of prayers said for every Muslim who is dead were recited by Alhajj Heshaam Jaaber, of Elizabeth, New Jersey. At the phrase "Allahu Akbar"—"God is most great"—all Muslims in the audience placed their opened hands at the sides of their faces.

An official cortege, with the hearse, of three family cars, eighteen mourners' cars, twelve police cars and six press cars —followed by about fifty other cars—briskly drove the eighteen miles out of Manhattan and along the New York Thruway, then off its Exit 7 to reach the Ferncliff Cemetery in Ardsley, N.Y. All along the route, Negroes placed their hats or hands over their hearts, paying their final respects. At each bridge crossing in Manhattan County, police cars stood watch; the Westchester County police had stationed individual patrolmen at intervals en route to the cemetery.

Over the coffin, final Moslem prayers were said by Sheik Alhajj Heshaam Jaaber. The coffin was lowered into the grave, the head facing the east, in keeping with Islamic tradition. Among the mourners, the Moslems knelt beside the grave to pray with their foreheads pressed to the earth, in the Eastern manner. When the family left the gravesite, followers of Malcolm X would not let the coffin be covered by the white gravediggers who had stood a little distance away, waiting. Instead, seven OAAU men began dropping bare handfuls of earth down on the coffin; then they were given shovels and they carried dirt to fill the grave, and then mound it.

The night fell over the earthly remains of El-Hajj Malik El-Shabazz, who had been called Malcolm X; who had been called Malcolm Little; who had been called "Big Red" and "Satan" and "Homeboy" and other names—who had been buried as a Moslem. "According to the Koran," the *New York Times* reported, "the bodies of the dead remain in their graves until the Last Day, the Day of Judgment. On this day of cataclysm the heavens are rent and the mountains ground to dust, the graves open and men are called to account by Allah.

"The blessed—the godfearing, the humble, the charitable, those who have suffered and been persecuted for Allah's sake or fought in religious wars for Islam—are summoned to the Garden of Paradise.

"There, according to the teaching of Mohammed, the Prophet, they live forever by flowing streams, reclining on silken cushions, and enjoying the company of dark-eyed maidens and wives of perfect purity.

"The damned—the covetous, the evildoer, the follower of gods other than Allah—are sent to Eternal Fire, where they are fed boiling water and molten brass. 'The death from which ye flee will truly overtake you,' the Koran says. 'Then will ye be sent back to the Knower of things secret and open, and He will tell you the truth of the things that ye did.' "

After signing the contract for this book, Malcolm X looked at me hard. "A writer is what I want, not an interpreter." I tried to be a dispassionate chronicler. But he was the most electric personality I have ever met, and I still can't quite conceive him dead. It still feels to me as if he has just gone into some next chapter, to be written by historians.

New York, 1965

OSSIE DAVIS

ON MALCOLM X

Mr. Davis wrote the following in response to a magazine editor's question: Why did you eulogize Malcolm X?

You are not the only person curious to know why I would eulogize a man like Malcolm X. Many who know and respect me have written letters. Of these letters I am proudest of those from a sixth-grade class of young white boys and girls who asked me to explain. I appreciate your giving me this chance to do so.

You may anticipate my defense somewhat by considering the following fact: no Negro has yet asked me that question. (My pastor in Grace Baptist Church where I teach Sunday school preached a sermon about Malcolm in which he called him a "giant in a sick world.") Every one of the many letters I got from my own people lauded Malcolm as a man, and commended me for having spoken at his funeral.

At the same time—and this is important—most of them took special pains to disagree with much or all of what Malcolm said and what he stood for. That is, with one singing exception, they all, every last, black, glory-hugging one of them, knew that Malcolm—whatever else he was or was not—*Malcolm was a man!*

White folks do not need anybody to remind them that they are men. We do! This was his one incontrovertible benefit to his people.

Protocol and common sense require that Negroes stand back and let the white man speak up for us, defend us, and lead us from behind the scene in our fight. This is the essence of Negro politics. But Malcolm said to hell with that! Get up off your knees and fight your own battles. That's the way to win back your self-respect. That's the way to make the white man respect you. And if he won't let you live like a man, he certainly can't keep you from dying like one!

Malcolm, as you can see, was refreshing excitement; he scared hell out of the rest of us, bred as we are to caution, to hypocrisy in the presence of white folks, to the smile that never fades. Malcolm knew that every white man in America profits directly or indirectly from his position vis-à-vis Negroes, profits from racism even though he does not practice it or believe in it.

He also knew that every Negro who did not challenge on the spot every instance of racism, overt or covert, committed against him and his people, who chose instead to swallow his spit and go on smiling, was an Uncle Tom and a traitor, without balls or guts, or any other commonly accepted aspects of manhood!

Now, we knew all these things as well as Malcolm did, but we also knew what happened to people who stick their necks out and say them. And if all the lies we tell ourselves by way of extenuation were put into print, it would constitute one of the great chapters in the history of man's justifiable cowardice in the face of other men.

But Malcolm kept snatching our lies away. He kept shouting the painful truth we whites and blacks did not want to hear from all the housetops. And he wouldn't stop for love nor money.

You can imagine what a howling, shocking nuisance this man was to both Negroes and whites. Once Malcolm fastened on you, you could not escape. He was one of the most fascinating and charming men I have ever met, and never hesitated to take his attractiveness and beat you to death with it. Yet his irritation, though painful to us, was most salutary. He would make you angry as hell, but he would also make you proud. It was impossible to remain defensive and apologetic about being a Negro in his presence. He wouldn't let you. And you always left his presence with the sneaky suspicion that maybe, after all, you *were* a man!

But in explaining Malcolm, let me take care not to explain him away. He had been a criminal, an addict, a pimp, and a prisoner; a racist, and a hater, he had really believed the white man was a devil. But all this had changed. Two days before his death, in commenting to Gordon Parks about his past life he said: "That was a mad scene. The sickness and madness of those days! I'm glad to be free of them."

And Malcolm was free. No one who knew him before and after his trip to Mecca could doubt that he had completely abandoned racism, separatism, and hatred. But he had not abandoned his shock-effect statements, his bristling agitation for immediate freedom in this country not only for blacks, but for everybody.

And most of all, in the area of race relations, he still delighted in twisting the white man's tail, and in making Uncle Toms, compromisers, and accommodationists—I deliberately include myself—thoroughly ashamed of the urbane and smiling hypocrisy we practice merely to exist in a world whose values we both envy and despise.

But even had Malcolm not changed, he would still have been a relevant figure on the American scene, standing in relation as he does, to the "responsible" civil rights leaders, just about where John Brown stood in relation to the "responsible" abolitionist in the fight against slavery. Almost all disagreed with Brown's mad and fanatical tactics which led him foolishly to attack a Federal arsenal at Harpers Ferry, to lose two sons there, and later to be hanged for treason.

Yet, today the world, and especially the Negro people, proclaim Brown not a traitor, but a hero and a martyr in a noble cause. So in future, I will not be surprised if men come to see that Malcolm X was, within his own limitations, and in his own inimitable style, also a martyr in that cause.

But there is much controversy still about this most controversial American, and I am content to wait for history to make the final decision.

But in personal judgment, there is no appeal from instinct. I knew the man personally, and however much I disagreed with him, I never doubted that Malcolm X, even when he was wrong, was always that rarest thing in the world among us Negroes: a true man.

And if, to protect my relations with the many good white folks who make it possible for me to earn a fairly good living in the entertainment industry, I was too chicken, too cautious, to admit that fact when he was alive, I thought at least that

460 THE AUTOBIOGRAPHY OF MALCOLM X

now, when all the white folks are safe from him at last,
I could be honest with myself enough to lift my hat for one
final salute to that brave, black, ironic gallantry, which was
his style and hallmark, that shocking *zing* of fire-and-be-
damned-to-you, so absolutely absent in every other Negro
man I know, which brought him, too soon, to his death.

Pulitzer Prize Winner

Carl Sagan's

THE DRAGONS OF EDEN

SPECULATIONS ON THE EVOLUTION OF HUMAN INTELLIGENCE

At last in paperback!
The entertaining and acclaimed bestseller
that takes us on a compelling voyage
inside the human brain. Combining
daring speculations and great fun,
The Dragons of Eden
is a masterpiece of scientific writing
for non-scientists.

(BB) Ballantine Books   26031/$2.25

LG-8

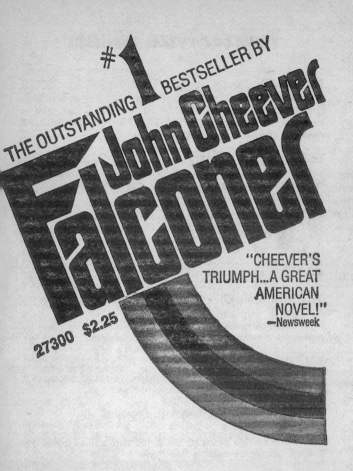

LG-2